FROM SCENES LIKE THESE

FROM SCENES LIKE THESE

Scottish Anecdotes and Episodes

Compiled and edited by
DAVID ROSS

Birlinn

First published in 2000 by
Birlinn Limited
8 Canongate Venture
5 New Street
Edinburgh
EH8 8BH

www.birlinn.co.uk

ISBN 1 84158 101 1

British Library Cataloguing-in-Publication Data
A catalogue record for this book is available from the British Library

Typeset by Initial Typesetting Services, Edinburgh
Printed and bound by Creative Print and Design, Ebbw Vale

'From scenes like these Auld Scotia's grandeur springs,
That makes her loved at home, revered abroad'
Robert Burns, *The Cottar's Saturday Night*

'So much, then for the Scots' boundless, insatiable
interest in their fellow men and women; they are tireless
gossips and anecdotists.'
Edwin Muir, *The Scots and Their Country*

'Sit up, and A'll tell ye an awn-ecdote.'
Anonymous minister quoted in Anne Gordon,
Candie for the Foundling

CONTENTS

INTRODUCTION

A small boy stands on a footbridge, watching as an old coal-burning engine gets its goods train under way. On the wintry moor, a solitary walker endures long moments of panic when he stumbles into a snow-filled hole. A merry-hearted society lady indulges in 'mystifications' for her own diversion. Unlucky chance ensures that a king in hiding does not escape his murderers. In a manner as elegant as that of any of his experiments, an eighteenth-century natural philosopher expires at his supper-table. After another killing – this has been, perhaps in some ways still is, a rough country – one of the assassins urinates into the dead man's face, in order to make a prophecy come true. Far out on a Hebridean isle, a naturalist shares the rapture of the petrels' nightly dance. Among the trees, in a misty stillness after rain, a piper plays the 'Lament for the Children'.

There are many scenes, many events, many characters. The little arc of the earth's surface between The Cheviot and Muckle Flugga has a human history as varied as its geology. In the human record too there are petrified cores of ancient fire, layered strata of long habitation and language, sudden abruptnesses, wildernesses, revelations of a primeval bleakness; as well as green glades and sunny nooks, and occasional veins of gold.

'Things unpublished' is what the Greek root of the word anecdote means, and the word still retains a faint sense of revealing a secret, or at least a confidence, which was its original English meaning. Later it came to signify the narrative of an interesting or striking incident or event; and then – following the law that the value of words goes only downwards – merely an item of gossip. 'Anecdotal' nowadays means at best unprovable, at worst invented. But a proper anecdote should be a true story, and preferably one that certain people would like to remain untold. This is the quality that gives an anecdote its savour: it lifts the veil on what we are not supposed to be allowed to see.

Most anecdotes do not give away dark and terrible, or shameful, or even exciting secrets. More often they simply show us the intriguing details that formal history leaves out, because it is too pompous, or in too much of a hurry, or anxious to avoid complicating detail. But the devil can be in the detail, as the tennis-loving James I found on the night of his assassination. Humour is also often in the detail; and much entertainment for the latter-day reader can be found there.

This book concerns itself with Scotland and the Scots – a rich source of material. The lack of a modern collection of Scottish anecdotes has been a glaring gap in the range of reference works that support us in the eternal quest of exploring what being Scottish is all about. The contents of such a collection would not fit well into a modern History – most of them fall foul of the considerations mentioned in the preceding paragraph, and might be false or irrelevant to boot. Many others are 'episodes' of sharp individual interest but with no claim to bear on the national story. But many of the items here were once considered to be part of Scottish history – Patrick Fraser Tytler's monumental mid-nineteenth-century *History of Scotland* is immensely anecdotal in style and content – and some of them still are; and, just as its myriad scales combine to clothe the herring, so does each one of these tales add its glistening mite of detail to the Scottish experience.

They are of two main kinds: either about events, or about people. Scottish history, like all history, is full of small happenings which, for one reason or another, have a significance that extends beyond their immediate circumstances and makes them of interest even hundreds of years later. The assassination of Archbishop Sharp is a good example; sharpened further by its effect on such a mind as that of Robert Louis Stevenson. Yet it was an apparently minor aspect of that affair which fired Stevenson's imagination: the inactivity of one man in a scene of hasty, panicky butchery. And Scottish history has its share of persons whose predicaments, thoughts or actions are worth reading about and remembering. Some of these people are only half-remembered, like Grizel Hume, a heroine of the Covenant – but the Covenant no longer exerts the mandatory claim on the Scottish mind that it once did. Others remain famous names, but in their cases we are on the lookout for the interesting human details. David Hume is immortal for his philosophy, but his fart shows him to be on a level with the rest of us, and yet transcending it by his honesty and compassion. Scottish history also has its full share of episodes that are probably completely untrue, or at least unverifiable. The Douglas Dinner is an example. It certainly happened, and the arrogant young Earl, his brother and their improvident counsellor were summarily slaughtered, to the distress and horror of the boy-king James V. But the placing of a black bull's head upon the table by Chancellor Crichton – as a sign of death, an assertion glibly repeated in many histories of Scotland – where does it come from? There is no other recorded instance of this happening, as an indication to unsuspecting diners that their lives are about to be violently truncated. It is an anecdotal appendage to a true and tragic story. Scottish history is rich in such details, and as the patient work of historians sloughs them off the factual record, the national collection of anecdotes, already possessed of Bruce's spider, Jenny Geddes' stool, and James Watt's kettle, grows ever richer. Such things do not belong in history, but have some claim for preservation as part of the national mythology. Knowledge of them, spoken or unspoken, is integral with centuries of Scottish life, thought and writing. Part of the function of this collection, under its thirty-nine headings, is thus to be a Scottish *mythotèque*, though it by no means claims to contain them all.

The modern anecdote began in France, in the seventeenth century, but was quickly picked up in England and, a little later, in Scotland. It is linked to the memoir and the *Essai*, as exemplified by the writing of Montaigne, and to the diary. There is much of the anecdotal in such a seventeenth-century work as James Fraser's *Policratica Temporum*, though written as a record of events; and more in Boswell's *Journal*, in the next century. In the early history of Scottish anecdotage, the prime eighteenth-century figure is Henry Mackenzie, though his collection of *Anecdotes and Egotisms* was not published until the twentieth century. His anecdotes are chiefly based on his personal observation, or on what was told him by older persons; unlike some later anecdotists, he is not an anthologiser, but an observer and a recorder of people and events.

Already in Mackenzie's time the definition of the anecdote was becoming looser. The appetite among readers for such tasty snippets of life was strong, and, since golden ones were in fairly short supply, the currency inevitably became debased. The characters ceased to be distinctive, named individuals and instead became types. The situations, epithets and responses became anonymous and bland. This trend is very clear in the Scottish anecdote. The form began to lose its identity and combined with another established story tradition, that of the jest, the aim of which was humorous rather than informative. Jest books and chap-books which included quaint or humorous stories had been circulating since the mid-sixteenth century. Now, collections of more or less pithy tales accreted around such stock-figures as the laird, the minister, the kenspeckle old wife, and, not least, the village idiot. Many of them celebrate the artlessness of the lower or uneducated elements in society, like the story of the traveller in a country inn, who, provided with a large breakfast, said to the serving girl, 'All I want now is an appetite.' 'Losh, sir', said she, 'I don't know if we have one in the house, but I'll away and ask the cook'. The editors of the *Laird of Logan* collection, which went through numerous editions in the nineteenth century, have several hundred more where that one came from, as does Alexander Hislop's *Scottish Anecdotes*, published in 1857. The indefatigable Robert Chambers produced a collection of *Scottish Jests and Anecdotes* as early as 1832, though his *Scottish Biographical Dictionary* is a far better source of real anecdotal material. But the Grand Anecdotist of the Nineteenth Century is undoubtedly Dean Ramsay, the genial Episcopalian clergyman whose *Reminiscences of Scottish Life and Character* went through many editions, the later ones adorned with genre colour plates of his character types. Ramsay is more selective, his standards a little higher. Nevertheless he and the others, with their relentlessly prosy, sententious, often witless humour, have much to answer for. Patronising, self-admiring, the object of their tales always at one remove from themselves, sucking up to the aristocracy (the more rural lairds can sometimes be laughed at, but lords or dukes never), they wallow with arid satisfaction in the chaff-tub of their own pawkiness. Just as much as the 'Kailyard' novelists, they share responsibility for degrading the intellectual spirit of three generations. 'No expression or allusion having the least tendency to offend correct morals has been admitted', said the editor of the 1863 edition of *Laird of Logan*, which was dedicated to none other than Prince Albert. Yet this literary equivalent of a trouser-legged piano portrays a country inhabited by sly morons, henpecked husbands, drunks, vagrants and ignorant rustic Highlanders with outlandish pronunciation of English, bestridden by dourly high-minded ministers who always get the last word against their admittedly brainless collocutors. There are few jewels amidst all this dross, and not much from these collections is to be found in this one.

A few stories of the generalised, unascribable type so popular in the nineteenth and early twentieth centuries are included. They are here on their merits, and in the interest of making the collection a representative one. There are also one or two entries, like Stuart Piggott's musing on the origins of Scottish song, or young James Clerk Maxwell's inventory of his laboratory, that are scarcely anecdotal, but which, once discovered, were impossible to omit.

Two aspects of the true anecdote have been borne in mind in the compiling of this anthology. The first is intrinsic: the form. An effective anecdote is succinct, holds to its point, and however long or short has an internal unity and energy of its own. The second is extrinsic: anecdotes are items that need to mature before consumption. Episodes from the present or very recent past are too near, too fluid in their associations. Beguiling they may seem, but they must exhibit staying power outside the immediate context to be seen and appreciated in a true perspective. They need to stand a decade or two – then we'll judge their sauce.

There is no end to the collecting of anecdotes, but the reader may feel that an end to the introducing of them is overdue. It only remains to be said that the editor and the publishers will welcome comments and suggestions which will improve the usefulness and enjoyability of future editions.

ANGLERS AND STALKERS

A Conscientious Water-Bailiff

There is a man now, I believe, living in Selkirk, who in times of yore used certain little liberties with the Tweed Act, which did not become the virtue of his office. As a water bailiff he was sworn to tell of all he saw; and indeed, as he said, it could not be expected that he should tell of what he did not see. When his dinner was served up during close time his wife usually brought to the table a platter of potatoes and a napkin; she then bound the latter over his eyes so that nothing might offend his sight. This being done, the illegal salmon was brought in smoking hot, and he fell to, blindfolded as he was, like a conscientious water bailiff – if you know what that is; nor was the napkin taken from his eyes till the fins and bones were removed from the room, and every visible evidence of a salmon having been there had completely vanished: thus he saw no illegal act committed, and went to give in his annual report at Cornhill with his idea of a clear conscience.

William Scrope (1772–1852), Days and Nights of Salmon Fishing in the Tweed *(1843)*

The Poet-Angler of Teviotdale

At the age of 23 he became an Advocate, although he does not appear to have held a brief at any time. His legal training was of some value, however: it enabled him to study with a proper understanding the various complicated Acts of Parliament which dealt with rivers and fishing. His parents, recognising where his real interests lay, provided him with a modest competency so that he could henceforth follow his particular bent and heart's desire. He settled down in Kelso, near to his beloved Tweed and Teviot.

'Well, Tom, and what are you doing now?' asked his old friend Sheriff Glassford Bell.

'Doing? Man, I'm an angler', was Stoddart's swift reply, and an angler he remained to the end of his days.

James Robb, Notable Angling Literature *(1947). Thomas Tod Stoddart (1810–1880) wrote in verse and prose on fishing topics; his angling verses are still appreciated.*

The Bloody Doctor

The loch, to be plain, is almost unfishable. It is nearly round, and everywhere, except in a small segment on the eastern side, is begirt with reeds of great height. These reeds, again, grow in a peculiarly uncomfortable, quaggy bottom, which rises and falls, or rather which jumps and sinks, when you step on it, like the seat of a very luxurious armchair. Moreover, the bottom is pierced with many springs, wherein if you set foot you shall have thrown your last cast.

. . . On this day, by a rare chance, the wind blew from the east, though the sky at first was a brilliant blue, and the sun hot and fierce. I walked round to the east side, waded in, and caught two or three small fellows. It was slow work, when suddenly there began the greatest rise of trout I ever saw in my life. From the edge of the loch as far as one could clearly see across it there was that endless plashing murmur, of all sounds in this world the sweetest to the ear. Within the view of the eye, on each cast, there were a dozen trout rising all about, never leaping, but seriously and solemnly feeding. Now is my chance at last, I fancied; but it was not so – far from it. I might throw over the very noses of the beasts, but they seldom even glanced at the (artificial) fly. I tried them with Greenwell's Glory, with a March brown, with 'the woodcock wing and hare-lug', but it was to almost no purpose . . . From twelve to half past one the gorging went merrily forward, and I saw what the fish were rising at. The whole surface of the loch, at least on the east side, was absolutely peppered with large, hideous insects. They had big grey-white wings, bodies black as night, and brilliant crimson legs, or feelers, or whatever naturalists call them. The trout seemed as if they could not have too much of these abominable wretches, and the flies were blown across the loch, not singly, but in populous groups. I had never seen anything like them in any hookbook, nor could I deceive the trout by the primitive dodge of tying a red thread round the shank of a dark fly. So I waded out, and fell to munching a frugal sandwich and watching Nature, not without a cigarette.

. . . Out in the middle, where few flies managed to float, the trout were at it till dark. But near shore there was just one trout who never stopped gorging all day. He lived exactly opposite the nick in the distant hills, and exactly a yard further out than I could throw a fly. He was a big one, and I am inclined to think he was the Devil. For, if I had stepped in deeper, and the water had come over my wading boots, the odds are that my frail days on earth would have been ended by a chill, and I knew this, and yet that fish went on tempting me to my ruin. I suppose I tried to reach him a dozen times, and cast a hundred, but it was to no avail. At length, as the afternoon grew grey and chill, I pitched a rock at him, by way of showing that I saw through his fiendish guile, and I walked away.

There was no rise now, and the lake was leaden and gloomy. When I reached the edge of the deep reeds I tried, once or twice, to wade through them within casting distance of the water, but was always driven off by the traitorous quagginess of the soil. At last, taking my courage in both hands, I actually got so near that I could throw a fly over the top of the tall reeds, and then came a heavy splash, and the wretched little broken rod nearly doubled up. 'Hooray, here I am among the big ones!' I said, and held on. It was now that I learned the nature of Nero's diversion when he was an angler in the Lake of Darkness. The loch really did deserve the term 'grim'; the water here was black, the sky was ashen, the long green reeds closed cold about me, and beyond them there was a trout that I could not deal with. For when he tired of running, which was soon, he was as far away as ever. Draw him through the forest of reeds I could not. At last I did the fatal thing. I took hold of the line, and then 'plop', as the poet said, he was off. A young sportsman on the bank who had joined me expressed his artless disappointment. I cast over the confounded reeds once more. 'Splash!' – the old story! I stuck to the fish, and got him into the watery wood, and then he went where the lost trout go. No more came on, so I floundered a yard or two further, and climbed into a wild-fowl's nest, a kind of platform of matted reeds, all yellow and faded. The nest immediately sank down deep into the water, but it stopped somewhere, and I made a cast. The black water boiled, and the trout went straight down and sulked. I merely held on, till at last it seemed 'time for us to go', and by cautious tugging I got him through the reedy jungle, and 'gruppit him', as the Shepherd would have said. He was simply but decently wrapped round, from snout to tail, in very fine water-weeds, as in a garment. Moreover, he was black as your hat, quite unlike the comely yellow trout who live on the gravel in Clearburn. It hardly seemed sensible to get drowned in this gruesome kind of angling, so, leaving the Lake of Darkness, we made for Buccleugh, passing the cleugh where the buck was ta'en. Surely it is the deepest, the steepest, and the greenest cleugh that is shone on by the sun! Thereby we met an angler, an ancient man in hodden grey, strolling home from the Rankle burn. And we told him of our bad day, and asked him concerning that hideous fly, which had covered the loch and lured the trout from our decent Greenwells and March browns. And the ancient man listened to our description of the monster, and he said: 'Hoot, ay: ye've jest forgathered wi' the Bloody Doctor.'

Andrew Lang (1844–1912), Angling Sketches (1891). 'The Shepherd' is James Hogg, poet and novelist.

'Gang Quiet, Sir'

The new kind of gillie, who has usually served in the war, can point out a stag with the precision of an artillery observer. The old type used to labour heavily.

'D'ye see yon white stone?' 'I see a million white stones.' 'Ah, but d'ye see another?'

But he often had wonderful phrases. 'Gang quiet, sir,' I remember one telling me. 'Gang quiet, as if ye was something growing.'

John Buchan (1874–1940), Memory-Hold-the-Door (1940)

A Middle-Aged Novelist's First (and Only) Stag

I have only once shot a red deer, and I am fortunate indeed that it did not happen till I was fifty: too late, that is, to form a habit. That excitement was deeper, as the labour to attain it was more strenuous. There was hard walking, for several hours, over a great treeless forest, there was a long stalk that brought no result, for the day was almost breathless but little draughts of air circled about the flanks of the hills, and the deer winded us, and galloped off with that easy, leaping tread that swallows a valley and devours a mountain with no effort. Again we approached them and an aeroplane, an Anson trainer, flew low and frightened them. There was one last chance, said the stalker, and that was to reach the far side of a hill, round whose circumference they seemed to be moving, in time to meet them. And now we really walked. We had not been loitering before, but now we covered the heather in long strides like men who had some purpose of high honour to compel a punctual arrival; and after walking till my heart seemed swollen to the size of a rugby football, I had to crawl, uphill, in soft black peat and keep my head and backside low to the ground and still obey the keeper's injunction to make haste. And when I saw the stag I admitted I could not hit him.

He was couched in the heather and all that showed was his branching head and the back of his neck. He was facing the other way, but a little youngling stag was moving about and sometimes looking towards us. The stalker said there was a hind as well, and the hind would surely wind us, or see us, and give the alarm. But I thought I could not hit the back of a stag's neck, the breadth of a girl's thin hand, at rather more than a hundred yards, and I must wait, I said, till he rose. 'Then for God's sake keep still,' muttered the stalker fiercely. 'There's the hind now,' I whispered, when suddenly she appeared and stood staring straight at me, her long ears a menace of intelligence, her round black eyes a stare of imminent detection. 'Keep still, keep still,' murmured the stalker, a little behind and below me; not fiercely now, but in the voice of a man praying in secret. And for a long minute, with my chin on the peat and a fly tormenting my neck, I endured the accusing gaze of the hind – and then she stamped her foot, and on the instant the stag was up, and for a moment stood superb, his great head high and turned a little towards me, his off fore-leg crooked at the knee for action. I put up my rifle, and fired. I saw the up-flung tail of the hind, and as she disappeared the stag fell sideways in a ponderous, absolute descent.

We ran towards him – 'Re-load,' said the stalker – and there he lay on grey moss and a grey boulder, quite still. We watched him for a few seconds, and he made no movement. He was dead, and I loved him dearly. For a moment, I suppose, I loved myself, and him I loved because he contributed to me. But whatever the niceties and shadows of the sensation, it was both a profound and exalted feeling – profound because its origin lay in the heart of an ancestral Pict, perhaps, and exalted because I had driven my body to an extertion far beyond its custom and killed my stag – my only stag – with the cleanness of instant death.

Eric Linklater (1899–1974), A Year of Space (1953)

Snowdrift

I had been out, on a day of deep, soft snow, stalking hinds. The glen bottom, white and featureless, was empty of deer, and I had to climb the hill face to where a wide flat stretched behind it, a flat seamed and channelled by peat hags. Reaching the top, an unbroken prospect of white stretched before me, every landmark changed and obliterated by the depth of snow, while a spindrift of fine, gritty snow was being wind-blown across it. It was bitterly cold in that wind and I got going across that flat as fast as the clinging depth of snow and stinging head wind would allow. Without warning, about the middle of the flat, I floundered to my knees in seemingly bottomless snow. My rifle was slung on my back or I must have lost it in my sudden fall. Not yet realizing the seriousness of my situation I at once tried to get to my feet, only to find that as soon as I put my weight on one foot I started to sink and could find no purchase or bottom in the snow. I tried to edge myself forward on my knees and again began to sink. Only where I had packed the snow hard below my knees in my fall could I remain without sinking. My next attempt, at crawling out on hands and knees, was wellnigh disastrous. As soon as I put weight on my outstretched widespread hands I sank quickly forward until my face was pressed hard into the white, cold softness, nose and ears full of snow. It was with the utmost difficulty and in near panic that I somehow levered myself back to my former position, on my knees. I had realized by this time where I had landed. I had stumbled in the featurelessness of that white expanse into the middle of a large, deep peat hag which was drifted full of soft snow. I was in a drift of about seven feet of snow with an unknown depth of semi-liquid peat below that. Fear began to oust reason; was I to freeze thus on my knees or struggle and smother in a welter of snow and peat?

No matter how I manoeuvred I simply could not, absurd as it may sound, regain my feet. My fall had taken me well out into the drift, and there it seemed I was stuck. There was no-one out on the winter hills but myself, no shepherd even, as the sheep were lower down. It would be dark before any anxiety was felt, and even then my exact whereabouts would be unknown. Rescue would probably arrive too late; in that wildness of wind-blown snow my tracks would have been covered long ago. Almost in despair I remembered reading of how, in quicksand, one should lie flat and present the largest area of one's body to its softness. Reluctant though I was to try it, remembering all too vividly the suffocating feeling as my face sank in the snow in my attempt at crawling, something had to be tried, and quickly. I unslung my rifle and gripped it at the muzzle with one hand and at the butt with the other. Then I gradually eased forward and extended rifle and arms ahead of me. I pulled and edged myself bodily forward, and to my joy made headway without sinking too much. My progress was painfully slow and to any onlooker must have looked ludicrous, a human frog spreadeagled, breast-stroking his way across the snow.

At length I judged I must be clear of the hag and tentatively essayed a leg below me. What glorious relief to find, after an initial sinking, solid ground below me, and with what care I made for the nearest hard ridge, avoiding like poison any suggestion of drain or hag. So buoyant is the human spirit that I spied, stalked and bagged two hinds from a herd on my way home.

Lea McNally, Highland Year *(1968)*

ANIMALS

Queen Mary's Dog

Then one of the executioners, pulling off her garters, espied her little dog, which was crept under her clothes, which could not be got furth by force, yet afterwards would not depart with the dead corpse, but came and lay between her head and her shoulders, which being imbrued with her blood was carried away and washed, as all things else were that had any blood was either burned or clean washed.

From the official record of Mary I's beheading, February 1587

An Aberdeen Dog-fight

The conflicting religious doctrines of presbyterian and episcopalian, and of course the political doctrines of whig and tory, found in Aberdeen a more equal balance than perhaps in any other part of Scotland... Gibbs being a Roman Catholic, was the friend of neither party, and an object of peculiar antipathy to the presbyterians, who testified their sense of his importance and wickedness, by instructing the children in the neighbourhood to annoy the old gentleman in his premises, and hoot him on the streets. Gibbs, to show his respect for both parties, procured two fierce dogs for his personal protection, and engraved on the collar of the one, 'Luther', and on that of the other, "Calvin"; the compliment was understood by neither party; and the dogs and their master being summoned before the bailies to answer for their respective misdemeanours, the former were delivered over to the proper authorities, and executed according to law, at the cross, the public place of execution.

Robert Chambers, Scottish Biographical Dictionary. *Peter Gibbs, a merchant, was the father of James Gibbs (1682–1754), the celebrated architect.*

Rat-free in Ross-shire

. . . the inhabitants will flatter you with an absurd opinion (an old tradition received from their ancestors) that the earth in Ross hath an antipathy against rats, as the Irish oak has against the spider: And this curiosity, if you please to examine, you may, for the natives do; but had they asserted there are no mice in Ross, every tongue had contradicted them. Now mice and rats are cousins-german, everybody knows that knows any thing, and for the most part they keep house together: But what difference has happened among them here, to make such a feud in this county of Ross, that the rats in Ross should relinquish their country, and give possession wholly to the mice; this is a mystery that I understand not.

Besides this fond opinion of the natives hereabouts, some others more remote (as ignorant as themselves) transport the earth of Ross into most parts of Scotland; perswading themselves, that if they do but sprinkle it in the fields, fens, moors, mountains, morish or boggy ground (all is one as to that) . . . it still retains a certain antipathy against that enormous vermin the rat, nay, the very scent on't shall force him to become an exile. This odd kind of creed they had when I was resident amongst them; yet to the best of my observation I never saw a rat; nor do I remember of any one that was with me ever did; but for mice, I declare, so great is their plenty, that were they a commodity, Scotland might boast on't.

Richard Franck, Northern Memoirs, etc. *(1658), reprinted in P. Hume Brown,* Early Travellers in Scotland *(1891)*

Lord Gardenstone's Pig

Lord Gardenstone seemed to have had two favourite tastes: he indulged in the love of pigs and the love of snuff. He took a young pig as a pet, and it became quite tame and followed him about like a dog. At first the animal shared his bed, but when, growing up to advanced swinehood, it became unfit for such companionship, he had it to sleep in his room, in which he made a comfortable couch for it of his own clothes.

Dean E. B. Ramsay (1793–1872), Reminiscences of Scottish Life and Character. *The Dean claims personal knowledge of Gardenstone's life (d.1793). He was a judge of the Court of Session and the proprietor of Laurencekirk, where he set up an inn, and maintained a visitor's book, until Professor Stuart of Aberdeen inserted the following lines 'in the style of the prophecies of Thomas the Rhymer':*

> Frae sma' beginnings Rome of auld
> Became a great imperial city,
> 'Twas peopled first, as we are tauld,

By bankrupts, vagabonds, banditti.
Quoth Thamas, Then the time may come
When Laurencekirk shall equal Rome.

The 'Ettrick Shepherd' and His Dog

My dog was always my companion. I conversed with him the whole day – I shared every meal with him, and my plaid in the time of a shower; the consequence was, that I generally had the best dogs in all the country. The first remarkable one that I had was named Sirrah. He was beyond all comparison the best dog I ever saw. He was of a surly unsocial temper – disdained all flattery, and refused to be caressed; but his attention to his master's commands and interests never will again be equalled by any of the canine race. . .

I had always about 700 lambs put under my charge every year at weaning time. As they were of the short, or black-faced breed, the breaking of them was a very ticklish and difficult task. I was obliged to watch them night and day for the first four days, during which time I always had a person to assist me. It happened one year, that just about midnight the lambs broke loose, and came up the moor on us, making a noise with their running louder than thunder. We got up and waved our plaids, and shouted, in hopes to turn them, but we only made matters worse, for in a moment they were all round us, and by our exertions we cut them into three divisions; one of these ran north, another south, and those that came up between us, straight up the moor to the westward. I called out, 'Sirrah, my man, they're a' away'; the word, of all others, that set him most on the alert, but owing to the darkness of the night, and the blackness of the moor, I never saw him at all. As the division of the lambs that ran southward were going straight towards the fold, where they had that day been taken from their dams, I was afraid they would go there, and again mix with them; so I threw off part of my clothes, and pursued them, and by great personal exertion, and the help of another old dog that I had besides Sirrah, I turned them, but in a few minutes afterwards lost them altogether. I ran here and there, not knowing what to do, but always, at intervals, gave a loud whistle to Sirrah, to let him know I was depending on him. By that whistling, the lad who was assisting me found me out; but he likewise had lost all trace whatsoever of the lambs. I asked him if he had never seen Sirrah? He said he had not, but that after I left them, a wing of the lambs had come round with a swirl, and that he supposed Sirrah had then given them a turn, though he could not see him for the darkness. We both concluded that whatever way the lambs ran at first, they would finally land at the fold where they left their mothers, and without delay we bent our course towards that; but when we came there, there was nothing of them, nor any kind of bleating to be heard, and we discovered with vexation that we had come on a wrong track.

My companion then bent his course towards . . . the north, and I ran away westward for several miles, along the wild tract where the lambs had grazed when following their dams. We met after it was day, far up in a place called the Black Cleuch, but neither of us had been able to discover our lambs, nor any traces of them. It was the most extraordinary circumstance that had ever occurred in the annals of the pastoral life! We had nothing for it but to return to our master, and inform him that we had lost his whole flock of lambs, and knew not what was become of one of them.

On our way home, however, we discovered a body of lambs at the bottom of a deep ravine, called the Flesh Cleuch, and the indefatigable Sirrah standing in front of them, looking all round for some relief, but still standing true to his charge. The sun was then up; and when we first came in view of them we concluded that it was one of the divisions of the lambs, which Sirrah had been unable to manage until he came to that commanding situation, for it was about a mile and a half distant from the place where they first broke and scattered. But what was our astonishment when we discovered by degrees that not one lamb of the whole flock was wanting! How he had got all the divisions collected in the dark is beyond my comprehension. The charge was left entirely to himself from midnight until the rising of the sun; and if all the shepherds in the Forest had been there to assist him, they could not have effected it with greater propriety. All that I can say farther is, that I have never felt so grateful to any creature below the sun as I did to Sirrah that morning.

James Hogg (1770–1835), The Shepherd's Calendar

'Maida' and Art

Sir Walter Scott, on being asked to sit for his portrait for Terry, the comedian, said that both he and his dog, Maida, were tired of that sort of thing – Maida particularly so; for she had been so often sketched, that whenever she saw an artist unfurl his paper and arrange his brushes, she got up, and walked off with a dignity and an expression of loathing that was almost human.

John Timbs, A Century of Anecdote, 1760–1860 *(1864)*

The Christian and the Lion

The lions here are very numerous and very troublesome, and besides having attacked us here and destroyed some of the cattle of our people, one of them destroyed nine sheep and goats in broad daylight on a little eminence opposite our hut last Wednesday. The natives came screaming to us as we were engaged in the watercourse, and as all operations were immediately suspended I very imprudently ventured across the valley in order to encourage them to destroy him. This very nearly cost me my life, for after he was wounded he rushed down, bit Mabalwe badly on the thigh, another native on the shoulder, and myself on the arm. The humerus is splintered, and his teeth have produced deep wounds which may trouble me for a long time. Had it been directly in the way of duty I should not have cared for the pains, but I have not that consideration to comfort myself by. It was, too, so contrary to my regular rules of acting I don't know what induced me to go. However, I have great cause for thankfulness that I escaped with my life. He shook me as a cat does a mouse, and had the mercy of the Lord not prevented could easily have torn me to peices.

David Livingstone (1813–1873), letter to Robert Moffat, 15 February 1844. This was Livingstone's first account of the incident, also described in his Missionary Travels. *He was writing from his mission station at Mabotsa.*

Bull Terrier Meets Mastiff

. . . the Chicken's blood is up, and his soul unsatisfied; he grips the first dog he meets, but discovering she is not a dog, in Homeric phrase, he makes a brief sort of amende, and is off. The boys, with Bob and me at their head, are after him; down Niddry Street he goes, bent on mischief; up the Cowgate like an arrow, Bob and I, and our small men, panting behind.

There, under the large arch of the South Bridge, is a huge mastiff, sauntering down the middle of the causeway, as with his hands in his pockets: he is old, grey, brindled; as big as a little Highland bull, and has the Shakespearian dewlaps shaking as he goes.

The Chicken makes straight at him, and fastens on his throat. To our astonishment, the great creature does nothing but stand still, hold himself up, and roar – yes roar; a long, serious remonstrative roar. How is this? Bob and I are up to them. He is muzzled! The bailies had proclaimed a general muzzling, and his master, studying strength and economy mainly, had encompassed his huge jaws in a home-made apparatus, constructed out of the leather of some ancient breechin. His mouth was open as far as it could; his lips curled up in rage – a sort of terrible grin; his teeth gleaming, ready, from out of the darkness; the strap across his mouth tense as a bowstring; his whole frame stiff with indignation and surprise; his roar asking us all round, 'Did you ever see the like of this?' He looked a statue of anger and astonishment, done in Aberdeen granite.

We soon had a crowd; the Chicken held on. 'A knife!' cried Bob, and a cobbler gave him his knife: you know the kind of knife, worn away obliquely to a point, and always keen. I put its edge to the tense leather; it ran before it, and then! one sudden jerk of that enormous head, a sort of dirty mist about his mouth, no noise – and the bright and fierce little fellow had dropped, limp and dead. A solemn pause – this was more than any of us had bargained for. I turned the little fellow over, and saw he was quite dead; the mastiff had taken him by the small of the back like a rat, and broken it.

He looked down at his victim, appeased, ashamed, and amazed; snuffed him all over, stared at him, and taking a sudden thought, turned round and trotted off. Bob took the dead dog up and said, 'John, we'll bury him after tea.' 'Yes,' said I, and was off after the mastiff. He made up the Cowgate at a rapid swing: he had forgotten some engagement. He turned up the Candlemaker Row, and stopped at the Harrow Inn.

There was a carrier's cart ready to start, and a keen, thin, impatient, black-a-vised little man, his hand at his grey horse's head, looking about angrily for something. 'Rab, ye thief!' said he, aiming a kick at my great friend, who drew cringing up, and avoiding the heavy shoe with more agility than dignity, and watching his master's eye, slunk dismayed under the cart – his ears down, and as much as he had of tail down too.

What a man this must be – thought I – to whom my tremendous friend turns tail! The carrier saw the muzzle hanging, cut and useless, from his neck, and I eagerly told him the story, which Bob and I always thought, and still think, Homer or King David, or Sir Walter, alone were worthy to rehearse. The severe little man was mitigated, and condescended to say, 'Rab, my man, puir Rabbie' – whereupon the stump of a tail rose up, the ears were cocked, the eyes filled, and were comforted; the two friends were reconciled. 'Hupp!' and a stroke of the whip were given to Jess; and off went the three.

John Brown (1810–1882), Rab and His Friends, *from* Horae Subsecivae *(1858). This story is almost contemporaneous with the tale of 'Greyfriars Bobby', and occupies precisely the same territory, but Dr Brown was first on the scene.*

Horse Psychology

Dr Reid of Peebles . . . a true Philip, a lover of horses, saw one Fair day a black horse, entire, thoroughbred. The groom asked a low price, and would answer no questions. At the close of the fair the doctor bought him, amid the derision of his friends. Next morning he rode him up Tweed, came home after a long round, and had never been better carried. This went on for some weeks; the fine creature was without a fault. One Sunday morning he was posting up by Neidpath at a great pace, the country people trooping into the town to church. Opposite the fine old castle, the thoroughbred stood stock still, and it needed all the doctor's horsemanship to counteract the law of projectiles; he did, and sat still, and not only gave no sign of urging the horse, but rather intimated that it was his particular desire that he should stop. He sat there a full hour, his friends making an excellent joke of it, and he declining, of course, all interference. At the end of the hour, the Black Duke, as he was called, turned one ear forward, then another, looked aside, shook himself, and moved on, his master intimating that this was exactly what he wished; and from that day till his death, some fifteen years after, never did these two friends allude to this little circumstance, and it was never repeated; though it turned out that he had killed his two men previously. . . Had he given the horse one dig with his spurs, or one cut with his whip, or an impatient jerk with his bit, the case would have failed. When a colt it had been brutally used, and being nervous, it lost its judgment, poor thing, and lost its presence of mind.

John Brown, Presence of Mind, *from* Horae Subsecivae

Skuas at Work

. . . the firth, as we expected, was filled with sea-gulls wheeling about in detached flocks and feeding on the shoals of young seth or coal-fish as they 'boiled up', to use the expressive Gaelic phrase, or played here and there along the surface of the rapid, eddying stream. It was an interesting and beautiful sight, but we had seen it hundreds of times before, and it wasn't exactly what we had come to see. In a short time, however, the flock of gulls nearest us was thrown into a state of wild commotion by the arrival in their midst of what we took at first to be a pair of herring-gulls in the dark-grey marbled plumage of last year's birds; but a second and keener look, and the screams of the gulls that scattered in all directions, convinced us that what we took to be young gulls were in truth a pair of skuas – birds which bear about the same relationship to the ordinary gull that the Bedouin Arab of the desert does to the peaceful trading caravan, or rather that the pirate schooner, with her skull and cross-bones flag, bears to the honest merchantman. The skuas were not long in selecting their first victims. Two large black-backed gulls, separating themselves from the rest, flapped and flew away with loud screams of honest execration at the disturbers of their peace, and after them darted the dusky skuas, each coursing his selected victim with all the ardour and all the staunchness of a well-bred hound. The gulls were strong of wing, and in their efforts to outdistance their pursuers, exerted themselves to the utmost, but without avail; the skuas were not to be shaken off. They soon overtook the gulls, and wheeling rapidly above and around them, struck at them and buffeted them unmercifully. . . They stuck to their game right through the centre of the loud-screaming flock, and out and beyond began again to strike and buffet them as before, until at last, thoroughly tired out, and seeing that no better might be, the gulls almost at the same instant vomited in one large half-digested lump all the fish they had caught that morning, which was just what the skuas wanted, for they now poised themselves for a moment, falcon-wise, on quivering wings, and then, with a graceful sweep and lightning-like velocity of descent, they darted each after the falling mass which properly belonged to itself, and cleverly catching them before they touched the water, bore them away with a loud shriek of exultation, to be devoured at leisure somewhere among the solitudes of the opposite shore.

Alexander Stewart ('Nether Lochaber', 1829–1901), 'Twixt Ben Nevis and Glencoe (1885)

Wee Captain

Once this dear little chap saved my life. He and I were on our way to the coal face with a 'rake' of empty hutches. We had to pass a 'drift' – an old working that has fallen in and been cut through, leaving above a fearsome-looking vaulty space some twenty or thirty feet high. I always felt creepy when we came to this great gloomy cavern, and I think Captain did the same. In any case, we always rushed it. But came a time when the pony stopped dead just in front of the drift. Without thinking what I was doing I urged him to get on with the job in hand. He still refused. I gave him a sharp cut with my little whip. Wincing, he looked round and stared me full in the face. 'What's wrong, Captain?' I asked. Simultaneously with the question I heard the most terrifying sound that can assail the miner's ears – the creak and groan of the world above him before the earth and stone comes crashing down to fill the vacuum. Captain turned completely round in his tracks, pulling one of the hutches off the rails, and sought the comparative safety of the tunnel we were just about to leave. I did the same. Next moment five hundred tons of material fell with a noise like thunder into the cavern in front of us. How near we both were to disaster can be judged by the fact that the hutch pulled round off the rails by the pony was afterwards found to be filled with jagged stones and rock! Safe in the tunnel I turned and hugged and kissed Captain again and again. . . Years afterwards I would have given my right hand to be able to buy Captain and present him with his freedom in God's sunlight. But he died in the pit, as he had lived in it. Brave heart! I have forgotten many men and I'll forget many more. I shall never forget 'Wee Captain!'

Sir Harry Lauder (1870–1950), Roaming in the Gloaming (1928). In his youth the great entertainer worked in the coal pits.

An Otter Slide

'Did you ever get a really good view of an otter?' I asked my companion, my thoughts reverting to a fine sea-trout which we had found, earlier in the day, in a sadly mutilated condition in one of the small tributaries.

'I never did,' he admitted, 'no' in all the years I've been on the lochside – an' it's no' that they're no' that plentifu' either. But I'll tell you whit I hev seen,' he continued.

'What?' I asked.

'An otter slide,' he replied.

'An otter slide?' I echoed. 'What's that?'

'Jist whit I'm tellin' ye – an otter slide. . . It wis when I wis a bit laddie in Glesca – ye maun ken I wis an apprentice cabinet-maker in thae days – that I first heard tell o' otters slidin'. Yin o' thae weeklies had aye a bit verse in't, an' yin o' the poems tuk my fancy – me being frae the country, like enough – it wis a' aboot the wilds in the Rockies or some o' thae regions. But there wis wan verse in't aboot otters I couldna un'erstaun'. Whit wis't noo? Aye –

> "The bars, the wolves, they know my track,
> The otters knows my face,
> An' thinks that slidin's risky fun
> When I am near their place."

'That's jist no' hoo it began; but, whit was "otters slidin"?'

'I've really no idea,' I confessed.

'Weel,' said my companion, 'it lang bothered me, an' it wis no' for ten or fifteen year later that I fun' oot. I seen it masel' – Man, there a braw fish up!'

I had been watching it, a great big male, but I had hesitated to interrupt the narrative.

'It wis the winter o' 1885,' he resumed, 'an' auld Hugh an' me had gane oot on the loch for a shot at the duicks, roon' by the Back o' the Ross. It had been snawin' in the nicht, ye ken, an' keepin' the boat close in by the point o' Frechlan, I sees the track o' an otter quite plain, leavin' the loch an' leadin' up the rocks in by the trees. So, comin' hame, efter we'd had a shot or twa – Man, there anither! – I ses tae Hugh, "We'll awa' in by, Hugh, an' pit him oot." So we rin the boat ashore, an' landed jist whaur he'd left the watter, an' we followed his tracks in an' oot an' roon' aboot the trees till we cam' on yin o' thae bare sklents o' rock – An' there wis the otter slide.'

'Really?' I interjected.

'Man, I'm tellin' ye,' – but I had not meant to hint a doubt. 'Richt doon the face o' the rock, mebbe echt fit, mebbe mair, the beast had been slidin' on the snaw. Ye cud see the track whaur he had slid doon, an' then rin aboot the stane, an' up the back o't, an' doon again. He micht a been a wee laddie slidin' doon a brae face. . . Thur wis nae doots aboot it. The lad that writ thur verses kent whit he wis writin' aboot.'

'Do you remember any more of the poem?' I inquired.

'It's birlin' in ma heid,' – my friend knitted his brows – 'but I'll mind it yet. . . It wis ca'd – I min' it noo – "Injun Joe", an' it began: "What odds if

in the settlement . . . I'm only Injun Joe I can gie ye the hale o't the morn',
he added.

Henry Lamond, Days and Ways of a Scottish Angler (*1932*)

An Eagle's Nesting-Place

In a western glen is a rock which bears the name Creag na h-Iolaire, the
Eagle's Rock. For long the rock was empty, then one season the King of
Birds returned to the rock and brought his Queen with him.

It was evening when, after a long walk through the hills, I came in sight
of the Eagle's Rock. Three eaglets had been hatched in the eyrie, and I learned
that this particular eagle had laid three eggs, and had hatched and reared
three young, during each of the six preceding years. On the occasion of my
visit I found that she had again hatched three eaglets, but one of them lay
dead at the edge of the nest; it had probably been pecked to death by the
survivors. During early life golden eaglets are most pugnacious. I have
watched one eaglet daily attack the other, hammering it unmercifully on the
head, neck and back, so that it barely escaped with its life, and have no
doubt that the weaker bird is on occasion actually killed.

Around the two surviving eaglets a feast of food was spread – six mountain hares and two grouse. Although the eaglets were still in white down and
had not grown their feathers, one of them was already fierce and
advanced without hesitation to the attack, waddling across the eyrie and opening its beak wide in defiance. The parent eagles had brought to the eyrie
several green-leaved rowan branches, freshly torn from some distant tree.

Perhaps twenty-five yards from the eyrie was a large boulder, half-
embedded in the heather of the steep hillside. This was evidently used by the
eagles as a site on which to disembowel their pray, for upon it were scattered
the entrails and legs of many hares, some fresh, others old and dried.

My companion told me that this pair of eagles fed almost entirely on
hares, but that on one occasion the previous year he had seen no fewer than
seven grey crows, all neatly skinned, in the eyrie. Since the grey crow is the
arch-enemy of the game preserver, the killing of these pests by the eagle
should be a mark in its favour.

The eagle had left the eyrie, and now gave a fine display of soaring. Higher
and higher she rose, leaaning on the wind, until she disappeared over the
summit of a neighbouring hill. Her mate had by now joined her, and before
they vanished the two sailed in wide spirals. From the hillside opposite I saw
her return, but before this I watched a battle in the eyrie, one eaglet attacking
the other and driving it from the nest on to the ledge. Here it had room to
conceal itself, for the ledge was a broad one, and in places wild hyacinths
were in flower upon it; below the eyrie oak ferns grew among the rocks.

Seton Gordon (*1886–1968*), A Highland Year (*1947*)

'Seobhrag's Begun!'

She had an innate facility for succouring sick animals or people and the house was surrounded by aged dogs, stray cats, a wild goose with a broken wing that fed with her domestic fowls, and a formidable tame ewe called Rachel that had the freedom of the house. It had been rescued as a lamb from a local shepherd who wrongly decided that it was too sickly to survive. There was also an obscene-looking old parrot of unknown age, who lived in a cage in the porch and startled unwary customers with a raucous 'Hullo, darling' when they entered. Four or five ponies grazed with the cows, one of which was a young Highlander due to have her first calf.

One Sunday, at Uilleamena's suggestion, we dressed for a very special dinner – she was a genius at cooking – and afterwards relaxed over coffee and gramophone records. Suddenly the maid burst into the room with an excited cry, 'Miss Macrae, Miss Macrae, Seobhrag's begun!'

There was a bellowing from the byre at the back of the house. In two shakes of a lamb's tail my hostess had pinned up her velvet gown, kicked off the silver slippers, torn off a wrist watch, and in old waterproof coat, wellington boots and a headscarf rushed off to the byre.

About fifteen minutes later the maid came back with the prim message: 'Miss Macrae's compliments, and would you please to come out to the byre and see the new calf?'

I went and found my hostess busily cramming an egg, whole, down the mother's throat, while the new calf, still damp, was trying to jump the wooden partition that divided him from his proud mother's stall.

Helen B. Cruickshank (1886–1975), Octobiography. Miss Uilleamena Macrae kept the inn at Inverailort. Seobhrag, 'Primrose', is a favourite Highland name for a cow.

The Dance of the Petrels

There is no quiet on Rona in summer, day or night; the harsh rattle of the guillemots and shags, the cackle of fulmars, the high-pitched cries of kittiwakes, the coarse complaint of black-backs and the high, chittering scream of Arctic terns, all are blended into a splendid paean in our ears.

There are also the little storm petrels churring in the walls of the fank at night-time, and from midnight on, the sound of the Leach's fork-tailed petrel may be heard . . . usually it was good to get into the shelter of the main house and wait until the first-comers arrived from the sea. Several were flitting about by half-past twelve, then more came in rapid succession, and those already in their burrows in the dry-stone walls began to sing in an ascending trill most pleasant to hear. It seemed to me that more petrels gathered near the place immediately after these trillings. Soon the birds in the air began to scream, but this was no unpleasant sound like that of the

Manx shearwaters. It was a succession of eight or ten notes in a definite cadence and of varying pitch, rather like a staccato, musical laugh. The swift-flying shapes increased in number and the volume of sound grew. We could feel the excitement waxing in this community of little black birds. Their flight is erratic and swift, and when two or three hundred are flying in this way within a restricted space, collisions are common. Our faces were brushed by the soft wings smelling strongly of the characteristic petrel musk. A pitch of excitement is reached after one o' clock in the morning, and the laughter and erratic movements wane before dawn.

How exciting it was for us the first night we went to see and hear this aerial dance! We stood silent a long time, and I was thinking how few people in Britain have experienced this phenomenon of the northern summer night. St Kilda, the Flannans, Sula Sgeir and North Rona; after these you must go to Iceland or Greenland, the Labrador coast or the Aleutian Islands in the Northern Pacific Ocean. I shone a torch into one hole in a dry-stone dyke when I heard that little trill coming forth, and there was the full black eye of the petrel, its lovely grey face and the shining black bill with its nostrils set in a tube above it.

Sir Frank Fraser Darling (1903–1979), Island Years (1940)

Rosie the Cow Comes Home

A man had once told me the story of a cow he had sold to a stalker beyond the mountains. The cow had been driven in stages along the main road – a circuitous route but easy. A few nights after the sale, his wife nudged him awake. 'That's Rosie the cow come home again,' said his wife. 'Don't talk nonsense and go to sleep – wakening me like this!' said he. 'I know her moo,' said his wife. In the end she got him wakened properly, and out he had to go in the grey of the morning. There was Rosie, and she bellowed to him in greeting. Later it was proved beyond doubt that Rosie had taken the short-cut by mountains and through glens she had never seen before, and manifestly had not been troubled by indecision on the way.

Neil M. Gunn (1891–1973), Highland Pack (1949)

Ice, Mink and Moonlight

The snow hadn't come to much, so it was no more than inch-deep, and frozen, and the walking was easy. On our left we passed the wa-gang tracks of a hare, followed the neat prints of a walking fox, then stopped where two roe deer had crossed our front. But there was no sign of them.

I veered off down to the frozen burn. In the burnside trees a tawny owl was calling, but there was nothing moving in the spectral radiance. Until the black shape appeared from under the washed-out roots of a beech tree. . .

I sat down with the dog, holding her close to me for warmth as well as to restrain her in case she had the notion to investigate. The black shape appeared from a clump of white-furred thistles, ferret-like, not cat-like. It bellied low across the ice on the burn, then bounded, weasel-like, back to the beech tree. The moon leered frozenly down; the black fur sheened. The beast was mink-wrapped against the cold. It was a mink.

. . . The minutes froze on, and the temperature dived still further below zero; and the stars winked mirthlessly, and the moon laughed in its sleeve, and the bitch poked my arm with her muzzle, and my big toe sent waves of warning up my tibia and fibula. I was nearing the point where sitting still would be about as easy as not breathing. Then the mink reappeared.

It was going up the bank backwards, like a badger dragging in bedding. But it wasn't dragging bedding. It was dragging a body, a body as big as itself. And the body was a rabbit. It dragged the rabbit under the beech roots. I listened to my toe and rose. I walked, with the bitch at heel, along the middle ice of the burn and stopped opposite the beech tree.

The dog knew as well as I did where the mink was, and I had to *wheesht* her to stay still. I could see nothing, and I could hear nothing. But my nose suddenly owned to a smell I could recognise, the sort of camphory funk scent of a mink. So it had got the dog smell, and my smell, and was letting off.

I left it at that, and walked home on feet I couldn't feel, and with fingers I didn't want to own.

David Stephen, The World Outside (*1983*)

ARMED FORCES

The Escape of Archibald Douglas

Archibald Douglas, having been made prisoner along with the rest, appeared in more sumptuous armour than the other Scottish prisoners; and, therefore, he was supposed by the English to be some great lord. Late in the evening after the battle, when the English were about to strip off his armour, Sir William Ramsay of Colluthy, happening to be present, fixed his eyes on Archibald Douglas, and, affecting to be in a violent passion, cried out, 'You cursed, damnable murderer, how comes it, in the name of mischief, that you are thus proudly decked out in your master's armour? Come hither, and pull off my boots!' Douglas approached trembling, kneeled down, and pulled off one of the boots. Ramsay, taking up the boot, beat Douglas with it. The English bystanders, imagining him out of his senses, interposed, and rescued Douglas. They said that the person whom he had beaten was certainly of great rank, and a lord. 'What, he a lord?' cried Ramsay; 'he is a scullion, and a base knave, and, as I suppose, has killed his master. Go, you villain, to the field, search for the body of my cousin, your master, and when you have found it, come back, so that at least I may give him a decent burial.' Then he ransomed the feigned serving-man for forty shillings; and, having buffeted him smartly, he cried, 'Get you gone: fly.' Douglas bore all this patiently, carried on the deceit, and was soon beyond the reach of his enemies.

Lord Hailes (1726–1792), Annals of Scotland. *The two kinsmen had been fighting on opposite sides at the Battle of Poitiers, 1356.*

General Tam Dalyell Comes to London

He was bred up very hardy from his youth, both in diet and in clothing. He never wore boots, nor above one coat, which was close to his body, with close sleeves. . . He never wore a peruke, nor did he shave his beard since the murder of King Charles the first. In my time his head was bald, which he covered only with a beaver hat, the brim of which was not above three inches broad. His beard was white and bushy, and yet reached down almost to his girdle. He usually went to London once or twice in a year, and then only to kiss the king's hand, who had a great esteem for his worth and valour. His unusual dress and figure when he was in London never failed to draw after him a great crowd of boys and other young people, who constantly attended at his lodgings, and followed him with huzzas as he went to court or returned from it. As he was a man of humour, he would always thank them for their civilities, when he left them at the door to go into the king; and would let them know exactly at what hour he intended to come out again and return to his lodgings. When the king walked in the park, attended by some of his courtiers, and Dalyell in his company, the same crowds would always be after him, showing their admiration at his beard and dress, so that the king could hardly pass on for the crowd; upon which his majesty bid the devil take Dalyell, for bringing such a rabble of boys together, to have their guts squeezed out, while they gaped at his long beard and antic habit; requesting him at the same time (as Dalyell used to express it) to shave and dress like other christians, to keep the poor bairns out of danger. All this could never prevail on him to part with his beard; but yet, in compliance to his majesty, he once went to court in the very height of fashion; but as soon as the king and those about him had laughed sufficiently at the strange figure he made, he reassumed his usual habit, to the great joy of the boys, who had not discovered him in his fashionable dress.

Memoirs of Captain Creichton, 17th century, *quoted in Robert Chambers, Scottish Biographical Dictionary. Chambers notes that Dalyell's beardcomb was preserved at his home, The Binns. It was a foot wide, with teeth six inches deep.*

General Hugh Mackay and the Bayonet

Casting aside their plaids and other impediments, the line set forward in characteristic fashion, and with a loud and ringing shout which told of assured victory. With their fire, especially on the right wing, the Covenanters did much execution, but the Highlanders sped on without flinching, and reserved their fire till they were close at hand, when they poured in a murderous volley. Then, casting away their firelocks, they rushed down the incline, broadsword in hand, and hurled themselves upon the enemy ere the latter had succeeded in unscrewing their unhandy bayonets. . . It should be remembered, to the credit of General Mackay, that the lesson taught by the battle led to his devising the simple plan of fixing the bayonet by means of a socket to the outside of the barrel, instead of being inserted in the inside as formerly – one of the most important inventions of war.

Dugald Mitchell, History of the Highlands and Gaelic Scotland *(1900). The reference is to the Battle of Killiecrankie in 1689, when a Highland force under Viscount Dundee defeated the government army led by Hugh Mackay of Scourie.*

The Marshal Meets the Grand Vizier

In 1739, the Russians and Turks, who had been at war, met to conclude terms of peace. The commissioners were Marshal Keith for the Russians and the Grand Vizier for the Turks. These two personages met, and carried on their negotiations by means of interpreters. When all was concluded they rose to separate, but just before leaving the Grand Vizier suddenly went to Marshal Keith, and, taking him cordially by the hand, declared in the broadest Scotch dialect that it made him 'unco' happy to meet a countryman in his exalted station'. As might be expected, Keith, who was himself a Scotsman in the service of Russia, stared with astonishment, and was eager for an explanation of the mystery. 'Dinna be surprised,' the Grand Vizier exclaimed; 'I'm o' the same country wi' yoursell, mon! I mind weel seein' you and your brother, when boys, passin' by to the school at Kirkaldy; my father, sir, was bellman o' Kirkaldy.'

James Settle, Anecdotes of Soldiers in Peace and War *(1905). James Keith (1696–1758), brother of the Earl Marischal, was a major-general in the Russian army, and later a Prussian field marshal. The Grand Vizier is a hazier figure altogether, though interestingly, one Thomas Keith of the 78th Highlanders (The Ross-shire Buffs), taken prisoner in Egypt in 1807, converted to Islam, and became governor of the holy city of Medina. The anecdote may be a conflation of the two men's stories.*

Breaking the Line

The revolutionary manoeuvre of 'breaking the line' – cutting across the battle line of an enemy fleet and bombarding it from both sides – was developed by the Royal Navy in the eighteenth century. Two Scotsmen claimed credit for this concept – one was the land-bound naval theoretician John Clerk of Eldin, the other was Sir Charles Douglas, captain of Admiral Sir George Rodney's flagship *Formidable* at the battle of the Isle of Saints in 1782.

Being one of the aides-de-camp to the commander-in-chief on that memorable day, it was my duty to attend both on him and the captain of the fleet, as occasion might require. It so happened, that some time after the battle had commenced, and whilst we were severely engaged, I was standing near Sir Charles Douglas, who was leaning on the hammocks . . . his head leaning on his one hand, and his eye occasionally glancing on the enemy's line, and apparently in deep meditation, as if some great event were crossing his mind: suddenly raising his head, and turning quickly round, he said, 'Dash, where's Sir George?'

'In the after-cabin, Sir,' I replied. He immediately went aft: I followed and on meeting Sir George coming from the cabin, close to the wheel, he took off his cocked hat with his right hand, holding his long spy-glass in his left, and, making a low and profound bow, said, 'Sir George, I give you joy of the victory!'

'Poh!' said the chief, as if half angry, 'the day is not half won yet.'

'Break the line, Sir George!' said Douglas, 'the day is your own, and I will ensure you the victory.'

'No,' said Sir George, 'I will not break my line.' After another request and another refusal, Sir Charles desired the helm to be put a-port; Sir George ordered it to starboard. On Sir Charles again ordering it to port, the admiral sternly said, 'remember, Sir Charles, that I am commander-in-chief – starboard, Sir,' addressing the master, who during this controversy had placed the helm amidships. The admiral and captain then separated; the former going aft, and the latter going forward. In the course of a couple of minutes or so, each turned and again nearly met on the same spot, when Sir Charles quietly and coolly again addressed the chief – 'Only break the line, Sir George, and the day is your own.' The admiral then said in a quick and hurried way, 'Well, well, do as you like,' and immediately turned round, and walked into the after cabin. The words 'Port the helm' were scarcely uttered, when Sir Charles ordered me down with directions to start firing on the starboard side. On my return to the quarter deck, I found the *Formidable* passing between two French ships, each nearly touching us. We were followed by the *Namur*, and the rest of the ships astern, and from that moment the victory was decided in our favour.

Sir Charles Dashwood, quoted in Robert Chambers, Scottish Biographical Dictionary

Duchess Jean Goes Recruiting

Her only surviving son, George, Marquis of Huntly, entered the army early in life. To assist him in raising his regiment, the 92nd Highlanders, it is reported of her that she headed a recruiting party in the Highlands, and at the fairs, dressed in plaid and Highland bonnet with sword in hand, she held a shilling in her teeth, and every handsome Highlander she saw in the crowd she enlisted by placing it in his mouth.

Joseph Mitchell (1803–1883), Reminiscences of My Life in the Highlands. *Jane Maxwell, glamorous and unconventional, 'The Flower of Galloway', married the fourth Duke of Gordon.*

Admiral Duncan Deals with a Mutineer

On 13th May . . . there was a serious rising on board the *Adamant*, but it was not of long duration. The Admiral proceeded on board, hoisted his flag, and mustered the company. 'My lads,' he said, 'I am not in the least degree apprehensive of any violent measures you may have in contemplation; and though I assure you I would rather acquire your love than incur your fear, I will with my own hands put to death the first man who shall display the slightest signs of rebellious conduct.' He then demanded to know if there was any man aboard who dared to presume to question or dispute the authority of his officers or himself. One man pushed his way forward and said in an insolent voice, 'I do!' Duncan raised his mighty arm and seizing the mutineer by the collar swept him off the deck and lifted him bodily over the side. He held him suspended there by one arm and turning to the ship's company he said, 'My lads, look at this fellow who dares to deprive me of the command of the fleet.'

Geoffrey Callender, Sea Kings of Britain *(1924). This was in 1797. Despite his stern view of duty, the Dundee-born Duncan was a popular and compassionate figure among the seamen, and his attitude to them helped him to victory over the Dutch at Camperdown later that year.*

Steadiness Under Fire

In the landing near Pigeon Island, he was among the first who jumped ashore, under a heavy fire of grape and round shot from a battery so posted as to almost sweep the beach. 'A cannon-ball', says he, in a letter addressed to Sir John Sinclair, 'passed Lord Hopetoun's left shoulder, and over my head. He observed that a miss was as good as a mile, to which I cordially agreed; and added, that it was fortunate for me that I was only five feet six inches; as if I were like him, six feet five inches, I would have been a head shorter.'

Robert Chambers, Scottish Biographical Dictionary, *quoting Major-General David Stewart of Garth (1772–1829), in a recollection of Sir Ralph Abercromby's West Indian Expedition of 1796*

The Death of Sir John Moore

. . . Sir John Moore was struck to the ground by a cannon-ball, which lacerated his left shoulder and chest.

He had half-raised himself when Hardinge, having dismounted, caught his hand, and the general grasped his strongly, and gazed with anxiety at the Highlanders, who were fighting courageously; and when Hardinge said, 'They are advancing,' his countenance lightened.

Colonel Graham now came up, and imagined, from the composure of the General's features, that he had only fallen accidentally, until he saw blood welling from his wound. Shocked at the sight, he rode off for surgeons. Hardinge tried in vain to stop the effusion of blood with his sash; then, by the help of some Highlanders and Guardsmen, he placed the General upon a blanket. In lifting him, his sword became entangled, and Hardinge endeavoured to unbuckle the belt to take it off, when he said with soldierly feelings, 'It is as well as it is; I had rather it should go out of the field with me.'

His serenity was so striking, that Hardinge began to hope the wound was not mortal; he expressed his opinion, and said that he trusted the surgeons would confirm it, and that he would still be spared to them.

Sir John turned his head and cast his eyes steadily on the wounded part, and then replied, 'No, Hardinge, I feel that to be impossible . . .'

The soldiers had not carried Sir John Moore far, when two surgeons came running to his aid. They had been employed in dressing the shattered arm of Sir David Baird, who, hearing of the disaster which had occurred to the commander, generously ordered them to desist, and hasten to give him help. But Moore, who was bleeding fast, said to them, 'You can be of no service to me: go to the wounded soldiers, to whom you may be useful'; and he ordered the bearers to move on. But as they proceeded, he repeatedly made them turn round to view the battle, and to listen to the firing, the sound of which, becoming gradually fainter, indicated that the French were retreating.

The Life of Lieutenant-General Sir John Moore, Vol. 2 (*1834*). *Moore's death, in the successful rearguard action at Corunna, occurred on 16 January 1809.*

Marshal MacDonald Visits the Field of Culloden

The marshal, having carefully examined the ground and position of the respective armies, asked, 'Where was the artillery?' He was told that there was virtually no artillery. 'What! No artillery?' said the marshal, and then added, 'Where was the cavalry?' and was answered, 'There was no cavalry.' Upon this he became greatly excited, struck his forehead with his clenched fist, and exclaimed, 'Those idiots of generals, les perruques, if they had brought out these men on purpose to be slaughtered they would have done exactly what they did. They would have led them into these open moors without cavalry and practically without artillery against an enemy supplied with both.' Then, turning round and pointing to the mountains in the south-west, he continued, 'Why not occupy these fastnesses? Who can tell how long our brave Highlanders in their vantage ground might have kept the English at bay?'

Inverness Courier, 18 February 1875, quoted in Joseph Mitchell (1803–1883), Reminiscences of My Life in the Highlands. MacDonald was the son of the Jacobite exile Neil MacDonald. Brought up as a Frenchman, he became one of Napoleon's Marshals and the Duke of Tarentum. His visit to the land of his fathers was made in 1825.

Conqueror of Sind

It was, and still is, the custom in the British army for the general to list in his after-action reports the names of officers who distinguished themselves. Such officers were said to have been mentioned in dispatches. After his battles in Sind, Napier not only gave the names of officers who had been particularly brave but also, for the first time in British history, listed the names of men from other ranks, both British and Indian, who had performed valiantly.

Byron Farwell, Eminent Victorian Soldiers (1985). Sir Charles James Napier (1782–1853), is often credited with the Latin message Peccavi ('I have sinned') to announce his conquest of the Indian province of that name. In fact it was invented for him by Punch.

The Thin Red Line

Five hundred and fifty men of the Argylls and 100 invalids were now left to stand between the Russian army and Balaclava, and Sir Colin rode down the line telling them, 'Men, remember there is no retreat from here. You must die where you stand.'

To the Russian cavalry as they came on, the hillock appeared unoccupied, when suddenly, as if out of the earth, there sprang up a line two deep of Highlanders in red coats – the line immortalised in British history as 'the thin red line'. Every man in that line expected to be killed and, determined to sell his life as dearly as possible, faced the enemy with stern steadiness.

The Russians were taken aback. Their intelligence service was quite as inadequate as the British; they had no idea of the strength and disposition of the British troops and they suspected once more that they had fallen into an ambush. Indeed the gorge ahead would have been perfect for that purpose had the idea of an ambush ever occurred to the British command.

The Russian cavalry checked, halted, and from the thin red line came a volley of the deadly musket-fire, every bullet aimed, which formation in line made possible. The Russians wavered, steadied, advanced, and a second volley was fired. Once more the Russians wavered, and such was the eagerness of the Argylls that there was a movement forward; the men wanted to dash out and engage the enemy hand to hand, and Sir Colin Campbell was heard shouting sternly, 'Ninety-third! Ninety-third! Damn all that eagerness.' The British line steadied, a third volley was fired, and the Russians wheeled and withdrew in the direction of the main body of their cavalry. The Highlanders burst into hurrahs. Balaclava, for the moment, was saved.

Cecil Woodham Smith, The Reason Why *(1957)*

'Fighting Mac' and the Dervishes

By eight o'clock it seemed to Kitchener that the battle was over, and he ordered the cease-fire to be sounded. Half an hour later most of the brigades and batteries had swung into marching columns and were echeloned across the plain, moving towards Omdurman. Kitchener thought the Dervish army had been destroyed. He was wrong.

Macdonald's brigade was to bring up the rear of the army, and he had not yet put his four battalions into marching order when a screaming mass of 15,000 men of the Khalifa Abdullahi bin Said Mohammed's bodyguard, hand-picked fanatics, emerged from a series of rolling sand-hills. Only Macdonald's brigade stood between them and the marching columns. While Kitchener, in a white heat, flew about, trying to reverse his army and put it back into fighting formations, Macdonald coolly steadied his men and beat off the attack. No sooner was this accomplished than another, even larger, force of Dervishes appeared from a new direction. Macdonald moved his troops with parade-ground precision to meet this new threat. It was a difficult manoeuvre carried out in the presence of an aggressive enemy that outnumbered his own brigade by more than seven to one.

. . . Macdonald had clearly saved the day and was the hero of the hour. The correspondents fell over themselves in praising him. One reported that Macdonald had received an order to retreat but had said, 'I'll no do it. I'll see them damned first. We maun just fight!'

Byron Farwell, Eminent Victorian Soldiers *(1985). Sir Hector Macdonald (1853–1903), born at Rootfield on the Black Isle, rose from the ranks to become a major-general.*

Flanders, May 1915

We were in our places by 1 a.m. The whine of a shell came down to us on the wind. Flares from the enemy, bathing the earth in a cold, white glare, disclosed little. Mounds looked like men, and distant avenues of trees like massed battalions. Fears too fantastic to be real assailed the faint of heart. Our nerves, strung to the highest pitch, kept us constantly peering over the parapet. Our ignorance was phenomenal. We did not know at what distance lay the enemy. Some were unaware even of the enemy's direction! We longed for dawn to come. About 2 a.m., above the sullen roar of the guns, pealed a terrific blast of thunder. The lightning flashed down the bayonets with a weird effect. As it was dawning a little more could be distinguished – an open field of fire of about 600 yards, torn up by shells, and a frontage of ruins. A group of trees on the left, sadly shattered and stripped of their branches and leaves, alone mitigated the loneliness of these waste places. The dead lay thick in front. . . As day advanced we became more and more accustomed to our surroundings. Our neighbours on either flank were the 5th Seaforths and the 7th Black Watch. They, too, had experienced the same initial difficulties. We were tyros in those days. Whenever we heard a shell approaching we jumped up to see it burst. Appreciative or deprecating remarks greeted each missile. 'That was a good one!' . . . 'bad shot, Fritz, try again!' . . . and so on, *usque ad nauseam.*

Robert B. Ross, The Fifty-First in France (*1918*)

Doctors at War

. . . when preparing for the Passchendaele battle, a group of medical officers in our division met unofficially to exchange ideas. One difficulty was that of getting water to the front line. Most of the men had nearly emptied their water bottles owing to their thirst after sweating on the march carrying heavy loads in the sunshine. It was suggested that the stretcher bearers who were going up to the line with empty stretchers should take a full petrol can of water up with them, and when the water was finished the empty tin could be put on a stretcher going back with a wounded man until it reached the place where the wounded were transferred to the Red Cross vehicles taking them to hospital and where there was always a watering point. The refilled petrol cans could then come up again with the empty stretchers. When this was suggested to the Chief Medical Officer of the division he said it was impossible. We replied that water was the most urgently needed medical comfort, especially for wounded men who had lost blood, and could well be regarded as a Red Cross medical necessity. 'But', said he, 'it is against the army regulations for water to be carried in an ambulance vehicle.' One of us, being a little impertinent, suggested that if the driver would stick it under his seat neither the Secretary of State for War nor the King would know anything about it. At this the Chief lost his temper and said, 'By God, sir, I will have you sent home.' There was a roar of laughter: there was nothing the medical officers wanted more than to get home!

Lord Boyd Orr (1880–1971), As I Recall (1966). Boyd Orr's point was that in this as in other matters, the volunteer and conscripted officers were far more flexibly minded than the regulars, and that the winning of the war was largely due to this.

Admiral Cunningham in the Mediterranean

Had Italy thrown all her forces into battle with Admiral Cunningham's fleet in the opening stages of the Mediterranean war it is difficult to see how the enemy could have failed to establish complete domination of the Mediterranean, seize the Suez Canal and so link up with the Italian forces in the Red Sea, and carry the war across the Arab world to India while severing the British Empire's eastern lifeline. . .

This was the prospect with which Andrew Cunningham was faced. The cards were heavily stacked against him, but he was far from being intimidated. He was quite determined that the enemy should not have things their own way, however much they held the geographical and material advantage.

> He either fears his fate too much,
> Or his deserts are small,
> Who dare not put it to the touch
> To win or lose it all.

Those lines, written by James Graham, Marquis of Montrose, in the first half of the seventeenth century, sustained another Scot, Admiral Cunningham, three hundred years later. They hung on the bulkhead of Admiral Duncan's cabin in his flagship, HMS *Warspite*.

Cunningham's interpretation of these lines was the reverse of an exhortation to take the unjustified risks of a desperate gambler. It was by bold but calculated action that he saved the situation in the Mediterranean and established first a moral ascendancy over the enemy, and then set about destroying the enemy's material superiority.

Kenneth Edwards, Men of Action (1943). When Cunningham (1883–1963) was twelve, his father sent him a telegraph: 'Would you like to join Royal Navy?' The boy replied: 'Yes. Would very much like to be an Admiral.'

ART AND ARTISTS

William Berry Rises to a Challenge

In this department (the cutting of heraldic seals) he was, without dispute, the first artist of his time, but even here that modesty which was so peculiarly his own, and that invariable desire of giving perfection to everything he put out of his hand, prevented him from drawing such emoluments from his labours as they deserved. Of this the following anecdote will serve as an illustration, and as an additional testimony of his very great skill. Henry, Duke of Buccleuch, on succeeding to his title and estates, was desirous of having a seal cut, with his arms properly blazoned upon it. But as there were no fewer than thirty-two compartments in the shield, which was of necessity confined to a very small space so as to leave room for the support-ers and other ornaments, within the compass of a seal of ordinary size, he found it a matter of great difficulty to get it executed. Though a native of Scotland himself, the noble Duke had no idea that there was a man of first-rate eminence in this art in Edinburgh; and accordingly he had applied to the best seal-engravers in London and Paris, all of whom declared it to be beyond their power. At this time, Berry was mentioned to him with such powerful recommendations that he was induced to pay him a visit, and found him, as usual, seated at his wheel. The gentleman who had men-tioned Mr Berry's name to the Duke, accompanied him on his visit. This person, without introducing the Duke, showed Mr Berry the impression of a seal which the Duchess-Dowager had got cut a good many years before, by a Jew in London, now dead, and which had been shown to others as a pattern, asking him if he would cut a seal the same size as that. After exam-ining it a little, Mr Berry answered readily that he would. The Duke, at once pleased and astonished, exclaimed, 'Will you, indeed?' Mr Berry, who thought this implied some doubt of his ability to perform what he under-took, was a little piqued, and turning round to the Duke, whom he had never before seen, he said, 'Yes, Sir; if I do not make a better seal than this, I will charge no payment for it.' The Duke, highly pleased, left the pattern with Mr Berry, and went away. The original contained, indeed, the various devices of the thirty-two compartments distinctly enough to be seen; but none of the colours were expressed. Mr Berry, in proper time, finished the seal, on which the figures were not only done with superior elegance, but the colours on every part so distinctly marked that a painter could delineate the whole, or a herald blazon it, with perfect accuracy. For this extraordinary and most ingenious labour, he charged no more than thirty-two guineas, though the pattern seal had cost seventy-five.

Robert Chambers, Scottish Biographical Dictionary. Berry lived from 1730–1783, and was also a portrait-engraver of great accomplishment.

The Foulis Art Collection

In 1753 the brothers Robert and Andrew Foulis, who had begun as the University's printers, established in one of the College's largest rooms an acad-emy for the training of painters, sculptors, and engravers. . . As samples of the highest excellence Robert, an ardent if somewhat gullible collector, accumulated some 450 pictures including thirty-eight which he believed to be by Raphael, twenty-one by Titian, thirty-five by Rubens, eight by Rembrandt, and others, in smaller quantities, labelled as by Leonardo, Michelangelo, Correggio, Andrea del Sarto, Veronese, Tintoretto, Poussin, Claude, Van Dyck and Bruegel. The venture, with a catalogue that read like a dictionary of artists, was, of course, absurdly over-ambitious. After Robert Foulis's death and the academy's demise in 1776, the collection was sold at Christie's where, even in an age when grandiose attributions were more acceptable than they are today, it realized a paltry £398 5s.

Andrew Mclaren Young, Glasgow University Pictures *(Introduction to an Exhibition at Colnaghi's, 1973). This was the academy whose faltering existence James Boswell discussed with Voltaire, who remarked that it is hard to paint when your feet are cold.*

Andrew Geddes at the Art Auction

Although his inclination for the profession of a painter was not encouraged, he devoted all his spare time to the study of art, rising at four o'clock in the morning in summer, for the purpose of drawing and painting, his studio being an attic adjoining his bedroom.

Even at this time he was a collector of prints, and constantly attended the print sales of Mr William Martin, bookseller and auctioneer in Edinburgh. This personage was a character in his way. He had been bred a shoemaker, but like the celebrated Lackington of London, became a bookseller, and held a regular auction-mart of prints and old books. He knew the general extent of funds of young Geddes, and when a lot of prints were generally going for ninepence or tenpence, he would encourage him by such words as 'Noo, my bonny wee man – noo's your time,' and, on the contrary, would give him a most significant shake of the head when he saw him looking wistfully after a lot that seemed likely to bring a higher sum.

W. Anderson, Scottish Nation, *1863. Andrew Geddes (1783–1844), painter and etcher, spent most of his working life in London.*

Duncan Grant Hoaxes the Admiralty

As a young man Duncan Grant showed extraordinary high spirits. The most striking manifestation was his participation in the 'Dreadnought' hoax of 1910. With Horace Cole, the instigator, Adrian Stephen and his sister, Virginia, he spent two or three hours disguised as an Abyssinian notable, after a telegram, purporting to have come from the Admiralty, advised the Captain of the visitors' arrival. They were shown the wireless, then regarded as a species of 'secret weapon', but owing to their make-up they did not dare accept an invitation to luncheon. The exploit startled the whole country and echoed round the world. Duncan Grant apologised to the First Lord of the Admiralty, Reginald MacKenna. King Edward was greatly distressed and expressed the hope that none of the culprits would ever come to Court.

Sir John Rothenstein, Modern English Painters, Volume II (1956). Duncan Grant (1885–1978) was a prominent member of the Bloomsbury literary/artistic group. The telegram was purportedly from the Foreign Office, not the Admiralty. In the heat of the battleship's interior, Grant's moustache almost came off. His biographer, Frances Spalding (Duncan Grant, 1998) records an aftermath, when three officers from HMS Dreadnought briefly abducted Grant, intending to give him a beating. Discountenanced by his mild behaviour, they gave him two token taps and offered him a lift home.

James McBey Wins a Prize

Every July a Flower Show was held in the village Public Hall. Prizes were offered by various patrons for the best vegetables or fruit or flowers. The village grocer, Willie Murray, offered one year a prize of 2s 6d for a drawing of the local antiquity – the ruined keep, Knockhall Castle, built in 1565 – with the cautious proviso that the winning drawing 'would become the property of the donor'.

Furtively I studied that ruin until I had memorized it.

At home I got a large sheet of cartridge paper, made the outlines and painstakingly filled in between with as stony-looking stones as I knew how. I knew it would improve it vastly if only I could make one part of the ruin look near and the other recede, but how to do this? The subtleties of perspective and chiaroscuro were unknown to me. Anyway, it was unmistakably Knockhall Castle. Meticulously I printed my name in the bottom corner. Misgivings assailed me as I took it, rolled in a newspaper, to the show. I felt I was exposing myself, naked, to the eyes of a hostile world.

It won the prize. There were no other entries.

When the show opened, there it was, pinned on the wall with, on it, an impressive prize label. Apart from the 2s 6d, which meant wealth to me, the effect produced was astonishing. Sacrosanct dignitaries of the village who, till now, would not have seen me had they looked my way, graciously bestowed on me words of recognition and congratulation.

James McBey (1883–1959), The Early Life of James McBey, Nicolas Barker (ed.) (1977). McBey noted, sadly, that the one person who uttered no word of praise or interest was his mother. He began work in an Aberdeen bank, but later became an artist and etcher of distinction.

MacIan's Singing

... he was a clever reciter of Scottish songs, being especially great in 'Donald Caird' and 'We arena fou'. The latter song he at one time interpreted so naturally in the house of the late Mr S. C. Hall, that the servant made a confidential enquiry to his master as to whether he ought to procure a cab to convey the gentleman home.

Robert Brydall, Art in Scotland *(1889). Robert Ronald MacIan (d.1856), was the artist of the much-reproduced* Costumes of the Clans, *the publication of which began in 1843.*

The Discovery of 'The Four'

In 1896, the English Arts and Crafts Society invited a Glasgow group of designers, known as 'The Four', to show their work at its annual London exhibition. The four were the sisters Frances and Margaret Macdonald, with Herbert MacNair and Charles Rennie Mackintosh.

Their work raised a storm of protest from public and critics alike. Everyone was shocked ... except Gleeson White, editor of *The Studio*... The English Arts and Crafts society, however, maintained its attitude of scornful derision, and the Scottish designers were not invited again to exhibit south of the Border.

When the exhibition ended, White determined to visit Glasgow and meet the artists on their own ground, to discover if possible their aims and objectives, and to find the sources on which they drew for inspiration. He travelled north with an open mind and, no doubt, not a little curiosity, for he comments later on the 'legend of a critic from foreign parts' who attempted to deduce the character and apppearance of the Macdonald sisters from their works – they were visualised as 'middle-aged sisters, flat-footed, with projecting teeth and long past the hope (which in them was always forlorn) of matrimony, gaunt unlovely females'. In all probability White too imagined the artists as a coterie of languid aesthetes, if not middle-aged, at least effete sophisticates, surrounded by *objets d'art* from Egypt and the Orient, and brooding over Swinburne and Wilde. Instead, he found 'two laughing comely girls, scarce out of their teens' and a pair of serious architectural draughtsmen with a penchant for decorative arts and craftwork.

Thomas Howarth, Charles Rennie Mackintosh and the Modern Movement *(1952). Soon afterwards, MacNair married Frances and Mackintosh married Margaret. White's enthusiastic support was instrumental in arousing European interest in the work of the Glasgow designers and of Mackintosh in particular.*

Charles Rennie Mackintosh – Spy

As soon as war was declared stringent security regulations were imposed on the East Anglian coastal areas. Every stranger was treated with suspicion and many artists immediately left the district; in any case the summer visitors usually departed by the end of September at the latest. The Mackintoshes, however, stayed on through October, November and December. They could not go back to Glasgow and as yet had no definite plans for the future. During the day they worked hard in a tiny studio by the river and in the evenings went for long walks into the country. The unaccountable presence of the two strangers, both speaking with a foreign accent – the pleasant vernacular of Central Scotland being a rarity in the marshlands of Suffolk – and wandering about the countryside at dusk, soon aroused suspicion, and brought them under observation as enemy agents.

Mackintosh's taciturn manner, swarthy complexion, drooping eyelid and pronounced limp, and, most of all, his openly acknowledged friendships in Austria, added to this impression, and the police began to take an active interest in his movements. On returning from a walk one evening the artists found a soldier guarding their lodgings: all their papers had been examined and some correspondence with the Viennese Secessionists discovered. Their explanations were unavailing and, to his chagrin, Mackintosh was summoned to appear before a local tribunal. This he did, and only with difficulty was he able to establish his *bona fides*. In fact Professor Patrick Geddes of Edinburgh sent his daughter, now Lady Norah Mears, to the War Office to speak with the authorities on his behalf. Mackintosh, needless to say, was bitterly affronted at the injustice of the charge, and could hardly be restrained from taking the matter to a higher court.

Thomas Howarth, Charles Rennie Mackintosh and the Modern Movement. *In summer and autumn 1914 the Mackintoshes were staying in the Suffolk village of Walberswick.*

'The Call'

To travel to Edinburgh in bitter weather for the express purpose of spending some silent moments beside the soldier statue in Princes Street Gardens may seem to some mere eccentricity of sentiment.

That Dickensian spectacle of snow-clad Edinburgh, busy with Christmas shopping, was delightful; but it did not lift the queer dowieness that lay upon my thoughts. There was something I had to do ere I could enter into the jollity of that charming scene.

Beside the wicket opening from the street into the whitely glimmering gloom of the Gardens I could imagine myself saying to a stranger, 'I have to go in here for a little. I've to see someone. Will you mind my leaving you? I want to be my lonesome.'

Not even the indescribably noble and pathetic Shrine at the Castle can touch the war-scarred heart of Scotland as does the figure of the well set-up bonnie soldier lad, bareheaded and solitary, sitting with his rifle on his knee, looking up to the Castle, listening and eagerly ready for 'The Call' – the bugle clarion that summoned him to sacrifice.

If ever sculptor's vision and skill made bronze to live, it is in that soldier figure all alone, though so close to the crowds that pour along the most beautiful street in the world. The frosty snow lay on his bare head, in his kilted lap and on the hands that grasped the ready rifle. Christmas had come to 'our lad'. It was bitterly cold where he sat; but as I stood there beside him, I was aware of a warmth as of ten thousand Christmas fires in Scotland lighting the faces of those he had loved, and who loved him and care for him now more than ever.

Was it only fancy on my part that he knew I was there and was glad that I had come? It was no mere bronze that moved me. The sculptor has symbolized Scotland's young soldier manhood in a family portrait, and the portrait comes to life in the experience of every Scot who sees it. The bareheaded lad sitting there becomes the lad that went away from ten thousand Scottish firesides, and to thousands of them he never returned. Only the poor earth-grubbing materialist says our lad is dead. . .

With a salute I left him, looking and listening – the snow on his bare head.

Norval Scrymgeour, The Sunday Post, *25 December 1927, reprinted in Christopher Hussey,* Tait McKenzie: Sculptor of Youth *(1929). The statue is on the Scots-American war memorial in Princes Street Gardens, and is one of many such figures executed by the Canadian-Scots sculptor Tait McKenzie.*

Samuel Peploe's Aspidistra

It was probably about this time (1927) that he acquired an aspidistra, that plant the butt of humorists, but the one green spot in many a dreary wilderness. It was perhaps its greenness that attracted Peploe, or he may have recognized how its full rich colour harmonized with the dull grey-reds of the common clay flower-pot. It is not a plant with obvious pictorial interest, its very intractability acted as a challenge, its sword-like blades made a definite and different pattern, but there was also perhaps some hint of championship of a misunderstood and harmless vegetable. He may have regarded it as a symbol. It was not a plant to combine easily with others; he may have surmised that on some higher plane it shared with him a fellow-feeling, or he may have acknowledged in the slim polished leaves, so straight and up-right but curled in on themselves, some reflection of his own inner self. More probably he bought it merely as something to paint on a winter's day, little knowing that he had entered on a combat which had its parallel in Jacob's struggle with the Angel. That aspidistra dominated his studio for years. His friends laughed at it; it stood about in corners. It sprouted and spread, neglected and pampered by turns, but ever its sharp leaves goaded him on to further battles. He knew that somewhere in that plant there was a picture. At times it found a subsidiary place in a still-life group, but his ambition was to paint that aspidistra in all its austere and lonely dignity. In spite of all remonstration he persevered. He painted it several times, and in at least one version he enshrined for all time the very soul of all aspidistras.

Stanley Cursiter, Peploe (1947). *Samuel John Peploe, painter, lived from 1871–1935.*

Sir Henry Raeburn Finds a Wife

One day, a young lady presented herself at his studio, and desired to sit for her portrait. He instantly remembered having seen her in some of his excursions, when, with his sketchbook in his hand, he was noting down some fine snatches of scenery; and, as the appearance of anything living and lovely gives an additional charm to a landscape, the painter, like Gainsborough in similar circumstances, had readily admitted her into his drawing. This circumstance, he said, had its influence. On further acquaintance, he found that, besides personal charms, she had sensibility and wit. His respect for her did not affect his skill of hand, but rather inspired it, and he succeeded in making a fine portrait. The lady, Anne Edgar, daughter of Peter Edgar, Esq., of Bridgelands, was much pleased with the skill, and likewise with the manners of the artist; and about a month or so after the adventure of the studio, she gave him her hand in marriage; bestowing at once an affectionate wife and a handsome fortune.

Allan Cunningham, Lives of British Painters. *James Greig in his* Sir Henry Raeburn: Life and Works *(1911) admires but dismisses this tale; the couple had known each other for some time and the lady, a widow, was twelve years Raeburn's senior.*

David Wilkie at a Loss

Among the Letters of Introduction that Wilkie brought to London was one to Caleb Whiteford, celebrated at that time as a wit. Whilst opening the letter and looking at the bearer, he asked his age. 'Weel, I don't exactly know', was the reply. 'What!' said Caleb, 'You come to London to wrestle with so many celebrated men, and you don't even know your own age!' This remark made so strong an impression on him at the time, that out of it he afterwards painted his 'Letter of Introduction'.

John Burnet, The Art Journal *(1860) on the arrival in London of the future Sir David Wilkie (1785–1841). 'The Letter of Introduction' is one of Wilkie's most famous and typical paintings.*

David Wilkie's 'Blind Fiddler'

Old Mrs Wilkie loved to be asked questions about her son Davie. A friend enquired one day whether he had early displayed much talent in drawing.

'Aweel,' said she, 'I mind that he was ae scrawling, and scratching, I did na ken what, and he had an idle fashion o' making likenesses and caricatures, like of all the folk as came. And there was an auld blind man, Willie, the fiddler, just an idle sort of a beggar-mon, that used to come wi' his noise, and set all the woman servants a-jigging wi' his scratching and scraping; and Davie was ae taking this puir bodie into the hoose, and gieing him a drap o' toddy: and I used to cry shame on the lad for encouraging such lazy vagabonds about the hoose. Weel', pursued the old lady, 'but ye maun ken he was an ill-favoured, daft sort of a creatur, that puir blind bodie, weel eno' in his way, but not the sort o' folk to be along wi' Davie; yet the lad was always a-saying to me, "Mither, gie's a bawbee for puir blind Willie." This, sir,' she added with a sigh, 'was when we lived at the Manse.'

'A-weel, sir, they told me – it was mony years after the puir blind bodie was gane hame, sir – that Davie had painted a grand pictur; and he wrote me to go to Edinburgh to see it; and I went, and sure eno' there was puir old Willie, the very like o' him, his fiddle and a'. I was wud wi' surprise; and there was Davie standing and laughing at me, and saying, "Mither, mony's the time that ye ha heard that fiddle to the toon o' 'The Campbells Are Coming'."'

John Timbs, A Century of Anecdote, 1760–1860 (1864)

BORDER REIVERS

The Reivers' Humour 1 – 'Geordie Blackdowp'

They seem to have possessed, however, the same wry sense of humour, sardonic, often macabre and slanted against themselves, that their descendants have today. . . The Armstrongs, no doubt, were greatly tickled at the thought that while Carey was making his famous expedition against them at Tarras Moss, they were engaged in lifting some of the warden's cattle; or to see Jock o' the Side riding sidesaddle 'like ony bride' on his return from Newcastle gaol. Indeed many of the reivers' jokes were inspired by their ability to outwit the common enemy, as when Nicholas Rutherford stole five horses from the garrison at Norham under their very noses, or when that notable reiver, 'Geordie Blackdowp' earned his nickname. Geordie was returning home to Redesdale one day well satisfied with a foray that he had conducted, when his party was overtaken and roughly handled, and in the scuffle he lost part of his breeches. After his companions had dispersed in order to throw off their pursuers, his horse went lame and he was forced to squat down in the rushes with only his bare backside showing; 'An they ken my face,' he explained afterwards, 'they dinna ken my dowp.'

Geoffrey Watson, The Border Reivers (1974). Sir Robert Carey was a Warden of the Marches on the English side. Jock o' the Side came home sidesaddle because his legs were still in irons. The 'Geordie Blackdowp' anecdote may have an ancestral affinity to the Oxford story of the don Maurice Bowra when a boatload of ladies inadvertently came by the all-male swimming site of Parson's Pleasure. Whilst all around sought to hide their private parts, he covered his face, explaining afterwards that whilst he could not speak for his colleagues, he himself was known in Oxford by his face.

The Reivers' Humour 2 – Archie Armstrong's Oath

One of the best examples of reiver wit comes from that Archie Armstrong who later became court jester to Charles I. Archie lived at Stubholm, near the River Esk, whence he sallied forth one day to replenish his larder with one of his neighbour's sheep. Having cut its throat and borne it home, he was much put out to see the shepherd approaching the house. Looking round for somewhere to hide the animal, he lit upon the empty cradle, into which he hastily stuffed it. When the shepherd appeared, Archie, according to his own story, managed to dull his suspicions by taking his oath (which he subsequently immortalized in verse), that –

> If e'er I did sae fause a feat
> As thin my niebour's faulds,
> May I be doom'd this flesh to eat
> This vera cradle haulds.

Geoffrey Watson, The Border Reivers

To Ask Grace at a Graceless Face

... the interview between the outlaw chief and the King has so much of human nature in it that it is hard to disbelieve.

They met at Carlanrig in Teviotdale, Armstrong with perhaps fifty riders at his back, all hoping to get their pardons. One historian says that as soon as the King saw them he ordered his troops to close in, but in Pitscottie's account there seems to be a suggestion that it was only when they came face to face that the King made up his mind how to deal with the formidable robber.

Johnnie came 'reverentlie', but he and his men were so splendidly equipped and dressed, and so evidently self-confident, that His Majesty's reaction was the celebrated: 'What wants yon knave that a king should have?'

And then he 'turned about his face and bade take that tyrant out of his sight'. Armstrong, no doubt bewildered, pleaded for his life; he swore his loyalty, protested that he had never robbed in Scotland or despoiled a Scot, and offered to bring the King any English subject, from a duke downwards, on any stated day, dead or alive. It was perhaps not such an idle boast as it may have sounded, but the King would have none of him. The Armstrongs must die. Whether this interchange really happened, or is just the stuff of legend, there is a startlingly genuine ring about Pitscottie's account of the reiver's final retort before he was led to the gallows:

> He seeing no hope of the King's favour towards him, said very proudly, 'I am but a fool to ask grace at a graceless face. But had I known, sir, that you would have taken my life this day, I should have lived on the Borders in spite of King Harry and you both, for I know King Harry would down-weigh my best horse with gold to know that I were condemned to die this day.'

. . . Johnnie and his followers without trial were promptly 'all hangit apoun growand trees', and whether they were taken by treachery or not, they had it coming to them. One of the reivers Sandy Scott, 'a prowd thief', was burned alive because he himself had burned a house containing a woman and her children; it is worth remembering things like that, when considering the heroic eminence that folk-lore has given to Johnnie Armstrong and his riders.

George Macdonald Fraser, The Steel Bonnets (1971). *King James V's punitive visitation of the Borders took place in 1530.*

The Lifting of Kinmont Willie

He had been present at Dayholm, near Kershopefoot, on the occasion of a day of truce, in the month of March, in the year 1596. The business which called them together having been finished, he was returning home, accompanied by a few of his friends, along the banks of the Liddle, when he was suddenly attacked by a body of two hundred English Borderers, led by Salkeld, the deputy of Lord Scrope, the warden of the East March, chased for some miles, captured, tied to the body of his horse and thus carried in triumph to Carlisle castle.

> They led him thro' the Liddel-rack,
> And also through the Carlisle sands;
> They brought him to Carlisle castell
> To be at my Lord Scrope's commands.

This proceeding was clearly in direct violation of Border law, which guaranteed freedom from molestation to all who might be present at a warden court, or day of truce, between sunrise on the one day and sunrise on the next. We can easily understand the overmastering desire of the warden's deputy to lay Kinmont by the heels, as he had long been notorious for his depredations on the English Border. . . An account of what had happened was speedily conveyed to Branxholme, where the Bold Buccleuch was residing. When he heard what had occurred he was highly indignant. The picture drawn by the balladist is graphic in the extreme. For intense realism it has rarely ever been surpassed:

> He has ta'en the table wi' his hand,
> He garr'd the red wine spring on hie –
> 'Now Christ's curse on my head,' he said,
> 'But aveng'd on Lord Scrope I'll be!'

Before resorting to extreme measures Buccleuch did everything in his power to bring about an amicable settlement of the case. He first of all applied to Salkeld for redress, but Salkeld could only refer him to Lord Scrope, who declared that Kinmont was such a notorious malefactor that he could not release him without the express command of Queen Elizabeth. Buccleuch then brought the matter under the consideration of James, who made an application through an ambassador, for Kinmont's release; but this also proved unavailing.

It looked as though the imprisoned freebooter was likely to pay his 'lodging mail' in a very unpleasant fashion. The English government seemed determined to detain him until such time as they could conveniently put a period to his career by hanging him on Haribee hill. But Buccleuch, while anxious to effect his purpose, if possible by constitutional means, was determined that Kinmont should be rescued, whatever might be the method he was under necessity of adopting. To accomplish his purpose he was prepared to 'set the castle in a low, and sloken it with English blood'. This threat was regarded as a mere piece of bravado. The castle was strongly garrisoned and well fortified. It was in the centre of a populous and hostile city, and under the command of Scrope, who was regarded as one of the bravest soldiers in England. The Bold Buccleuch, however, was not easily daunted. He had a strong arm and a brave heart, and he knew that he could summon to his aid a small band of followers as brave and resolute as himself. On a dark tempestuous night, two hundred of his followers met him at the tower of Morton, a fortalice in the Debatable land, on the water of Sark, some ten miles or so from Carlisle. Their plans had been carefully considered and determined upon a day or two before, when they had met at a horse race near Langholm. The Armstrongs, of course, were ready to adventure their lives in such a laudable undertaking, and the Graemes, to whom Will of Kinmont was related by marrriage, were also forward with promises of assistance. They were all well mounted, and carried with them scaling ladders and crowbars, hand-picks and axes, prepared to take the castle by storm. The rain had been falling heavily, and the Esk and the Eden were in roaring flood, but boldly plunging through their turbid waters they soon came within sight of the 'Corbie's Nest' which they had come to 'herry' . . . When Buccleuch and his men reached the castle they were dismayed to find that the ladders they had brought with them were too short; but finding a postern they undermined it, and soon made a breach big enough for a soldier to pass through. 'In this way a dozen stout fellows passed into the outer court (Buccleuch himself being the fifth man who entered), disarmed and bound the watch, wrenched open the postern from the inside, and thus admitting their companions, were masters of the place. Twenty-four troopers now rushed to the castle jail, Buccleuch meanwhile keeping the postern, forced the door of the chamber where Kinmont was confined, carried him off in his irons, and sounding their trumpet, the signal agreed on, were answered by loud shouts and the trumpet of Buccleuch, whose troopers filled the base court. All was now terror and confusion, both in town and castle. The alarum-bell rang and was answered by his brazen brethren of the cathedral and the town-house; the beacon blazed upon the top of the great tower; and its red, uncertain glare on the black sky and the shadowy forms and glancing armour of the Borderers, rather increased the terror and their numbers. None could see the enemy to tell their real strength.'

The suddenness of the attack and the terrific noise made by Buccleuch and his troopers as they laid siege to the castle, created confusion and dismay among the defenders of the stronghold. Lord Scrope, with commendable prudence, kept close within his chamber. He was convinced, as he afterwards declared, that there were at least five hundred Scots in possession of the castle.

Kinmont, as he was borne triumphantly forth on the broad shoulders of Red Rowan, shouted a lusty 'good night' to his bewildered lordship.

> 'Farewell, farewell, my gude Lord Scroope!
> My gude Lord Scroope, farewell,' he cried –
> 'I'll pay you for my lodging maill,
> When first we meet on the Border side.'

Robert Borland, Border Raids and Reivers (*1898*). *The interpolated quotation is from P. F. Tytler's* History of Scotland, *and the verses are from one of the ballads recounting the exploit. Walter Scott of Buccleuch, Keeper of Liddesdale, organised the raid to free Willie Armstrong of Kinmont, in April 1596. George Macdonald Fraser, in* The Steel Bonnets, *puts Buccleuch's*

troop at around eighty, and also suspects internal connivance in the open-
ing of the gate.

Clean Spurs

We are told that when the last bullock which Auld Wat had provided from
the English pastures was consumed, The Flower of Yarrow placed on her
table a dish containing a pair of clean spurs: a hint to the company that they
must bestir themselves for their next dinner.

*J. G. Lockhart, Life of Sir Walter Scott. Auld Wat was Walter Scott of
Harden, who is said to have commented, as he rode past an English hay-
stack close to the Border, 'If ye had legs, ye wadna stand there lang.' The
Flower of Yarrow was his wife Mary.*

CHILDHOOD

Early Scepticism

At night after we were in bed, Veronica spoke out from her little bed and
said, 'I do not believe there is a God. . . I have thinket it many a time, but
did not like to speak of it.' I was confounded and uneasy, and tried her with
the simple argument that without GOD there would not be all the things
we see. 'It is HE who makes the sun shine.' Said she: 'It shines only on good
days.' Said I: 'GOD made you.' Said she: 'My mother bore me.'

James Boswell (1740–1795), Journal, 17 December 1779

Not Caught So Young

He was the eleventh child of the fifth Lord Stormont, descended from the
Murrays of Tullibardine, and connected with the houses of Buccleuch and
Montrose. The family fortune was not great, and in the tumble-down castle
of Scone, where he was born, the bringing-up of the fourteen children must
have been spartan. For some reason or other, a story got about that he was
taken to London as a child, which is as accurate as the other legend, that he
was born at Bath and educated at Lichfield. Dr Johnson believed it, and
used to say that 'much may be made of a Scotsman if he be caught young';
but there is little doubt that the young Murray was first sent to the grammar school of Perth, and abode there till his fourteenth year. Scots grammar
schools of that time may have been deficient in many things, but they could
teach Latinity; and Mansfield used to declare that it was there, also, that he
first learned the genius and structure of his mother tongue. At first he lived
at home, riding to school on a pony, and running about barefoot with the

small boys of the place. Long afterwards Grub Street pamphleteers made merry with this early training. 'Learning was very cheap in his country,' wrote one scribbler; 'and it is very common to see a boy of quality lug along his books to school, and a scrap of oatmeal for his dinner, with a pair of brogues on his feet, posteriors exposed, and nothing on his legs.'

John Buchan (1875–1941), Some Eighteenth-Century Byways. *Buchan was writing of William Murray, Lord Mansfield (1705–1793), who became Lord Chief Justice of England. At the age of fourteen, he was indeed sent to Westminster School, but perhaps by then a little too old for Dr Johnson's mot, which did refer to him, to have the same bite.*

The Peril of Having a Nanny

One of our earlier nannies was a girl of character called Nurse Kate. . . She would enter the nursery of a morning and say: 'You're naughty.' Elizabeth and I suspected she might be right, but weren't sure how much she knew. So we would ask, 'Why?' She had the standard grown-up riposte to this: 'Don't answer back.' Then she used to fill our mouths with mustard, put sticking plaster across them, and lock us up alone in the dark in our separate bedrooms.

Being lazy, this didn't bother me much; except that I couldn't breathe well through my nose which was usually blocked by scabs, and so had to ease one end of the plaster loose so that I could breathe through the corner of my mouth. While we lay in the dark, in my case having placid daydreams about treasure islands and the like, Nurse Kate was off on her usual joy ride and picnic with the chauffeur. On her return, as she unlocked our bedroom doors, I used to smooth the end of the sticking plaster back into place; just in time for her to be able to rip it off savagely in the often vain hope that it hurt.

Nurse Kate's fun life came to light when Uncle Guy, who had been a submarine commander and loved mechanical contraptions, took in that his prized motor car was clocking up too many miles. Poor Nurse Kate was sacked with words of contumely. Uncle Guy and Aunt May sent for me and Elizabeth, and asked why on earth we hadn't reported all this long since. We had no adequate reply, as most things grown-ups did seemed so mad to us, we had thought it was everyday life.

Sir Ian Moncrieffe of that Ilk (1919–1985), *from* Kidnapped, *in A. Kamm and A. Lean,* A Scottish Childhood (1985)

Youthful Reading

A child's imagination is unbelievably vivid, and I do not know whether it was a benefit or a calamity when my brother Willie, out of pure kindness, began taking *Chums* for me. *Chums* was at that time the chief rival of *The Boy's Own Paper,* which I did not see until years later, when it bored me with its stories of public-school life, filled with incomprehensible snobbery. The line of *Chums* was adventure stories in savage lands. There was always a hero with a pointed beard, sailors with soft bushy beards and honest faces, and a boy called Frank. This small company passed through sunless canyons, forded alligator-infested rivers, cut their way through dense jungles, and fought savage tribes set on by bad, white, clean-shaven men, meanwhile foiling the attacks of lions, tigers, bears and serpents. Returned to England with their riches, they dropped through trapdoors in rotting wharves and languished in dripping dungeons, until the sailors, having broken out, returned like a benevolent music-hall chorus to rescue the others, with a vast tattoo of sturdy fists on villainous faces. The excitement of following these adventures was more a pain than a pleasure, and everything was so real to me that when I was herding the cows on the side of the hill I would often glance over my shoulder in case a tiger might be creeping up behind me. I knew with one part of my mind that there were no tigers on Orkney, but I could not resist that nervous backward jerk of the head.

Edwin Muir (1887–1959), Autobiography

Family Prayers

Then we turned and knelt at our chairs while Uncle George said his prayer. This might last anything from five minutes to half an hour, while we weaker vessels drifted into vague reflections, or into secret games of patience. Easy chairs and high-backed chairs each had their particular advantages. The high-backed chair was not so comfortable, but it was also less secluded, and, peering through the interstices in the woodwork, one could take unobtrusive observations on the room and on the attitudes of the others. Little things which in the ordinary scurry of activity went unnoticed became fascinating and delightful. You watched a coal teetering on the bars of the grate, and waited to see out of the corner of your eye how many would start when it fell. You made little optical tests, like seeing how many titles of books in the bookcase you could read without moving your head. Or there was simple pleasure to be had in seeing that Uncle George knelt with his toes bent back so that his slippers stuck out at an angle exposing the heel of a sock in which there was a big round hole. That was the sort of thing that Aunt Maggie would notice, too, for in the very act of rising from her knees she would be issuing her orders to the maid, and instructing the minister to go straight away and change his socks . . .

These adventures in inattentiveness were insignificant compared with the more constructive idlesse of two of Aunt Maggie's younger brothers. Once at worship in my grandfather's house, they miscalculated the length of time that a visiting good man would pray, and when the family and guests rose after an unexpected 'Amen' the two boys were discovered, back to back, standing on their heads on the hearthrug. It was Uncle Dan, who was older, and who, I think, envied them their misdemeanour, who told me of the incident, adding, 'By faith, they got an awful lundering for that one.'

Alastair Philips, My Uncle George

Home Life of the Raeburns

Sir Henry and Lady Raeburn, and their son and his wife with three children, comprised the family party at this time. The great portrait-painter, as far as I can recollect him, had a very impressive appearance, his full, dark, lustrous eyes, with ample brow and dark hair, at this time scant. His tall frame had a dignified aspect. I can well remember him, seated in an arm-chair in the evening, at the fireside of the small drawing room, newspaper in his hand, with his family around him. His usual mode of address to us when we were spending the evenings, while he held out his hand with a kind smile, was, 'well my dears, what is your opinion of things in general today?' These words always filled us with consternation, and we all huddled together like a flock of scared sheep, vainly attempting some answer by gazing from one to the other; and with what delight and sense of freedom we were led away to be seated at the tea-table, covered with cookies, bread and butter and jelly! After tea we were permitted to go away for play to another room; we made as much noise as we liked, and generally managed to disturb old Lady Raeburn. This old lady was quite a character, and always spoke in broad Scotch; then common among the old families, now extinct. I can never forget the manner in which we uproarious little creatures tormented her, flinging open the door of her snug little room, whither she had fled for a little quiet from our incessant provocations and unwearied inventions at amusement, which usually reached the climax by throwing bed-pillows at her and nearly smothering her small figure. At this juncture she would rise up, and, opening the door of a cupboard, would bring out of it a magnificent bunch of grapes which she endeavoured to divide among us with these words of entreaty, 'Hoot, hoot, bairns, here's some grapes for ye; no' gang awa' an' behave yersels, like gude bairns, and dinna deave me any mair.'

Mrs Ferrier, as related to Dr John Brown and reprinted in James Greig, Sir Henry Raeburn: His Life and Works (*1911*). *Raeburn died in 1823.*

Filial Pride

Scott's young son was ignorant of his father's fame as a novelist, but loved and admired him for reasons closer to a boy's heart. Once when he was in his teens he was in the company of some older people who were discussing

Scott's genius. 'Aye,' put in young Scott, 'it's commonly him is first to see the hare.'

G. *Davenport,* Geography of the Imagination

Fisherfolks' Children

When I started work at eight years old I had to take a chair and climb on to the roof of our house, covering all the tiles with gutted and split salted fish to dry in the warm sun. The yellow fish were smoked in our own hanging lum in the house. Apart from my father's catch my mother bought much extra fish at Fraserburgh harbour; these were spread out on the rocks, from Broadsea shore to the Manshaven; the whole beach was white with salt fish. All the little loons and quinies had a lot of fun and daffin as they watched their charges. We were experts at stoning the marauding seagulls who would devour the newly salted fish. When we saw moisture on the rock it was time to turn the fish over, and threatening rain we gathered the whole cure under a tarpaulin. There were aye folk with tarry fingers who stole other people's fish, but most were honest; and there were the lazy who wanted to scrounge a living off others; if a person was old or sick or a widow with bairns it was your duty to help them out.

Christian Watt (1833–1923), The Christian Watt Papers, *edited by David Fraser (1983)*

Renée Houston Lights a Candle

On Sundays we always went to church. And when we left the house, Grannie always gave us a shilling to light two blessed candles for the repose of her husband's soul. Now, a shilling was a small fortune in those days and the temptation to put it to another use was something we struggled with.

But we only yielded once.

On the way to church, we met our companions, Rosina and Mattie, and as we walked along, Billie kept looking at the shilling. 'Let's get penny candles,' she said suddenly.

'No. We can't do that,' I protested weakly. 'It's cheating.'

'Don't be daft,' Billie replied, 'Grandpa won't know. He's dead, isn't he?'

Well, the logic of it was unassailable. We got penny candles and after church rushed off to spend our ill-gotten gains. The first stop was the Italian ice-cream shop where we bought four McCallums. They consisted of sponge biscuits, smothered in ice-cream, a piece of cream chocolate and a topping of raspberry sauce. We got that lot down then went and bought a plate each of hot peas and vinegar!

Needless to say, we were all violently ill. When Billie and I got home, I miserably confessed the truth and waited for Grannie to explode. But she couldn't help but laugh.

'That's the kind of thing your Grandpa would have done,' she admitted. 'He was a bloody villain too.'

Renée Houston (1902–1980), Don't Fence Me In *(1974). Born in Johnstone to a theatrical family, and baptised Katerina Valorita, she and Billie Houston were a celebrated sister act in variety theatre for many years.*

Robert Garioch is Innocent

I was brought up as a Scottish Episcopalian, maybe because my mother went 'not for the doctrine, but the music there', and a very good reason too. Also, I understand, she was influenced by a churchman named, I assure you, Canon Ball. I thought I would rather have been a Presbyterian, that being more Scottish. . . An embarrassing situation arose when the time came for me to be confirmed. I was expected to confess my sins. But I hadn't any. I ran my eye down the list. I had nothing to be proud about, and did not envy anybody; what would be the use of that? Anger, no; I had a pretty good temper, and loved peace better than war. I didn't covet anything either, not having much chance of getting it anyway. I had recently dug as much as I could of our allotment. It was full of couch grass, or rack, as we called it. That was a poor bit of ground named 'the Sandies', opposite our house, a disused sand-pit. No, I was not slothful. Lust, oh no, that was quite out of the question, and so was Gluttony. The Rector grew impatient. 'You don't mean to tell me you're perfect?' he said. I said no, but whatever was wrong with me, it was not on the list. Seemingly only the Seven Deadly Sins would do. I was confirmed just the same, and have a certificate to prove it, which goes to show something, but I'm not sure what.

Robert Garioch (Robert Garioch Sutherland, 1909–1981), Early Days in Edinburgh, *from* As I Remember, *edited by Maurice Lindsay (1979)*

At the Socialist Sunday School

The ILP Sunday School opened with a song from the Socialist Sunday School Song Book. Then the minutes of the last meeting were read followed by the attendance being taken. We then recited some of the precepts before singing another song. On the day the Young Socialist newspaper was sold we had something read to us from it. We always had a collection of one penny each. We were then invited to sing or recite on our own. The Youth Section had a social evening frequently and the Sunday School were invited to it. We always finished every Sunday singing 'The Red Flag' accompanied by the organ. The ILP precept was:

> Love Learning Which Is the Food of the Mind
> Be as grateful to your teachers

As to your parents
We desire to be just and loving
To all our fellow Men and Women
To work together as Brothers and Sisters
To be kind to every living creature
And so help to form a New Society
With Justice as its Foundation
And Love its Law.

The Proletarian Sunday School which I attended later did not have such a large attendance. . . The attendance was taken then the precepts were learnt. I cannot remember them all but here are some I do remember.

1. Thou shalt inscribe on your banner:
'Workers of all lands unite',
You have nothing to lose but your chains;
You have a world to win.

2. Thou shalt not be a patriot;
For a patriot is an international Blackleg.
Your duty to yourself and your class
Demands that you be a citizen of the World.

3. Thou shalt not take part in any bourgeois war
For all modern wars are the result of the clash of economic
    interest
Your duty as an Internationalist is to wage class war
Against all such wars.

. . . I enjoyed the Proletarian Sunday School much better than the ILP. It was less formal and more working class and down to earth.
   Mary Docherty, A Miner's Lass (1992), *describing her 1920s childhood in the Fife mining villages.*

Windy Days in Lewis

Lewis is a windy place. It was not difficult to feel that the whole island was in motion, being birled about in the general movement of the planet, and with a definite danger of being blown off, into the sea, into space. In winter gales it had a loud, eerie howl, which one grew to love. My mother used to put a coat over her head, and a jacket over mine, and we would go out and stand at the end of the house for a while, in the dark, listening to the wind and enjoying it. It was a sensuous and emotional need, not like the doctrinaire theory of an old Lewis bachelor of whom I heard, who made a practice of going out first thing on a winter morning, in his nightshirt, in the belief that if you got a good chill then you wouldn't feel so cold for the rest of the day.

Derick Thomson (1921–), A Man Reared in Lewis, from As I Remember, *edited by Maurice Lindsay (1979)*

The Contents of Granny's Pocket

Now Granny was an old lady, and every old traveller woman in these by-gone days never carried a handbag. But around their waist they carried a big pocket. I remember Granny's – she made it herself, a tartan pocket. It was like a large purse with a strap, and she tied it around her waist. It had three pearl buttons down the middle, no zip in these days. Granny carried all her worldly possessions in this pocket.

Now, Granny smoked a little clay pipe. And when she needed tobacco, she would say, 'Weans, I want you to run to the village for tobacco for my pipe.' And she'd give us a threepenny bit, a penny for each of us and a penny for tobacco. The old man used to have a roll of it on the counter, and he cut off a little bit for Granny for her penny. We came back and our reward was, 'Granny, tell us a story!'

She sat there in front of her little tent, and she had a little billy-can and a little fire. We collected sticks for her, and she'd boil this strong, black tea. She lifted the can off, placed it by the side of the fire and said, 'Well, weans, I'll see what I have in my pocket for you this time.' She opened up that big pocket by her side with the three pearl buttons. I remember them well, and she said, 'Well, I'll tell you this story.' Maybe it was one she'd told three nights before. Maybe it was one she had never told for weeks. Sometimes she would tell us a story three–four times; sometimes she told us a story we'd never heard.

So, one day my sister and I came back from the village. We were playing and we came up to Granny's little tent. The sun was shining warm. Granny's little can of tea was by the fire: it was cold, the fire had burned out. The sun was warm. Granny was lying, she had her two hands under her head like an old woman, and her little bed was in front of the tent. By her side was the pocket. That was the very first time we'd ever seen that pocket off Granny's waist. She probably took it off when she went to bed at night-time. But never during the day!

So my sister and I crept up quietly and we said, 'Granny is asleep! There's her pocket. Let's go and see how many stories are in Granny's pocket.' So very gently we picked the pocket up, we took it behind the tree where we lived in the forest and opened up the three pearl buttons. And in that pocket was like Aladdin's Cave! There were clay pipes, threepenny pieces, rings, halfpennies, farthings, brooches, pins, needles, everything an old woman carried with her, thimbles . . . but not one single story could we find! So we never touched anything. We put everything back inside, closed it and put it back, left it by her side. We said, 'We'll go and play and we'll get Granny when she gets up.' So we went off to play again, came back about an hour later and Granny was up. Her little fire was kindling. She was heating up her cold tea. And we sat down by her side. She began to light her pipe after she drank this strong, black tea. We said, 'Granny, are you going to tell us a story?'

'Aye, weans,' she said, 'I'll tell you a story.' She loved telling us stories because it was company for us, forbye it was good company for her to sit there beside us weans. She said, 'Wait a minute noo, wait till I see what I have for you tonight.' And she opened up that pocket. She looked at me and my little sister for a while, for a long time with her blue eyes. She said, 'Ye ken something, weans?'

We said, 'No, Granny.'

She said, 'Somebody opened my pocket while I was asleep and all my stories are gone. I cannae tell ye a story the nicht, weans.' And she never told us a story that night. And she never told us another story. And I was seventeen when my granny died, but eleven when that happened. Granny never told me another story, and that's a true story!

Duncan Williamson, The Horsieman (1994)

The Way It Was

We didn't understand how things worked, and we took things too far. Our most serious purpose was the search for fun, and this became an increasingly dangerous business, and often a notably violent one. In that year, I think, we found out how bad we could be.

Around that time, I was in the habit of walking to school in the company of a blonde girl from the other side of the square. I'll call her Katie. We were in the same class, and she was sort of my girlfriend. We liked to play at offices on her doorstep, with loads of pads and typewriters, but we'd often get fed up with that and imagine ourselves into something else. We got to taking a little boy to school in the morning, little David, and we were fond of taunting him along the way. The workies on the building sites would give us lemonade bottles to cash in for sweets, and we'd scoff the sweets, and leave David out. We started to play at being his mummy and daddy, and hitting him for being bad. It was just a few slaps at first, but it got worse. There were freshly planted trees around the place, tied to stalks with rubber belts. We started taking them off on the journey, and whipping David with them. Eventually, one morning, very late for assembly, we were caught on a railway bridge near the school, practically skinning the boy's legs. He was screaming and we were laughing and hitting like crazy. The teachers caught us and our parents battered us in return, but it was nowhere near the end of it.

... We'd go camping on the school playing-fields at night, and never go to sleep. A game of hide and seek with torches would sometimes turn into a game of hunting down small animals or cats to worry or kill. We got into petty vandalism on these trips, and loved to wreck gardens, break countless milk bottles and panes of glass. There was a place called Todhill Farm on the outskirts of our estate. It was a training farm for young men with Down's Syndrome, and it sat just under the dual carriageway that was being built in 1976. We'd go down there with our torches – the Toadies, we'd whisper, the Toadies are loonies – and wreck their work. They had fields of carrots and strawberries which they tended every day, and there we'd be, leaping and tearing in the dark, and carrying off bags of fat strawberries in plastic bags brought specially for the purpose. Kids like us gave those Down's boys a terrible time. Even in broad daylight, we'd terrorise them, and chase them over the fields on our Grifters or Choppers or whatever these chunky bikes were called. It became difficult to see the difference between fun and brutality, between bad-boyish misdemeanours and hellish bad-bastardness. Now and again, when you'd a certain group of marauding kids bouncing malevolent sparks off each other, you would think you were untouchable. There's no pride in it, but that's the way it was.

Andrew O'Hagan, The Missing (1995)

THE CHURCH AND CHURCHMEN

Adamnan's Powers

... the Irish Life of Adamnan contains the following strange legend:

The body of Bruide, son of Bile, king of the Cruithnigh, was brought to Ia (Iona), and his death was sorrowful and glorious to Adamnan, and he desired that the body of Bruide should be brought to him into the house that night. Adamnan watched by the body till morning. Next day, when the body began to move and open its eyes, a certain devout man came to the door of his house and said, 'If Adamnan's object be to raise the dead, I say he should not do so, for it will be a degradation to every cleric who shall succeed to his place, if he too cannot raise the dead.' 'There is somewhat of right in that,' said Adamnan, 'therefore, as it is more proper, let us give our blessing to the body and soul of Bruide.' Thus Bruide resigned his spirit to heaven again, with the blessing of Adamnan and the congregation of Ia.

W. F. Skene, Celtic Scotland, *Vol. I (1886). The story brings to mind another Irish legend of Iona, of how St Oran, having been buried alive and then exhumed after three days, sat up and said that there was no such great wonder in death, neither was hell what it had been described, causing Columba to cry: 'Earth, earth to stop Oran's mouth,' and the saint was speedily re-interred.*

Aidan is Picked to Convert the English

While the priest Segenius ruled as Abbot of Iona, Aidan was raised to the dignity of the episcopate, and was sent out from this island monastic community to preach the Faith of Christ to the English people. Among other evidences of holy life, he gave his clergy an inspiring example of self-discipline and continence, and the highest recommendation of his teaching to all was that he and his followers lived as they taught. . . It is said that when King Oswald originally asked the Scots to send a bishop to teach the Faith of Christ to himself and his people, they sent him another man of a more austere disposition. Meeting with no success in his preaching to the English, he returned home and reported to his superiors that he had been unable to teach anything to the nation to whom they had sent him because they were an uncivilized people of an obstinate and barbarous temperament. The Scots fathers therefore held a great conference to decide on the wisest course of action, for although they regretted that the preacher whom they had sent had not been acceptable to the English, they still wished to meet their desire for salvation. Then Aidan, who was present at the conference, said to the priest whose efforts had been unsuccessful: 'Brother, it seems to me that you were too severe on your ignorant hearers. You should have followed the practice of the Apostles, and begun by giving them the milk of simpler teaching, and gradually instructed them in the word of God until they were capable of greater perfection and able to follow the sublime precepts of Christ.' All who were at the conference paid close attention to all he said, and realized that here was a fit person to be made bishop and sent to instruct the ignorant and unbelieving, since he was particularly endowed with the grace of discretion, the mother of virtues. They therefore consecrated him bishop, and sent him to preach.

St Bede, Ecclesiastical History of the English People *(731). St Aidan's mission to Northumbria was successful. He died in 651.*

St Cuthbert's Lack of Hygiene

It seems he had a marked reluctance to take off his skin-boots more than once a year, for the ritual annual foot-washing on Maundy Thursday . . . It sounds almost too revolting to contemplate, but Bede justifies this conspicuous disregard for hygiene on the ground that 'he had so far withdrawn his mind from the care of his body and fixed it on the care of his soul alone that, having once been shod with the boots of skin that he was accustomed to use, he would wear them for whole months together'.

Magnus Magnusson, Lindisfarne (*1984*). *St Cuthbert lived from c.635–687.*

The Miracle of Queen Margaret's Book

She had a book of the Gospels beautifully adorned with jewels and gold, and ornamented with the figures of the four Evangelists, painted and gilt. The capital letters throughout the volume were also resplendent with gold. For this volume she always had a greater affection than she had for any others she was in the habit of reading. It happened that while the person who was carrying it was crossing a ford, he let the volume, which had been carelessly folded in a wrapper, fall into the middle of the stream, and, ignorant of what had occurred, he quietly continued his journey. But when he afterwards wished to produce the book, he, for the first time, became aware that he had lost it. It was sought for a long time, but was not found. At length it was found at the bottom of the river, lying open, so that its leaves were kept in constant motion by the action of the water, and the little coverings of silk which protected the letters of gold from being injured by the contact of the leaves, were carried away by the force of the current.

Who would imagine that the book would be worth anything after what had happened to it? Who would believe that even a single letter would have been visible? Yet of a truth it was taken up from the river so perfect, uninjured and free from damage, that it looked as though it had not even been touched by the water . . . let others consider what they should think of this, but as for me I am of the opinion that this miracle was wrought by our Lord because of His love for this venerable Queen.

Turgot, The Life of St Margaret, Queen of Scotland (*early 12th century*)

The Burning of the Bishop of Caithness

In 1222 . . . the bishop's exactions of tithes of butter reached such a pitch that the Caithness folk met at his house at Halkirk, and demanded that the earl should protect them against the bishop's rapacity, and, either at the earl's suggestion or without any opposition on his part, they attacked the bishop in his house, which was close to Breithivellir (now Brawl) Castle, where John lived. The Saga gives the following description of this affair:

They then held a Thing on the fell above the homestead where the earl was. Rafn the Lawman was then with the bishop, and prayed the bishop to spare the men; also he said he was afraid how things might go. Then a message was sent to Earl John with a prayer that he would reconcile the bishop and the freemen; but the earl would never come near the spot. Then the freemen ran down from the fell and fared hotly and eagerly. And when Rafn the Lawman saw that, he bade the bishop devise some plan to save himself. He and the bishop were drinking in a loft, and when the freemen came to the loft, the monk went out at the door, and was immediately struck across the face, and fell down dead inside the loft. And when the bishop was told that, he answered, 'That had not happened sooner than was likely, for he was always making our matters worse.' Then the bishop bade Rafn tell the freemen that he wished to be reconciled with them. When this was told to the freemen, all of the wiser among them were glad to hear it. Then the bishop went out and sought to be reconciled. But when the worse kind of men, those who were most inflamed, saw that, they seized Bishop Adam, and put him in a little house and set fire to it. The house burned so quickly that those who wished to save the bishop could do nothing. Thus Bishop Adam died, and his body was little burnt when it was found. Then a fitting grave was bestowed on it, and a worthy burial. But those who had been the greatest friends of the bishop sent men to the King of Scots. Alexander was then King of Scots, son of King William the Saint.

. . . it appears that Earl John, who was responsible for law and order in Caithness at the time, although invited by Rafn the Lawman to intervene, and although he was on the spot, did nothing, saying 'he could give no advice' and 'that he thought it concerned him very little', and adding that 'two bad things were before them, that it was unbearable' . . . King Alexander, urged by the remainder of the bishops in Scotland, at once marched into Caithness with an army, and took vengeance on the bishop's murderers by mutilating a large number of those concerned and seizing their lands, while in 1223 the Pope excommunicated them and also interdicted them from their lands.

James Gray, Sutherland and Caithness in Saga-Time (*1922*)

The Hospitality of Bishop Wardlaw

Wardlaw was celebrated for his charity; and though he laboured to suppress the riotous living which had become so general in the kingdom, he was yet a man of boundless hospitality. It is recorded of him, that the stewards of his household, on one occasion, complained to him of the numbers that resorted to his table, to share in the good things which it afforded; and requested that, out of compassion for his servants, who were often quite worn out with their labours, he would furnish them with a list of his intended guests, so that they might know how many they had to serve. To this he readily assented, and sent for his secretary, to prepare the required document. The latter having arranged his writing materials, inquired who was to be put down. 'Put down, first,' replied the bishop, 'Fife and Angus' (two large counties). This was enough: his servants, appalled by anticipations of a list which began so formidably, instantly relinquished their design of limiting the hospitality of their generous master.

Robert Chambers, Scottish Biographical Dictionary. *Henry Wardlaw (c.1380–1440), Bishop of St Andrews, was the founder of St Andrews University.*

John Knox, Preaching in Old Age

In the opening up of his text he was moderat, the space of ane half houre, but when he enterit to application, he made me so to grew and tremble, that I could not hold a pen to wryte. He was very weik. I saw him everie day of his doctrine go hulie and fear; with a furring of marticks round his neck, a staff in the ane hand, and gud godlie Richart Ballanden, his servant, holding up the uther oxter, from the abbey to the parish kirk; and he, the said Richart, and another servant, lifted up to the pulpit, where he behovit to lean, at his first entrie; bot ere he haid done with his sermone, he was sa active and vigorous that he was lyk to ding the pulpit in blads, and flie out of it.

James Melville (1556–1614), Life of John Knox. *Written in 1571, the year before Knox's death.*

The Preservation of Glasgow Cathedral

In Glasgow, the next Spring, 1578, there happened a little disturbance by this occasion. The magistrates of the city, by the earnest dealing of Mr Andrew Melville and other ministers, had condescended to demolish the Cathedral, and build with the materials thereof some little churches in other parts, for the ease of the citizens. Divers reasons were given for it, such as the resort of superstitious people to do their devotions in that place; the huge vastness of the Church, and that the voice of a preacher could not be heard by the multitudes that convened to sermon; the more commodious service of the people; and the removing of that idolatrous monument (as they called it) which was of all the Cathedrals in the country the only one left unruined, and in a possibility to be repaired. To do this work, a number of quarriers, masons and other workmen was conduced, and the day assigned when it should take beginning. Intimation being made thereof, and the workmen by sound of drum warned to go unto their work, the craftsmen of the city in a tumult took arms, swearing with many oaths, that he who did cast down the first stone should be buried under it. Neither could they be pacified till the workmen were discharged by the magistrates.

Archbishop John Spottiswoode (1565–1639), History of the Church of Scotland. *Spottiswoode's story, used by Sir Walter Scott in* Rob Roy, *is refuted by James Paton in* The Book of Glasgow Cathedral (1898), *who found no evidence whatever that the Glasgow magistrates had considered demolishing*

the Cathedral. Incidentally, the Archbishop seems to have been unaware of
St Magnus Cathedral in Kirkwall, also preserved intact.

A Presbyterian's Magnanimity

An instance of the generosity of Melville's disposition, which occurred about
this time, cannot be passed over . . . Archbishop Adamson, one of his most
irreconcilable enemies, having lost the favour of the king, was reduced by
the sequestration of his annuity, which immediately followed, to great
pecuniary distress. He applied to Melville for relief, and he did not apply in
vain. Melville immediately visited him, and undertook to maintain himself
and his family at his own expense, until some more effective and permanent
assistance could be procured for him, and this he did for several months,
finally obtaining a contribution for him from his friends in St Andrews.

Robert Chambers, Scottish Biographical Dictionary. *Andrew Melville*
(1545–1622) was the leader of the Presbyterians, and this incident happened
around 1590, while Melville and his party were very much in the ascendant.

'God's Sillie Vassal'

. . . he frequently addressed King James in language much more remarkable
for its plainness than its courtesy. He had no sympathy whatever for the
absurdities of that prince, and would neither condescend to humour his
foibles nor flatter his vanity. A remarkable instance of this plain dealing
with his majesty, occurred in 1596. In that year, Melville formed one of a
deputation from the commissioners of the General Assembly, who met at
Cupar in Fife, being appointed to wait upon the king at Falkland, for the
purpose of exhorting him to prevent the consequences of certain measures
inimical to religion, which his council were pursuing. James Melville . . .
was chosen spokesman of the party, on account of the mildness of his manner and the courteousness of his address. On entering the presence, he
accordingly began to state the object and views of the deputation. He had
scarcely commenced, however, when the king interrupted him, and in passionate language denounced the meeting at Cupar as illegal and seditious.
James Melville was about to reply with his usual mildness, when his uncle,
stepping forward, seized the sleeve of the king's gown, and calling his
sacred majesty 'God's silly vassal', proceeded to lecture him on the impro-
priety of his conduct, and to point out to him the course which he ought to
pursue. . . 'Sir,' he said, 'we will always humbly reverence your majesty in
public; but since we have this occasion to be with your majesty in private,
and since you are brought in extreme danger of your life and crown, and
along with you, the country and the church of God are likely to go to wreck,
for not telling you the truth, and giving you faithful counsel, we must dis-

charge our duty or else be traitors both to Christ and you. Therefore, Sir, as divers times before I have told you, so now again I must tell you, there are two kings and two kingdoms in Scotland: there is King James, the head of this commonwealth, and there is Christ Jesus the king of the church, whose subject King James the Sixth is, and of whose kingdom he is not a king, nor a lord, nor a head, but a member.'

Robert Chambers, Scottish Biographical Dictionary. *Andrew Melville's eloquence had only a negative effect on James VI. 'Sillie' at that time had the sense of 'mere'.*

A Royal Confrontation with Knox's Daughter

Mr Welch was at this period seized with an illness which his physicians declared could could be removed only by his returning to breathe the air of his native country. Under these circumstances he ventured, in 1622, to come to London, hoping that when there he should be able to obtain the king's permission to proceed to Scotland. This request, however, James, dreading Welch's influence, absolutely refused. Among those, and there were many, who interceded with the king in behalf of the dying divine, was his wife. On obtaining access to James, the following extraordinary, but highly characteristic, conversation, as recorded by Dr McCrie, in his *Life of Knox*, took place between the intrepid daughter of the stern reformer and the eccentric monarch of England: his majesty asked her, who was her father. She replied, 'Mr Knox.' 'Knox and Welch,' exclaimed he, 'the devil never made such a match as that.' 'It's right like, sir,' she said, 'for we never speired his advice.' He asked her how many children her father had left, and if they were lads or lasses. She said three, and they were all lasses. 'God be thanked!' cried the king, lifting up both his hands, 'for an they had been three lads, I had never bruicked my three kingdoms in peace.' She again urged her request that he would give her husband his native air. 'Give him his native air,' replied the king. 'Give him the devil!' a morsel which James had often in his mouth. 'Give that to your hungry courtiers,' said she, offended at his profaneness. He told her at last, that if she would persuade her husband to submit to the bishops, he would allow him to return to Scotland. Mrs Welch, lifting up her apron, and holding it towards the king, replied, in the true spirit of her father, 'Please your majesty, I'd rather kep his head there.'

Robert Chambers, Scottish Biographical Dictionary. *John Welch (c.1570– 1622), a prominent Presbyterian clergyman, had been banished to France in 1606.*

A Curse Upon James Sharp

Mr Sharp makes (for the fashion) a visit to Mr Robert Douglass at his own house, where, after his preface, he informed him it was the king's purpose to settle the church under bishops, and that for respect to him his majesty was very desireous Mr Douglass would accept the archbishopric of St Andrews. Mr Douglass answered, he would have nothing to doe with it. . . Sharp insisted and urged him; Mr Douglass answered as formerly, whereupon Sharp arose and took leave. Mr Douglass convoyed him to his gallery door; and after he hade passed the door, Mr Douglass called him back, and told him, James, (said he) I see you will engadge, I perceive you are clear, you will be bishop of St Andrews: take it, and the curse of God with it. So clapping him upon the shoulder, he shutt his door upon him.

James Kirkton (c.1620–1699), The Secret and True History of the Church of Scotland from the Restoration to the Year 1678, *from J. G. Fyfe,* Scottish Diaries and Memoirs, 1550–1746 *(1907). James Sharp (1613–1679) did become Archbishop, and met his death at the hands of assassins on Magus Muir.*

The Capture of James Renwick

Coming to Edinburgh in the beginning of the year 1688, to give in a testimony to the synod of tolerated ministers against the toleration which they had accepted . . . he passed over to Fife, where he continued preaching at different places, till the end of January, when he returned to Edinburgh, and took up his lodgings in the house of a friend on the Castle hill, a dealer in uncustomed goods. A party coming to search for these discovered Mr Renwick and apprehended him. He did not, however, surrender himself into the hands of his enemies without resistance. He drew out and fired a pocket pistol, and having thus made an opening among his assailants, escaped into the Castle wynd, and ran towards the head of the Cowgate; but, one of the party having hit him a violent stroke on the breast with a long staff as he passed out, he was staggered, and fell several times, and having lost his hat, was laid hold of by a person in the street, who probably knew nothing of the man, or the crimes laid against him. Being taken to the guard-house, he was kept there for a considerable time, and suffered much from the insolence of some that came to see him. The captain of the guard seeing him of little stature, and of a comely countenance, exclaimed, 'Is this the boy which the whole nation has been troubled about?'

Robert Chambers, Scottish Biographical Dictionary. *James Renwick (1662–1688), leader of the extreme Covenanters, was hanged in Edinburgh in February 1688.*

The Destruction of the Chapel Royal

Holyrood House, the ancient palace of James (VII)'s ancestors, and his own habitation when in Scotland, had been repaired with becoming splendour, when he came to the throne. But it was within its precincts that he had established his royal chapel for the Catholic service, as well as a seminary of Jesuits . . . a printing establishment was also erected, from which were issued polemical tracts in defence of the Catholic religion, and similar productions. The palace and its inmates were on all these accounts very obnoxious to the Presbyterian party, which now began to obtain the ascendancy.

The same bands, consisting of the meaner class of people, apprentices, and others, whose appearance had frightened the Chancellor out of the city, continued to parade the streets with drums beating, until, confident in their numbers, they took the resolution of making an attack on the palace, which was garrisoned by a company of regular soldiers, commanded by one Captain Wallace.

As the multitude pressed on this officer's sentinels, he at length commanded his men to fire, and some of the insurgents were killed. A general cry was raised through the city, that Wallace and his soldiers were committing a massacre of the inhabitants; and many of the citizens, repairing to the Earl of Athole and his colleagues, the part of the Privy Council which remained, obtained a warrant from them for the surrender of the palace, and an order for the King's heralds to attend in their official habits to intimate the same. The city guard of Edinburgh was also commanded to be in readiness to enforce the order; the trained bands were got under arms, and the provost and magistrates, with a number of persons of condition, went to show their goodwill to the cause. Some of these volunteers acted a little out of character. Lord Mersington, one of the Judges of the Court of Session . . . was girt with a buff belt above five inches broad, bore a halbert in his hand, and (if a Jacobite eyewitness speaks truth) was 'as drunk as ale and brandy could make him'.

On the approach of this motley army of besiegers, Wallace, instead of manning the battlements and towers of the palace, drew up his men imprudently in the open courtyard in front of it. He refused to yield up his post, contending that the warrant of the Privy Council was only signed by a small number of that body. Defiance was exchanged on both sides, and firing commenced; on which most of the volunteers got into places of safety, leaving Captain Wallace and the major of the town guard to dispute the matter professionally. It chanced that the latter proved the better soldier, and finding a back way into the palace, attacked Wallace in the rear. The defenders were at the same time charged in front by the other assailants, and the palace was taken by storm. The rabble behaved themselves as riotously as might have been expected, breaking, burning, and destroying, not only the articles which belonged to the Catholic service, but the whole furniture of the chapel; and finally, forcing their way into the royal sepulchres, and pulling about the bodies of the deceased princes and kings of Scotland. These monuments, to the great scandal of the British Government, were not closed until ten or twelve years since, before which time, the exhibition of the wretched relics of mortality which had been dragged to light on this occasion, was a part of the show offered for the amusement of strangers who visted the palace.

Sir Walter Scott (1771–1832), Tales of a Grandfather

A Romantic Marriage

Mary, eldest daughter of Colonel John Erskine, married in 1739 the Rev. Alexander Webster, minister of the Tolbooth Church, Edinburgh. Connected with this marriage is a romantic incident. Prior to his settlement at Edinburgh Dr Webster was minister of Culross, Perthshire. Mary Erskine resided in that parish with her aunt Lady Preston . . . A young gentleman of the neighbourhood was attracted by her charms, but being unsuccessful in his addresses, begged Dr Webster to intercede on his behalf. The Doctor consented, and waiting on Miss Erskine, pled his friend's cause with energy. The lady listened patiently but expressed a decided negative. 'Had you spoken as well for yourself', she added, 'I might have answered differently.' To his friend Dr Webster reported the particulars of this interview, and soon afterwards presented himself at Valleyfield to plead his own suit . . . The marriage took place on the 13th June, 1737; Miss Erskine possessing a dowry of £4,000.

Charles Roger, Boswelliana (1874). *Dr Alexander Webster conducted the first scientific census of Scotland in 1755 and was one of the chief proponents of the New Town in Edinburgh.*

Dr Webster's Drinking Habits

Dr Webster was of the rigid Presbyterian Calvinistic party of the Church, and extremely popular with his congregation, to whom indeed he was very attentive. He was, however, of a social and rather a jovial disposition, and sometimes drank a good deal of wine, tho' the strength of his head was such as rarely to betray any of its effects. Going home one night at a late hour from a long supper at a tavern, and somewhat elevated with the good claret and the joyousness of the company, one of them who was attending him home said, 'Dr Webster, what would any of your parishioners say if they saw you now?' – 'Sir,' replied the Doctor, 'they would not believe their eyes.'

Henry Mackenzie, The Anecdotes and Egotisms of Henry Mackenzie

A Touch of the Tar-brush

. . . it was women in particular who were given to falling asleep during church services. Having slaved at home throughout the week, worked extra hard on Saturday to get ready for Sunday and then walked possibly a long way to church, they were exceedingly tired, if not exhausted, when they got there ... In 1643 Monifieth Kirk Session gave their beadle, Robert Scott, 5 s with which to buy a pint of tar so that he might slap it with a brush on to the face of anyone asleep or with a plaid about their heads... A far kinder way was that of a minister who once stopped abruptly during his sermon and addressed the congregation thus: 'Try and sit up! Sit up and A'll tell ye an awn-ecdote ...'

Anne Gordon, Candie for the Foundling (1992)

John Brown Buys a Greek Testament

He had now acquired so much knowledge of Greek as encouraged him to hope that he might at length be prepared to reap the richest of all rewards which classical learning could confer on him, the capacity of reading, in the original tongue, the Blessed New Testament ... Full of this hope, he became anxious to possess a copy of the invaluable volume. One night, accordingly, having folded his flocks in safety, and his fellow-shepherd ... having undertaken to discharge his pastoral duties for the succeeding day, he set out on a midnight-journey to St Andrews, a distance of twenty-four miles. Having reached his destination in the morning, he repaired straightway to the nearest bookseller, and asked for a copy of the Greek New Testament. The master of the shop, though, situated as he was in a provincial Scottish University, he must have been accustomed to hear such books inquired for by youths whose appearance and habiliments were none of the most civilised, was nevertheless somewhat astonished by such an application from so unlikely a person, and was rather disposed to taunt him with its presumption. Meanwhile a party of gentlemen, said to have been professors in the university, entered the shop, and having understood the matter, one of them desired the bookseller to bring the volume, who accordingly produced it, and throwing it down on the table, 'Boy,' said he, 'read that book, and you shall have it for nothing.' The offer was too good to be rejected, and young Brown having acquitted himself to the admiration of his judges, carried off his cheaply-purchased Testament in triumph, and ere the evening arrived, was studying it in the midst of his flock upon the hills of Abernethy.

Robert Chambers, Scottish Biographical Dictionary. *John Brown (1722–1787), became author of* The Self-Interpreting Bible *and many other popular religious works. This same story is told about other auto-didacts in other countries. In similar vein Sir D'Arcy Wentworth Thompson's daughter Ruth, in her biography of her father, recalls how 'He was seen standing outside a second-hand bookshop on George IV Bridge in Edinburgh, accompanied by three small ragamuffins who were gazing eagerly at a copy of* Robinson Crusoe. *D'Arcy was heard to say that if they could read him half a page, the*

book would be theirs; this they did and were soon darting down the
Candlemaker Row with their trophy. The curious thing was it was the very
copy D'Arcy himself had read as a child.'

Misunderstood Kipper

When Dr d'Aubigné was staying with the Scottish divine and preacher Thomas
Chalmers, he was served a kippered herring for breakfast. He asked his
host the meaning of the word 'kippered' and was told 'kept' or 'preserved'.
This item of information had a sequel at morning prayer, when the guest,
leading the household in their devotions, prayed that Dr Chalmers might be
'kept, preserved, and kippered'.

L. Missen, After Dinner Stories and Anecdotes, *quoted in C. Fadiman,*
The Little, Brown Book of Anecdotes *(1985). Jean Henri Merle d'Aubigné*
(1794–1872) was a leading Swiss Calvinist divine.

The Rev. Ebenezer Brown Fails to Hold his Audience

When he was on a missionary tour in the north, he one morning met a band of
Highland shearers on their way to the harvest; he asked them to stop and hear
the word of God. They said they could not, as they had their wages to work for.
He offered them what they said they would lose; to this they agreed, and he
paid them, and closing his eyes engaged in prayer; when he had ended, he
looked up, and his congregation had vanished! His shrewd brother Thomas, to
whom he complained of this faithlessness, said, 'Eben, the next time ye pay folk
to hear you preach, keep your eyes open, and pay them when you are done.'

John Brown (1810–1882), letter to John Cairns, D.D., from Horae
Subsecivae *(1861)*

The Disruption

The morning levee had been marked by an incident of a somewhat extraordinary nature, and which history, though in these days little disposed to
mark prodigies and omens, will scarce fail to record. The crowd in the
Chamber of Presence was very great, and there was, we believe, a considerable degree of confusion and pressure in consequence. Suddenly – whether
brushed by some passer by, jostled rudely aside, or merely affected by the
tremor of the floor communicated to the partitioning – a large portrait of
William the Third, that had held its place in Holyrood for nearly a century
and a half, dropped heavily from the walls. 'There,' exclaimed a voice from
the crowd, 'there goes the Revolution Settlement.'

. . . The Moderator rose and addressed the House in a few impressive
sentences. There had been an infringement, he said, on the Constitution of

the Church – an infringement so great, that they could not constitute its General Assembly without a violation of the union between Church and State, as now authoritatively defined and declared. He was therefore compelled, he added, to protest against proceeding further; and, unfolding a document which he held in his hand, he read, in a slow and emphatic manner, the protest of the Church.

For the first few seconds, the extreme anxiety to hear defeated its object, the universal hush, hush, occasioned considerably more noise than it allayed; but the momentary confusion was succeeded by the most unbroken silence; and the reader went on till the impressive close of the document, when he flung it down on the table of the House, and solemnly departed. He was followed, at a pace's distance, by Dr Chalmers; Dr Gordon and Dr Patrick Mcfarlan immediately succeeded; and then the numerous sitters on the thickly occupied benches behind filed after them, in a long unbroken line, which for several minutes together continued to thread the passage to the eastern door, till at length only a blank space remained. As the well-known faces and forms of some of the ablest and most eminent men that ever adorned the Church of Scotland glided along in the current, to disappear from the courts of the State institution for ever, there rose a cheer from the galleries, and an impatient cry of 'Out, out,' from the ministers and elders not members of Assembly, now engaged in sallying forth, to join with them, from the railed area behind. The cheers subsided, choaked in not a few instances by tears. The occasion was far too solemn for the commoner manifestations of either censure or approval; it excited feelings that lay too deep for expression. There was a marked peculiarity in the appearance of their opponents – a blank, restless, pivot-like turning of head from the fast-emptying benches to one another's faces; but they uttered no word, not even in whispers. At length, when the last of the withdrawing party had disappeared, there ran from bench to bench a hurried, broken whispering – 'How many?' – 'How many?' – 'A hundred and fifty?' 'No'; 'Yes'; 'Four hundred?' 'No'; – and then for a moment all was still again. The scene that followed we deemed one of the most striking of the day.

The empty vacated benches stretched away from the Moderator's seat in the centre of the building, to the distant wall. There suddenly glided into the front rows a small party of men whom no-one knew, obscure, mediocre, blighted-looking men, that, contrasted with the well-known forms of our Chalmerses and Gordons . . . reminded one of the thin and blasted corn-ears of Pharaoh's vision, and, like them too, seemed typical of a time of famine and destitution. Who are these? was the general query; but no one seemed to know. At length the significant whisper ran along the house, 'The Forty'. There was a grin of mingled contempt and compassion visible on many a broad Moderate face, and a too audible titter shook the gallery. There seemed a degree of incongruity in the sight that partook highly of the ludicrous. For our own part, we were so carried away by a vagrant association, and so missed Ali Baba, the oil kettle, and the forty jars, as to forget for a time that at the doors of these unfortunate men lies the ruin of the Scottish establishment.

Hugh Miller (1802–1856), report in The Edinburgh Witness, *20 May 1843*

A Ministerial Sacrifice

. . . the Disruption caused much excitement, and also much talk throughout the country, and no doubt much pain and misery to the ministers who deprived themselves of their livings. It was said that one of these Sutherland ministers, in discussing the sacrifice they had made for conscience' sake, mentioned that no man had made greater sacrifices than he had, for besides the comfortable manse and glebe he had vacated he had to relinquish a snug farm requiring three pairs of horses, as well as the honour of a dinner twice a year with the Duke of Sutherland. He ended by asking, 'What were the sacrifices the Apostle Peter made compared to these? A coble and a few nets!'

Joseph Mitchell (1803–1883), Reminiscences of My Life in the Highlands

The Rev. Mr Baird and Marriages of Necessity

My father had a strong dislike for marriages of necessity, common enough at one time in Scotland. He was called to officiate at one of these, and arrived with reluctance and disgust half an hour late.

'You are very late, Mr Baird,' said the bridegroom.

'Yes, about six months too late,' replied Mr Baird.

John Logie Baird (1888–1946), Sermons, Soap and Television

Funding of the Iona Community

Early the next year Dr Macleod was laying plans for a kind of religious organisation new to modern Scotland. The little isle of Iona had been the home of the greatest of early Celtic missionaries, St Columba, and his monks. George MacLeod had known and loved the island's peculiar air of sanctity and remoteness, its medieval abbey and nunnery whose remains still rose above its village street and the narrow waters of its sound. The abbey church had been restored, but the monastic buildings were still in ruins. It was now proposed that Iona should become the centre of a community once more. This would consist partly of craftsmen, partly of divinity students. Together they would rebuild the monastery and worship in the great church during the long days of the western summer. The students would spend part of their time in study and discussion. Having learned to live and work with other men and know what a worshipping society could do, they would return to the cities in the autumn to approach the work of evangelism and church organisation in a new communal spirit.

Having thought out his plan, Dr MacLeod reckoned that £5,000 would be needed to begin, but the rich churchmen whom he approached would hear nothing of it. Finally he wrote to Sir James Lithgow. To Sir James, too, Iona meant a good deal. He had often visited it by sea from his sister's home, Glengorm. On an evening when Dr Macleod's appeal was being framed James Lithgow had suggested to his wife that the Scottish Church was not imaginative enough. It was also too poor. It had gathered money for good works, from hospitals to foreign missions, but had not provided properly for itself. There ought, they agreed, to be some new approach to the people of the mid-twentieth century, which would surely need more money. When the MacLeod letter arrived it was clear to him that the new project, of which he had heard nothing when he spoke, was very much in character.

'Will you give up your damned pacifism if I give you a start?' he asked. This was the type of test which both Lithgow brothers are known to have applied when they were considering an application of some kind. If the man one of them was dealing with compromised himself by some too eager concession he would not get what he wanted.

Dr Macleod's reply, however, was 'Not on your life!'

He got his £5,000 and was told to come back in a year's time if more was needed.

J. M. Reid, James Lithgow: Master of Works *(1964). Dr Macleod was then minister of Govan, where the Lithgow shipyard was situated. In the previous year (1937) he had refused Lithgow's request to bless the launch of a warship, but said he would be proud to give a blessing to a merchant vessel, which Lithgow duly invited him to do.*

CLANS AND CLANSFOLK

The Fairy Flag

'What is yon music I am hearing, if it is hearing I am?' said the Lady of Macleod to herself, as she sat in her hall, spinning the wool. And she arose, and made for the music, and whither drew it her but, step by step, to the sleep-chamber of her baby son. What saw she there but the Little Woman of the Green Kirtle swathing the child in a silk Banner of many colours, and singing over him a Cradle Spell.

Ho-ro veel-a-vok, Bone and flesh o' me,
Ho-ro veel-a-vok, Blood and pith o' me.
Skin like falling snow, green thy mail-coat,
Live thy steeds be, dauntless thy following.

'God sain us!' cried out the Lady of Macleod, 'it is I who am the mother to yon child.' And at the sound of the Good Name she vanished, the Little Woman of the Green Kirtle.

But the Cradle Spell remained; the Banner, likewise, and, together, they made of a clan the something more than a clan. The women nursed the children and crooned the songs and did the day's work, with a thought somewhere in the heart of each that on a day of days she might be called to Dunvegan Castle to sing the Cradle Song over the young heir. And the men, going forth to battle, fought in the hope that now was the day on which the Banner would appear at their head, putting rout on the enemy. Outwardly, at any rate, the luck was mostly with the women. Baby heirs came often; the Banner came but twice. The end of the tale is not yet, however. 'What came twice will come thrice,' say the Islesfolk, 'and on a day to be, it is the Fairy Flag, going forth for the last time, that will be overcoming the world for us, Gaels.' Which may well be, if one remembers that its first burden was a little child, its first victory a song, and its weaving not of the flesh.

Kenneth Macleod (1871–1955), The Road to the Isles

How The MacLeods Gained St Kilda

Long ago the MacLeods of Harris and the MacDonalds of Uist, both desirous of owning St Kilda, decided that a curach from Harris and a curach from Uist should race each other across the intervening fifty miles of sea, and that the crew of the boat arriving first should have the right to claim Hirta. The long race was a close one, and the boats approached Hirta with the MacDonalds leading by a few yards. When it seemed certain that the MacLeods would be defeated . . . their leader, Colla MacLeod, chopped off his left hand at the wrist and hurled it ashore over the heads of the rival crew.

Seton Gordon (1888–1977), Afoot in the Hebrides. *Versions of this story are told about other characters in similar situations.*

The Origin of the Macintyres

After his victory in Morvern, and in spite of a little opposition in Argyllshire, Somerled had mastered the lands of 'Lorn, Argyle, Kintyre and Knapdale; most of the inhabitants knowing these lands were his by right, as formerly belonging to and possessed by his predecessors'. About this time

'Olay, surnamed the Red' (Olaf in the *Chronicle of Man*) the king of Man had sailed north with his fleet to quell a rising in the more northerly of the isles, and had encamped on the shore of Loch Stornua, at the point of Ardnamurchan.

'Somerled came to the other side of the loch, and cried out, if Olay was there, and how he fared?

'Olay replied that he was well.

'Then said Somerled: "I come from Somerled, Thane of Argyle, who promises to assist you conditionally in your expedition, provided you bestow your daughter on him."

'Olay answered, that he would not give him his daughter, and that he knew he, himself, was the man; but that he and his men should follow him in his expedition.

'So Somerled resolved to follow Olay. There was at that time a foster-brother of Olay's, one Maurice MacNeill, in Olay's company, who was a near friend of Somerled; and when Somerled brought his two galleys near the place where Olay's ship lay, this Maurice aforesaid came to where he was, and said that he would find means by which he might come to get Olay's daughter. So, in the night-time, he bored Olay's ship under water with many holes, and made a pin for each hole, overlaying them with tallow and butter.

'When they were up in the morning and set to sea, after passing the point of Ardnamurchan, Olay's ship sprang a leak, casting the tallow and butter out of the holes by the ship tossing on the waves, and, beginning to sink, Olay and his men cried out for help to Somerled. Maurice replied that Somerled would not save him unless he bestowed his daughter upon him.

'At last Olay, being in danger of his life, confirmed by an oath that he would give his daughter to Somerled, who received him immediately into his galley.

'Maurice went into Olay's galley, and fixed the pins in the holes which he had formerly prepared for them, and by these means they landed in safety. From that time the posterity of Maurice are called the Macintyres (from saor = wright) to this day.'

I. F. Grant, The Lordship of the Isles (*1935*), *quoting from the* Chronicle of Man. *Somerled, Lord of Argyll, (d. 1164) was the ancestor of the Lords of the Isles.*

The Slaughter on the North Inch

Two clans, or rather two leagues or confederacies, composed each of several separate clans, fell into such deadly feud with each other, as filled the whole neighbourhood with slaughter and discord.

When this feud or quarrel could be no otherwise ended, it was resolved that the difference should be decided by a combat of thirty men of the Clan

Chattan, against the same number of the Clan Kay; that the battle should take place on the North Inch of Perth, a beautiful and level meadow, in part surrounded by the river Tay, and that it should be fought in the presence of the King and his nobles. Now, there was a cruel policy in this arrangement; for it was to be supposed that all the best and leading men of each clan would desire to be among the thirty which were to fight for their honour, and it was no less to be expected that the battle would be very bloody and desperate. Thus, the probable event would be, that both clans, having lost very many of their best and bravest men, would be more easily managed in future. Such was probably the view of the King and his counsellors in permitting this desperate conflict, which however was much in the spirit of the times.

The parties on each side were drawn out, armed with sword and target, axe and dagger, and stood looking on each other with fierce and savage aspects, when, just as the signal for fight was expected, the commander of the Clan Chattan perceived that one of his men, whose heart had failed him, had deserted his standard. There was no time to seek another man from the clan, so the chieftain, as his only resource, was obliged to offer a reward to anyone who would fight in the room of the fugitive. Perhaps you think it might be difficult to get a man, who, for a small hire, would undergo the perils of a battle which was likely to be so obstinate and deadly. But in that fighting age men valued their lives lightly. One Henry Wynd, a citizen of Perth, and a saddler by trade, a little bandy-legged man, but of great strength and activity, and well accustomed to use the broadsword, offered himself, for half a French crown, to serve on the part of the Clan Chattan in the battle of that day.

The signal was then given by the sound of the royal trumpets, and of the great war-bagpipes of the Highlanders, and the two parties fell on each other with the utmost fury, their natural ferocity of temper being excited by feudal hatred against the hostile clan, zeal for the honour of their own, and a consciousness that they were fighting in presence of the King and nobles of Scotland. As they fought with the two-handed sword and axe, the wounds they inflicted on each other were of a ghastly size and character. Heads were cloven asunder, limbs were lopped from the trunk. The meadow was soon drenched with blood, and covered with dead and wounded men.

In the midst of the deadly conflict, the chieftain of the Clan Chattan observed that Henry Wynd, after he had slain one of the Clan Kay, drew aside, and did not seem willing to fight more.

'How is this?' said he, 'art thou afraid?'

'Not I,' answered Henry; 'but I have done enough of work for half a crown.'

'Forward and fight,' said the Highland chief; 'he that doth not grudge his day's work, I will not stint him in his wages.'

Thus encouraged, Henry Wynd again plunged into the conflict, and, by his excellence as a swordsman, contributed a great deal to the victory, which at length fell to the Clan Chattan. Ten of the victors, with Henry Wynd, whom the Highlanders called the Gow Chrom (that is, the crooked or bandy-legged smith, for he was both a smith and a saddler, war-saddles being then made of steel), were left alive, but they were all wounded. Only one of the Clan Kay survived, and he was unhurt. But this single individual dared not oppose himself to eleven men, though all more or less injured, but, throwing himself into the Tay, swam to the other side and and went off to carry to the Highlands the news of his clan's defeat. It is said that he was so ill received by his kinsmen that he put himself to death.

Sir Walter Scott (1771–1832), Tales of a Grandfather. *This event happened in 1392, in the reign of Robert III.*

The Munros Dispute a 'Road Collop'

John Munro, the tutor of Foulis, in travelling homeward from Edinburgh to Ross, stopped in a meadow in Strathardle that he and his servants might obtain some rest. While they were asleep, the owner of the meadow cut off the tails of their horses. To revenge this insult, on his return to Ross, he summoned his whole kinsmen and followers, and having selected 350 of the best men among them, he returned to Strathardle, which he wasted and spoiled, killing some of the inhabitants and carrying off their cattle. In passing by the castle of Moy, on his way home, the laird of Macintosh sent a message to him demanding a share of the spoil. This was customary among the Highlanders when a party drove cattle so taken through a gentleman's land, and the part so exacted was called a *Staoig Rathaid*, or *Staoig Creich*, that is, a road collop. Munro offered Macintosh a reasonable share of the booty, but the latter would not accept of less than half. This Munro refused, and drove off the cattle. Collecting his clansmen, Macintosh went in pursuit of him, and came up with him at Clach-na-haire, near Inverness. On perceiving his approach, Munro sent home fifty of his men with the cattle, and in the contest that ensued, Macintosh and the greater part of his men were killed. Several of the Munros were also slain, and John Munro himself was left for dead on the field of battle, when Lord Lovat had him carried to his house in the neighbourhood, where he was cured of his wounds. One of his hands was so mutilated that he lost the use of it, on which account he was called John Bac-Laimh, or Ciotach (Left-handed).

W. Anderson, Scottish Nation *(1863). This event occurred in 1454. The 'tutor' of a clan was the guardian of an underage chief.*

Macleod of Assynt

The name of the laird of Assynt lives in Scottish history with that of Sir John Menteith, who sold Wallace. It is remembered as the solitary case of a

Gael who betrayed a suppliant for gold. Ian Lom, the bard of Keppoch, has left bitter verses on the 'stripped tree of the false apples, Neil's son of woeful Assynt'. He made little of his infamy. His lands were raided by Glengarry, the Macleods, and the penitent Mackenzies. After the restoration he was a good deal in gaol, and was twice tried for his life. His castle was burned, and no children survived to bear his name. He was awarded 25,000 pounds Scots for his services, of which 20,000 were to be paid in coin and the rest in oatmeal. It does not appear that he ever got the money, but the receipts for the meal were long extant, and Highland tradition is positive that two-thirds of it were sour.

John Buchan (1875–1940), Montrose. Neil Macleod of Assynt handed the Marquis of Montrose over to the Covenant leaders after the Battle of Carbisdale in 1650. The destruction of his castle of Ardvreck is itself the subject of a legend, recorded in Polson's Scottish Witchcraft Lore: A ball was given in the castle one Saturday night, and the fun, which was fast and furious, was continued to the early hours of the Sunday morning. The revellers, to prevent the dawn reminding them of the approach of the Sunday morning, had heavy blinds drawn across the windows, and the cocks' tongues cut out lest they should herald the morning. A dispute, however, arose between some of the guests, bloodshed was threatened, and it was agreed to ask the presence of the devil in bodily form to settle the matter. After the chanting of incantations, the Prince of Darkness did appear, but at the same moment the castle was found to be on fire, and in a few minutes the whole building was a mass of blackened ruins. It has never been rebuilt.

A Strange Confrontation

Upon the west coast a highly dramatic incident occurred in 1527, which was in later years productive of much strife and bloodshed. The scene of it was a rock at the south end of Lismore, and the chief actors Lachlan Cattanach MacLean of Duart, and his wife the Lady Elizabeth, sister of the then Earl of Argyll. The union of this couple proved unhappy, and, as the eye of the chief fell upon a daughter of MacLean of Treshnish, a comely lady of his own clan, he conceived the idea of ridding himself of the Lady Elizabeth by exposing her on an isolated rock which, at high water, was deeply covered. With the aid of several clansmen the savage chief placed her on the rock in the evening hour and, on this place of certain death, left her to her fate. But just as the waves were breaking over her, a deliverer came, and she was rescued by the crew of a boat sent out by one of the chief's bodyguard, who had come to hear of the villainy that was being perpetrated. By these men the unhappy lady was taken to the mainland, and escorted to her brother's stronghold at Inveraray. Of the rescue, Lachlan knew nothing, but communicated to the Earl the news of the death of his sister from natural causes, and his desire that she should be interred in the tomb of her ancestors. For the time the Earl kept his counsel, and within a few days the tearful husband, accompanied by many followers, arrived at the castle, bearing a coffin containing a lay figure. But the tables were turned on the thunderstruck monster when, on being ushered into the dining hall where the family sat at dinner, he found the Lady Elizabeth seated at the head of the table. Cattanach was allowed to escape, and no dramatic catastrophe occurred, but the resentment of the Campbells at the odious act burned deeply into their souls. Many years afterwards, when MacLean was an old man of eighty years, that resentment found expression in his murder at the hands of Sir John Campbell of Calder, brother of the Lady Elizabeth. The deed of vengeance was perpetrated while the aged chief was resting in his bed in Edinburgh, to which city he had come under letters of protection.

Dugald Mitchell, History of the Highlands and Gaelic Scotland (1900)

Lochiel's Toothsome Morsel

One of the last of the Highland chiefs to lay down his arms (against Cromwell's Commonwealth) was the renowned head of the Camerons, Evan Cameron of Lochiel, or Evan Dubh, as he was commonly called. On more than one occasion, this distinguished Highland chief, while serving under Middleton, found it necessary to withdraw from the general body, and return to Lochaber to protect his property against the depredations of the garrison of Inverlochy. On the first of these occasions, Lochiel had a rencontre with an English officer of great personal strength, who, during the fight, marked him out for single combat. 'Lochiel', says Scott, in telling the story, 'was dexterous enough to disarm the Englishman; but his gigantic adversary suddenly closed in on him, and in the struggle which ensued both fell to the ground, the officer uppermost. He was in the act of grasping at his sword, which had fallen near the place where they lay in deadly struggle, and was naturally extending his neck in the same direction, when the Highland chief, making a desperate effort, grasped his enemy by the collar, and snatching with his teeth at the bare and outstretched throat, he seized it as a wild-cat might have done, and kept his hold so fast as to tear out the windpipe. The officer died in this singular manner. Lochiel was so far from disowning or being ashamed of this extraordinary mode of defence, that he was afterwards heard to say, it was the sweetest morsel he had ever tasted.'

Some years later, when Evan Dubh went up with Monk to London, he had a curious experience which very vividly brought back to him the scene just described. One day when being shaved in a barber's shop, the operator observed, 'You are from the North, sir?' 'Yes,' said Lochiel, 'I am. Do you know people from the North?' 'No,' replied the barber, 'nor do I wish to: they are savages there. Would you believe it, sir, one of them tore the throat out of my father with his teeth, and I only wish I had the fellow's throat as near me as I have yours just now.' Evan Dubh never again entered a barber's shop.

Dugald Mitchell, History of the Highlands and Gaelic Scotland

The Betrayal of Alastair MacGregor of Glenstrae

To the Earls of Argyll and Atholl were now entrusted the active proceedings to be taken against the (MacGregor) rebels, who, after a brave and stubborn resistance, were at last overcome. Early in the year 1604 Alastair MacGregor surrendered himself to Argyll on the condition that the latter should grant him a safe-conduct into England, that he might there lay his case before the King, and crave his mercy. What Argyll did, however, was to send him over the Border and then immediately bring him back to Edinburgh, where, after a few days, he and some hostages whom he had previously delivered up to Argyll were hanged – 'himself being chieff he was hangit his awin hicht above the rest of his friendis'.

Dugald Mitchell, History of the Highlands and Gaelic Scotland

'Another for Hector'

In the battle of Inverkeithing, between the Royalists and Oliver Cromwell's troops, five hundred of the followers of the Laird of Maclean were left dead on the field. In the heat of the conflict, seven brothers of the clan sacrificed their lives in defence of their leader, Sir Hector Maclean. Being hard pressed by the enemy, he was supported and covered from their attacks by these intrepid men; and as one brother fell, another came up in succession to cover for him, crying 'Another for Hector'.

David Stewart of Garth (1772–1829), Sketches of the Character, Institutions and Customs of the Highlanders of Scotland. *The seven were traditionally Hector's foster-brothers. But he too was killed in the battle, which was fought in 1648.*

Rob Roy and the Duke of Montrose

When Macgregor required a supply of meal, he sent notice to a certain number of the Duke's tenants to meet him at the girnal, on a certain day, with their horses to carry home his meal. They met accordingly, when he ordered the horses to be loaded, and, giving a regular receipt to his Grace's storekeeper for the quantity taken, he marched away, always entertaining the people very handsomely, and careful never to take the meal till it had been lodged in the Duke's store-house, in payment of rent. When the money rents were paid, Macgregor frequently attended. On one occasion, when

Mr Graham of Killearn (the factor) had collected the tenants to receive their rents, all Rob Roy's men happened to be absent except Alexander Stewart, 'the Bailie' . . . With this single attendant, he descended to Chapellairoch, where the factor and tenants were assembled. He reached the house after it was dark, and, looking in at a window, saw Killearn, surrounded by a number of the tenants, with a bag full of money, which he had received, and was in the act of depositing in a press or cupboard; at the same time saying, that he would cheerfully give all in the bag for Rob Roy's head. This notification was not lost on the outside visitor, who instantly gave orders in a loud voice to place two men at each window, two at each corner, and four at each of two doors, thus appearing to have twenty men. Immediately the door opened, and he walked in with his attendant close behind, each armed with a sword in his right and a pistol in his left hand, and with dirks and pistols slung in their belts. The company started up, but he requested them to sit down, as his business was only with Killearn, whom he ordered to hand down the bag and put it on the table. When this was done, he desired the money to be counted and proper receipts to be drawn out, certifying that he had received the money from the Duke of Montrose's agent, as the Duke's property, the tenants having paid their rents, so that no after demand could be made against them, on account of this transaction; and finding that some of the people had not obtained receipts, he desired the factor to grant them immediately, 'to show his Grace', said he, 'that it is from him I take the money, and not from these honest men who have paid him'. After the whole was concluded, he ordered supper, saying, that as he had got the purse, it was proper he should pay the bill; and after they had drank heartily together for several hours, he called his bailie to produce his dirk and lay it naked upon the table. Killearn was then sworn that he would not move from that spot for an hour after the departure of Macgregor, who thus cautioned him: 'If you break your oath, you know what you are to expect in the next world and in this,' pointing to his dirk. He then walked away, and was beyond pursuit before the hour expired.

David Stewart of Garth, Sketches of the Character, Institutions and Customs of the Highlanders of Scotland. *Graham of Killearn experienced other harassments from Rob Roy in his feud with the Duke. When Montrose complained that the Duke of Argyll gave the outlawed Rob Roy safe haven on his land, Argyll was able to riposte that it was Montrose who supplied him with food and money.*

Duncan Bán MacIntyre's First Poem

Duncan had just reached manhood when the memorable Rising of 1745 took place, and ignorant alike of book-learning and the ways of men, though ever on the alert and shrewdly observant, he was easily lured into the great struggle. For the paltry sum of 300 merks Scots, or £16, 17s. 6d., he engaged to act in the army of King George as substitute for Mr Fletcher, a tacksman of Glenorchy, and in this capacity served under Colonel Campbell of Carwhin at the battle of Falkirk, 17th January 1746.

But the young hunter's heart was not with the army he joined. Fain would he have been on that occasion with the lads who followed Prince Charlie. And lacking enthusiasm for the fight he was hired to uphold against his own countrymen, he thought no shame, on the sudden repulse of the red coats, to fling away his sword and fly with the vanquished. Indeed in his first poem on the battle he is playfully humorous in describing the retreat and his own undignified share in the rout. . . The sword with which Macintyre so lightly parted had been given him by Fletcher, and because he had lost it, that irate gentleman refused to pay him his bounty. Yet in this affair the substitute was more than a match for his principal. In the above-mentioned poem, which became widely-known and popular, he satirised the missing weapon and its stingy owner in a provokingly ingenious fashion. The sword he described as an edgeless lump of iron with a twist in the hilt; so heavy, that it bruised his side, and like an alder-tree in size. One that could neither hew nor cut, it carried the soot and rust of ages on its blunt, lack-lustre blade. And not content with the simple power of sarcasm, the defrauded youth submitted his grievance to the Earl of Breadalbane, who commanded the tacksman to hand over the money.

Stung by this humiliation the foolish Fletcher harboured revenge, and meeting the object of his ire at a local market, he struck him with his staff, shouting, 'Go, rascal, and make a song on that.' Duncan might have retaliated, but being of a peaceable and non-pugnacious nature he quietly withdrew. The publicity which those who were witnesses gave the incident in the district won for the bard additional sympathy and respect, while it served to lower his assailant considerably in the popular esteem.

Magnus Maclean, The Literature of the Highlands (*1903*)

A Chief's Discomfiture

. . . as the meanest among them pretended to be his relations by consanguinity, they insisted on the privilege of taking him by the hand wherever they met him. Concerning this last, I once saw a number of very discontented countenances, when a certain Lord, one of the chiefs, endeavoured to evade this ceremony. It was in the presence of an English gentleman, of high station, from whom he would willingly have concealed the knowledge of such seeming familiarity with slaves of wretched appearance; and thinking it, I suppose, a kind of contradiction to what he had often boasted at other times, viz., his despotic power in his clan.

Edmund Burt (c.1692–1755), Letters of a Gentleman from the North of Scotland

John F. Campbell Visits a Story Man in the Isles

Let me describe one of these old story men as a type of his kind. . . . His name is MacPhie; he lives at the north end of South Uist, where the road ends at a sound, which has to be forded at the ebb to get to Benbecula. The house is built of a double wall of loose boulders, with a layer of peat three feet thick between the walls. The ends are round, and the roof rests on the inner wall, leaving room for a crop of yellow gowans. A man might walk round the roof on the top of the wall. There is but one room, with two low doors, one on each side of the house. The fire is on the floor; the chimney is a hole above it; and the rafters are hung with pendants and festoons of shining black peat reek. They are of birch from the mainland, American drift wood, or broken wreck. They support a covering of turf and straw, and stones, and heather ropes, which keep out the rain well enough.

. . . The owner of the house, whom I visited twice, is seventy-nine. He told me nine stories, and like all the others, declared that there was no man in the islands who knew them so well. 'He could not say how many he knew'; he seemed to know versions of nearly everything I had got; and he told me plainly that my versions were good for nothing.

'Huch! Thou hast not got them right at all.' They came into his mind, he said, sometimes at night, when he could not sleep – old tales that he had not heard for threescore years.

He had the manner of a practised narrator, and it is quite evident that he is one; he chuckled at the interesting parts, and laid his withered finger on my knee as he gave out the terrible bits with due solemnity. A small boy in a kilt, with large round glittering eyes, was standing mute at his knee, gazing at his wrinkled face, and devouring every word. The boy's mother first boiled, and then mashed, potatoes; and his father, a well grown man in tartan breeks, ate them. Ducks and ducklings, a cat and a kitten, some hens and a baby, all tumbled about on the clay floor together, and expressed their delight at the savoury prospect, each in his own fashion; and three wayfarers dropped in and listened for a spell, and passed their remarks till the ford was shallow. The light came streaming down the chimney, and through a single pane of glass, lighting up a tract in the blue mist of the peat smoke, and fell on the white hair and brown withered face of the old man, as he sat on a low stool with his feet to the fire; and the rest of the dwelling, with all its plenishing of boxes and box-beds, dishes and dresser, and gear of all sorts, faded away through shades of deepening brown, to the black darkness of the smoked roof and the 'peat corner'. There we sat, and smoked and talked for hours, till the tide ebbed; and then I crossed the ford by wading up to the waist, and dried my clothes in the wind in Benbecula.

J. F. Campbell, from the Introduction to Popular Tales of the West Highlands, Orally Collected (*1890*)

CRIME AND THE LAW

The Angus Cannibals

About this tyme thair was ane briggant tane, with his haill familie, quho haunted a place in Angus. This mischeivous man had ane execrabe faschione to tak all young men and childrene aither he could steall away quietlie, or tak away without knawledge, and eat thame, and the younger they war, esteemed them the more tender and delitious. For the quhilk caus, and damnable abuse, he with his wayff and bairnes, war all brunt, except ane young wench of a yeir old, wha was saiffed, and brought to Dundie, quhair shoe was broucht up and fosterred, and when shoe cam to ane vomanes yeires, shoe was condemned and brunt quick for that cryme. It is said, that when shoe was cuming to the place of execution, thair gathered ane hudge multitud of people, and speciallie of vomen, cursing hir that shoe was so unhappie, to commit so damnable deidis. To quhom shoe turned about, with an irefull countenance, saying, 'Quhairfor chyd yea with me, as if I had committed ane unworthy act; give me credence and trow me, if yea had experience of eating men and vomenis flesch, yea wold think it so delitious, that yea would never forbear it againe.'

Robert Lindsay of Pitscottie (c.1532–1580), Chronicles of Scotland, *writing about events in the reign of James II*

Nobbling the Judge

The Armstrongs, almost without exception, were noted thieves. They seem to have possessed a rare genius for reiving. . . One of the last, and most noted of this reiving clan, was William Armstrong, a lineal descendant of the famous Johnie of Gilnockie, who was known on the Borders by the name of Christie's Will, to distinguish him from the other members of his family and clan. He flourished during the reign of Charles I, a circumstance which shows that moss-trooping did not altogether cease at the Union of the Crowns. It is related that, on one occasion, Christie's Will had got into trouble, and was imprisoned in the Tolbooth of Jedburgh. The Lord High Treasurer, the Earl of Traquair, who was visiting in the district, was led to inquire as to the cause of his confinement. The prisoner told him, with a pitiful expression of countenance, that he had got into grief for stealing two *tethers* (halters). The eminent statesman was astonished to hear that such a trivial offence had been so severely punished, and pressed him to say whether this was the only crime he had committed. He ultimately reluctantly acknowledged that there were two *delicate colts* at the end of them! This bit of pleasantry pleased his lordship, and through his intercession the culprit was released from his imprisonment.

It was a fortunate thing for Lord Traquair that he acted as he did. A short time afterwards he was glad to avail himself of the services of the man whom he had thus been the means of setting at liberty. The story is one of the most romantic on record. . . A case, in which the Earl was deeply interested, was pending in the Court of Session. It was believed that the judgment would turn on the decision of the presiding judge, who has a casting vote in the case of an equal division among his brethren. It was known that the opinion of the president was unfavourable to Traquair; and the point was, therefore, to keep him out of the way when the question should be tried. In this dilemma the Earl had recourse to Christie's Will, who at once offered his services to *kidnap* the president. He discovered that it was the judge's usual practice to take the air on horseback, on the sands of Leith, without an attendant. One day he accosted the president, and engaged him in conversation. His talk was so interesting and amusing that he succeeded in decoying him into an unfrequented and furzy common, called the Frigate Whins, where, riding suddenly up to him, he pulled him from his horse, muffled him in a large cloak which he had provided, and rode off with the luckless judge trussed up behind him. Hurrying across country as fast as he could carry him, by paths known only to persons of his description, he at last deposited his heavy and terrified burden in an old castle in Annandale, called the Tower of Graham. The judge's horse being found, it was concluded he had thrown his rider into the sea; his friends went into mourning, and a successor was appointed to his office. Meanwhile the disconsolate president had a sad time of it in the vault of the castle. His food was handed to him through an aperture in the wall, and never hearing the sound of human voices, save when a shepherd called his dog, by the name of *Batty*, and when a female domestic called upon *Maudge*, the cat. These, he concluded, were invocations of spirits, for he held himself to be in the dungeon of a sorcerer. The law suit having been decided in favour of Lord Traquair, Christie's Will was directed to set the president at liberty, three months having elapsed since he was so mysteriously spirited away from the sands at Leith. Without speaking a single word, Will entered the vault in the dead of night, again muffled up in the president's cloak, set him on a horse, and rode off with him to the place where he had found him. The joy of his friends, and the less agreeable surprise of his successor, may be more easily imagined than described, when the judge appeared in court to claim his office and honours. All embraced his own persuasion that he had been spirited away by witchcraft; nor could he himself be convinced to the contrary, until, many years afterwards, happening to travel in Annandale, his ears were saluted once more with the sounds of *Maudge* and *Batty* – the only notes which had reached him during his long confinement.

Robert Borland, Border Raids and Reivers (1898). *The judge's name is given as Sir Alexander Gibson, Lord Durie, who became a Lord of Session in 1621. A further story about the Earl of Traquair is found under Lairds, Lords and Ladies.*

A Tricky Brief

. . . in 1661, his third year at the bar, he was selected as one of the counsel of the marquis of Argyle, then tried by a commission of parliament for high treason. On this occasion, he acted with so much firmness, and even boldness, as at once established his character. As the counsel for Argyle were appointed by parliament, they presented a petition under form of protest, that in the defence of their client, they might not be made responsible for every expression they might utter, but that a latitude and freedom of expression, suitable to the extent and difficulty of the charges they were called upon to canvass, might be allowed them. This being peremptorily refused, Sir George and his associates took such steps, in consequence, as subjected them to the imminent risk of a charge of treason: 'It is impossible to plead for a traitor,' said the young lawyer, 'without speaking treason!', an antithesis certainly more bold than true, but calculated to make a considerable impact on the multitude. The counsel only escaped from the consequences of their rashness by the special mercy of the court.

Robert Chambers, Scottish Biographical Dictionary. *The young lawyer was Sir George Mackenzie of Tarbat (1630–1691), later notable for his severity against the Covenanters.*

The Trial of Hackston of Rathillet

In the barbarous spirit of the age, the seizure of Hackston was celebrated as a kind of triumph, and all possible insult was heaped on the unhappy man. He was brought into Edinburgh, mounted on a horse without a saddle, and having his face to the tail. The head and hands of Richard Cameron were borne before him on pikes. But such insults rather arouse than break the spirits of brave men. Hackston behaved with great courage before the Council. The Chancellor having upbraided him as a man of libertine habits, 'While I was so,' he replied, 'I was acceptable to your lordship; I only lost your favour when I renounced my vices.'

Sir Walter Scott (1771–1832), Tales of a Grandfather. *Rathillet was captured at the Battle of Airds Moss, and executed, with a barbarity disgraceful even for the period, in July 1680.*

A Scot Abroad

He now deserted Scotland for France, with which, like all his countrymen, he claimed a cousinship; and so profoundly did he impose upon Paris with

his immense stature, his elegant attire, his courtly manners (for he was courtesy itself, when it pleased him), that he was taken for an eminent scholar,
or at least a soldier of fortune.

Prosperity might doubtless have followed a discreet profession, but
Gilderoy must still be thieving, and he reaped a rich harvest among the
unsuspicious courtiers of France. His most highly renowned exploit was
performed at St Denis, and the record of France's humiliation is still treas-
ured. The great church was packed with ladies of fashion and their devout
admirers. Richelieu attended in state; the king himself shone upon the assembly. The strange Scotsman, whom no man knew and all men wondered at,
attracted a hundred eyes to himself and his magnificent equipment. But it
was not his to be idle, and at the very moment whereat Mass was being
sung, he contrived to lighten Richelieu's pocket of a purse. The king was a
delighted witness of the theft; but Gilderoy, assuming an air of facile intimacy, motioned him to silence; and he, deeming it a trick put upon Richelieu
by a friend, hastened, at the service-end, to ask his minister if perchance he
had a purse of gold upon him. Richelieu instantly discovered the loss, to the
king's uncontrolled hilarity, which was mitigated when it was found that
the thief, having emptied the king's pocket at the unguarded moment of his
merriment, had left them both the poorer.

Charles Whibley, A Book of Scoundrels (1897). *Gilderoy, whose real name
was Patrick MacGregor, was a notorious highwayman and robber, credited
with many exploits. He was hanged in Edinburgh in 1636 on especially
high gallows, giving rise to the phrase 'to be hanged higher than Gilderoy's
kite', and remaining famous in song:*

> Of Gilderoy sae fraid they were,
> They bound him mickle strong,
> Till Edenburrow they led him thair
> And on a gallows hong;
> They hong him high aboon the rest,
> He was so trim a boy. . .

But the French story, first found in Captain Johnson's History of the Most
Famous Highwaymen (1734), *is a fabrication. Gilderoy was no man of the
world. He did not even speak English and required a Gaelic interpreter at
his trial.*

The Aberdeen Advocates

Some (English) lawyer expressed to Lord Elibank an opinion, that at the
Union the English law should have been extended all over Scotland. 'I cannot say how that might have answered our purpose,' said Lord Patrick,

who was never nonsuited for an answer, 'but it would scarce have suited *yours*, since by this time the *Aberdeen Advocates* would have possessed themselves of all the business in Westminster Hall'.

Sir Walter Scott *(1772–1832)*, Journal *(March, 1826)*

Lord Monboddo Stays Put

About 1780, he first began to make an annual journey to London, which he continued for a good many years, indeed, till he was upwards of eighty years of age. As a carriage was not a vehicle in use among the ancients, he determined never to enter and be seated in what he termed a box. He esteemed it degrading to the dignity of human nature to be dragged at the tails of horses instead of mounted on their backs. In his journeys between Edinburgh and London he therefore rode on horseback, attended by a single servant. . . Lord Monboddo being in London in 1785, visited the King's bench, when some part of the fixtures giving way, a great scatter took place among the lawyers, and the very judges themselves rushed towards the door. Monboddo, somewhat near-sighted, and rather dull of hearing, sat still, and was the only man who did so. Being asked why he had not bestirred himself to avoid the ruin, he coolly answered, that he 'thought it was an annual ceremony, with which, being an alien, he had nothing to do'.

Robert Chambers, Scottish Biographical Dictionary. *James Burnet (Lord Monboddo, 1714–1799) was a Judge of the Court of Session, and an independently minded philosopher. His theorising on human beings' one-time possession of tails resulted in much mockery, behind his back.*

The Discovery and Execution of Deacon Brodie

After the robbery . . . he escaped into Holland; but his being a sort of public crime, the Dutch were persuaded by the remonstrance of our Ambassador to deliver him up, and he was brought to Edinburgh where he was tried and executed. The place of his concealment was unknown (indeed it was supposed he had gone to America, the common refuge of such offenders against the laws of Great Britain), but discovered himself by writing to one of his associates in cockfighting (that being a province of gambling which he was supposed to be master of) anxious to know how the issue of a battle at a main of cocks then going on in Edinburgh between two cocks, one of which was a favourite of his. His handwriting being known, the letter was opened at the post-office and thence the place of his retreat discovered.

He employed part of his wealth in bribing (as was suspected) the executioner to favour his escape, by allowing him to have a steel collar under his neck-cloth to prevent strangulation; and after he was cut down he was brought rapidly to the village of Musselburgh by the advice of an anatomist, the shake of the motion being supposed favourable to reanimation. By the same advice he had eaten a solid meal of beef-steak before his execution, another expedient for the same purpose; but these means did not avail, and he died like any other less favoured felon.

Henry Mackenzie (1745–1831), Anecdotes and Egotisms. Another unusual aspect of Brodie's execution (1 October 1788) is that he is credited with inventing the 'drop' – the system of trapdoor and lever that replaced the method of pushing the condemned man off a ladder; Brodie himself was the first to experience its efficacity. Similar tales are told of the Earl of Morton, who introduced the 'Maiden' beheading machine to Scotland and was in due course executed by it; and of course of Dr Guillotin himself.

Lord Hermand and the Improving Effects of Liquor

Lord Hermand was convivial to the point of believing that drinking could improve one's behaviour. He was a member of a panel of judges trying a young man who had accidentally killed a drinking companion. A verdict of culpable homicide was brought in and the majority of the panel thought a lenient sentence would be appropriate; a short term of imprisonment was imposed. Lord Hermand dissented: 'We are told there was no malice, and that the prisoner must have been in liquor. In liquor! Why, he was drunk! And yet he murdered the very man who had been drinking with him! They had been carousing the whole night; and yet he stabbed him! After drinking a whole bottle of rum with him! Good God, my laards, if he will do this while he's drunk, what will he not do when he's sober?'

Dictionary of National Biography. George Fergusson, Lord Hermand (1743–1827) was one of a clutch of highly idiosyncratic judges of his time.

Lord Braxfield – a Powerful Judge

Lord Braxfield was powerful, with his beetle-brows, his red face, his glowering eyes, his thick lips and growling voice which made his victims in the dock to tremble. There would come from him the coarse jokes, which in private jovial talk were seldom decent, the fleering interjections, the insolent gibes in vulgarest Scots, spoken without heart or pity. 'You're a vera clever chiel, maun; but ye wad be nane the waur o' a hanging,' was his reply to a prisoner who had pleaded ably for his life.

H. Grey Graham, Scottish Men of Letters in the Eighteenth Century (1908). Unlike some of his learned colleagues, Robert MacQueen (1722–1799), appointed to the Court of Session as Lord Braxfield, had no aspirations to history or antiquarianism. The Braxfield quotations, like the one above, taken from J. G. Lockhart's life of Scott, are mostly apocryphal. Another such, quoted in Lord Cockburn's Memorials of His Time (1856), is his comment during the trial of a political reformer in 1794. When the prisoner said that Jesus Christ too had been a reformer, the judge remarked: 'Muckle he made of that: he was hangit.' An intemperate, prejudiced and bullying judge, he was at least no coward, walking home alone to his house in Edinburgh after delivering sentence, despite occasional bloody threats from the relatives of those victimised by him.

'Trochter'

There was no Lunatic Asylum or Poor House in the North, and five or six half-witted creatures used to go about the streets, tormented often by idle boys. A poor creature was kept for many years in the jail, who was said to have committed murder in a fit of insanity, and was condemned to confinement for life. He was placed in a cell with a small grated aperture for air and light, a pallet of straw for his bed, and bread and water his food. He lay there for many years, the community perfectly indifferent to his condition, till in 1816 he was removed to the Lunatic Asylum of Dundee, where in a few years he died. We children were told that if we were not good we would be sent to 'Trochter'; such was the name he was called, being the Gaelic for murderer. He used, in a stentorian voice, which was heard a long way off, up and down the street, to cry out in Gaelic, 'Oh yea, yea, Thighearna nan gras dean trochair orm,' translated 'O Lord of Grace, have mercy on me.' The people became so accustomed to the cry that they thought nothing of it; but in the middle of the night, when the shouts were frequent, the noise was very appalling.

   Joseph Mitchell (1803–1883), Reminiscences of My Life in the Highlands, *on his boyhood in Inverness*

Boozing on the Bench

At Edinburgh, the old judges had a practice, at which even their barbaric age used to shake its head: they had always wine and biscuits on the bench when the business was plainly to be protracted beyond the usual dinner hour. The modern judges – those I mean who were made after 1800 – never gave in to this; but with those of the preceding generation, some of whom lasted several years after 1800, it was quite familiar. Black bottles of strong port were set down beside them on the bench, with glasses, carafes of water, tumblers and biscuits; and this without the slightest shame or attempt at concealment. The refreshment was generally allowed to stand untouched, and as if despised, for a short while, during which their lordships seemed to be intent only on their notes. But in a little some water was poured into the tumbler, and sipped quietly, as if merely to sustain nature. Then a few drops of wine were ventured upon, but only with the water. Till at last patience could restrain no longer, and a full bumper of the pure black element was tossed over, after which the thing went on regularly, and there was a comfortable munching and quaffing, to the great envy of the parched throats in the gallery. The strong-headed ones stood it tolerably well. Bacchus never had an easy victory over Braxfield. But it told, plainly enough, upon the feeble or the twaddling, such as Eskgrove and Craig. Not that the ermine was absolutely intoxicated. But it was certainly very muzzy.

Lord Cockburn (1779–1854), Circuit Journeys (*1888*)

Not Taking a Loan

When, at a change of government, the Whig advocate Henry Erskine became Lord Advocate, he encountered his Tory predecessor, Henry Dundas, in the Parliament House of Edinburgh (at that time, the headquarters of the legal profession). Erskine explained he was off to order his silk gown of office. Dundas said it was hardly worth his while, since he was likely to be in office such a short time, and offered to lend Erskine the gown he himself had worn.

'I have no doubt,' replied Erskine, declining the offer, 'that your gown may fit any *party*, but it shall never be said that while in office, Henry Erskine put on the *abandoned habits* of his predecessor.'

Henry Erskine (1746–1817), brother of Thomas (see below), orator, wit and supporter of democratic causes, became Lord Advocate in 1783 and again in 1806–7. Another sartorial quip was made by him when he was told one day his coat was too short. 'It will be long enough before I get another,' he said.

Thomas Erskine Worsted for Once

Erskine was warm-hearted, generous, and open, not hard or greedy. If he had sometimes to listen to gibes against his origin, they were never cruel. On one occasion, when appearing in a case relating to a patent for a knee-buckle, he held it up to the jury, exclaiming, 'How would my ancestors have admired this specimen of dexterity.' Mingay, who was opposed to him, was ready with a retort. 'Gentlemen,' he said, 'you have heard a good deal today of my learned friend's ancestors and their probable astonishment at his knee-buckles. But gentlemen, I can assure you, their astonishment would have been quite as great at his breeches.'

J. A. Lovat-Fraser, Erskine (1932). Thomas Erskine (1750–1823), youngest of three notable brothers (the eldest was the earl of Buchan: see Lairds, Lords and Ladies), and a brilliant performer at the English Bar, ended his career as Lord Chancellor.

The Dumfriesshire Murderess

It was about 1811 when I began to be familiar with the figure of Jeffrey, as I saw him in the Courts; it was in 1812 or 1813 that he became universally famous, especially in Dumfriesshire, by his saving from the gallows one 'Nell Kennedy', a country lass who had shocked all Scotland, and especially that region of it, by a wholesale murder, done on her next Neighbour and all his Household in mass, in the most cold-blooded and atrocious manner conceivable to the oldest artist in such horrors. Nell went down to Ecclefechan one afternoon, purchased a quantity of arsenic; walked back with it towards Burnswark Leas, her Father's Farm; stopped at Burnswark Farm, which was 'old Tom Stoddart's', a couple of furlongs short of her own home; and sat there gossiping till she pretended it was too late and that she would now sleep here with the maid. Slept, accordingly, old Tom giving no welcome, only stingy permission; rose with the family next morning; volunteered to make the porridge for breakfast; made it, could herself take none of it, went home instead, 'having headache' – and in an hour or so after, poor old Tom, his Wife, maid and every living creature in the house (except a dog who had vomited, and *not* except the cats, who couldn't) was dead or lay dying. Horror was universal in these solitary quiet regions; on the third day, my Father, finding no lawyer take the least notice, sent a messenger express to Dumfries; whereupon the due 'precognitions' due *et ceteras,* due arrestment of Helen Kennedy with strict questioning and strict locking-up, as the essential element. I was in Edinburgh that summer of 1812, but heard enough of the matter there; in the Border regions, where it was the universal topic, perhaps not one human creature doubted but Nell was the criminal, and would get her doom. Assize-time came, Jeffrey there; and Jeffrey, by such a play of advocacy as was never seen before, bewildered the poor jury into temporary deliquium, or loss of wits (so that the poor foreman, *Scotticè* 'chancellor', on whose casting-vote it turned, said at last, with the sweat bursting from his brow, 'Mercy, then, mercy!'), and brought Nell clear off – home that night, riding gently out of Dumfries in man's clothes to escape the rage of the mob. The jury-chancellor, they say, on awakening next morning, smote his now dry brow, with a gesture of despair, and exclaimed, 'Was I mad?' I have heard from persons who were at the trial that Jeffrey's art in examining of witnesses was extreme, that he made them seem to say almost what he would, and blocked them up from saying what they evidently wished to say; his other great resource was urging the 'want of motive' on Nell's part – no means of fancying how a blousy rustic lass should go into such a thing; thing *must* have happened otherwise! And indeed, the stagnant stupid soul of Nell, awake only to its own appetites, and torpid as dead bacon to all else in this universe, had needed uncommonly little motive: a blackguard young farmer of the neighbourhood, it was understood, had answered her, in a trying circumstance, 'No, oh no, I cannot marry you: Tom Stoddart has a bill against me for £50; I have no money, how can I marry?' 'Stoddart; £50?' thought Nell to herself; and without difficulty decided on removing that small obstacle!

Thomas Carlyle (1795–1881), Reminiscences. Francis Jeffrey's advocacy had the effect of leaving Nell Kennedy free first to murder her baby, for which she again was acquitted; and then to maintain a career of arson and other crime until she eventually disappeared from her native area.

'Not Proven'

The judges had already taken their seats, and now the fifteen jurymen entered the court and took their places; and one by one they answered a roll-call of their names.

The Clerk of the court then called upon their foreman, William Moffat, the teacher from the High School, to deliver the verdict.

He rose to his feet, his eyes filled with tears, and consulted the piece of paper which he held in his hand. Then without glancing in the direction of the prisoner, he said:

'The jury find the panel not guilty on the first charge in the indictment by a majority. Of the second charge not proven. And by a majority find the third charge also not proven.'

On the two charges on which the verdict had not been unanimous the majority had been thirteen to two.

All eyes had been on the prisoner as this verdict was given, but the prisoner herself had kept her gaze upon the speaker, staring at him steadily but with no signs of agitation, but an observer in the court, who was watching her intently at this moment, noted that 'when the verdict of not proven on the third charge was pronounced, her head slightly fell, and her face broke into a bright but somewhat agitated smile'.

But, if the effect on the prisoner was only slight, the reaction among those in the court was tumultuous.

The tension was broken at last, and pandemonium broke out. The court-room echoed to thunderous applause, and while some stood to cheer the slight figure standing motionless in the dock, others ran out into the street to carry the news to the immense crowds waiting outside.

At his table beneath the dock the Dean of Faculty sat with his head bent and his shoulders bowed, too deeply moved to speak. He did not raise his eyes towards the dock, nor make any sign as his client prepared to leave the Court for the last time.

For a moment she stood undecided, as though unable at first to appreciate the meaning of the words that the foreman of the jury had just spoken. Then she found herself surrounded by her well-wishers, who were clapping and cheering and seeking to clasp or to kiss her hands. Some had tears in their eyes, others were white-faced and overcome with emotion.

She smiled down at them, gave a slight bow in the direction of the judges and the jury, and then gathered her skirts about her as she prepared to leave the Court. But before she stepped down through the trap-door which led into the passage beneath the Court and thence to freedom, she cast one look backwards in the direction of her advocate, who sat with his head still bowed and seemingly unmindful of the tumult around him. But he did not raise his eyes.

She gave him a fleeting, quizzical smile and then disappeared from sight.

Henry Blyth, Madeleine Smith: A Famous Victorian Murder Trial *(1975). The trial in Glasgow of Madeleine Smith in 1857 for the murder of her lover by arsenic still prompts controversy, partly because of the uniquely Scottish verdict which concluded it. Madeleine Smith's advocate was John Inglis, Dean of the Faculty of Advocates. The nuances of 'not proven' had been tested even further in the famous 'St Fergus' murder trial, in Aberdeen in 1854, when the Lord Justice Clerk asked the jury, having returned this verdict, whether it lay 'between Not Proven and Not Guilty, or between Not Proven and Guilty'. A juryman replied that it was the latter.*

DARK DEEDS

The Douglas Larder

While Robert the Bruce was engaged in rousing the men of Carrick to take up arms in his cause, Sir James Douglas was permitted to repair to his patrimonial domains in Douglasdale, for the purpose of drawing over the ancient and attached vassals of his family to the same interest, and, in the first place, of avenging, should an occasion occur, some of the particular wrongs himself and family had sustained from the English. Disguised, therefore, and accompanied only by two yeomen, Sir James, towards the close of an evening in the month of March, 1307, reached the alienated inheritance of his house, then owned by the Lord Clifford, who had posted within the castle of Douglas a strong garrison of English soldiers. . . The day of Palm Sunday . . . was fixed upon by Douglas, as then being near at hand, and as furnishing, besides, a plausible pretext for the gathering together of his adherents. The garrison, it was expected, would on that festival attend divine service in the nearby church of St Bride. The followers of Douglas having arms concealed upon their persons, were, some of them, to enter the building along with the soldiers, while the others remained without to prevent their escape. Douglas himself, disguised in an old tattered mantle, having a flail in his hand, was to give the signal of onset, by shouting the war-cry of his family. When the concerted day arrived, the whole garrison, consisting of thirty men, went in solemn procession to attend the service of the church, leaving only the porter and the cook within the castle. The eager followers of the knight did not wait for the signal of attack; for, no sooner had the unfortunate Englishmen entered the chapel, than, one or two raising the cry of 'a Douglas, a Douglas!' which was instantly echoed and returned from all quarters, they fell with the utmost fury upon the entrapped garrison. They defended themselves bravely, till two-thirds of their number lay either dead or mortally wounded. Being refused quarter, those who yet continued to fight were speedily overpowered and made prisoners, so that none escaped. Meanwhile, five or six men were detailed to secure possession of the castle gate, which they easily effected: and being soon after followed by Douglas and his partisans, the victors had now only to deliberate as to the use to which their conquest should be applied. Considering the great power and numbers of the English in that district, and the impossibility of retaining the castle should it be besieged; besides, that the acquisition could then prove of no service to the general cause, it was determined that that which could be of little or no service to themselves, should be rendered equally useless and unprofitable to the enemy. This measure, so defensible in itself, and politic, was stained by an act of singular and atrocious barbarity, which, however consistent with the rude and revengeful spirit of the age in which it was enacted, remains the sole stigma which even his worst enemies could ever affix to the memory of Sir James Douglas. Having plundered and stripped the castle of every article of value which could be conveniently carried off and secured, the great mass of the provisions, with which it then happened to be amply provided, were heaped together within an apartment of the building. Over this pile were stored the puncheons of wine, ale and other liquors which the cellar afforded; and lastly the prisoners who had been taken in the church, having been despatched, their dead bodies were thrown over all; thus in a spirit of savage jocularity, converting the whole into a loathsome mass of provision, then, and long after, popularly described by the name of the Douglas' Larder. These savage preparations gone through, the castle was set on fire, and burned to the ground.

Robert Chambers, Scottish Biographical Dictionary. *This event occurred in 1307.*

The End of the First Duke of Rothesay

Rothesay, as he rode towards St Andrews, accompanied by a small retinue, was arrested near Stratyrum, by Ramorgny and Lindsay, and subjected to a strict confinement in the castle of St Andrews, until the duke and the Earl of Douglas should determine upon his fate.

This needed little time, for it had long been resolved on; and when masters of his person, the catastrophe was as rapid as it was horrible. In a tempestuous day, Albany and Douglas, with a strong party of soldiers, appeared at the castle, and dismissed the few servants who waited on him. They then compelled him to mount a sorry horse, threw a coarse cloak over his splendid dress, and hurrying on, rudely and without ceremony, to Falkland, thrust him into a dungeon. The unhappy prince now saw that his death was determined, but he little anticipated its cruel nature. For fifteen days he was suffered to remain without food, under the charge of two ruffians named Wright and Selkirk, whose task it was to watch the agony of their victim till it ended in death. It is said that, for a while, the wretched prisoner was preserved in a remarkable manner, by the kindness of a poor woman, who, in passing through the garden of Falkland, and attracted by his groans to the grated window of his dungeon, which was level with the ground, became acquainted with his story. It was her custom to steal thither at night, and bring him food by dropping small cakes through the grating, whilst her own milk, conducted through a pipe to his mouth, was the only way he could be supplied with drink. But Wright and Selkirk, suspecting from his appearance that he had some secret supply, watched and detected the charitable visitant, and the prince was abandoned to his fate. When nature at last sunk, his body was found in a state too horrible to be described, but which showed that, in the extremities of hunger, he had gnawed and torn his own flesh. It was then carried to the monastery of Lindores, and there privately buried, while a report was circulated that the prince had been taken ill and died of a dysentery.

P. F. Tytler, History of Scotland (1841). *This event occurred in 1401. The 'Duke' was the duke of Albany, younger brother of King Robert III and effective ruler of the kingdom. Rothesay was Robert III's son and heir apparent to the throne.*

Boiling a Royal Sheriff

Another of the Melvilles is said to have been John, Sheriff of Kincardineshire (but more probably a sheriff-depute, if indeed either) in the time of James I. Of his horrible death by being boiled in a caldron on the hill of Garvock, Sir Walter Scott, in noticing the similar fate of Lord Soulis, says:

> The tradition regarding the death of Lord Soulis, however singular, is not without a parallel in the real history of Scotland. The same extraordinary mode of cookery was actually practised *(horresco referens)* upon the body of a Sheriff of the Mearns. This person, whose name was Melville of Glenbervie, bore his faculties so harshly that he became detested by the barons of the county. Reiterated complaints of his conduct having been made to James I (or, as others say, to the Duke of Albany), the monarch

answered, in a moment of unguarded impatience, 'Sorrow gin the Sheriff were sodden and supped in broo!' The complainers retired perfectly satisfied. Shortly afterwards, the lairds of Arbuthnot, Mathers, Lauriston, and Pitarrow decoyed Melville to the top of the Hill of Garvock, under pretence of a grand hunting party. Upon this place, still called the Sheriff's Pot, the barons had prepared a fire and a boiling caldron, into which they plunged the unlucky Sheriff. After he was 'sodden', as the king termed it, for a sufficient time, the savages, that they might literally observe the royal mandate, concluded the scene of abomination, by actually partaking of the hell-broth. The three lairds were outlawed for the offence, and Barclay, one of their number, to screen himself from justice, erected the Kaim (*i.e.* the fortress) of Mathers, which stands upon a rocky and almost inaccessible peninsula overhanging the German Ocean. The Laird of Arbuthnot is said to have eluded the royal vengeance, by claiming the benefit of the law of the clan Macduff. A pardon, or perhaps a deed of replegiation founded on that law, is said to be still extant. . .

Andrew Jervise, Memorials of Angus and the Mearns (*1885*), *quoting from Sir Walter Scott's* Border Minstrelsy. *This event is somewhat better attested than the similar boiling of William de Soulis, Lord of Hermitage Castle in the Borders, who had conspired against Robert I in 1320, and had the reputation of being a warlock. To the many complaints about him, the king was reputed to have said: 'Boil him if you please, but let me hear no more of him.' The 'law of the clan Macduff', exempting its members from the process of royal justice, was abolished by James I in 1426.*

The Douglas Dinner

The earle Douglas . . . cam forwardis to Edinburgh, and entred within the castle, quhair, with fainzied and colloured countennance, he was receaved with gritt joy and blythnes, and banquetted royallie with all delicatis that could be gottin: and evir that he sould not have any suspitione of ony deceit to fallow thairupone. Than at the last manie of the earles friendis being skailled aff the toun, and opportunitie servand, with adwyse and consent of the governour, quha came then of sett purpos to Edinburgh. Than the chancellour, eftir the coursis war takin away from the dinner, presented ane bullis head befoir the earle Douglas, quhilk was ane signe and tokin of condemnatorie to the dead. But this earle and his brother, beholding the manifold treasone, with sad myndis and drearie countenances, start up from the boord, and maid them to loup at any place they might gett out. But then fra hand ane companie of armed (men) rusched round about thame, quha breaking all kynd of law and hospitalitie, led thame out to the Castle hill, with Sir Malcolme Fleming of Cumbernald, and utheris gentlmen, thair familiaris, and strak the heidis from thame. . . It is said the king being bot ten yeires of age, grat very sore quhan he saw the men of weir bind the earle's handis and his brotheris with cordes, and lamented verie heavilie; and prayed the chancellour for Goddis sak to latt them allone and save thair lyves for ony plesour he wold desir of him. . .

    Robert Lindsay of Pitscottie (c.1532–1580), Chronicles of Scotland. *This event occurred in 1440, in the boyhood of King James II. The earl was aged about seventeen; his brother two years younger.*

'It is Ill Talking Between a Full Man and a Fasting'

In 1452, at the height of the tension between King James II and the mighty Earl of Douglas, Douglas was outraged that a Galloway noble, Maclellan, the Tutor of Bombie, should support the King rather than himself.

    The earl, incensed at his opposition, suddenly assaulted his castle, made him prisoner, and carried him to the strong fortress of Thrieve, in Galloway, situated on an island in the river Dee. The King took a particular interest in Maclellan's fate, the rather that he was petitioned to interfere in his favour by a personal favourite of his own. This was Sir Patrick Gray, the commander of the royal guard, a gentleman much in James's confidence, and constantly attending on his person, and who was Maclellan's near relative, being his uncle on the mother's side. . . The King wrote a letter to the Earl of Douglas, entreating as a favour, rather than urging as a command, that he would deliver the person of the Tutor of Bomby, as Maclellan was usually entitled, into the hands of his relative, Sir Patrick Gray.

    Sir Patrick himself went west with the letter to the castle of Thrieve. Douglas received him just as he had arisen from dinner, and, with much apparent civility, declined to speak with Gray, on the occasion of his coming, until Sir Patrick also had dined, saying, 'It was ill talking between a full man and a fasting.' But this courtesy was only a pretence to gain time to do a very cruel and lawless action. Guessing that Sir Patrick Gray's visit respected the life of Maclellan, he resolved to hasten his execution before opening the King's letter. Thus, while he was feasting Sir Patrick, with every appearance of hospitality, he caused his unhappy kinsman to be led out, and beheaded in the courtyard of the castle.

    Sir Walter Scott (1771–1832), Tales of a Grandfather

'The Cursed Cardinall'

Efter this the cursed cardinall passed over to the abbey of Ardbroath, quhair he mett the earle of Crawford, and married his eldest dochter upoun the maister of Crawford, with great solemnitie. Thairefter he returned to Sanct Androis to his awin castle, quhair he gott word that the Inglisch men were preparing ane great navie to cum upoun the coast of Scotland, to cum and distroy the same, and in speciall about Sanct Androis, Fyfe, and within that coast; quhairunto he sett his intent to find remeid, and sent for all the gentlmen that dwelt near the coast, to have their counsall. . .

Bot in this mean tyme Normand Leslie cam to him for certane bussiness; bot they fell shortlie in alteration of wordis, quhikis war uncharitable amongest Christiane men. Nothwithstanding, Normand Leslie depairted to his ludging that night, quhill on the morne, betuixt four and five houres, syne cam doun to the castle with his complices, and dang the porter from the yettis, and isched all the place at his pleasour: and Petir Melvill past up to the east blokhous chamber, quhair the cardinall lay, and rusched at the door. The cardinall inquired, quho? Then they shew thair names unto him, and then he was affrayed, and said to thame, 'Will yea slay me?' and they answeired, 'No.' Then he opined the doore and lett thame in; and als soone as they entered they stickit him. Then the cry raise in the toun that the cardinall was slaine, and they rane to gett ledderis to ledder the wallis, thinkand that he had beine alive, and to have reskewed him. Bot they that war in the castle laid the cardinall over the wallis to put all men out of doubt, and the people. And when he was lying over the wall, ane called Guthrie pisched in his mouth, that the people might see ane part of Mr Georger Wishartis prophecie fuflfilled, quho said, that within few dayes he should ly als ignominious out over that wall head, as he was glorious that day of his martyrdome.

Robert Lindsay of Pitscottie (c.1532–1580), Chronicles of Scotland. *Cardinal David Beaton was the Chancellor of Scotland. On 1 March 1546, he had supervised the burning of the Protestant George Wishart, who prophesied on his pyre that the cardinal, then in all his splendour, would soon perish in ignominy. Beaton was assassinated on 29 May of that year by Norman Leslie, Peter Melville, and others.*

'Kilchrist'

After much plundering in Brae Ross under Allan Macranald of Lundie, the MacDonalds proceeded to the church of Kilchrist, in which the MacKenzies were at the time worshipping. Surrounding the building they at once set it on fire, and burned to death the whole congregation, the piper the while marching round the building, and drowning the cries of the victims in the shrill notes of that pibroch which, under its name of Kilchrist, has been employed ever since as the clan tune of the Clanranald of Glengarry.

Dugald Mitchell, History of the Highlands and Gaelic Scotland (1900). *This atrocity, committed in 1603, was the worst one in a series of raids and*

*ambushes in the long MacDonald-MacKenzie feud. Alexander Mackenzie,
in* Historical Tales and Legends of the Highlands (1878) *recounts the story
in detail, and says that the Mackenzies, in pursuit of the escaping
MacDonalds, cornered thirty-seven of them in an inn at Torbreck, near Inverness, and burned them with the house. But Allan escaped, by leaping the
chasm of Alltsaigh by Loch Ness and swimming across the loch until he was
picked up by his ally Fraser of Foyers.*

The Well of the Heads

In the autumn of 1663, young Alexander, thirteenth chief of the MacDonells
of Keppoch, and his brother, Ranald, were foully done to death by Alexander
MacDougall MacDonald of Inverlair, and six accomplices. And it is because Iain Lom had sworn to avenge this death with the seven heads of the
perpetrators that he was pushing on through Lochaber in the summer of
1665, almost two years after the incident had occurred. . .

Had Iain Lom been given the support he wanted, this matter would have
been settled finally a year or two previously. His earlier demand that retri-
bution should be sought had met with no response. Therefore, he had been
compelled to leave Keppoch in the hope of finding an ally elsewhere. He
found, in the person of Sir James MacDonald of Sleat, a chieftain ready to
render him the assistance he craved. In the Highlands the old folks still
pretend to quote the conversation that passed between Iain Lom and
MacDonald of Sleat, when they met in Skye –

'Whence come you, Iain Lom?' enquired MacDonald of Sleat.

'From Laodicea,' replied Iain.

'And how are they there? – hot or cold?' asked MacDonald.

'Abel is cold; and the blood of him is crying for vengeance', continued
Iain; 'but Cain is warm, and his hands are red.'

. . . There is a tradition still current in the Highlands that, when Iain
Lom's attack became imminent, the seven murderers barricaded themselves
in Inverlair House.

. . . There exists no actual record of the attack made on Inverlair House,
so far as I am aware. That it was singularly successful in its purpose, however, is obvious. They say in Keppoch that, not until the besiegers put flame
to the house, were they able to dislodge the murderers. As the latter rushed
forth from the blazing house, they were slain to a man. And their seven
heads were cut off by Iain Lom . . . As to Iain Lom's subsequent action,
tradition in the Highlands is persistent. He ran a heather rope through the
seven heads, slung them over his shoulder, and proceeded with them by the
shore of Loch Oich to the threshold of Glengarry, thus to testify his having
avenged the foul murder of his kinsmen. Anxious that the heads should
present a less bloody appearance ere he exhibited them, he tarried by the

wayside, and washed them in the well. And ever since that day, the well has been known as Tobar nan Ceann, Well of the Heads. If you examine carefully the monument now standing over this wayside well, you will see that it is crowned by a hand grasping seven heads beautifully fashioned in stone. And protruding a little from the hand is the sharp point of a dirk.

Alasdair Alpin MacGregor, Somewhere in Scotland (revised edition, 1948). *Iain Lòm MacDonald (c.1625–c.1707), the celebrated bard, warlike as he undoubtedly was, is more likely to have instigated the revenge than to have led it. The Well of the Heads may still be seen by the side of Loch Oich.*

Magus Muir

I still see Magus Muir two hundred years ago; a desert place, quite unenclosed; in the midst, the primate's carriage fleeing at the gallop; the assassins loose-reined in pursuit, Burley Balfour, pistol in hand, among the first. No scene of history has ever written itself so deeply on my mind; not because Balfour, that questionable zealot, was an ancestral cousin of my own; not because of the pleadings of the victim and his daughter; not even because of the live bum-bee that flew out of Sharpe's 'bacco-box, thus clearly indicating his complicity with Satan; nor merely because, as it was after all a crime of a fine religious flavour, it figured in Sunday books and afforded a grateful relief from *Ministering Children* or *The Memoirs of Mrs Katherine Winslowe*. The figure that always fixed my attention is that of Hackston of Rathillet, sitting in the saddle with his cloak about his mouth, and through all that long, bungling, vociferous hurly-burly, revolving privately a case of conscience. He would take no hand in the deed, because he had a private spite against the victim, and 'that action' must be sullied with no suggestion of a worldly motive; on the other hand, 'that action' in itself was highly justified, he had cast in his lot with 'the actors', and he must stay there, inactive but publicly sharing the responsibility. 'You are a gentleman – you will protect me!' cried the wounded old man, crawling towards him. 'I will never lay a hand on you', said Hackston, and put his cloak about his mouth. It is an old temptation with me, to pluck away that cloak and see the face – to open that bosom and read the heart. . . whenever I cast my eyes backward, it is to see him like a landmark on the plains of history, sitting with his cloak about his mouth, inscrutable. How small a thing creates an immortality! I do not think he can have been a man entirely commonplace; but had he not thrown his cloak about his mouth, or had the witnesses forgot to chronicle the action, he would not thus have haunted the imagination of my boyhood, and today he would scarce delay me for a paragraph.

Robert Louis Stevenson (1850–1894), 'The Coast of Fife', *from* Random Memories

The Appin Dirk

About two months after the battle (of Culloden) – about June, 1746 – a detachment of Red Coats, in passing through Lochaber and Appin on their way to Inveraray, found amusement in burning and pillaging as they went. When moving through the Strath of Appin in the evening, one of the soldiers noticed a young woman milking her cows in a field by the roadside. The sergeant in charge of the detachment leapt over the dyke into the field, and shot the cow dead without any explanation or provocation. He then turned his attention to the young woman, who defended herself with great courage. As she retreated towards the Appin shore, she picked up a stone which she hurled at the sergeant with such accuracy and force that it stunned him, thus allowing her to escape to a boat floating by the shore. Out of reach she rowed to an island, the Gaelic name of which signifies the Island of the Goats' Township. There she remained some time, free from further persecution. The heroine's name to this day is given in Appin as Julia MacColl.

The stunned sergeant was soon picked up by his men, and borne to the place of halt for that night. In the morning he succumbed to the wound inflicted by the stone. He was buried in the old churchyard of Airds; but the wrathful men of Appin were determined that the corpse should not remain there for long. And so, when the Red Coats had gone their way, they exhumed the body and cast it into the sea – but not before the brother of Julia MacColl had flayed the right arm of it for the purpose of making a dirk sheath from it. When the dirk sheath was seen in 1870 by the Rev. Alexander Stewart (better known in the Highlands by the pen-name of 'Nether Lochaber'), it was dark-brown in colour, limp and soft, with no ornament except a small piece of brass at the point, and a thin edging of the same metal round the opening, on which were inscribed the date, 1747, and the initials D.M.C.

Alasdair Alpin MacGregor, Somewhere in Scotland (revised edition, 1948)

The Body-Snatchers

All Edinburgh is alarmed by a very odd and horrid discovery. Some Irish people have been for some time in the habit of decoying into secret places and murdering such wretches as they thought would be least missed for the sole purpose of selling their bodies for dissection and it would seem that the Anatomists have been in the habit of giving them from £7 to £10 for any corpse whatever, no questions asked, and, what seems shocking, that they saw marks of violence on the bodies without being startled or making enquiry how the party came to his end. It is supposed that upwards of twenty persons have perished in this most miserable manner. But it is certain that three cases can be distinctly proved against Burke and his wife who kept a subterranean cellar in the Grassmarket where this horrid trade was driven. Their usual mode was to intoxicate the poor creatures and so strangle or smother them. But the fate of a poor idiot well known by the name of daft Jamie was particularly shocking. Having in that respect more wit than wiser folks he refused the liquor which they tried to forc(e) upon him and after a desperate defence was subdued and strangled by main forc(e). The trial comes on Monday. I am sorry I cannot be there. The murtherers are all Irish of the lowest ranks. There is a generall terror among the servant maids who think their pretty persons are especially aimd at. And two of Glengarry's savage Highlanders were so completely cow'd that they dared not stir out after sunset for fear of being caught up and dissected.

They keep the thing as quiet as they can for fear of riot but if I were a Doctor I would be afraid of my windows on Monday and well if they got off with a pebbling.

I was shockd in the midst of all this by receipt of a very polite card from the Medical Society inviting me to dine with them.

Sir Walter Scott (1771–1832), letter to his son Charles, December 1828. Burke was executed in 1829, and his body was sent to the anatomy school. The Edinburgh mob threatened to burst in, and eventually the naked corpse, on a black marble table, was publicly exhibited to some 25,000 spectators.

The Eigg Massacre

According to MacLeod historians, the escalation in violence occurred when the entire crew of a Clanranald galley, driven ashore in Harris by a storm, were beheaded by their MacLeod host who presented the heads on a rope to the governor of the island. In reprisal, a MacLeod birlinn was captured and its thirty-six men – including an illegitimate son of the chief of Dunvegan – were thrown into a Uist dungeon and starved to death. Consequently, when bad weather forced a MacLeod galley to seek shelter in the lee of Eigg, the crew decided against landing on the island and took refuge on Eilean Chasteil, off the coast of Galmisdale. Led by a MacAskill and a foster-son of Alastair Crotach, the chief of Dunvegan, the thirty men helped themselves to a few cattle which they proceeded to roast, molesting the girls who were looking after them. But as they were enjoying their dinner, the inhabitants of Eigg descended on them and massacred the entire crew, except their leaders. For them they reserved a slow and painful death: their arms and legs broken, the two men were set adrift in a boat without rudders or oars.

But what the MacDonalds did not count on was that, carried by the currents, the boat drifted all the way back to Dunvegan. When he heard what had happened on Eigg, Alastair Crotach vowed not to change his clothes until he had taken his revenge on every soul on the island. With his son Uilleam, who was no less outraged by the treatment his foster-brother had received, he set sail immediately for Eigg at the head of a force of several galleys full of armed men. As soon as the galleys were sighted, the inhabitants of Eigg knew what was in store for them and took to their traditional hiding place, Uamh Fhraing, the cave on the south side of the island which once gave shelter to St Donnan, to sit the raid out. The cave was an ideal refuge, deceptively spacious inside, but with an entrance concealed by a waterfall and small enough to be easily overlooked.

Landing on Eigg, the MacLeod landing party conducted a thorough search for three whole days. They did not find a soul save one old woman at the north end of the island who had not bothered to hide because she was too lame to walk. They tried to make her tell where the rest of the islanders had gone, but the obstinate old woman would always answer in the same way: 'If it comes through my knee, it can't be helped but it shall not come through my mouth.' They burned her house and destroyed her crops, but still she would not tell. She taunted them even more: why, she had a home under every rock and she had all the cockles of Laig bay to eat if she wanted. Enraged, the MacLeods ploughed the sands in the bay – to this day, there are no shellfish to be found there, maintains tradition – but undaunted, the old woman laughed at them: she could live, and live well at that, on the dulse of the rock pools and the watercress of the well of Hulin. The raiders gave up in the end, persuaded that the islanders had taken refuge on another island, and left under her curses: 'Humpback is the heir of MacLeod today and as long as dry straw will burn, many a hump and crook there will be in the clan hereafter!' shouted the old woman as they made their way to their galleys.

Meanwhile, the islanders, who had spent three days in the cave, thought it safe enough to send a scout outside. But it was a cold spring day and there had been a fresh snowfall in the night. No sooner had the MacLeods rounded the south side of the island on their way back to Dunvegan than they spotted the scout against the snow. They turned straight back and had no difficulty in finding the cave even though the poor scout had taken the precaution of retracing his steps backwards. The MacLeods decided to smother the islanders in their refuge and set about diverting the waterfall in front of it, piling up at the entrance all the heather and thatching they could find. Just as they were about to set fire to it, Alastair Crotach hesitated: willing to show some mercy, he wanted to let the women and children go unharmed, but his son Uilleam was unmoved; he would spare only one life, the life of the Eiggach who had been merciful to his half-brother when he had starved in Clanranald's dungeon. The man asked if he could bring his son out with him but Uilleam would not allow even this, so he preferred to perish with the rest. Once again Alastair Crotach hesitated, deciding to ask for God's judgement: they would wait another six hours and if at the end of this delay, the wind blew away from the cave, the islanders would be spared. But the wind rose and blew towards the land, sealing the islanders' fate. The chief sailed away, leaving his son to set the blaze alight, a deed for which he was known as 'Uilleam of the Cave' for ever after. Thus perished the entire population of the island, save the old woman in Hulin.

Camille Dressler, Eigg, Story of an Island (*1998*). *The story of the massacre was told to Alexander Smith, author of* Summer in Skye (*1865*). *'Don't you think it was a very barbarous act?' he asked. 'I don't know,' said the narrator, 'I am a MacLeod myself.'*

Tourists in the Cave of the Bones

On Eigg they were shown the cave in which the entire population were smoked to death by a party of vengeful MacLeods on a day trip from Skye. 250 years later the grisly evidence was still lying around.

The bones of the victims lay scattered about the floor in various places, a considerable number at the far narrow end, to which it may be supposed the wretched creatures had retreated when the horrid choking smoke began to roll its fatal wreaths upon them. A good many lie also near the entrance, being the skeletons of those who had clung to the hope of fresh air or freedom or mercy from without. In the intermediate spaces they are few in number and apart, as if certain individuals from the huddled masses at either end had tried by a last desperate effort to change their respective positions when too late, and life had failed after a few faltering footsteps.

We found the scalp of a little child at the back of a large stone, and between the stone and the cavern side, close to its opening, as if it had been making a vain attempt to creep outward from the smoke, in ignorance of the clearer though not less deadly breath of 'the lightning of fiery flame'. Most of the skulls were gone, and, what struck us as curious, there were scarcely any teeth lying among the stones. These melancholy remains consist chiefly of the bones of legs and arms and a good supply of shoulder blades.

That they are a high-minded and romantic race these islanders, and extremely tenacious of their ancestral glories, is evident from this, that during the potato harvest the pigs are put out of the way of doing mischief by being all cooped up in this same ancestral cave – and fine mumbling work they will make of it, while grumphing to each other – de mortuis nil nisi bones. Now as the people eat the pigs and the pigs the people's predecessors, it follows logically that the present natives are a race of cannibals of the very worst description.

Yet they seemed a pleasant, courteous, good-looking set of lads, such of them as we came in contact with, and one little fellow of about ten years of age, who followed us into the cave, was most assiduous in dragging out the

hind legs of an old lady from an obscure corner, into which she had probably retired to be out of the crowd during the night of the great fire. He told
us that strange sights were sometimes dimly seen flitting about the mouth
of the cavern during the darker hours, and that dreadful groans and shrieks,
especially of women, were often heard. We were really glad to embark again
on board the Cutter.

   James Wilson, A Voyage Round the Coasts of Scotland and the Isles (*1842*),
quoted in Derek Cooper, Road to the Isles: Travellers in the Hebrides, 1770–
1914 (*1979*)

The Massacre of Glen Coe

. . . on the 13th day of February, being Saturday, about four, or five, in the
morning, Lieutenant Lindsay, with a party of the foresaid soldiers, came to
old Glenco's house, where, having call'd, in a friendly manner, and got in,
they shot his father dead, with several shots, as he was rising out of his bed;
and, the mother having got up, and put on her clothes, the soldiers stripped
her naked, and drew the rings off her fingers with their teeth; as likewise
they killed one man more, and wounded another grievously, at the same
place.

   . . . And the said John, Alexander and Archibald Macdonalds do all
depone that, the same morning, there was one Serjeant Barber, and a party,
at Auchnaion, and that Auchintriaten being there, in his brother's house,
with eight more, sitting about the fire, the soldiers discharged upon them
about 18 shot, which kill'd Auchintriaten, and four more; but the other
four, whereof some were wounded, falling down as dead, Serjeant Barber
laid hold on Auchintriaten's brother, one of the four, and ask'd him if he
were alive? He answer'd, that he was, and that he desir'd to die without,
rather than within. Barber said that, for his meat that he had eaten, he
would do him the favour to kill him without; but, when the man was
brought out, and soldiers brought up to shoot him, he, having his plaid
loose, flung it over their faces, and so escap'd; and the other three broke
through the back of the house, and escap'd. And this account the deponents
had from the men that escap'd. And, at Innerriggin, where Glenlyon was
quartered, the soldiers took nine other men, and did bind them, hand and
foot, (and) kill'd them, one by one, with shot; and, when Glenlyon inclin'd
to save a young man, of about 20 years of age, one captain Drummond
came, and ask'd how he came to be sav'd in respect of the orders that
were given, and shot him dead; and another young boy, of about 13 years,
ran to Glenlyon, to be sav'd. He was likewise shot dead. And, in the same
town, there was a woman, and a boy about four or five years of age,
kill'd; and, at Auchnaion, there was also a child missed, and nothing found
of him but the hand.

From Official Depositions made at the Inquiry into the Glencoe Massacre, 1694, Maitland Club Papers. Glenlyon was Robert Campbell of Glenlyon, in command of the soldiers, and recipient of the orders to carry out the massacre.

The Monster of Glamis Castle

The Dowager Lady Granville, elder sister of the Queen Mother, recalled that when she lived there children often awoke at night screaming because a huge bearded man had leant over their beds and looked at them.

There was one story, however, which Lady Granville admitted they were never allowed to discuss when they were children and which her father and grandfather absolutely refused to speak to her about. This was the story of the Castle Monster, an eldest son of the family born in a hideous form with a massive body covered in matted black hair, tiny arms and legs and a head sunk deep into his barrel chest. Obviously such a creature could not inherit the title and he was kept in a secret room and exercised on the roofs at night. He was believed to have lived to be well over a hundred and died in the early part of this century.

To keep the dreadful secret only four men at any one time were allowed to know of the Monster's existence. They were the Earl, the family lawyer, the agent to the estate and the eldest son who was shown the Monster, the rightful Earl, on the day that he came of age.

Jean Goodman, in collaboration with Sir Iain Moncrieffe of that Ilk, Debrett's Royal Scotland

DEATHS AND FUNERALS

Known Unto God

Some miles south of Lossit (in Kintyre) is a small bay called Aenan, where, in the summer of 1917, a shepherd found a body washed ashore, presumed to be that of a sailor lost at sea. The local folks buried the body above the shore; and over the grave they erected a wooden cross. And, since no one could identify the corpse, they carved upon the wooden cross only the words, 'God Knows'.

Aladair Alpin MacGregor, Somewhere in Scotland (revised edition, 1948)

The Tranquil Demise of Dr Joseph Black

In the latter days of Dr Black, he sunk into a low state of health, and only preserved himself from the shocks of the weather in this variable climate by a degree of care almost fantastic. Thus he spun out the thread of life to the last fibre. It was his generous and manly wish that he might never live to be a burden to his friends; and never was the wish more completely gratified. On the 26th of November, 1799, and in the seventy-first year of his age, he expired, without any convulsion, shock, or stupor, to announce or retard the approach of death. Being at table with his usual fare, some bread, a few prunes, and a measured quantity of milk, diluted with water, and having the cup in his hand when the last stroke of his pulse was to be given, he had set it down upon his knees, which were joined together, and kept it steady with his hand in the manner of a person perfectly at ease, and in this attitude expired, without spilling a drop, and without a writhe in his countenance; as if an experiment had been required, to show his family and friends the facility with which he departed.

   Robert Chambers, Scottish Biographical Dictionary. *Joseph Black (1728–1799) the discoverer of latent heat, was one of the founders of modern chemistry.*

The Death of Saint Columba

(Columba speaks to his attendant, Diormit).

> In the Sacred Volumes this day is called Sabbath, which is, interpreted, rest. And this day is truly a Sabbath day for me, because it is for me the last day of this present laborious life, on which I rest after the fatigues of my labours; and this night, at midnight, when begins the solemn day of the Lord, according to the saying of the Scriptures, I shall go the way of my fathers. For already my Lord Jesus Christ deigns to invite me, to Whom, I say, in the middle of this night, He himself inviting me, I shall depart. For so it has been revealed to me by the Lord himself.

... After this the Saint goes out of the granary, and, returning to the monastery, sits down half-way at the place where afterwards a cross, fixed to a millstone, and standing to this day, is to be seen at the roadside. And while the Saint, weary with age as I have said, rested there, sitting for a little while, behold the white horse, a faithful servant, runs up to him, the one which used to carry the milk pails to and fro between the byre and the monastery. He, coming up to the Saint, wonderful to tell, lays his head against his breast – inspired, as I believe, by God, by whose dispensation every animal has sense to perceive things according as its Creator himself has ordained – knowing that his master was soon about to leave him, and that he would see him no more, began to whinny and to shed copious tears into the lap of the Saint as though he had been a man ...

And then, going on and ascending the knoll that overlooks the monastery, he stood for a little while on its top, and there standing and raising both hands he blessed his monastery, saying: 'Upon this place, small though it be, and mean, not only the kings of the Scotic people, with their peoples, but also the rulers of barbarous and foreign races, with the people subject to them, shall confer great and no common honour: by the Saints also even of other churches shall no uncommon reverence be accorded to it.'

After these words, coming down from the knoll and returning to the monastery, he sat in his hut transcribing the Psalter . . . After transcribing the verse at the end of the page, the Saint enters the church for the vesper mass of the vigil of the Lord's Day, and as soon as this is over, he returns to his cell and sits up throughout the night on his bed, where he had the bare rock for pallet and a stone for pillow, which to this day stands by his grave as his monumental pillar. And so, there sitting up, he gives his last commands to the Brethren. . .

After which, as the happy last hour gradually approached, the Saint was silent. Then, when the bell began to toll at midnight, rising in haste he goes to the church, and running faster than the others he enters it alone, and on bended knees falls down in prayer at the altar. At the same moment, Diormit, his attendant, who followed him more slowly, sees from a distance the whole church filled within with Angelic light round about the Saint. And as he drew near to the door, the same light which he had seen suddenly withdrew, and this light a few others of the Brethren who stood afar off also saw. Diormit, therefore, entering the church, moans out with mournful voice: 'Where art thou, Father?' And as the lights of the Brethren had not yet been brought in, groping his way in the dark he finds the Saint lying before the altar, and raising him up a little and sitting down by him, he lays the holy head on his bosom. And meanwhile the community of monks, running up with lights, began to weep at the sight of their dying Father. And as we have learned from some who were there present, the Saint, his soul not yet departing, with open eyes upturned, looked round about on either side with wonderful cheerfulness and joy of countenance on seeing the holy Angels coming to meet him. Diormit then lifts up the holy right hand of the Saint that he may bless the choir of monks. But the venerable father himself at the same time moved his hand as much as he was able, so that what was impossible for him to do with his voice at his soul's departure he might still do by the movement of his hand, namely, give his blessing to the Brethren. And after thus signifying his holy benediction, immediately breathed forth his spirit. And it having left the tabernacle of the body, the face remained so ruddy and wonderfully gladdened by the vision of the Angels that it seemed not to be that of one dead, but of one living and sleeping.

St Adamnan (679–704), Life of St Columba, *translated from Latin by Wentworth Huyshe*

Wake for a Lord of Session

Old Dr Clark told my father the day Lord Forglen died he called at his door and was met by David Reid, his clerk.

'How does my lord do?'

'I hope he's weel.'

So the Doctor knew he was dead. David conducted him into a room and when he looked beneath the table there was two dozen of wine. In a little in came the rest of the Doctors. So they all sat down, and David gave them some of my lord's last words, at the same time putting the bottels about very busily. After they had taken a glass or two they arose to go away.

'No, gentlemen,' said David, 'not so; it was the express will o' the dead that I should fill you a' fou, and I maun fulfil the will o' the dead.'

All the time the tears were running down his cheeks.

'And indeed,' said the Doctor, 'he did fulfil it, for there was na ane o' us able to bite his ain thumb.'

Lord Auchinleck (d.1787), quoted in Charles Rogers, Boswelliana (1874). *Alexander Ogilvy, Lord Forglen, a Judge of the Court of Session, died in* 1727.

The Last Days of Marjorie Fleming

You are quite correct in stating that measles were the cause of her death. My mother was struck by the patient quietness manifested by Marjorie during this illness, unlike her ardent, impulsive nature; but love and poetic feeling were unquenched. When Dr Johnstone rewarded her submission with a sixpence, the request speedily followed that she might get out ere New Year's day came. When asked why she was so desirous of getting out, she immediately rejoined, 'Oh, I am so anxious to buy something with my sixpence for my dear Isa Keith.' Again, when lying very still, her mother asked her if there was anything she wished: 'Oh, yes! if you would just leave the room door open a wee bit, and play "The Land o' the Leal", and I will lie and think, and enjoy myself' (this is just as stated to me by her mother and mine). Well, the happy day came, alike to parents and child, when Marjorie was allowed to come forth from the nursery to the parlour. It was Sabbath evening, and after tea. My father, who idolised this child, and never afterwards in my hearing mentioned her name, took her in his arms; and while walking her up and down the room, she said, 'Father, I will repeat something to you: what would you like?' He said, 'Just choose yourself, Maidie.' She hesitated for a moment between the paraphrase, 'Few are thy days and full of woe', and the lines of Burns already quoted, but decided on the latter, a remarkable choice for a child. The repeating these lines seemed to stir up the depths of feeling in her soul. She asked to be allowed to write a poem; there was a doubt whether it would be right to allow her, in case of hurting her eyes. She pleaded earnestly, 'Just this once'; the point was yielded, her slate was given to her, and with great rapidity she wrote an address of fourteen lines, 'to her loved Cousin on the author's recovery', her last work on earth:

> Oh! Isa, pain did visit me
> I was at the last extremity
> How often did I think of you
> I wished your graceful form to view
> To clasp you in my weak embrace
> Indeed I thought Id run my race.
> Good Care Im sure was of me taken
> But indeed I was much shaken
> At last I daily strength did gain
> And O at last away went pain
> At length the docter thought I might
> Stay in the Parlour till the night
> I now continue so to do
> Farewell to Nancy and to you.
>   Wrote by M. F.

She went to bed apparently well, awoke in the middle of the night with the old cry of woe to a mother's heart, 'My head, my head!' Three days of the dire malady, 'water in the head,' followed, and the end came.

Letter from Elizabeth Fleming to Dr John Brown, circa 1863, quoted in Frank Sidgwick, The Complete Marjory Fleming *(1934). Elizabeth Fleming was Marjorie's younger sister.*

The Funeral of Mrs Forbes of Culloden

Formerly in Scotland a funeral was a feast, and sometimes a fortune was well-nigh consumed in celebrating the great event. . . At the funeral of Mrs Forbes, of Culloden, the mourners all got drunk. The festivities were conducted by her son Duncan, well known as the Lord President Forbes. The company sat so long and drank so freely, that when the word was given for the procession to form, and for the mourners to march to the burial ground, the coffin was forgotten. The whole troop of jolly mourners found themselves at the grave with nothing to put in it. Special messengers were sent back for the poor dead lady, whose remains were 'then deposited in the grave with all the decorum which could be mustered in such anti-funereal circumstances'.

John Timbs, A Century of Anecdote *(1864). The hospitality of Culloden House was legendary (see Burt's* Letters of a Gentleman from the North of

Scotland). *Similar tales of Highland funerals are common, but this one seems well authenticated.*

A Filial Toast

A man well known to the writer of these pages was remarkable for his filial affection, even among the sons and daughters of the mountains, so distinguished for that branch of piety. His mother being a widow, and having a numerous family, who had married very early, he continued to live single, that he might the more sedulously attend to her comfort, and watch over her declining years with the tenderest care. On her birth-day, he always collected his brothers and sisters, and all their families, to a sort of kindly feast, and, in conclusion, gave a toast, not easily translated from the emphatic language, without circumlocution – An easy and decorous departure to my mother, comes nearest to it. This toast, which would shake the nerves of fashionable delicacy, was received with great applause, the old woman remarking, that God had always been good to her, and she hoped to die as decently as she had lived . . .

    Anne Grant (1755–1838), Superstitions of the Highlanders

The Death of King James V

The king passed out of Hallirudhouse to Falkland, and thair became so heavie and dolorous that he neither ate nor drank that had guide digestioun, and became so vehement seik that no man had hope of his lyff. Then he sent for certain of his lordis, both spiritual and temporal, to have thaire counsall. But or thay cam, he was very near strangled to the death by extreme melancholie. Be this, the post cam out of Linlithgow schowing the king guid tidings, that the queen was deliverit. The king inquired whidder it was a man or woman. The messenger said it was ane fair dochter. He answeired and said, 'Fairweill, it cam with ane lass and it will pass with ane lass'; and so he commendit himself to the Almightie God, and spak little from thenforth, but turned his back to his lordis and his face to the wall.

    At this time Sir David Beaton, Cardinal of Scotland, standing in presence of the king, seeing him begin to fail of his strength and natural speech, held ane throughe of papir to his grace, and caused him to subscribe the same, whairin the cardinal writ what he pleased for his ain perticular weil; thinkand to have had the auctorite and preheminence in the government of the countrie. Bot we may knaw hereby that the king's legacie was verie schort; for in this meantime he depairted. As I have shown you, he turned upon his back, and lookit and beheld his lordis all about, and gave ane little lauchter, syne kissed his hand and gave it till all his lordis about him, and thairefter held up his hands to God, and yeildit the spirit.

    Robert Lindsay of Pitscottie (c.1532–1580), Chronicles of Scotland

The Execution of Montrose

The sentence . . . was then read to the undaunted prisoner, on which he observed, he was more honoured in having his head set on the prison, for the cause in which he died, than he would have been had they decreed a golden statue to be erected to him in the market-place, or in having his picture in the King's bedchamber. As to the distribution of his limbs, he said he wished he had flesh enough to send some to each city of Europe, in memory of the cause in which he died. He spent the night in reducing these ideas into poetry.

Early on the morning of the next day he was awakened by the drums and trumpets calling out the guards, by orders of Parliament, to attend on his execution. 'Alas!' he said, 'I have given these good folks much trouble while alive, and do I continue to be a terror to them on the day I am to die?'

The clergy importuned him, urging repentance of his sins, and offering, on his expressing such compunction, to relieve him from the sentence of excommunication, under which he laboured. He calmly replied, that though the excommunication had been rashly pronounced, yet it gave him pain, and he desired to be freed from it, if a relaxation could be obtained, by expressing penitence for his offences as a man; but that he had committed none in his duties to his prince and country, and, therefore, had none to acknowledge or repent of.

Johnstone of Warriston, an eminent Covenanter, intruded himself on the noble prisoner, while he was combing the long curled hair, which he wore as a cavalier. Warriston, a gloomy fanatic, hinted as if it were but an idle employment at so solemn a time. 'I will arrange my head as I please today, while it is still my own,' answered Montrose; 'tomorrow it is yours, and you may deal with it as you list.'

The marquis walked on foot, from the prison of the Grassmarket, the common place of execution for the basest felons, where a gibbet of extraordinary height, with a scaffold covered with black cloth, were erected. Here he was again pressed by the Presbyterian clergy to own his guilt. Their cruel and illiberal officiousness could not disturb the serenity of his temper. To exaggerate the infamy of his punishment, or rather to show the mean spite of his enemies, a book, containing the printed history of his exploits, was hung around his neck by the hangman. This insult, likewise, he treated with contempt, saying, he accounted such a record of his services to his prince as a symbol equally honourable with the badge of the Garter, which the King had bestowed on him. In all other particulars, Montrose bore himself with the same calm dignity, and finally submitted to execution with such resolved courage, that many, even of his bitterest enemies, wept on the occasion. He suffered on the 21st of May, 1650.

Sir Walter Scott (1771–1832), Tales of a Grandfather

The Trial and Execution of Argyll

Argile was very bold and confident in his own defence, with some reflections upon severalls, especially the Kings Advocat, who told him openly, Archibald, it is not with yow now as when yow set up the flesh stocks betuixt the Cross and the Tron. All that Argil replied was, A flesher dog bittes sore.

. . . [Upon the scaffold of the Maiden] Then, turning about to his friends, he said these few words: Many Christians may stumble at this, and my friends may be discontented; but, when things are rightly considered, my friends have no discredit of me, nor Christians no stumbling block, but rather an incurragement.

The four friends, with a scarlet cloath, received the head. It lay uppon the scaffold untill the dead body, being put in a coffin, was taken away: and one cried, Deliver the head of Archibald Campbell, late Marques of Argil, into the hands of the common hangman to be set up uppon the middle iron pin on the top of the wester gavel of the tolebooth of Edinburgh . . . It is observable that Pet. Grham [sic] of Morphy, glad of the occasion, stept up the leather to the gavel of the tolebooth, and, with his own hand, took down the Marques of Montross his head off the pin, and set up Argiles head in its place. . . But its reported that the foresaid Morphay Graham, by the excessive joy dyed soon after.

James Fraser (1634–1699), Policratica Temporum, *from the Wardlaw Manuscript. The King's Advocate at Argyll's trial was Sir John Flesher, hence Argyll's bitter pun. Montrose's head was up on the tolbooth for twelve years before it was replaced by that of his opponent.*

An Experiment that Failed

Among the intimate friends of Sir James at this period of his life was Mr Alexander Trotter. . . Mr Trotter was cut off early in life; and during his last illness, made a promise to Sir James, that, if possible, he would come to him after his death, in an enclosure near the house of Coltness, which in summer had been frequently their place of study. It was agreed, in order to prevent mistake or misapprehension, that the hour of meeting should be noon; that Mr Trotter should appear in the dress he usually wore; and that every other circumstance should be exactly conformable to what usually happened when they met together. Sir James laid greater stress on this engagement than sound reason would warrant. Both before and after his exile, he never failed, when it was in his power, to attend at the place of appointment, even when the debility arising from gout rendered him hardly able to walk. Every day at noon while residing at Coltness, he went to challenge the promise of Mr Trotter, and always returned extremely disappointed that his expectation of his friend's appearance had not been gratified. When rallied on the subject, he always observed seriously, that we do not know enough of 'the other world' to entitle us to assume that such an event as the reappearance of Mr Trotter was impossible.

Robert Chambers, Scottish Biographical Dictionary. *Sir James Steuart (1713–1780), was a pioneer of the subject of political economy. His exile, between 1746 and 1763, was occasioned by his active support of the Jacobite rising of 1745.*

The Last Fight of Sigurd the Powerful

Melbrigda Tönn, or of the Tooth, a Scottish jarl, and Earl Sigurd made an arrangement to meet in a certain place with forty men each in order to come to an agreement regarding their differences. On the appointed day Sigurd, suspicious of treachery on the part of the Scots, caused eighty men to be mounted on forty horses. When earl Melbrigda saw this, he said to his men, 'Now we have been treacherously dealt with by Earl Sigurd, for I see two men's legs on one side of each horse, and the men, I believe, are thus twice as many as the beasts. But let us be brave and each kill his man before we die.' Then they made themselves ready. When Sigurd saw it, he also decided on his plan, and said to his men, 'Now let one half of your number dismount and attack them from behind when the troops meet, while we shall ride at them with all our speed to break their battle-array.' There was hard fighting immediately, and it was not long till Earl Melbrigda fell, and all his men with him. Earl Sigurd and his men fastened their heads to the saddle-straps in bravado, and so they rode home triumphing in their victory. As they were proceeding, Earl Sigurd, intending to kick at his horse with his foot, struck the calf of his leg against a tooth protruding from Earl Melbrigda's head, which scratched him slightly; but it soon became swollen and painful, and he died of it.

W. F. Skene, Celtic Scotland, Volume I (1886). *Sigurd was the first Earl of Orkney, under the King of Norway.*

The Wigtown Martyrs

Margaret McLauchlan, who is said to have now manifested great fortitude, though, when in prison, she had offered to make concessions, was tied to the stake placed nearest the advancing tide, that she might perish first; for the obvious purpose of terrifying into submission the younger sufferer, who was bound to a stake nearer the shore. The multitude looked on, thrilled with horror. The flood gradually made its way to the aged matron, rising higher and higher at each successive wave, 'mounting up from knee, waist, breast and chin, lip', until it choked and overwhelmed her. Margaret Wilson witnessed the whole scene, and knew that she would soon share the same fate; but her steadfastness remained unshaken; and so far from exhibiting any symptoms of terror, she displayed a calm courage . . . When her fellow-sufferer was struggling in the waters with the agonies of death, a heartless by-stander, perhaps one of the soldiers, asked the youthful Margaret, to whom the tide had not yet advanced so far, what she thought of the spectacle before her. 'What do I see,' she answered, 'but Christ, in one of his members, wrestling there? Think you that we are the sufferers? No, it is Christ in us; for he sends none at warfare upon their own charges.'

When bound to the stake, Margaret Wilson sang several verses of the 25th Psalm, beginning at the 7th verse:

> Let not the errors of my youth,
> Nor sins remembered be:
> In mercy for thy goodness' sake,
> O Lord, remember me.

. . . She next engaged in prayer; and, while so employed, the waters had risen upon her so high as to reach her lips, and she began to struggle with the agonies of death. At this moment, by the command of her murderers, who pretended to be willing to preserve her life, provided she should swear the abjuration oath, the cords which bound her to the stake were unloosened, and she was pulled out of the waters. As soon as she recovered and was able to speak, it was asked her, by Major Windram's orders, if she would pray for the king. With the christian meekness which formed so engaging a feature in her character, she answered, 'I wish the salvation of all men, and the damnation of none.' 'Dear Margaret,' exclaimed a friend, deeply moved with pity, and anxious to save her life, 'say, God save the king!' With the greatest composure she replied, 'God save him, if he will; for it is his salvation I desire.' Immediately her friends called out to Windram, 'Sir, she hath said it! she hath said it!' But with this her murderers were not satisfied. Lagg, we are told, bellowed out, 'Damned bitch! we do not want such prayers; tender the oath to her'; and Windram, coming near her, demanded that she should swear the abjuration oath, else she should be instantly cast again into the sea. She needed not long to deliberate; in an instant her resolve was taken; preferring to die rather than do what she believed would be a denial of Christ and his truth, she firmly replied, 'I will not; I am one of Christ's children; let me go.' And so, after her sufferings were thus inhumanly protracted, and after being thus cruelly tantalized with the hope of life, she was, by Windram's orders, thrust into the waters, which speedily closed over her for the last time.

J. Anderson, Ladies of the Covenant *(1851)*

DOCTORS AND MEDICINE

Michael Scott's Pills

As a practising physician, Scot enjoyed a great reputation, being specially celebrated for his treatment of leprosy, gout and dropsy. . . One of his pills, known as 'Pilulae Magistri Michaelis Scoti', is noted by a 13th century copyist as effective to relieve headache, purge the humours wonderfully, produce joyfulness, heighten the intellect, improve the vision, sharpen hearing, preserve youth and retard baldness. These pills were composed of aloe, rhubarb, and nine fruits and flowers, made into a confection, and might fairly be described as excellent after-dinner pills.

John D. Comrie, History of Scottish Medicine *(1927)*. Michael Scott's *medical text* Liber Physionomiae, *composed at the start of the 13th century, was still current up to the 17th century.*

Dr Beaton and the Spanish Captain

James Beaton (Dr Bethune) was born in Skye, where he was the hereditary physician to the Lord of the Isles. He became a herbalist of European reputation. When the *Florida*, a Spanish galleon of the Armada, sought refuge in Tobermory bay, Mull, her Captain took ill, and Beaton was summoned. He was a keen observer, and after examining the patient prescribed regular doses of Bog-bean along with dulse-carragee. While he was standing on the poop the powder-magazine exploded and he was blown sky-high, but he fell into the sea and was rescued none the worse, for he survived twenty years.

Arnold Fleming, The Medieval Scots Scholar in France *(1952)*

Dr Pitcairn's Trick

Pitcairn seldom troubled the inside of any church, but every Sabbath morning his jug of claret was to be seen on its way from the tavern to his house, just as the more staid portion of the population was going to morning service. The kirk elders were greatly scandalised, and under the pretence of preventing Sabbath desecration, used to seize the jug, and confiscate the claret. Pitcairn, having doubts of the purity of the motive for this seizure, one morning put into the wine a dose of tartar emetic. It was as usual seized. The doctor, who was an Episcopalian, to the astonishment of the Presbyterians on that eventful day, took his place in the kirk. His eyes were directed to the seat of the elders. Worship had not proceeded far when one of the Sabbatarians rushed out of the church, as pale as death – another followed, and in a few minutes the elders' seat was empty, to the bewilderment of all but the contriver of the mischief.

James Maidment, A Book of Scottish Pasquils (*1868*). *Dr Archibald Pitcairn (1652–1713) was a notable satirical author as well as an eminent Edinburgh physician.*

John Hunter – Collector

He bought a country-house at Earl's Court . . . one which no one could pass without standing at gaze. Never before had so many kinds of animals been seen in the grounds of a country mansion. Behind it was a meadow where birds of all sorts were walking about, especially a great number of geese, whose eggs Hunter wanted for his embryological studies; but there were also pigs, goats, hedgehogs, an opossum, buffaloes, a zebra, an ostrich. The more dangerous beasts – leopards, jackals, serpents – were kept in cages. Many of the birds were rare specimens. There was a pond, for the study of fresh-water life. In the house there were dissecting-rooms, rooms for physiological experiments, and rooms for the storage of collections.

Hunter was perpetually on the look-out for rare beasts. If a gipsy passed by with a dancing bear, Hunter would make a bargain with the man to bring him the creature for dissection when it died. The Irish giant cost him much labour and a great deal of money. He was absolutely determined to have O'Bryan's skeleton for his collection. When the giant fell sick, Hunter had him kept under observation. But the Irishman scented danger, and, regarding with horror the thought that his body would be cut up, he made his friends promise that when he died they would never lose sight of his corpse until it had been sealed up in a leaden coffin and sunk in the sea. We are told that bribery and corruption to the tune of £500 were needed before Hunter could get his way. The upshot was that the skeleton is in the Royal College of Surgeons' museum, and that O'Bryan's name has become immortal.

H. E. Sigerist, Great Doctors (*1933*). *John Hunter (1728–1793), was founder of the Hunterian Museum. His experimental zeal was strong enough for him to inoculate himself with venereal disease.*

Dr Cullen on Patients

Neither the acutest genius, not the soundest judgment, will avail in judging of a particular science, in regard to which they have not been exercised. I have been obliged to please my patients sometimes with reasons, and I have found that any will pass, even with able divines and acute lawyers; the same will pass with the husbands as with the wives.

William Cullen (1710–1790), quoted in John Brown, Preface to Horae Subsecivae (*1858*). *Cullen was Professor of Medicine first in Glasgow, then for many years in Edinburgh; a physician of European renown, and a founder of the modern Scottish medical tradition.*

The Burning of the 'Burking-house'

A severe blow had been dealt to medical studies connected with the Aberdeen colleges by an occurrence known as 'the burning of the burking-house' in 1831. Early in the 19th century, before the passing of the Anatomy Act (1830), the supply of bodies for dissection had been very difficult to obtain and had only been made possible by the enthusiastic though often ill-directed 'Resurrectionist' activities of the Aberdeen medical students in the surrounding country churchyards, which vied with those recorded of Liston and other surgeons in Edinburgh. The terror inspired by the Burke and Hare affair of 1828 in Edinburgh had spread to Aberdeen, where Andrew Moir was lecturer in anatomy in 1831. The anatomist was apparently not too careful in his work, and one day a dog scraping in the open ground behind the anatomical theatre in St Andrew Street revealed a dissected human limb to some women passing to the bleach-green. A crowd gradually collected, and it was found that the fragments of a dead body had been carelessly buried. The theatre appears to have had a sinister appearance, with three false windows to the front and receiving its lighting from behind. An excited and furious mob gradually collected, broke into the theatre, and found three bodies laid out ready for dissection, which were borne off through the streets in triumph. The place was ransacked, instruments and furnishings destroyed and the mob, swelled to thousands, filled the neighbouring streets. Among them were jostled the protesting Provost of Aberdeen, members of the Town Council, policemen, and soldiers from the barracks, incapable of any action amid a mob of twenty thousand howling people. Andrew Moir, appearing on the spot, was pursued by a section of the crowd, thirsting for his life, but finally managed to conceal himself beneath a tombstone in the churchyard of St Nicholas. Tar barrels and other combustible materials were brought and set on fire, the walls of the building were undermined, and in an hour literally not one stone was standing upon another of the blazing theatre.

John D. Comrie, History of Scottish Medicine (*1927*)

Dr Bell's Trick

Bell used a standard experiment to test the powers of observation of each new class of medical students. He held up a tumbler of liquid, explaining that it contained a potent drug with a very bitter taste. 'We might easily analyse this chemically,' he said, 'but I want you to test it by smell and by taste, and, as I don't ask anything of my students which I wouldn't be willing to do myself, I will taste it before passing it around.' The students watched uncomfortably as Dr Bell dipped a finger into the liquid, put his finger to his lips, and sucked it. Grimacing, he then passed the tumbler around the class and each student in turn dipped a finger into the unknown substance, sucked it, and shuddered at the bitter taste. The experiment over, Dr Bell announced, 'Gentlemen, I am deeply grieved to see that not one of you has developed this power of perception, which I so often speak about. For, if you had watched me closely, you would have found that, while I placed my forefinger in the bitter medicine, it was the middle finger which found its way into my mouth!'

I. Wallace, The Fabulous Originals, *quoted in C. Fadiman*, The Little, Brown Book of Anecdotes, *which remarks that in a variant of the tale, the liquid is found to be urine. Dr Joseph Bell (1837–1911), of Edinburgh University, was Sir Arthur Conan Doyle's chief model for Sherlock Holmes*

Professor Gemmel's Lectures

Samson Gemmel, Professor of Clinical Medicine, was, I think, the man with the widest outlook on medical and world affairs generally that I ever met. He was an old man at the beginning of the present century, and must have graduated in medicine before the new era introduced by Pasteur. He lectured mainly in infectious diseases, leaving the lectures on the other aspects of medicine to his younger asssistants. He must have realised that the infectious diseases were on the way out, and usually in his lectures, after beginning to talk on some disease, he would wander off in reminiscences of medicine in his early days when all types of diseases were rampant in the industrial cities. He told us that the insurance companies were reluctant to accept a doctor for life insurance, unless he had had typhus fever and recovered from it. In those days, the Glasgow water supply from Loch Katrine had only recently been introduced, with water taps at different points in the city which were available to those who could pay five shillings for a key to the tap. Much of the water was still got from wells. There was one at the bottom of the eminence where there was an old cemetery. In describing conditions there, Professor Gemmel put it like this: 'The rain falls from heaven, percolates through the graves, comes out in the well at the bottom of the hill, and there the people were quite happily drinking a solution of their forefathers!'

Lord Boyd Orr (1880–1971), As I Recall *(1966)*

The 'Cruel Coins' of Shetland

In Shetland, scrofula, known as 'The Cruels', was very common, and coins of the various Stewart sovereigns were kept to be employed as remedies. At one time there were probably one or two in every parish, and many of them were used within living memory. I had first-hand knowledge of one such coin, an English half-crown of Charles II, dated 1672. It had been handed down in a family for at least four generations, and in spite of its age careful treatment had kept it in excellent condition. When anyone was affected by scrofula, this 'Cruel Coin' was sent for. To have effect, it had to be used by the third son or third daughter in a family and it was applied to the wound on three successive mornings while the person using it was fasting. The last occasion of its use seems to have been about 1902 or 1903, when it was applied by a little girl, a third daughter. The patient of that time . . . told me of it when she was a woman of about eighty, and recollected little of the occurrence, but was confident that the coin was effective as a cure. It can have done no harm, for she lived until 1942, when she was 93. The coin is still preserved, and quite recently, on the death of its previous holder (a third daughter), it was handed on to her third son.

Gordon Donaldson (1913–1993), Isles of Home: Seventy Years of Shetland

DWELLERS ON THE LAND

The First Gaels

In the Life of St Brandane it is found that in the city of Athens in Greece there was a noble chevalier who had one son whose name was Gaidel, who had for his wife the daughter of Pharao, king of Egypt, whose name was Scota, by whom he had fair offspring. Gaidel was chivalrous; he gathered the youth of his city, put to sea in a vessel with his wife Scota and their children, sought a dwelling on chance, with desire to conquer it, arrived in Spain, where on a high mountain, on the coast of the Hibernian sea, he built a strong castle and called it Brigance. He lived with his people upon rapine of the peasants of the country. His fishermen were driven one day by a deep tempest on the sea, and on their return announced that they had seen by the floating of flowers, thistles and other signs, that there was land near, beyond the sea. Gaidel with his sons, who had the surname of Scoti, from their mother Scota, put to sea in three vessels, sailed over the sea, found a large isle, landed on it, found the land grassy and pleasant, with woods and rivers, but not well peopled. . . Gaidel repaired to his castle of Brigance, proposing to return to the discovered island; but he was attacked by a grievous sickness, of which he must die; he desired his sons to go to that island, and to inhabit it, as a country without great defence and easy to conquer. Eberus, the eldest son of Gaidel and Scota, the daughter of Pharao, departed with his brothers for the said Isle, which he seized, and they slew, or subjected to their obedience, those whom they found there, and then called the Isle Hibernia, from the eldest brother Eberus, or from the sea Eberiaco, thus named by the Spanyards; but the surname Scoti remained with the other brothers, and their issue a long time in that Isle which among us is called Irrelande.

Chronicles of the Picts, *translated from* Scalacronica, *in W. F. Skene,* Chronicles of the Picts and Scots (1867)

The Fair Isle Knitters

. . . to this day there still survives a relic of the long winter evenings when the sailors of the great Armada crouched about the hearths of the Fair-Islanders, the planks of their own lost galleon perhaps lighting up the scene, and the gale and the surf that beat about the coast contributing their melancholy voices. All the folk of the north isles are great artificers of knitting: the Fair-Islanders alone dye their fabrics in the Spanish manner. To this day, gloves and nightcaps, innocently decorated, may be seen for sale in the Shetland warehouse at Edinburgh, or on the Fair Isle itself in the catechist's house; and to this day, they tell the story of the Duke of Medina Sidonia's adventure.

Robert Louis Stevenson (1850–1894), 'The Coast of Fife', *from* Random Memories

Family Life of the Selkirks

Alexander Selkirk was a favourite of his mother, on account of his being a seventh son born without the intervention of a daughter. The boy's own wish was to go to sea, in which he was encouraged by his mother, while his father's desire was to keep him at home as an assistant in his own trade.

One day he committed an assault on his brother Andrew, for which he was brought before the kirk-session of his native parish, and the following extracts from the session-book are curious, as giving the particulars of the quarrel, and also showing the pertinacity with which kirk-sessions in those days followed up any subject they had once taken in hand:

> 1701, Nov. 25. The session mett. John Selcraig, elder, compeared, and being examined what was the occasion of the tumult that was in his house, he said he knew not, but that Andrew Selcraig having brought in a canful of salt water, of which his brother Alexander did take a drink by mistake, and he laughing at him for it, his brother Alexander came and beat him; upon which he ran out of the house and called his brother John. John Selcraig, elder, being again questioned what made him sit on the floor with his back to the door? said it was to keep down his son Alexander, who was seeking to go up to get his pistole, and being inquired what he was going to do with it, he said he could not tell.
>
> Alexander Selcraig compeared not, because he was at Coupar. John Selcraig, younger, being questioned concerning the foregoing tumult, declared, that he being called by his brother Andrew,

came into his father's house, and when he entered his mother went out, and he seeing his father sitting on the floor with his back to the door, was much troubled, and offered to help him up, and to bring him to the fire, at which time he did see his brother Alexander in the other end of the house casting off his coat and coming towards him; whereupon his father did get betwixt them, but he knew not what he did otherwise, his head being borne down by his brother Alexander, but being liberated by his wife, did make his escape.

Margaret Bell, the wife of John Selcraig the preceding witness, declared that Andrew Selcraig came running for her husband John, and desired him to go to his father's house, which he doing, the said Margaret did follow her husband, and coming into the house she found Alexander Selcraig gripping both his father and her husband, and she labouring to loose Alexander's hands from her husband's head and breast, her husband fled out of doors, and she followed him, and called back again, 'You false loun, will ye murder your father and my husband both?'

November 29. Alexander Salcraig compeared, and confessed that he having taken a drink of salt water out of the cann, his younger brother Andrew laughing at him, he did beat him twice with a staffe. He confessed also that he had spoken very ill words concerning his brothers, and particularly he challenged his elder brother John to a combate, as he called it, of dry neiffells, which afterwards he did refuse and regret; moreover, he said several other things – whereupon the session appointed him to compear before the pulpit against tomorrow, and to be rebuked in the face of the congregation for his scandalous carriage.

November 30. Alexander Salcraig, according to the session's appointment, compeared before the pulpit, and made acknowledgement of his sin in disagreeing with his brothers, and was rebuked in the face of the congregation for it: he promised amendment in the strength of the Lord, and so was dismissed.

M. F. Connolly, Fifiana (1869). See also Sea and Seafaring.

Deterrence

Mr Walter Ross, Writer to the Signet, Edinburgh, by way of protecting his property from midnight marauders, published the following handbill:

Thou shalt not steal! All persons whom it may concern are desired to take notice, that steel traps, of the largest size, for catching breakers of the eighth commandment, are every night placed in the garden of St Bernard's, between Stockbridge and the Water of Leith, on the north side of the water; that spring-guns are set to rake the walls with shot upon the touch of a wire, and that a tent, having in it an armed watchman, is pitched in the middle, with orders to fire without mercy. If, therefore, any evil-disposed person or persons shall attempt to break into the grounds of St Bernard's, their blood be upon their own heads! – Amen.

This seemed very well for some time; but, at length, a suspicion arose that the arrangements were all of a fictitious nature, and the boys and black-guards of the city began to pick up their scattered courage. On learning that such was the state of matters, Mr Ross adopted the strangest expedient that could perhaps have entered the head of a country gentleman. He procured the limb of a corpse from the Royal Infirmary, dressed it in a stocking, shoe and buckle, and sent it through the streets of the city with the public crier, proclaiming that it had been found last night in the grounds at St Bernard's, and that it would be restored to the owner on being properly vouched. The garden of St Bernard's was no more broken.

Robert Chambers, Scottish Jests and Anecdotes (*1832*)

In the Land of the Fairies

It was a delightful evening – still, breathless, clear – as we swept slowly across the broad breast of Loch Maree; and the red light of the sinking sun fell on many a sweet wild recess, amid the labyrinth of islands purple with heath, and overhung by the birch and mountain-ash; or slanted along the broken glades of the ancient forest; or lighted up into a blush the pale stony faces of the tall pyramidal hills. A boat bearing a wedding party was crossing the lake to the white house on the opposite side, and a piper stationed in the bows, was dis-coursing sweet music that, softened by distance, and caught up by the echoes of the rocks, resembled no strain I had ever heard from the bagpipe before. Even the boatmen rested on their oars, and I had just enough of Gaelic to know that they were remarking how very beautiful it was. 'I wish', said my comrade, 'you understood these men: they have a great many curious stories about the loch, that I am sure you would like. See you that large island? It is Island-Maree. There is, they tell me, an old burying-ground on it, in which the Danes used to bury long ages ago, and whose ancient tombstones no man can read. And yon other island beside it is famous as the place on which the good people meet every year to make submission to their queen. There is, they say, a little loch in the island, and another little island in the loch; and it is under a tree on that inner island that the queen sits and gathers kain for the Evil One. They tell me that, for certain, the fairies have not left this part of the country yet.'

Hugh Miller (1802–1856), My Schools and Schoolmasters. *It is on record that, even after the Reformation, bulls were sacrificed on this island (properly named Eilean Subhainn), ostensibly to St Maelrubha, whose name the loch bears.*

The Sutherland Clearances of 1819

The reckless lordly proprietors had resolved upon the expulsion of their long-standing and much-attached tenantry from their widely extended estates, and the Sutherland Clearance of 1819 was not only the climax of their system of oppression for many years before, but the extinction of the last remnant of the ancient Highland peasantry in the North. As violent tempests send out before them many a deep and sullen roar, so did the advancing storm give notice of its approach by various single acts of oppression. I can yet recall to memory the deep and thrilling sensation which I experienced, as I sat at the fireside in my rude little parlour at Achness, when the tidings of the meditated removal of my poor flock first reached me from head-quarters . . . Notwithstanding their knowledge of former clearances they clung to the hope that the 'Ban-mhorair-Chatta' would not give her consent to the warning as issued by her subordinates, and thus deprive herself of her people, as truly a part of her noble inheritance as were her broad acres. But the course of a few weeks soon undeceived them. . . The people received the legal warning to leave forever the homes of their fathers with a sort of stupor – that apparent indifference which is often the external aspect of intense feeling. As they began, however, to awake from the stunning effects of this first intimation, their feelings found vent, and I was much struck with the different ways in which they expressed their sentiments. The truly pious acknowledged the mighty hand of God in the matter. In their prayers and religious conferences not a solitary expression could be heard indicative of anger or vindictiveness, but in the sight of God they humbled themselves, and received the chastisement at His hand. Those, however, who were strangers to such exalted and ennobling impressions of the gospel breathed deep and muttered curses on the heads of the persons who subjected them to such treatment. The more reckless portion of them fully recognised the character of the impenitent in all ages, and indulged in the most culpable excesses, even while this divine punishment was still suspended over them. These last, however, were very few in number – not more than a dozen. To my poor and defenceless flock the dark hour of trial came at last in right earnest. It was in the month of April, and about the middle of it, that they were all – man, woman and child – from the heights of Farr to the mouth of the Naver, on one day, to quit their tenements and go – many of them knew not whither. For a few, some miserable patches of ground along the shores were doled out as lots, without aught in the shape of the poorest hut to shelter them. Upon these lots it was intended they should build houses at their own expense, and cultivate the ground, at the same time occupying themselves as fishermen, although the great majority of them had never set foot on a boat in their lives. Thither, therefore, they were driven at a week's warning. As for the rest, most of them knew not whither to go, unless their neighbours on the shore provided them with a temporary shelter; for, on the day of their removal, they would not be allowed to remain, even on the bleakest moor, and in the open air, for a distance of twenty miles around.

    Donald Sage, Memorabilia Domestica (1889). *Sage was the minister of Farr. His hand-wringing acquiescence in the 'God-given' clearance was typical of the ministers of the time. The Ban-mhorair-Chatta was the Gaelic name for the Countess of Sutherland.*

The Black Dwarf

His personal appearance seems to have been almost indescribable, not bearing any likeness to anything in this upper world. But as near as I can learn, his forehead was very narrow and low, sloping upwards and backward, something of the hatchet shape; his eyes deep set, small and piercing; his nose straight, thin as the end of a cut of cheese, sharp at the point, nearly touching his fearfully projecting chin; and his mouth formed nearly a straight line; his shoulders rather high, but his body otherwise the size of ordinary men; his arms were remarkably strong . . . His legs beat all power of description; they were bent in every direction, so that Mungo Park then a surgeon at Peebles, who was called to operate on him for strangulated hernia, said he could compare them to nothing but a pair of cork-screws; but the principal turn they took was from the knee outwards, so that he rested on his inner ankles, and the lower part of his tibias. . . He carried a long pole, or 'kent', like the Alpenstock, tolerably polished, with a turned top on it, on which he rested, placed it before him, he then lifted one leg, something in the manner that an oar of a boat is worked, and then the other, next advanced his staff, and repeated the operation, by diligently doing which he was able to make not very slow progress. . . Sir James Nasmyth, late of Posso, took compassion on the houseless, homeless *lusus naturae*, and had a house built for him to his own directions; the door, window and everything to suit his grotesque, diminished form; the door four feet high, the window twelve by eighteen inches . . . his sister, who lived in the same cottage with him, was separated by a stone and lime wall, and had a separate door of the usual size, and window to match, and was never allowed to enter his dwelling . . . His sister and he were on very unfriendly terms. She was ill on one occasion; Miss Ballantyne asked how she was today. He replied, 'I dinna ken, I ha' na been in, for I hate folk that are aye gaun to dee and never do't.'

Robert Craig, from letters quoted in John Brown, The Black Dwarf's Bones, *in* Horae Subsecivae *(1858). David Ritchie, or Bowed Davie, the Black Dwarf, lived from 1741 to 1811. Mungo Park (1771–1806) is the African explorer, who practised as a surgeon in Peebles between his two visits to Africa, on the second of which he was drowned during a fight with Africans.*

River Lore

With moor and mountain enough to preserve the feeling of wildness, the prevailing character of the range is that of advancing cultivation, interrupted by many a tumbling stream, and broken by innumerable hillocks, and streaks and masses of wood, by which the whole surface of this half Highland country is diversified.

A shepherd, with whom I had a crack, was much offended at the slight put on his river by my asking him if it was the 'Tarf'? 'Tarf? deil a drap o' Tarf's in't. That's the black water o' Dee! the auncientest water in Scotland.'

Lord Cockburn (1779–1854), Circuit Journeys. *The name Dee is indeed ancient, related to the* dea nigra, *or black goddess, mentioned in Adamnan's* Life of St Columba. *But then so is the Tarf: whose patron spirit is a water bull (Gaelic* tarbh).

Shepherds' Larder

I had often heard that shepherds made great use of eagles' nests to fill their larders, and my uncle corroborates as follows:

> Eagles sometimes built where not even a rope-dancer could get at them – a sad case for shepherds, who were accused of concealing the whereabouts of their nests when in accessible places. It was said that they tethered the eaglets to the nest long after they could fly, because until the young birds left the nest the parents never ceased to bring quantities of all sorts of game to feed them, quite half of which was said to go into the shepherds' larder. A shepherd admitted to me that he once took a salmon quite fresh out of a white-tailed eagle's nest. Fawns, hares, lambs and grouse were brought in heaps to the nest for months – an agreeable variety at the shepherd's daily dinner of porridge and potatoes and milk.

Osgood Mackenzie (1842–1922), A Hundred Years in the Highlands

An Old Scotch Gardener

The first time that I saw him, I fancy Robert was pretty old already; he had certainly begun to use his years as a stalking horse. Latterly he was beyond all the impudencies of logic, considering a reference to the parish register worth all the reasons in the world. 'I am old and well-stricken in years,' he was wont to say; and I never found any one bold enough to answer the argument. Apart from this vantage that he kept over all who were not yet octogenarian, he had some other drawbacks as a gardener. He shrank the very place he cultivated. The dignity and reduced gentility of his appearance made the small garden cut a sorry figure. He was full of tales of greater situations in his younger days. He spoke of castles and parks with a humbling familiarity. He told of places where under-gardeners had trembled at his looks, where there were meres and swanneries, labyrinths of walk and wildernesses of sad shrubbery under his control, till you could not help feeling that it was condescension on his part to dress your humbler garden plots. You were thrown at once into an invidious position. You felt that you were profiting by the needs of dignity, and that his poverty and not his will consented to your vulgar rule. Involuntarily you compared yourself with the swineherd that made Alfred watch his cakes, or some bloated citizen who may have given his sous and his condescension to the fallen Dionysius. Nor were the disagreeables purely fanciful and metaphysical, for the sway that he exercised over your feelings he extended to your garden, and, through the garden, to your diet. He would trim a hedge, throw away a favourite plant, or fill the most favoured and fertile section of the garden with a vegetable that none of us could eat, in supreme contempt for our opinion. If you asked him to send you in one of your own artichokes, 'That I wull, mem,' he would say, 'with pleasure, for it is mair blessed to give than to receive.' Ay, and even when, by extra twisting of the screw, we prevailed on him to prefer our commands to his own inclination, and he went away, stately and sad, professing that 'our wull was his pleasure' but yet reminding us that he would do it 'with feelin's' – even then, I say, the triumphant master felt humbled in his triumph, felt that he ruled on sufferance only, that he was taking a mean advantage of the other's low estate, and that the whole scene had been one of those 'slights that patient merit of the unworthy takes'.

   Robert Louis Stevenson (1850–1894), Memories and Portraits

The St Kildan Sense of Time

As you moved from pier to pier and island to island your progress was slow but you felt the rain and wind on your cheek and you smelt the sea. Villagers came on board and drammed up in the saloon, you were not insulated from life behind a windscreen, but thrown right into the midst of it. . .

   But even in those days of unhurried peace the ethos of the St Kildans was considered by most visitors to be eccentric in its lack of urgency. Had one been compiling an Olympic team to Go Slow for Britain the St Kildans would have sauntered slowly away with the all the golds leaving South Sea islanders and other tropical lotus eaters nowhere in the field. Norman Heathcote, who visted St Kilda in 1898 with a camera, a paint-box, and his intrepid sister, found it difficult to make up his mind whether they were lazy or not:

> There is no doubt that they waste a lot of time, but I am inclined to think that this is because they are as ignorant of the value of time as of the value of money.

> Sometimes they will take a whole day making up their minds to go fishing on the next, but when once started they are most industrious, and do not seem to mind hard work.

Most of the carrying of goods from the shore and peat from the hills was done by women who were broken into it at an early age: 'I have seen a girl of about eleven with a smaller child on one arm and a bucket of water in the other, or coming over the hill with a sheep on her back.'

From what Heathcote experienced, ten days (which was all they allowed themselves on their first visit) seems a very fleeting time in which to get anything done:

> If they were going to take us out in the boat they would say we must be ready by nine o'clock to get the benefit of the tide round a certain promontory. When we had sat for half an hour on the rocks two men would appear. They would look at the boat and talk for five minutes, then one of them returns to the village to fetch the others. When all have at length appeared and said what they want to say, they proceed to haul down the boat. Soon after ten we were seated in comparative comfort in the stern and have hopes that we are off. Not a bit of it. They have forgotten an oar. Then it is discovered that one of the rowlocks is broken, and a new one has to be made. This is done by whittling a bit of stick. A long conversation follows, and we find the question now is, what the lady is to sit on: some advocate a plank, others an empty box. Eventually the box carries the day and we are off, but of course we have missed the tide.

Derek Cooper, The Road to the Isles: Travellers in the Hebrides, 1770–1914 (1979), quoting Norman Heathcote, St Kilda (1900). The Gaelic proverb 'It's a whole day's work, getting started', comes to mind. The people of St Kilda were evacuated to the mainland and the Hebrides in August 1930.

A Totem from the Past

But who can tell from what deep well of tradition many of the half-expressed fears and traditional beliefs of the countryside may be drawn, how far back into prehistory their roots may stretch? It was at the beginning of this century that the weathered limb-bone of a whale, its half-human shape improved to form a face, was found on Bernera by a crofter who thought it was one of the old gods of the island fraught with ill-luck. It was given to a visitor, whose return journey was a tale of troubles, the whale-bone image only being accepted as a passenger by the boatman after protest and its concealment in a sack, and on the mainland it was hysterically denied accommodation with its owner in the hotel! It was still an object of terror: its date is unknown, and it could belong to any period. It is as timeless as the traditions and fears with which it was so lately endowed.

Stuart Piggott, Scotland Before History (1958)

A Lesson in Peat-Cutting

Saturday morning came with the sound of men's voices, the clattering of feet, and the ring of metal on stones near the house. My party of peat-cutters had assembled, fourteen of them all told, with Sandy at their head. I led the way into school where a long table improvised from school benches had been set for breakfast. They followed me, leaving their tools outside. My sister and Catriona were busy preparing fried ham and eggs, and strong tea in large pots and jugs. Piles of scones, butter, cheese and jam were already on the table at which the men seated themselves. A hot plate of ham and eggs with a cup of tea was placed before each and to my surprise they all sat solemnly still gazing in front of them without saying a word. I was wondering if they were waiting for me to say 'grace' when Catriona whispered in my ear: 'The whisky!' This was produced and white-haired Sandy passed round the table handing each a brimming wine-glass of whisky, the contents of which were tossed off without a blink or word and with the utmost solemnity. All sat silent till the last man had drained the glass, then first looking round at each other they began to eat heartily of all before them. Before long they were talking to each other in Gaelic and seemed more natural – the effect of the food and perhaps the whisky, thought I. When they had breakfasted to repletion – and I noticed each man said a grace of thanksgiving, signing himself with a cross as he did so – an ounce of tobacco was given to each from which they shaved and rolled a pipeful, then they sat comfortably smoking and talking in low tones. At a word spoken in Gaelic by Sandy, they all rose, and, putting on their caps at the school door, took up their tools and started for the peat banks.

I was curious to see this process of peat-cutting, so followed. We arrived on the raised piece of grass-covered ground which was intersected here and there with ditches. Four or five of the men threw off their coats and with spades removed the turf along the top of the bank bordering a ditch, while others with shovels removed the surface soil that lay beneath the turf. A smooth damp-looking close-fibred brown substance was then revealed. The white-haired leader told me that this first process was known as 'skinning the binks' and the ground was now ready for cutting the peat. Two men now came forward to the front edge of the raised peat bank and one of them jumped into the ditch below. The other man carried in his hand a most strange implement called 'the iron'. The upper part was just like that of the ordinary spade, but the lower part, made of heavy steel about fifteen inches long and three inches wide, had a ten-inch keen-looking knife-blade some eight or nine inches from its end. This man advanced to the front of the bank and placed the base of 'the iron' on the peat so that the knife-blade was directly to his front with its point exactly on the front edge of the bank. He then pressed a foot on a protuberance on the shank of his implement just above the blade and the iron part sank into the damp peat to its own depth. With a jerk of the handle a clean-cut piece of peat fell from the bank into the hands of the man waiting in the ditch below who immediately threw it with a sliding motion of the hands on to the bank of the other side of the ditch. Stepping back the length of the knife-blade the man on the bank cut another piece, and so on for the whole length of the peat-bank, one man cutting and jerking, the other catching and throwing with such regularity that the movements appeared to be automatic.

F. G. Rea, A School in South Uist (1964)

The Back Hill of the Bush

The Back Hill of the Bush must surely be what I have claimed for it – the remotest house in Scotland. The shepherd who lives there gets his supplies from the farm that employs him, away over the hill into the Glenkens; twice a month they are brought half-way to him, together with his mail, and left in an iron shelter, from which he has to fetch them. Months often pass without his seeing a soul, unless this modern Elijah's visits to the shelter happen to coincide with those of his ravens, or he foregathers with his colleague of the Glenhead or the Laggan over some strayed beasts. Once a year he goes to the Lanark lamb sales; once a year, perhaps, he may join with the other hill shepherds in the early spring in trying to shoot down some of the hundreds of foxes who infest the whole region. The rest of the time his business lies only in and around the Dungeon; so he is not sorry to hear a knock on his door of an evening, and to see a strange if usually dirty face.

The first time I came into the spotless kitchen of the Back Hill of the Bush, Adam was sitting by the fire toasting his toes, a metal-capped pipe in his mouth and a book in his hands. He gave me the usual greeting in these parts – a sidelong duck of the head – without rising from his chair; but he took his pipe out of his mouth and put it back again, by way of making me welcome. Later in the evening I stole a glance at his book: it was the *Vicomte de Bragelonne.*

I have no clear recollection of that evening, but I suppose it must have followed the same course as all the other evenings that I afterwards spent there. Supper, and an excellent one, of scones and bacon and eggs and tea – hottest and strongest imaginable – falling from pot to cup with that inimitable spluttering sound that only the hottest and strongest tea can achieve . . .

. . . I do not think we had any music that night; a fiddle hung, smoke-blackened, beside the fire-place, on one of the hooks intended for bacon or braxy mutton; but it was not till my second or third visit that I prevailed on Adam to play it, and we had an orgy of such tunes as The Flowers of Edinburgh, Cameron's Got His Wife Again, and Pop Goes the Weasel. I do not suppose he played it well, but with the atmosphere of that old-fashioned kitchen, the tap of his slipper on the floor and the music that he played, he might have been Neil Gow himself.

Bernard Fergusson, Galloway, *in* Scottish Country, *edited by George Scott-Moncrieff (1936)*

Island Moments

The sea is a sheet of silver tonight, and the old grey rocks of the island are silver too in this light. How bright the lights of the lighthouses gleam! We were up the hill watching them tonight – Ardnamurchan, two flashes every twenty seconds; Dhu Artach, two every thirty seconds; and Skerryvore, one every twenty seconds. Such is the land of change in which we live: last night we could hear only the howl of the wind, its thunder on our tent, and the roar of the sea below. Tonight the sea but murmurs, the wild geese talk as they settle to graze on Creag a'Chaisteal and Sgeir nan Erionnach, and the cheerful note of the snipe reaches us as the birds come down near the tent. . . And we remember the lovely sunsets which we used to watch from the Cruachan. At first the sky would be a blaze of gold, then the red came into it as the sun fell slightly to the west of the Dutchman. At the edge of lighted sky and the blue there was a patch of mother-of-pearl cloud of the finest texture. The upper thousand-foot cone of Ben More Mull was white with snow and now made roseate by the reflection from the south-west. How can I describe adequately the multitude of tints from violet, vermilion to red, rose and yellow which composed this great expanse of land, sea and sky?

Sir Frank Fraser Darling (1903–1979), Island Years. *The island was Lunga, in the Treshnish group.*

Potato Lifting

It was bright, windy and cold as we spilled from the lorry and began our apprenticeship as potato pickers. The field was divided into lengths or 'drills' marked out by sticks, and the tractor raced round the field turning up potatoes by the hundred. We filled the wicker baskets with an enthusiasm which owed everything to novelty. The grieve, or overseer, kept stalking round, exhorting us to 'Make a clean pick'. He had an eye of astonishing keenness for even the most fugitive potato.

The tractor made its second circuit. We picked. It came again. We picked. It was becoming more painful to straighten. There were local women with us in the field who picked with a practised economy of motion. The stark realisation dawned. There was nothing else to this job. The tractor would keep coming round and we would keep gathering, perhaps 20 times in a morning.

Lunch came at last, strong tea and sandwich spread, an anaemic vegetable concoction on our bread. There was a fierce short blatter of rain then we resumed picking. The afternoon crawled past until it was time to clamber up on the lorry, looking to sit directly behind the cabin out of the wind. . . The second and last day for me was noteworthy for my first taste of industrial action. We were far from being as patriotic as we should have been. Our thoughts should have been on the nation's larder, which we were helping to fill, aiding the fulfilment of the Government's expressed desire, 'Eat less bread, eat potatoes instead'. Our thoughts should have been so, but we were much more exercised by what we took to be sharp practice on the part of the farmer. It seemed to me that the drills were longer than they had been on the previous day. We were good at judging distances – penalty areas and cricket pitches were our everyday currency. I mentioned my thoughts to 'Quadie', my next in line. He took a look and agreed. We canvassed other side-of-mouth opinions like convicts in a James Cagney movie. There was unanimity. Also, to our partial eyes, the tractor driver was coming round faster than he had done the previous day. We had more to do and less time in which to do it. It was not to be borne. It was during the lunch-break that some forgotten genius, over the cheese sandwiches, conceived the idea of bunging a small potato up the tractor exhaust. This unpatriotic action gained us an hour's remission while the trouble was diagnosed and a court of inquiry conducted.

Bob Crampsey, The Young Civilian: A Glasgow Wartime Boyhood (*1987*)

The Carrots of Muck

Muck is immensely fertile. The laird, Mr Macewan, farms almost the whole of it, apart from the small croft lands about the harbour. He showed us enthusiastically round the rich knolls and valleys of his land. At that time he was spending his winters skiing in Switzerland and the rest of the year farming in Muck – an entrancing blend. In his hayfields, the haystacks jostled one another, so thick had been the growth. His fat sheep ambled and gorged the ripe grass. On the west side of the island we saw an agricultural prodigy – fields and fields of carrots flourishing. The carrot-fly disease is unknown here, and the endless wind lifts an endless spray of the powdered-shell sand from the beach on to the fields, which enjoy a steady snow of lime.

The carrots were mighty, and great also was our enthusiasm to spread the news of this fertility. This led us to overreach ourselves in the matter of press illustrations, for the story we got ready to send about Muck would be better, we judged, if one of the outsize carrots could accompany it. We obtained such a carrot from the laird and wedged it into the cardboard container from a whisky bottle, coiling its long delicate tail round the inside of the parcel. The whole was wrapped and tied, and addressed, along with the story, to the late celebrated John James Miller, at that time the agricultural editor of the *Daily Record*. We learned later that when the parcel arrived in his mail in its familiar shape, he tore it joyfully open. His rage was dreadful when he pulled forth, instead of a bottle, the earthy club of carrot which had been our proud exhibit, and hurled it from him. It lodged in one of the immense waste-paper containers which buoy editorial floors, and the Muck carrots never got a mention.

Alastair Dunnett, The Canoe Boys *(1995), recounting a trip in the 1950s*

ENCOUNTERS AND FAREWELLS

Goodbye to the Divines – and Reflections on Committees

When I took my leave of the Assemblie I spoke a little to them. The Proloquitor, in the name of the Assemblie, gave me ane honourable testimonie, and many thanks for my labours. I had been ever silent in all their debates; and however this silence sometimes weighted my mind, yet I found it the best and wisest course. No man there is desyred to speak: four parts of five does not speak at all; and among these are many most able men, and known by their wrytes and sermons to be much abler than sundrie of the speakers; and of these few that use to speak, sundry are so tedious, and thrusts themselves in with such misregard of others, that it were better for them to be silent. Also there are some eight or nyne so able, and ready at all times, that hardly a man can say anything, but what others, without his labour, are sure to say alse weell or better. Finding, therefore, that silence wes a matter of no reproache, and of great ease, and brought no hurt to the work, I wes content to use it.

Robert Baillie (1559–1662), Letters and Journals. *Baillie attended the Assembly of Divines at Westminster between 1644–47, the conclave which established the forms of Presbyterian worship.*

A Meeting with Rob Roy

This celebrated freebooter, towards the end of his career, being hunted from his own shire of Dumbarton, took refuge among the inaccessible mountains of Lochaber, and lived on shabby depredations among the few flocks of sheep supported by their pasturage, with now and then a deer which he shot where it might not alarm. At that time it was the custom of the War Office to send to Fort Augustus the monthly pay of that garrison by an orderly sergeant. One of those sergeants was travelling on this errand, with the monthly allowance in his pocket, across the mountain of Corryarrick, where the road to Fort Augustus separates from that to Inverness a little beyond the inn of Dalwhinny, when he overtook a stout good-looking man in the Highland garb and arms, who told him, on being accosted, that he was going towards Fort Augustus. 'I am glad of that,' said the sergeant, a very uncautious messenger, 'because I think you will serve me as a protector from a desperate fellow who, I am informed, frequents this district, called Rob Roy, who would have a good subject for his trade in me, as I am the bearer of the monthly pay of the garrison of Fort Augustus.'

'I do not believe', answered the Highlander, 'that Rob Roy would meddle with you, but you are welcome to such protection as I can afford.'

They journeyed on together, till they reached the high ground from which there is a bird's eye view of the Fort – 'Now,' said the Highlander, 'you cannot miss your way, and I must bid you farewell.'

'But we must not part so, my good friend,' replied the sergeant. 'You must be my guest tonight at the Fort, and shall have the best supper it can afford, as a reward for your good company.'

'That would not be quite convenient for me,' rejoined the stranger; 'but when you reach the Fort, make my compliments to the Governor, and tell him that Rob Roy escorted you in safety.'

Henry Mackenzie (1745–1831), The Anecdotes and Egotisms of Henry Mackenzie. *Mackenzie notes that the Highlander, according to Sir Walter Scott, was one Donald Gunn, and not Rob Roy MacGregor. David Stewart of Garth calls him John Dhu Cameron, the 'Sergeant Mor'. But one may doubt also whether a single redcoat soldier would have been sent with a large sum of money through the Highlands in the 1730s.*

Bear-leader's fee

When Boswell was bear-leading Samuel Johnson through Scotland, he introduced him, in the Parliament House at Edinburgh, to Henry Erskine, who after making his bow and a short conversation left the conductor and conducted, putting a shilling into Boswell's hand, being the common fee for a sight of wild beasts.

Henry Mackenzie, The Anecdotes and Egotisms of Henry Mackenzie

Dundonian Thrift

A respectable public functionary in Dundee, of parsimonious habits, was one day rallied by a friend from the country upon the extreme shabbiness of his attire. 'Hoot, man,' answered the bailie, 'it's nae matter; every body kens me here;' meaning that, his character being perfectly known in the place, it was quite unnecessary that he should fortify his pretensions by fine clothes. It happened that the same friend met him afterwards in the streets of London; and finding his clothes no better, expressed still greater surprise than before, adding that surely his former excuse would not avail him now. 'Hoots, man,' answered the pertinacious miser, 'naebody kens me here.'

Robert Chambers, Scottish Jests and Anecdotes (*1832*)

Lord Kames Says Goodbye to the High Court and the World

Each morning he was to be seen proceeding to Court from his house in the Canongate, attended by Sinkum, his favourite caddy, whose stumpy figure, with one leg shorter than the other, which caused him to duck at every step, contrasted with the tall, slouching lord, bending down to hear his companion's gossip of the day. It was on a December day that he finally quitted the old Court, on whose bench he had been so notable a figure for nearly thirty years, giving his not too dignified farewell as he closed the door behind him. Eight days afterwards he was dead – 'of old age' . . . Never was there a more industrious mortal, a more inquisitive person, than the old judge, who two days before he died told his old friend Dr Cullen that he wished earnestly to be away, because he was exceedingly curious to learn the nature and manners of the other world.

H. Grey Graham, Scottish Men of Letters in the Eighteenth Century (*1908*). *Henry Home, Lord Kames (1696–1782) was an agricultural improver and a widely read theorist of literature and aesthetics in his day, in addition to his long role as a judge who 'dearly loved a hanging circuit'. His notorious valediction to his Court colleagues was: 'Fare ye a' weel, ye bitches.'*

Scott says Goodbye to Mungo Park

There, to the north-east, is the place – Williamhope Ridge – where Sir Walter Scott bade farewell to his heroic friend Mungo Park. They had come up from Ashestiel, where Scott then lived, and where 'Marmion' was written . . . Well, it was on that ridge that the two friends – each romantic, but in such different ways parted, never to meet again. There is the ditch Park's horse stumbled over and all but fell. 'I am afraid, Mungo, that's a bad omen,' said the Sheriff; to which he answered, with a bright smile on his handsome, fearless face – 'Freits follow those who look to them' . . . Scott used to say, when speaking of this parting, 'I stood and looked back; but he did not.'

John Brown (1810–1882), Minchmoor, *from* Horae Subsecivae

A Vexed Question

On the 26th October I had the opportunity of attending a meeting at Dingwall of the Commissioners of Supply of Ross-shire. . . Accordingly I repaired to the County Hall, not exactly at the time appointed, but a good while after that; for I had observed that the Dingwall clock was exactly three-quarters of an hour behind my Lowland time. How long that cadaverous old timepiece may have told its fib to the people I cannot say; but it seemed to me not inappropriate after all, that the Dingwall clock should be three-quarters of an hour too slow, seeing that the county was that day to assemble for the purpose of considering whether they should commmence to do certain works which ought to have been accomplished three-quarters of a century ago. . . Mr Davidson, of Tulloch, in philabeg and plaid, at length ascended the rostrum, and formally opened the proceedings of the day . . . And now, thought I, for the roads; when up rose a thin-faced gentleman, whom I learned to be Major Robertson, of Glencalvie notoriety, and, in a slow and tremulous voice, propounded the following question: 'Gentlemen, since you have appointed me convener of this committee, may I ask what the duties of a convener are?'

Robert Somers, Letters from the Highlands *(1848)* on the Famine of 1846. *Robertson was the proprietor who evicted the inhabitants of Glencalvie, through the agency of his factor, Gillanders.*

The Source of the Tweed

When a boy I knew, and often think still, of a well far up among the wild hills – alone, without shelter of wall, or tree, open to the sun and all the winds. There it lies, ever the same, self-contained, all-sufficient; needing no outward help from stream or shower, but fed from its own unseen unfailing spring.

In summer, when all things are faint with the fierce heat, you may see it, lying in the dim waste, a daylight star, in the blaze of the sun, keeping fresh its circle of young grass and flowers.

The small birds know it well, and journey from far and near to dip in it their slender bills and pipe each his glad song.

The sheep-dog may be seen halting, in his haste to the uplands, to cool there his curling tongue.

In winter, of all waters, it alone lives; the keen ice that seals up and silences the brooks and shallows has no power there. Still it cherishes the same grass and flowers with its secret heat, keeping them in perpetual beauty by its soft warm breath.

Nothing can be imagined more sweetly sudden and beautiful than our well seen from a distance, set with its crown of green, in the bosom of the universal snow. One might fancy that the Infant Spring lay nestled there out of grim winter's way, waiting till he would be passed and gone.

Many a time, as a boy, have I stood by the side of this lonely well, 'held by its glittering eye', and gazing into its black crystal depths, until I felt something like solemn fear, and thought it might be as deep as the sea! It was said nobody knew how deep it was, and that you might put your fishing-rod over head and not find the bottom.

But I found out the mystery. One supremely scorching summer day, when the sun was at his highest noon, I lay poring over this wonder, when behold, by the clear strong light, I saw far down, on a gentle swelling like a hill of pure white sand (it was sand), a delicate column, rising and falling and shifting in graceful measures, as if governed by a music of its own. With what awful glee did I find myself the sole witness of this spectacle! If I had caught a Soul, or seen it winking at me out of its window, I could scarcely have been more amazed and delighted.

John Brown (1810–1882), Horae Subsecivae

Far from Home

We had been upon the road all evening; the coach-top was crowded with Lews fishers going home, scarce anything but Gaelic had sounded in my ears; and our way had lain throughout over a moorish country very modern to behold. Latish at night, though it was still broad day in our sub-arctic latitude, we came down upon the shores of the roaring Pentland Firth, that grave of mariners; on one hand, the cliffs of Dunnet Head ran seaward; in front was the little, bare white town of Castleton, its streets full of blowing sand; nothing beyond, but the North Islands, the great deep, and the perennial icefields of the Pole. And here, in the last imaginable place, there sprang up young outlandish voices and a chatter of some foreign speech; and I saw, pursuing the coach with its load of Hebridean fishers – as they had pursued *vetturini* up the passes of the Apennines or perhaps along the grotto under Virgil's tomb – two little dark-eyed, white-toothed Italian vagabonds, of twelve to fourteen years of age, one with a hurdy-gurdy, the other with a cage of white mice. The coach passed on, and their small Italian chatter died in the distance; and I was left to marvel how they had wandered into that country, and how they fared in it, and what they thought of it, and when (if ever) they should see again the silver wind-breaks run among the olives, and the stone-pine stand guard upon Etruscan sepulchres.

Robert Louis Stevenson (1850–1894), Random Memories, *from* Further Memories

Dancing al Fresco . . .

An example of concentrated joy was at Acharacle, when in front of a croft a young fellow was dancing the Highland Fling, with such whole-souled consuming zeal that I stood transfixed with wonder and awe. He was alone, and I came suddenly upon him at a sharp bend of the road. He threw his legs about him with such regardless glee that for a moment I was afraid that one of them might come spinning through the air to hit me. I watched him, fascinated, for fully ten minutes. When at length he saw me, the glory flowed suddenly off his legs; he subsided into a country bumpkin, and beat a hasty retreat indoors.

D. T. Holmes, Literary Tours in the Highlands and Islands *(1909)*

. . . and Dancing Indoors

It was, I remember, a perfect winter night when I left the bothy to return to the house. The mud in the yard was frozen into little rills and waves; the sky was a deep unfathomable dark out of which the stars shone in frosty splendour; and to the west the young moon rose in a narrow field of light. Even though I was only a child I stood still and held my breath for wonder at the brittle clearness of the night when even the silence seemed to crack, with a tiny silver noise, under the grip of the frost. But it was not only the frost I listened to. A loud noise was coming from the house, a bumbling rowdy noise that sounded strangely through the still night. It had in it something of an organ and something of the zoo and most of all it was like some force of nature suddenly set free. I stood in the close, a little frightened, wondering what horror had invaded the countryside. Then I realised it was the staid Scots farmers at their pleasure. I ran into the house afraid that I might miss something that sounded like tremendous fun.

Whatever I may have expected, the reality did not disappoint me. The scene in the parlour was like nothing I had ever imagined. The big low room was poorly lighted by a paraffin lamp that threw monstrous shadows on the roof and left the corners in obscurity. It was better so, for I could see legs and boots emerging from the darkness where their owners had retired from the melée or had slipped from the supporting corner to the safety of the floor in unmelodious slumber. At one side of the room a six-foot horse dealer was playing on the pianoforte and since he did not trust himself on the music stool he was on his knees at the keyboard. He was playing with an excellent sense of time but his fingers were so broad that each one hit a chord at a time. The result was very powerful. And it was wholly in keeping with the rest of the scene. For three farmers were dancing a barbaric dance, an extempore invention, in the middle of the room. So that they could dance the freer, they had stripped themselves entirely naked and were leaping fantastically between the shadows in the full glory of their manhood. I stood at the door, completely stricken; for the din of the piano, the shouts of the dancers and the hairy bodies prancing in the gloom made me feel that some ruthless elemental force had been let loose in the room.

My coming in disturbed them. One of them gave a shout and made at me. I just managed to dodge him so that he ran out through the door into the lobby beyond. The other two chased after him. I could hear them shouting and clattering among the pans in the dark kitchen and with great daring I ran after them. By that time they were out into the close, chasing each other with hideous shouts. Still daring, I followed; and, lurking in the darkest shadow, watched them make half a dozen rounds of the close. Then one of them found an open gate into a field; the others followed him; and, as I stood there in the icy close, I could see their white naked bodies go tearing over the frosty lea and hear their shouts diminish into the echoes of the night . . .

John R. Allan, Summer in Scotland (*1938*)

Bard Meets Bard

Long-haired men and short-haired women were not yet a common spectacle in the Island, and the more they multiplied on the roads the more the wonder grew. One of these explained to Murdo the bard that he wore his hair long because he was a poet. 'A poet, you know, is known in Wales and in the Highlands as a bard.'

'I always thought the beautiful poems come from the brain,' replied Murdo, 'and it is news to me that they come from the hair. The Good Book tells that Samson's strength lay in his long hair, and if that was so, it is quite as believable that the hair should be the source of lovely rhymes. But what will happen when the poet becomes bald?'

The long-haired poet looked at Murdo with astonishment. 'The long hair is just a sign to the world that a poet is not as other men: that he is an artist and feels and sees more than the others.'

'Oh, I see,' exclaimed Murdo. 'A poet can have his hair cut off by Delilah and he would lose nothing; he would be a poet still.'

The long-haired poet agreed. 'Do tell me,' he said, 'who was Samson and how did Delilah cut off his hair? There must be a story in that!'

But Murdo, there and then, ended the conversation. For, as he afterwards explained, a man with long hair who claimed to be a bard but was so ignorant as not to know the lovely stories in the Holy Book could not be worth talking to: he must be an impostor. 'I am a bard myself,' Murdo concluded his tale, 'and I know what I am talking about. The hair and poetry have nothing to do with each other. My father was as bald as an egg in his old age, and he was a bard to the last.'

Norman Maclean, The Former Days (*1945*)

A Gorbals Boy Sets off for Oxford

Father had left for work at seven. We had parted in an atmosphere of apocalyptic phlegm, overlaying an uneasy, hesitant, stilted kindliness. The hooded figure of the wounded past stood beside us counselling forbearance, generosity if not forgiveness, at this close of an epoch. . .

That parting in the cold grey kitchen, the imprisoned passion, the forlorn longing to recreate love and gentleness, still lacerates the spirit. Tumult roared within – the desire to erase the past, pity for him, remorse at leaving him, eagerness to take my chance away from him, the tingle of adventure, voices of doubt, foreboding. If only I could find the calm, the lucidity, to close the distance between us, spread out before him all that I felt about the present and the past and the future, smooth away all anger, all hurt, make him see that I had no choice but to go. I saw the disappointment in him, the defeat. I saw that he longed to understand and sympathise, to reach out to me, but that he could only come a fragment of the way. He knew why I was stricken dumb, but could not help me utter the truths that clamoured to be set free, perhaps because he too could not open his heart. We both had too much to say, and no words fitted.

. . . In the cold kitchen, in the grey morning light, as he stood ready to go to work, we faced each other, at the end, in silence. As always he was neatly dressed, navy blue overcoat, blue serge suit, white collarless shirt and grey woollen muffler, grey felt hat with black silk band. His tools were in a small Gladstone bag on the cracked oilcloth table cover. He looked deep into my eyes and then at the floor; would the Almighty send a sign to stop me going? At last he held out his hand and gripped mine hard: 'Gey gesunterheyt' (Go in health). He picked up the bag, blue-grey eyes looking at nothing, turned, squaring his shoulders, and strode out.

Ralph Glasser, Gorbals Boy at Oxford (*1988*)

A Curious Coincidence

. . . the greatest coincidence of which I have ever heard happened to the Lord Justice-Clerk of Scotland in the year 1937.

Staying at a well-known English spa, he was sitting in the lounge before dinner when a man, a total stranger, in immaculate evening dress, came in and sat down near him. After a time he said: 'Do you come from Scotland?'

'Yes,' said the Lord Justice-Clerk.

'Ah,' continued the affable stranger, 'I wonder if you happen to know my friend Lord Aitchison?'

Wondering if there might be a member of the peerage with the same name as himself, of whom he had not heard, the Lord Justice-Clerk replied: 'Do you mean the judge?'

'Yes – the Scottish judge.'

'Oh, yes', said Lord Aitchison, amazed at finding this new acquaintance. 'I have met him. When did you see him last?'

'As a matter of fact I was shooting with him last week.'

'Dear me! I didn't know he had a shoot.'

'Oh, rather, he's got a very good shoot down in Ayrshire.'

Shortly afterwards the dinner-hour arrived and the two went into the dining-room to sit at separate tables. During dinner the Lord Justice-Clerk told the head-waiter of the conversation in the lounge. The head waiter was a man of large experience of life who had met many strange characters in his day

'Well, my lord, do you mind if I mention the matter to the manager?'

'I wouldn't bother. I'm making no complaint. He's probably just a boaster and quite harmless.' Yet the Lord Justice-Clerk, from his knowledge of psychology and of criminals, reflected that if the man was a crook it was likely enough that he would know about judges and pretend to have a friend on the Bench. So he said to the head-waiter, 'Well, just as you like – but remember, I make no complaint.'

Next morning the affable stranger did not appear at breakfast . . . The manager had telephoned to the police giving them a description of the man. The police had sent a plain-clothes officer to the hotel, who on seeing the stranger thought he answered the description of a wanted man, and had then telephoned Scotland Yard. In the early morning a car with two of the CID arrived from London, the suspected man was interviewed in his bed, confessed his identity and was then arrested. He was a well-known jewel-thief . . .

Halliday Sutherland, Hebridean Journey (1939)

Backstage in the Usher Hall

It had struck me that Edinburgh's old Usher Hall might of itself provide the basis of an article. How many conductors, I wondered, had visited? How many great artists had gladdened its auditorium? I went along to talk to a hall attendant who had been there for many years.

We entered the green room where he spoke animatedly of the musicians he had met, their quirks and foibles. For some reason he wanted to show me the magnificent bathroom where many an artist had lain soaking and steaming away fatigue after an arduous concert. We were chatting happily there when we became aware of a presence behind us.

'What', asked Sir Thomas Beecham, 'are you doing in my bathroom?'

I could, I suppose, have told him I was the plumber, but I trundled out the truth instead. Beecham stories were legion. He had the gift of a sharp wit suited to most occasions. He did not fail me now. Jutting his goatee beard, he said: 'As a journalist you should know that the paper here is privately owned.'

Don Whyte, On the Lonely Shore (1977)

FESTIVALS AND CELEBRATIONS

The Riding of the Parliament

The procession, according to old feudal usage, began diminutively, and swelled in importance as it went. The representatives of the burghs went first; then, after a pause, came the lesser barons, or county members; and then the nobles – the highest in rank going last. A herald called each name from a window of the palace, and another at the gate saw that the member took his place in the train. All rode two abreast. The commoners wore the heavy doublet of the day unadorned. The nobility followed in their gorgeous robes. Each burghal commissioner had a lackey, and each baron two, the number increasing with the rank, until a duke had eight. The nobles were each followed by a trainbearer, and the Commissioner was attended by a swarm of decorative officers, so that the servile elements in the procession must have dragged it out to a considerable length. It seems, indeed, to have been borrowed from the French processions, and was full of glitter – the lackeys, over their liveries, wearing velvet coats embroidered with armorial bearings.

All the members were covered, save those whose special function it was to attend upon the honours – the crown, sceptre, and sword of state. These were the palladium of the nation's imperial independence, and the pomp of the procession was concentrated on the spot where they were borne ... before the Commissioner. Immediately before the sword rode the Lord Lyon, in his robe and heraldic overcoat, with his chain and baton. Behind him were clustered a clump of gaudy heralds and pursuivants, with noisy trumpeters proclaiming the approach of the precious objects which they guarded. Such was the procession which poured into that noble oak-roofed hall, which still recalls, by its name and character, associations with the ancient legislature of Scotland.

J. Hill Burton, History of Scotland

A Toast to Brother Burns

I went to a Mason-lodge yesternight where the Most Worshipful Grand Master Charters, and all the Grand lodge of Scotland visited. The meeting was most numerous and elegant; all the different Lodges about town were present in all their pomp. The Grand Master who presided with great solemnity, and honor to himself, as a Gentleman and Mason, among other general toasts gave, 'Caledonia and Caledonia's Bard, brother B——' which rung through the whole Assembly with multiplied honours and repeated acclamations. As I had no idea such a thing would happen, I was downright thunderstruck, and, trembling in every nerve, made the best return in my power. Just as I finished, some of the Grand Officers said, so loud as I could hear, with a most comforting accent, 'Very well indeed,' which set me something to rights again.

Robert Burns (1759–1796), letter to John Ballantine, January 14, 1787, from The Letters of Robert Burns, *selected by R. Brimley Johnson (1928). Burns was a keen Freemason and the Grand Lodge of Scotland preserves his signature on documents in its museum.*

Celtic Diversions

I presided last night at the dinner of the Celtic Society, 'all plaided and plumed in their tartan array', and such jumping, skipping and screaming you never saw. Chief Baron Shepherd dined with us and was very much pleased with the enthusiasm of the Gael when liberated from the thraldom of breeches.

J. G. Lockhart (1794–1854), letter to Sir Walter Scott, May 1821

The Carlyles Give a Soirée

In March (1839) Mrs Welsh persuaded her daughter to give a soirée in recognition of the fact that Carlyle – by now a literary celebrity – was being invited to dinners and breakfasts, and, as he put it, 'rather rising in society'. The house was accordingly polished and furbished, and refreshments prepared on a larger scale than anything Jane had dreamed of before: her entertainment of evening visitors had always been of the simplest. 'Tea is put down, and tiny biscuits; they sip a few drops of the tea, and one or two of the sugar biscuits "victuals" a dozen ordinary eaters.'

But now, as Carlyle put it, 'between twenty and thirty entirely brilliant bits of personages' were expected, and Mrs Welsh was determined that her daughter's party should be a success. After Jane had made her preparations, her mother sudddenly produced a fresh supply of delicacies that she had bought herself, together with an array of coloured candles for the table. Jane flew into a rage: such an extravagant display was ridiculous, would make her a laughing-stock, she cried as she removed dish after dish of sweetmeats. Then seizing two of the candles, she blew them out. 'They could be lit after her death,' she said, flinging them into a cupboard.

Mrs Welsh burst into tears. Jane, shaken and remorseful, pulled herself together in time to play hostess; but the memory of the incident lingered. The soirée went off, Carlyle reported, 'in the most successful manner: at midnight I smoked a peaceful pipe, praying that it might be long before we saw the like again'.

His prayer was answered. This was the first and the last soirée at Cheyne Row.

Thea Holme, The Carlyles at Home (*1965*)

The Invergarry Gathering

Such meetings are common enough now at Inverness and in other parts of the Highlands, but they were then unknown except in Glengarry . . . The scene of the games was very pretty and striking. There was an open space in the island surrounded with birch trees, and the clear river ran on each side, with mountains towering on both sides of the valley.

Lunch was provided in a tent for the gentry, and in a recess in the wood a rural kitchen was improvised, where cooking for some three or four hundred people, men, women and children, was carried on.

The games were of the usual sort now common – dancing, piping, lifting a heavy stone, throwing the hammer, and running from the Island to Invergarry and back, six miles. The young men who ran came in exhausted, and almost in a state of nudity, for they had thrown off their kilts on the way, and arrived in their shirts only. A blanket was cast over them and a glass of whisky administered.

One feat which I never saw since was twisting the four legs from a cow, for which a fat sheep was offered as a prize. The cow was brought up and felled before the multitude, and the barbarous competition began, several men making the attempt. At last one man succeeded. After struggling for about an hour, he managed to twist off the four legs, and as a reward received his sheep, with an eulogistic speech from the chief in Gaelic. . .

About five in the afternoon, when the games and feast had ceased, it was announced that the carriages for the chief and his party were on the road outside the island. A sort of procession was formed, the pipers leading, and the chief departed amidst loud cheers.

The country people were all regaled, dinner being laid out on the green consisting of basins of broth, boiled and roast beef and mutton, fowls, salmon, potatoes, and a large quantity of oaten bannocks. There were no knives or forks, but the men's dirks and skean dhus were called into requisition to assist their fingers. Afterwards they had dancing, which was entered into with great spirit.

Joseph Mitchell (1803–1883), Reminiscences of My Life in the Highlands, *describing a scene around 1820.*

The Hawick Common Riding

I went last week to the Hawick Common Riding. It was one of the most
exciting things I have ever seen or heard. Have you been there?

It is, of course, the Green Man in *The Golden Bough,* riding through the
town to bring in the leafing of the oak. They even wear oak leaves. Ostensibly it celebrates the Hornshole battle, the year after Flodden, when the
halflins of Hawick rode out on the plough horses and beat an English raid-
ing party and brought back the Hexham Abbey flag.

I had to give the oration at the Colour bussing. I cried like a cow and
could hardly get through my speech.

The town hall and the streets outside were packed and they had loud-
speakers for the people who couldn't get in. The Cornet's followers in the
gallery facing the platform sang like Hell for an hour before we arrived.
Then the fife band came up the middle aisle to lead in the Provost and his
Bailies in their red gowns. I used to think fifes sound like piddling in biscuit
tins but, when they play Teribus, they are really spirit-stirring all right.

They went out and came in again leading the Cornet's Lass and her
attendants, all dressed up to the nines. Then the Macer gave the colours to
a maid-of-honour, who pushed them up through crossed halberds to the
Lass who tied a favour to the flag and then handed it to the Provost, saying
that it had been well and truly bussed. The Provost said, 'Thank you, Gracie,'
and the band came back with the Cornet, between his green-coated Right
Hand and Left Hand Men.

The Lass hung on his sash and the Provost gave him the flag and ordered
him to carry it round the marches. He said he would, with great brevity and
dignity. He is a bar boy by profession.

I then made a really bloody awful speech and several songs were sung,
including the excellent PAWKIE PATTERSON'S AULD GREY YAUD, fin-
ishing up with TYR HAEBBE US TYR Y ODIN. The leader sings the first
two lines of each stanza and the audience take up the second two lines and
then slap into the chorus:

> Teribus y teri odin
> Sons of heroes slain at Flodden
> Imitating Border bowmen
> Aye defend your rights and Common

I wish to God they could find a better penultimate line, but there it is. Then
the audience filed out and the Riding was proclaimed from the balcony.

I went with the Provost – a fellow of infinite jest, of most excellent fancy – an exciseman – to the Callants' Club, where we had more songs and speeches and quite a lot of whisky . . .

Then we went to a party at the Provost's house.

I got to bed at five (between four and five we had about a dozen of champagne with the Jubilee Cornet who carried the flag in 1900). I told the porter to waken me at 6.30, as I had to attend the Provost's breakfast at 7.30. At 7.45 the Housekeeper woke me to say. 'The police are wanting ye.' I said, 'I've done nothing. Tell them to go to Hell,' and suddenly realised that I was already late for breakfast. I jumped up, shaved, and was round before eight. Ham and eggs, whisky, tea and some more speeches.

I told them that the only thing I had missed in their heathen rites was a human sacrifice; but that I was beginning to see that there might be one after all.

We then went in procession round the town and up a long, steep hill, the band playing in front of us like to bust themselves. At the top of the hill we stopped and watched the Cornet and his hundred followers coming up the road at full gallop. Hard on the beasts but very nice.

Into the cars again and up to the hill farm where we had curds and cream and rum and milk in a big hut to more speeches and songs.

Then at the racecourse, more whisky in the Provost's tent, a gallop round the course by the Cornet, and the planting of the flag. . . After lunch, I slept like a log till five. We drove back to Hawick to the Provost's and at six o' clock we were at the Cornet's Dinner in the Crown Hotel. That went on – better speaking than I have ever heard anywhere – till ten. Then there were two Balls.

I didn't see a parson and only one drunk man all the time I was there. The drunk man was a visitor from Glasgow.

I enjoyed it. It was very elegant – as good as THE THREE ESTATES. I thought I'd tell you.

It was a piece of natural religion, probably better and more sanitary than the A.D. variety. Indeed, God was hardly mentioned, except when He was asked – once, I think – to save the King.

James Bridie (Osborne Henry Mavor, 1888–1951), letter to Arthur Wallace, quoted in Ronald Mavor, Dr Mavor and Mr Bridie *(1988)*

Plumbers' Dinner

The lowest bid for the plumbing work was put in by a cheerful character called John McGruer, known locally as Johnny Plumb. So he got the job, and the scheme for passing all the pipes up through the chimney space was found to work quite well. Some time after the work was finished he did me the honour of inviting me to the Annual Plumbers' Dinner at Inverness – a slap-up affair at which no expense is spared, and a full bottle of whisky is put in front of every man. They have no time for your effete French wines in the Inverness and Northern District Master Plumbers' Association. . . We were chauffeured home in the plumbers' van – a necessary precaution in Ross, where the police are keen on the breathalyser.

Gerald Laing, Kinkell: The Reconstruction of a Scottish Castle (*1974*)

Judgment on a Piper

A story was told me by a friend, of a Highland concert at which the chairman proclaimed that the proceedings were to be opened by pipe music played by a certain piper. Now the skill of this piper was not rated too highly locally, and he had scarcely taken the pipes from their box and walked on to the platform, when one of the audience, with more vigour than taste, yelled at the top of his voice 'Sit doon, ye —— .' At once the chairman was on his feet and called out, in stern and disapproving tones, 'Who called the piper a —— ?' Came the answer instantly, in the broadest Scots, 'Fa caa'd the —— a piper?'

Seton Gordon (1886–1971), A Highland Year (*1947*)

FOOD AND DRINK

At Lucky Middlemass's

The favourite haunt of Robert Fergusson, and many other persons of his own standing, was Lucky Middlemass's tavern in the Cowgate, which he celebrates in his poem on Cauler Oysters. . .

> The entertainment almost invariably consisted of a few boards of raw oysters, porter, gin, and occasionally a rizzared haddock, which was neither more nor less than what formed the evening enjoyments of most of the citizens of Edinburgh. The best gin was then sold at about five shillings a gallon, and accordingly the gin at Lucky Middlemas's cost only threepence. The whole of the debauch of the young men seldom came to more than sixpence or sevenpence. Mr S—— distinctly recollects that Fergusson always seemed unwilling to spend any more. They generally met at eight o'clock, and rose to depart at ten; but Fergusson was sometimes prevailed upon to outsit his friends, by other persons who came in later, and, for the sake of his company, entreated him to join in further potations.

An eyewitness account of the poet Robert Fergusson (1750–1774) related by Robert Chambers in Scottish Biographical Dictionary

A Playwright's Faux-Pas

William Douglas-Home (1912–1992) and his wife Rachel were invited to join friends for dinner in London. He relates:

> Having been to Oxford for a matinee, I duly arrived, dined, chatted, and then rose to go around eleven.
> 'Thank you, Rachel, for a lovely dinner,' said my host.
> 'What do you mean?' I inquired. 'I brought it over from home,' Rachel explained, 'as their cook was off.'
> 'In that case', I said, 'I am at liberty to say that the fish was the most disgusting thing I've ever eaten.'
> 'That was the only dish I provided,' said my host.

Robert Morley, *A Book of Bricks*

The Scotch Pie

Mutton pies, which are still known tho' not so regularly called, formed another article of street merchandise. They were composed of scraps of mutton and a mixture of onions, and were sold for a halfpenny. It was strongly suspected that they were sometimes made of horse-flesh, and I certainly saw, in coming home from the Water of Leith on moonlight night, two bakers whom their jackets whitened by flour discovered to my view, performing some operations on the carcase of a dead horse, left, as was commonly the case at that time, after being skinned, on the bank at the back of the Castle; but what they were doing I had no leisure, nor indeed would it have been very safe, to examine.

Henry Mackenzie (1745–1831), The Anecdotes and Egotisms of Henry Mackenzie

The Social Need for Wine

When Sir James Stewart, the author of *Political Economy*, returned from abroad, he invited a select party of friends to dine with him to welcome his arrival. After dinner he said: 'Nobody seems inclined to drink and I have been accustomed to confine my drinking chiefly to the time of dinner. Suppose we order away these bottles and glasses, and sit sociably round the fire.' This plan was unanimously agreed to; but Sir James soon found the conversation to flag, and some of the company were almost asleep. 'I see, gentlemen,' said he, 'this won't do, in Scotland. We must have back the bottles and glasses, and with their inspiration our conversation will be revived.' That was accordingly done, and had the effect which he predicted.

Henry Mackenzie, The Anecdotes and Egotisms of Henry Mackenzie

Gauger and Smuggler

In some parts of the Highlands gauger and smuggler were on good terms though they watched one another like keeper and poacher. On one occasion a smuggler was cautioned by a gauger in a friendly manner. Both were Highlanders.

'Sandy,' said the gauger, 'you and I are well acquent and ye ken I'm a man o' my word. Weel, I'm telling you for your own good. Ye're going too far, and I've my orders. From now on I'm on your trail.'

'Thanks,' says Sandy. 'Ye'll admit my word's as good as your ain? Weel, I'll gie ye a chance. On Friday I'll bring in a firkin o' whisky under your very eyes and it'll be on the North road between Beauly and Inverness between 9 a.m. and 5 p.m.'

With much emphasis on the sanctity of the smuggler's word the two men parted, and by the Friday the gauger had gathered a strong band of excise officers and police to watch the road. From nine in the morning onwards there was a steady stream of traffic. First came carts with hay. Each cart was searched. Then came carts with turnips followed by carts with sheep, and later carts with wood. All were examined with infinite care but no whisky was found. Later, came a funeral cortege which held up the queue of carts for some time until a dray with a load of oats made a sudden dash to pass the procession. 'Stop that dray,' said the head gauger. The dray was searched in vain. The queue of carts continued until five in the evening when the gauger and his weary men were pleased to call a halt.

Later in the evening gauger and smuggler met to compare notes, and the gauger took Sandy to task.

'It's no' the playing of a trick on me that I mind,' he said. 'It's the fact that you broke your pledged word. Man, I trusted ye.'

'I kept my word,' said Sandy, 'and the whisky's in Inverness now'.

'Ye brought the whisky along the North road between nine and five. Have ye any witnesses?'

'Aye,' says Sandy, 'there's yersel. Man, ye took off your hat to it.'

Robert Bruce Lockhart, Scotch (1951)

Plain Fare at Achnasheen

Ere we reached the solitary inn of Auchen-nasheen – a true Highland clachan of the ancient type – the night had fallen dark and stormy for a night in

June; and a grey mist which had been descending for hours along the hills – blotting off their brown summits bit by bit . . . had broken into a heavy, continuous rain. As, however, the fair weather had lasted us until we were within a mile of our journey's end, we were only partially wet on our arrival, and soon succeeded in drying ourselves in front of a noble turf fire. My comrade would fain have solaced himself, after our weary journey, with something nice. He held that a Highland inn should be able to furnish at least a bit of mutton-ham or a cut of dried salmon, and ordered a few slices, first of ham, and then of salmon; but his orders served merely to perplex the landlord and his wife, whose stores seemed to consist of only oatmeal and whisky; and, coming down in his expectations and demands, and intimating that he was very hungry, and that anything edible would do, we heard the landlady inform, with evident satisfaction, a red-armed wench, dressed in blue plaiding, that 'the lads would take porridge'.

Hugh Miller (1802–1856), My Schools and Schoolmasters

Pure Water

The advent of pure Loch Katrine water was not, however, unanimously welcomed, for an old lady who all her life had been in the habit of fetching her water from a certain well which had been closed as polluted was most indignant, saying to a neighbour who urged her to take her new gravitation water and leave the well, 'I just canna thole that new water; it's got neither taste nor smell.'

Elizabeth Haldane, The Scotland of Our Fathers (*1933*)

The First Tea-room

According to some Glasgow stories, this city gave the world its first tea-room, as tea-rooms are known nowadays. At the east corner of Argyle Street and Queen Street stood a shop which specialised in selling tea. It was run by Stuart Cranston, a name to become famous in Glasgow temperance circles and even places in London where tea was drunk. Victorian ladies dropped into Cranston's to see what new tea had arrived, and Mr Cranston developed the idea of allowing them to taste each new infusion.

But this caused some confusion in the shop, and Mr Cranston decided to give the ladies their tea in another room. Accordingly, he opened up a room on the floor above, put in some tables and chairs, and, when his customers wanted to taste a new tea, he conducted them there so that they could sip in comfort.

After a while it seemed to him that many of the ladies were using this tea-tasting room as a, so to speak, convenience! And so he got the idea of charging them money for a cup of tea, whether they were trying it or not.

The ladies did not object in the least. Indeed, they flocked to Cranston's for tea. And behold! the tea-room was born.

Jack House, The Heart of Glasgow (*1968*). *It was under the management of Cranston's daughter that the tea-rooms were famously redesigned by Charles Rennie Mackintosh.*

The Effects of Atholl Brose

Atholl brose is a concoction which is drunk in company and on festive occasions like Hogmanay and St Andrew's Day. There are various recipes, but the simplest method is to mix an equal quantity of running heather honey and fine oatmeal in a little cold water. Then, according to the number of your guests, pour in very slowly a well-flavoured malt whisky. Stir the whole contents vigorously until a generous froth rises to the top. Then bottle and cork tightly, keep for two days, and serve in the finest silver bowl that you possess. A pound of oatmeal and a pound of honey will need four pints of whisky, and the quantity required can be reduced or increased in these proportions.

Atholl brose is a giant's drink, and I have vivid memories of the St Andrew's Day I organised in Prague, when we left the making of the brose to the Military Attaché. It was the first St Andrew's Day dinner ever held in the Czechoslovak capital, and the M.A., a Sassenach, resolved that it should not be forgotten. For several days he worked in secret. When the brose was passed round in a magnificent loving cup with two handles, with a guest standing up on each side of the drinker, the fumes were almost overpowering. The M.A. had laced the brose with an over-generous measure of slivovice, the potent plum vodka of Slovakia. He suffered for his intervention in Scottish affairs. After the dinner there were several casualties and the only standing survivors were three Scots and Jan Masaryk.

Robert Bruce Lockhart, Scotch (*1951*)

Two English Literary Gents Discover Highland Hospitality

Just before they reached the tenth milestone they saw a cottage on the left, fifty yards or so from the road, and decided that if the occupant would give them a cup of tea they would eat their sandwiches there. A young woman opened the door to them, and in a gentle voice said she would be delighted to make tea for them, inviting them to enter a parlour furnished with comfortable armchairs and a sofa. Pearson sank into an armchair and Kingsmill, flinging his rucksack on the floor, disposed himself on the sofa with his feet over the far end.

Pearson: What a stroke of luck! This is unquestionably the refuge I have been looking for.

Kingsmill: We must stop here at least an hour. The mistake the day before yesterday was not making a long enough halt for lunch, and today I've got that damned rucksack which weighs at least twice yours, though of course you have a brace of blisters.

A tray was brought in with tea, a large jug of milk, bread and butter, scones and various kinds of cakes. They had already taken out their sandwiches, and Pearson said, 'I hope you don't mind if we eat our own sandwiches, though we may sample your admirable cakes if we have any room to spare.' She smiled charmingly. 'Not at all,' she said, and left the room. They settled down to their sandwiches and soon emptied the teapot. 'I'll get some more tea,' said Kingsmill, 'and milk too, if we haven't cleaned her out.' He went into the kitchen and on returning with a replenished teapot and milk jug did not close the door properly. Presently a draught blew it open, and Pearson feebly pushed at it from the depths of his armchair. It opened again, and Pearson jabbed at it irritably. It opened for the third time, and Peasrson with a deep imprecation forced himself up a few inches and gave the door a blow which closed it with a crash that shook the house. When Pearson at the end of an hour suggested they should move, Kingsmill said it was a pity not to make the most of the place, and nearly another hour passed over two or three pipes and desultory talk before they at last heaved themselves up and went to pay the bill. 'No, no,' said their hostess, 'there is nothing to pay.'

'But I insist!' Pearson exclaimed.

'No, please! It was a pleasure.'

'But I can't possibly – I mean, it's preposterous . . . I should feel so frightfully – Really, you must take something.'

'I couldn't think of it. It's a pleasant break in the day. I have enjoyed being of service to you.' Pearson continued to protest, but gradually became inarticulate, and Kingsmill asked their hostess if they might send her the book they were writing on their tour. She said she would be very glad to read it, and told them her name was Mrs Campbell. Pearson, recovering his speech, joined Kingsmill in a babble of thanks, which Mrs Campbell accepted with a gentle smile.

They lurched down the road.

Hesketh Pearson and Hugh Kingsmill, Skye High (1937). *They were one of several pairs of writers who have set out to follow in the footsteps of Johnson and Boswell. Their tea-break occurred in Glen Shiel.*

Eating Cormorant

I once shot a cormorant and took it home. We roasted it, stuffed with oatmeal and potatoes which we threw away, as this stuffing is popularly supposed to draw the strong fishy taste out. Then we approached the corpse, holding our noses but we could not eat it. Next, with great courage, we hacked the flesh off the bones, curried it and put tomato sauce and pickles with it, but it was still uneatable and even the dogs would not touch it – though that may have been because of the curry. But when people tell you that cormorants are good, don't believe it.

Ruthven Todd (1914–1978), quoted by Louis MacNeice in I Crossed the Minch *(1938). MacNeice had been talking to a Barra boatman who, while he extolled the taste of cormorant, really felt there was nothing to beat a heron.*

John Grierson on Food

When Grierson was in Edinburgh at this time, the later 1950s, he was staying at 87a the West Bow, an upper floor of an old building near the Grassmarket. I called on him one afternoon there to discuss a film commentary and found him cooking – an Irish stew simmering in a pot and a joint roasting in the oven. I asked if this wasn't too much food for one man. It wasn't for him, he explained, but for the neighbours (who probably included some in need of a good meal). Unhappily, he insisted on me sampling the Irish stew which, however exquisite an example it was of his cooking, had little appeal as a mid-afternoon snack after an adequate lunch. He loved cooking, at all times and in any place, and it added greatly to his pleasure when there were appetites to satisfy.

He was once asked what was the strangest meal he had ever had. 'I was invited to a festival in a village not far from Mexico City with some American film men. The first course was cooked white worms. The second course was fried caterpillars. The main course was a goat dug out of a pit of mud where it had been cooked whole. The Americans got whiter and whiter with each course. Me? I found the meal strange – but delicious.' While in Edinburgh Grierson invariably bought fish as he was on the way to the airport for the flight south. It was his practice to ask where his selected haddock had been caught. 'Three miles nor'nor'east of Eyemouth, sir.' A month passed, another visit, another purchase and the same question. 'Three miles nor'nor'east of Eyemouth, sir.' Another month, etc., etc. I waited apprehensively for the answer. 'Three miles nor'nor'east of Eyemouth, sir.' Grierson did not ask again.

J. Forsyth Hardy, John Grierson: A Documentary Biography *(1979). John Grierson (1898–1972), producer of some classic Scottish films, was a pioneer of the 'documentary' film.*

HISTORIANS

Rude Awakening

He (David Hume) wanted a book out of the Advocates' Library, of which the learned antiquarian Goodall, author of the first Vindication of Queen Mary,

of Edinburg to Demand the keys of the Town and to tell them he intended to Enter it either that night or next day, and if their was any resistance made, whoever was found in Arms should be Severely treated; and besides, he Could not answere but if the town was taken by Storm his Soldiers would plunder it. At ten at night, their came four of the town Councill out to the Princes quarters to beg he would give them time to think on his demand. This was a messuage contrived to gain time, for they expected General Copes Army every hour to land at Leith from Aberdeen, and in case he landed time Enough, they intended to wait the Event of a Battle. The Prince, after they had kiss'd his hand, told them he was going to send of a detachment to Attack the town and let them defend it at their peril; that if they did the Consequences would be bad, and if they did not he intended no harm to the old Metropolis of his Kingdom. As Soon as they received this answere the Prince order'd Young Lochiel with 800 men to March & attack the town. Their Came out sometime after another deputation of Six Counsellors: Provost Coots was one of them. They Gott the same Answere as the first, and the Prince did not See them. The Coach that they came out in went in at the West port and sett down the Company, and as they were letting out the Coach at the Netherbow Lochiels party who were arrived their rush'd in, seized all the Gaurds of the Town, who made no resistance, and made themselves masters of Edinburgh without firing a Shot. They Establish'd Guards at the Gates, Guard house, Weigh house, and Parliament house. Notwithstanding of the towns being in this way taken without any Capitulation, the Highlanders did no mischief. The Prince Gott the news of Edinrs being taken the next morning 17 of Sept as he was upon his March and of their having seized 1000 Stand of Arms, which Gave him and his Army a Great deal of joy as they Stood in need of them. When the Army Came near town it was mett by vast Multitudes of people, who by their repeated Shouts and huzzas express'd a great deal of joy to see the Prince. When they Came into the Suburbs the Croud was prodigious and all wishing the Prince prosperity; in Short, nobody doubted but that he would be joined by 10,000 men at Edinburgh if he Could Arm them. The Army took the road to Dediston, Lord Strathallan marching first at the head of the horse, the prince next on horseback with the Duke of Perth on his right and Lord Elcho on his left, then Lord George Murray on foot at the head of the Colum of Infantry. From Dediston the Army enter'd the Kings park at a breach made in the wall. Lord George halted some time in the park, but afterwards marched the foot to Dediston, and the Prince Continued on horseback always followed by the Croud, who were happy if they could touch his boots or his horse furniture. In the Steepest part of the park Going down to the Abey he was oblidged to Alight and walk, but the Mob out of Curiosity, and some out of fondness to touch him or kiss his hand, were like to throw him down, so, as soon as he was down the hill, he mounted his horse and rode through St Anes yards into Holyroodhouse Amidst the Cries of 60,000 people, who fill'd the Air with the Acclamations of joy. . . He was joined Upon his Entring the Abby by the Earl of Kelly, Lord Balmerino, Mr Hepburn of Keith, Mr Lockart younger of Carnwath, Mr Graham younger of Airth, Mr Rollo younger of Powhouse, Mr Sterling of Craigbarnet, Mr Hamilton of Bangore and Younger of Kilbrackmont, Sir David Murray, and Several other Gentlemen of distinction, but not one of the Mob who were so fond of seeing him Ever ask'd to Enlist in his Service, and when he marched to fight Cope he had not one of them in his Army.

Lord Elcho (1721–1787), A Short Account of the Affairs of Scotland in the Years 1744, 1745 and 1746. *It was Elcho who shouted as he saw the Prince leave the field of Culloden: 'There you go for a damned cowardly Italian.'*

The Rout of Moy

Prior to the Battle of Culloden, Aeneas, the twenty-second chief (of Mackintosh) was a captain in the Black Watch, or 42nd Highlanders. At this time the regiment, along with a considerable royal force, was stationed at Inverness, under the command of the Earl of Loudoun. The main body of the royal army, under the Duke of Cumberland, was marching northward from Aberdeen. The Highland army, under the prince, was advancing through the central Highlands, along General Wade's military road. As the Highlanders approached Inverness, the prince and a small following were a little in advance. He took up his abode at Moyhall, twelve miles from Inverness, on February 16th, 1746.

The lady of the chief . . . who had strong Jacobite tendencies (notwithstanding that her husband was in arms for the Government), raised the clan in behalf of the prince, and placed them under the comand of a relative, Mr Macgillavry, of Dunmaglass.

The Earl of Loudoun, knowing that the Highland army was approaching Inverness, and hearing that the prince was to sleep at Moyhall on the 16th, conceived the idea of surprising him there and seizing his person. The enterprise required to be carried out with great secrecy, and with this view Lord Loudoun placed a cordon of guards round the town to prevent any alarm being given or notice sent. He gave orders that 1,500 men should be in readiness for a midnight expedition.

Some of the troopers, prior to their march, were drinking in a public house kept by a widow Baillie. She overheard their talk and conjectures that they believed the expedition was with the view of proceeding to Moyhall to capture the prince. On this she sent a messenger to the Dowager Lady Mackintosh, who was also a Jacobite, and was then residing in Inverness, to intimate what she had heard. The old lady immediately despatched one of her maidservants as messenger to Moyhall to warn them of the intended expedition and the danger to which the person of the prince would be exposed. This messenger, after many hairbreadth escapes, arrived in time to give the necessary alarm.

The lady of the chief at Moyhall, without ceremony and in great haste, sent the prince and his followers to a place of safety. She had previously instructed Fraser, the blacksmith of Moy, with a few trusty men under his command, to watch the approaches from Inverness.

Fraser concealed his men behind a series of hillocks which exist along the roadside, planting them at various distances as if there were a great body of men, and as Lord Loudoun's men approached in the dark, he gave orders to his men at the various distances to fire. The first shot killed MacLeod's piper, Macrimmon (said to be the best in the Highlands), Fraser at the same time calling out in the dark with a loud voice on the Macdonalds and Camerons to advance and protect the sacred person of their prince. The royalists were seized with panic, which passed along the whole body of the troops. They fled in great disorder, trampling on each other; and so complete was their rout and fear that they never stopped until they reached their headquarters at Inverness. . .

Immediately after the battle of Culloden a party of soldiers proceeded to Moyhall, seized the high-spirited lady who was the cause of this disaster, and carried her as prisoner to Inverness. The general, on the way back, in his polite and encouraging manner told her 'to be hung would be her fate, but from her pluck and spirit she was worthy to be swung from a golden cord and to stand on a mahogany gallows'.

Joseph Mitchell (1803–1883), Reminiscences of My Life in the Highlands. *The lady was said to be known afterwards as 'Colonel Anne'. She was imprisoned in Edinburgh for two years, and then released. The death of MacCrimmon was much regretted on both sides.*

Hiding Out in Badenoch

It was known to several Macphersons that Cluny, Lochiel, Dr Cameron, etc., were together in Badenoch, but then these Macphersons never once hinted to any person that they knew of any such thing; and when the Prince came to Cluny and Lochiel in Badenoch, it was known to none but to themselves and those that were with them; even the foresaid Macphersons never once suspecting that the Prince had ever come down the country to see Cluny, Lochiel, etc. None were admitted . . . but young Breackachie, and any such as they themselves ordered, or allowed him to introduce to them. This strictness continued still to be observed (rather more and more) after the Prince had come to them, and then none were admitted to them even by young Breackachie himself till a council was held to consider the necessity

or usefulness of having an interview with this or the other person that
Breackachie might happen to bring them notice of. So that it was scarce
possible that a discovery could be made of the Prince's being in Badenoch.

Breakachie said that the Prince used to tell his attendants in Badenoch,
that when Donald Cameron was about guiding him through the guards,
Donald would fall a-rubbing his nose, and would say to the Prince, 'O Sir,
my nose is yuicking, which is a sign to me that we have great dangers and
hazards to go through.' When they had passed through the guards, the prince
merrily said to Donald Cameron, 'Well, Donald, how does your nose now?'

'It is better now,' answered Donald, 'but it still yuicks a little.'

'Ay, Donald,' replied the Prince, 'have we still more guards to go through?'

This plainly shows how well the Prince kept up his spirits, even when
surrounded with the greatest dangers, of which indeed many instances can
be given.

Robert Forbes, The Lyon in Mourning (compiled *1746–85*)

Mackenzie's Self-Sacrifice

All who are acquainted with the events of the unhappy insurrection of 1745,
must have heard of a young gentleman of the name of Mackenzie, who had
so remarkable a resemblance to Prince Charles Stuart, as to give rise to the
mistake to which he cheerfully sacrificed his life, continuing the heroic deception to the last, and exclaiming, with his expiring breath, 'Villains, you
have killed your Prince!'

David Stewart of Garth (1772–1829), Sketches of the Character, Institutions and Customs of the Highlanders of Scotland

A Practical Reason for Incorruptible Fidelity

Of the many who knew of Prince Charles's places of concealment was one
poor man, who being asked why he did not give information, and enrich
himself by the reward of £30,000, answered, 'Of what use would the money
be to me? A gentleman might take it, and go to London or Edinburgh,
where he would find plenty of people to eat the dinners, and drink the wine
which it would purchase; but, as for me, if I were such a villain as to commit a crime like this, I could not remain in my own country, where nobody
would speak to me, but to curse me as I passed along the road.'

David Stewart of Garth, Sketches of the Character, Institutions and Customs of the Highlanders of Scotland.

A Jacobite Insurance Policy

In autumn 1746, Clerk Miller of Perth, a very able but unpopular man, much trusted at that time by the king's servants at Edinburgh, seeing Mr Anderson, factor to James Moray of Abercairney, on the street, beckoned to him. Taking him aside, he said, 'Anderson, do you not remember being in this town a year ago when the Highlanders were here?'

'Really, George, my memory is not as good as it has been.' Said the other, 'I will refresh it. Do you not remember carrying one thousand guineas to the Prince, and making a speech to him in your master's name?' Mr Anderson, who was a shrewd worthy man, got away as soon as he could, and mounting his horse, galloped home. On hearing what had passed, Abercairney said, 'Let my horses be got ready; I will set out directly for France or Holland.'

'That I hope,' said his sagacious factor, 'will be unnecessary. Take your bed and play the part of a sick man, to which your friend, Dr Smith of Perth, will give countenance, and leave the rest to me.' The good doctor entered readily into the plot, and pronounced his patient to be in great danger. Meanwhile Abercairney directed George Miller to be sent for in great haste. On his entering into the bedchamber, the supposed sick man addressed him thus in a tremulous voice, 'My dear George, thinking myself a dying man, it is most proper that I should settle my worldly affairs. In your abilities and integrity I have full confidence; let bonds of provision to the younger children, and a nomination of tutors and curators be drawn as soon as possible. I mean to make you factor on the estate till the heir be of age. Nor shall it be in the power of the tutors to remove you from that office.' The deeds were drawn, for which Miller received fifty guineas and then went home. In a competent time the laird recovered, and it may well be thought that for some months George was a frequent and welcome guest at Abercairney. Anderson judged soundly. Miller, who was sheriff as well as town-clerk, and supposed to be officious and over-harsh, took no steps to investigate Abercairney's conduct in September 1745. When the Act of Indemnity passed, in which he was not an excepted person, he sent for his friend Miller; but after giving him a good dinner and plenty of wine, loaded him with abuse, and then kicked him to the door.

John Ramsay of Ochtertyre (1736–1814), Scotland and Scotsmen in the Eighteenth Century

A Future Lord Chief Justice on the Hook

When Lord Mansfield (then Mr Murray) was examined before the Privy Council, about the year 1747, for drinking the Pretender's health on his knees (which he certainly did), it was urged against him, among other things, to show how strong a well-wisher he was to the cause of the exiled family, that, when he was employed as Solicitor-General against the rebels who were tried in 1746, he had never used that term, but always called them unfortunate gentlemen. When he came to his defence he said the fact was true; and he should only say that 'he pitied that man's loyalty who thought that epithets could add to the guilt of treason!' – an admirable instance of a dexterous and subtle evasion.

John Timbs, A Century of Anecdote (*1864*)

Jacobite Demonstrations in 1748

In the morning of Tuesday (December 20th, 1748), the Lion, the crest of the Scots arms placed above the outer entry of the Parliament house in Edinburgh, was found dressed in a white wig and a blue bonnet, with a large white cockade on one of the sides of the bonnet. When this was reported to the Magistrates, they ordered a party of the town-guard under the command of one of the captains, to march up to the Parliament Close and to pull down the blue bonnet and the wig. For that purpose a ladder was got, and the person who went up the ladder could not with all his strength pull off the wig and the bonnet, they having been well cemented to the Lion's head; upon which he told the captain that he behoved to have a knife to cut them off. It being some time before a knife could be got, the mob (a very numerous one) cried several times, 'Huzza! huzza! the blue bonnet has won the day! The blue bonnet has won the day for ever!' With the help of a knife, the business was at last made out.

In the foresaid morning, it was likewise observed that the eyes of the picture of the Duke of Cumberland (drawn upon each side of a sign-post at the Crown Tavern, in the entry of the Parliament Close) had been scraped out. Upon this the mob of Edinburgh had a witty saying, viz., 'That Cumberland had grutten out baith his een to see the lion better busked than himself.'

In the evening of the said day, a large bonfire was kindled on that point of Salisbury Craigs which is exactly opposite to the castle of Edinburgh. The bonfire flamed briskly for more than three hours, and several persons were seen dancing and skipping round it. . .

Throughout the whole of the said day, December 20th, all the streets of Edinburgh were crowded with cabals and processions of people, insomuch that it was dangerous for a redcoat to appear on the street. There was one company . . . who marched in great order down all the Canongate to the Abay gate, most of them being dressed in blue bonnets, with white cockades and in tartan cloaths. They marched up the Canongate again in the same order as they had marched down, one marching on the head of them, and another immediately at his back, and all the rest advancing in their several ranks at a proper distance from each other. In the center they had white colours displayed, the tops of the standards being decked with ribbands flying like streamers of a ship. They huzzaed several times in their marching up and down. No riot or squabble happened on any of the streets of Edinburgh throughout that whole night.

Robert Forbes, The Lyon in Mourning *(compiled 1746–1785). These manifestations took place at a time – two years after Culloden – when severe laws against wearing tartan were still in place.*

The Keeper of a Vow

There was another Highlander who resided near Kessock, who had vowed, immediately after the battle of Preston, that he would neither cut nor comb the hair of his head until Charles Stuart was placed on the throne of his ancestors. And he religiously observed this vow. My grandfather saw him twenty years after the battle. He was then a strange, grotesque-looking thing, not very unlike a huge cabbage out a-walking.

Hugh Miller (1802–1856), Notes and Legends of the North of Scotland

KINGS AND QUEENS

King Magnus Barelegs Gains Kintyre

Then men went between him and Malcolm, King of the Scots; and the kings made peace between them, to the effect that King Magnus should possess all the islands that lie to the west of Scotland, all between which and the mainland he could go, in a ship with the rudder in place.

But when King Magnus came north to Kintyre, he caused his men to draw a skiff across the isthmus of Kintyre, and to set the rudder in place: the king himself sat in the after-deck, and held the helm. And thus he took possession of the land that then lay to the larboard. Kintyre is a great land, and better than the best island in the Hebrides, excepting Man.

Heimskringla. Magnus Barelegs' Saga, *translated by A. O. Anderson. This supposed coup took place in 1098, five years after the death of Malcolm III, in the reign of Edgar. Magnus' adoption of the costume of the Western Isles, noted in* Heimskringla, *has often been hailed as an indication of the ancient tradition of the kilt, although another Scandinavian tradition calls him 'Barefoot' and ascribes the nickname to a hasty escape in the wars with Sweden.*

Malcolm Canmore and St Margaret

The King as it were feared to offend a Queen whose life was so venerable, since he clearly perceived that Christ was truly dwelling in her heart; he hastened all the more quickly to obey her wishes and prudent counsels. What she refused he refused, and what she loved, he loved for the love of her love. Hence even the books which she used in her devotions or for reading, the King, though unable to read, often used to handle and examine, and when he heard from her that one was dearer to her than others, this he regarded with kindlier affection, and would kiss and often fondle it. Sometimes also he would send for the goldsmith, and instruct him to adorn the volume with gold and precious stones, and when finished he would carry it to the Queen as proof of his devotion.

Turgot, The Life of St Margaret, Queen of Scotland (early 12th century)

Robert Bruce and the Spider

Every Scottish schoolchild used to be told the story of how the humble spider encouraged King Robert I to persevere in his efforts to establish himself. Defeated by the English soon after his coronation in 1307, Bruce was on the run for several months, kept hidden by friends in the Western Isles and in Galloway. Some stories say he even sailed to Norway. On one occasion he had to take refuge in a cave. It was the lowest point of his fortunes. His wife and sister were prisoners of the English king, Edward I. His supporters were being hunted down and executed. The struggle to re-establish Scotland as an independent kingdom seemed doomed to hopeless failure. It was then that Bruce's eye caught a spider, hanging by its thread from the roof of the cave. It was trying to swing to the cave wall. Several times it tried, but each time could not reach the wall and swung back again. It did not give up, and after many efforts, finally managed to reach and cling to the wall. Bruce was deeply impressed by its tenacity. He resolved that he too would keep on trying, until he had achieved his aim. Soon after that he returned to the Scottish mainland, and began his long, slow campaign which culminated in the Battle of Bannockburn in 1314 and the expulsion of the English from Scotland.

Although this story goes back almost to Bruce's own time, there is no evidence that it really happened. Like many other myths of Scottish history, it was made popular in Sir Walter Scott's Tales of a Grandfather *(1825), which ascribes it to a Bruce family tradition. Official propaganda and popular esteem created many stories around the king, including the famous 'I'll mak' siccar', remark of Roger Kirkpatrick, delivering the killing blow to John Comyn during the fatal meeting meeting between Comyn and Bruce in the Greyfriars Church of Dumfries in February 1306.*

'Kate Barlass' and the Death of James I

On this fatal evening the revels of the court were kept up to a late hour. The common sports and diversions of the time, the game of tables, the reading romances, the harp and the song, occupied the night; and the prince himself appears to have been in unusually gay and cheerful spirits. He even jested about a prophecy which had declared that a king should that year be slain; and when engaged in playing at chess with a young knight, whom in his sport he was accustomed to call the King of Love, warned him to look well to his safety, as they were the only two kings in the land. In the midst of this playful conversation, Christopher Chambers, one of the conspirators, being seized with remorse, repeatedly approached the royal presence, intending to warn James of his danger; but either his heart failed him, or he was prevented by the crowd of knights and ladies who filled the presence chamber, and he renounced his purpose. It was now long past midnight, and the traitors, Athole and Stewart, who knew by this time that Graham and the other conspirators must be near at hand, heard James express his wishes for the conclusion of the revels with secret satisfaction; when, at this moment, a last effort was made to save the unhappy prince, which had almost succeeded. The faithful highland woman who had followed the court to Perth, again presented herself at the door of the chamber, and so earnestly implored to see the king, that the usher informed him of her wishes. It was a moment on which his fate seemed to hang, but his evil genius presided; he bade her call again and tell her errand on the morrow; and she left the monastery, after solemnly observing that they would never meet again.

Soon after this James called for the parting cup, and the company dispersed. The Earl of Athole and Sir Robert Stewart the chamberlain, were the last to leave the apartment; and the king, who was now partly undressed, stood in his night-gown before the fire talking gaily with the queen and her ladies of the bedchamber, when he was alarmed by a confused clang of arms, and a glare of torches in the outer court. A suspicion of treason, and a dread that it was the traitor Graham, instantly darted into his mind, and the queen and the women flew to secure the door of the apartment, but to their dismay found the locks destroyed and the bolts removed. James thus became certain that his destruction was resolved upon; but his presence of mind did not forsake him, and commanding the women to obstruct all entrance as long as they were able, he rushed to the windows, but found them so firmly secured by iron bars, that all escape was impossible. The steps of armed men now came nearer and nearer, and in utter despair he seized the tongs of the fireplace in the apartment, and by main force wrenching up one of the boards of the floor, he let himself down into a small vault situated below; he then replaced the board, and thus completely concealed himself from observation. From this incommodious retreat there was a communication with the outer court by means of a drain or square hole used for cleansing the apartment, and of width enough to have permitted the king to escape; but it had unfortunately been built up only three days before by James's own direction, as the tennis court was near it, and the balls had frequently run in and been lost in the aperture. Meanwhile, Graham and his accomplices rushed towards the king's bedchamber, and having slain Walter

Straiton, a page, whom they met in the passage, began to force open the door amidst the shrieks of the queen and the women, who feebly attempted to defend it. One of the ladies, named Catherine Douglas, with heroic resolution thrust her arm into the staple from which the bolt had been treacherously removed; but it was instantly snapt and broken by the brutal violence of the conspirators, who, with furious looks and naked weapons stained with blood, burst into the chamber, and in their first attack had the cowardice to wound some of the queen's women, as they fled screaming into the corners of the apartment. The queen alone did not move . . . she would assuredly have been slain had the deed not been prevented by a son of Graham's. . . Every part of the chamber was now diligently examined, every place of probable concealment opened up without succcess; and after a tedious search, they dispersed through the outer rooms and passages, and from thence extended their scrutiny to the remoter parts of the building.

A considerable time had now elapsed since the first alarm, and although Graham had secured the gates and occupied the outer courts of the monastery by his highlanders, yet the citizens, and the nobles who were quartered in the town, already heard the noise of the tumult, and were hastening to the spot. It seemed exceedingly likely, therefore, that the king would still be saved, for his place of concealment had totally escaped the attention of the conspirators, and every moment brought his rescue nearer. But he was ruined by his own impatience. Hearing no stir, and imagining that they who sought his life had left the place not to return, he called to the women to bring the sheets from the bed, and draw him up again into the apartment; but in their attempt to effect this, Elizabeth Douglas, one of the queen's women, fell down. The noise recalled the conspirators, and at this moment Thomas Chambers, one of Graham's accomplices, who knew the monastery well, suddenly remembered the small closet beneath the bed-chamber, and conceiving, if James had not escaped, he must be there concealed, quickly returned to the apartment. In a moment he discovered the spot where the floor was broken, raised up the plank, and looking in, by the light of his torch perceived the king, and the unfortunate lady who had fallen in to the vault; upon which he shouted to his fellows with savage merriment to come back, for the bride was found whom they had sought and carolled all night. The dreadful scene was now soon completed; yet James, strong in his agony, although almost naked, and without a weapon, made a desperate defence. He seized Sir John Hall, who had leapt down, by the throat, and with main strength threw him under his feet; another of the murderers, Hall's brother, who next descended, met with the same fate; and such was the convulsive violence with which they had been handled, that at their execution, a month after, the marks of the king's grasp were seen upon their persons. But the villains being armed with large knives, James's hands and arms were dreadfully lacerated in the struggle. Sir Robert Graham now entered the chamber, and springing down with his drawn sword, threw himself upon his victim, who earnestly implored his mercy, and begged his life, should it be at the price of half his kingdom. 'Thou cruel tyrant,' said Graham, 'never hadst thou compasssion on thine own noble kindred, therefore expect none now.'

'At least,' said James, 'let me have a confessor for the good of my soul.'

'None,' cried Graham, 'none shalt thou have but this sword!' upon which he wounded him mortally in the body, and the unhappy prince instantly fell down, and, bleeding and exhausted, continued faintly to implore his life. The scene was so piteous, that it is said at this moment to have shook the nerves, and moved the compassion, of the ruffian himself, who was about to come up, leaving the king still breathing, when his companions above threatened him with instant death if he did not finish the work. He then obeyed, and, assisted by the two Halls, completed the murder by repeated wounds.

P. F. Tytler, History of Scotland (*1841*). *This event occurred in 1436. It may be noted that, in all the account of stabbings and gore, Tytler's nineteenth century sense of delicacy prevents him from saying that the hiding-place was in fact the outfall of the royal privy.*

Advice to King James II

So many great barons were engaged in alliance with the house of Douglas, that it is said to have been a question in the King's mind, whether he should abide the conflict, or fly to France, and leave the throne to the earl. At this moment of extreme need, James found a trusty counsellor in his cousin-german, Kennedy, Archbishop of St Andrews, one of the wisest men of his time. The archbishop showed his advice in a sort of emblem or parable. He gave the King a bunch of arrows tied together with a thong of leather, and asked him to break them. The King said it was beyond his strength. 'That may be the case, bound together as they are,' replied the archbishop; 'but if you undo the strap, and take the arrows one by one, you may easily break them all in succession. And thus, my liege, you ought in wisdom to deal with the insurgent nobility.'

Sir Walter Scott (1771–1832), Tales of a Grandfather

The Earl of Atholl Entertains King James V

In the meantime, the King resolved to set out on a summer progress through his dominions, in the course of which an entertainment was given to the yet youthful monarch by the Earl of Atholl, which is strikingly illustrative of the times. This potent Highland chieftain, who perhaps indulged in the hope of succeeding to a portion of the power so lately wrested from Argyll, received his sovereign at his residence in Atholl, with a magnificence which rivalled the creations of romance. A rural palace curiously framed of green timber, was raised in a meadow defended at each angle by a high tower, hung in its various chambers with tapestry of silk and gold, lighted by windows of stained glass, and surrounded by a moat, in the manner of a feudal fortress. In this fairy mansion the king was lodged more sumptuously than in any of his own palaces; he slept on the softest down; listened to the sweetest music; saw the fountains around him flowing with muscadel and hippocras; angled for the most delicate fish which gleamed in the little streams and lakes in the meadow; or pursued the pastime of the chase amid woods and mountains which abounded with every species of game. The queen-mother accompanied her son; and an ambassador from the papal court having arrived shortly before, was invited to join in the royal progress. The splendour, profusion, and delicacy of this feudal entertainment, given by those whom he had been accustomed to consider barbarians, appeared almost miraculous, even to the warmth of an Italian imagination; and his astonishment was not diminished, when Atholl, at the departure of the royal cavalcade, declared that the palace which had given delight to his sovereign should never be profaned by a subject, and commanded the whole fabric, with its innumerable luxuries, to be given to the flames.

P. F. Tytler, History of Scotland (*1841*). *This was in 1532, when James V was nineteen.*

The Return of Queen Mary

The 19th day of August, 1561, betwixt seven and eight hours before noon, arrived Mary queen of Scotland, then widow, with two gallies out of France. . . The very face of the heaven, at the time of her arrival, did manifestly speak what comfort was brought into this country with her, to wit, sorrow, dolor, darkness, and all impiety; for in the memory of man, that day of the year was never seen a more dolorous face of the heaven, than was at her arrival, which two days after did so continue: for, besides the surface wet, and corruption of the air, the mist was so thick and dark, that scarce might any man espy another the length of two pair of butts; the sun was not seen to shine two days before, nor two days after. That forewarning gave God unto us but alas the most part were blind.

John Knox (c.1513–1572), History of the Reformation in Scotland

John Knox Recounts a Conversation with Queen Mary

The Queen in a vehement fume began to cry out, that never Prince was used as she was. 'I have', said she, 'borne with you in all your rigorous manner of speaking, both against myself and against my uncles; yea, I have sought your favour by all possible means; I offered unto you presence and audience, whensoever it pleased you to admonish me, and yet I cannot be quit of you; I vow to God I shall be once revenged.'

And with these words scarce could Murdock, her secret chamber boy, get napkins to hold her eyes dry, for the tears and the howling, besides womanly weeping, stayed her speech. The said John did patiently abide all the first fume, and at opportunity answered, 'True it is, Madam, your Grace and I have been at divers controversies, into the which I never perceived your Grace to be offended at me; but when it shall please God to deliver you from that bondage of darkness and error, wherein ye have been nourished, for the lack of true Doctrine, your Majesty will find the liberty of my tongue nothing offensive. . .'

'What have you to do,' said she, 'with my marriage? Or, what are you within the Commonwealth?'

'A subject born within the same,' said he, 'Madam; and albeit I be neither Earl, Lord nor Baron within it, yet God hath made me (how abject that ever I be in your eyes) a profitable and useful member within the same; yea, Madam, to me it appertaineth no less, to forewarn of such things as may hurt it, if I foresee them, than it doth to any one of the nobility; for both my vocation and conscience craveth plainness of me; and therefore, Madam, to yourself I say, that which I spake in public, whensoever the nobility of this realm shall be content, and consent, that you be subject to an unlawful husband, they do as much as in them lieth to renounce Christ, to banish the Truth, to betray the freedom of this realm, and perchance shall in the end do small comfort to yourself.'

At these words, howling was heard, and tears might have been seen in greater abundance than the matter required. . . The said John stood still, without any alteration of countenance, for a long time, while that the Queen gave place to her inordinate passion; and in the end he said, 'Madam, in God's presence I speak, I never delighted in the weeping of any of God's creatures; yea, I can scarcely well abide the tears of mine own boys, whom my own hands correct, much less can I rejoice in your Majesty's weeping; But seeing I have offered to you no just occasion to be offended, but have spoken the truth, as my vocation craves of me, I must sustain your Majesty's tears, rather than I dare hurt my conscience, or betray the Commonwealth by silence.'

Herewith was the Queen more offended, and commanded the said John to pass forth of the cabinet, and to abide further of her pleasure in the chamber.

John Knox, History of the Reformation in Scotland

A Lesson for King James VI

The Scottish government was determined to bring up the youthful King

James as the model of a Calvinist monarch, and recruited the distinguished but elderly humanist George Buchanan as his tutor. The tetchy Buchanan is said to have often chastised the young king, leaving James with a deep horror of him (and no sympathy for Calvinism).

The Master of Erskine, who was the prince's playmate, had a tame sparrow, possession of which was coveted by James, and ineffectually entreated from the owner. James had recourse to violence in order to obtain what he desired, and the one boy pulled and the other held until the poor sparrow was killed in the struggle. The loss of his little favourite caused the Master of Erskine to shed tears, and make, as is usual in such cases, a lusty outcry. This brought the matter under the notice of Buchanan, who . . . 'gave the king a box on the ear, and told him that what he had done was like a true bird of the bloody nest of which he had come'.

. . . One of the earliest propensities which he (James) discovered, was an excessive attachment to favourites; and this weakness, which ought to have been abandoned with the other characteristics of childhood, continued to retain its ascendancy during every stage of his life. His facility in complying with every request alarmed the prophetic sagacity of Buchanan. . . He presented the young king with two papers which he requested him to sign; and James, after having slightly interrogated him concerning their contents, readily appended his signature to each, without the precaution of even a cursory perusal. One of them was a formal transference of the regal authority for the term of fifteen days. Having quitted the royal presence, one of the courtiers accosted him with his usual salutation: but to this astonished nobleman he announced himself in the new character of a sovereign; and with that happy urbanity of humour, for which he was so distinguished, he began to assume the high demeanour of royalty. He afterwards preserved the same deportment towards the king himself; and when James expressed his amazement at such extraordinary conduct, Buchanan admonished him of having resigned the crown. This reply did not tend to lessen the monarch's surprise; for he now began to suspect his preceptor of mental derangement. Buchanan then produced the instrument by which he was formally invested; and, with the authority of a tutor, proceeded to remind him of the absurdity of assenting to petitions in so rash a manner.

Robert Chambers, Scottish Biographical Dictionary

Princess Elizabeth and the Gunpowder Plot

The peaceful round of Elizabeth's country life was broken in the November of 1605 by the alarm of the Gunpowder Plot. Combe Abbey was in the centre of the conspirators' country, and they had planned to capture her and declare her Queen in her father's stead. It is an oft-told tale, how Sir Everard Digby invited the Catholic gentlemen of the neighbourhood to a meet at Dunchurch; how this party was to have hunted no smaller game than the princess herself; and how Lord Harington received warning of the plot only just in time to place her in safety at Coventry. We have the latter's own account of the episode in a letter addressed to his cousin: ' . . . Her Highness doth often say, "What a queen I should have been by this means! I had rather have been with my Royal Father in the Parliament House than wear his Crown on such conditions." This poor Lady hath not yet recovered the surprize, and is very ill and troubled.'

R. S. Rait, Five Stuart Princesses (1902). *Elizabeth was then aged nine. She went on to become, briefly, Queen of Bohemia, and lived to see the downfall and restoration of her family.*

King William, Dr Carstairs, and the Thumbikins

Besides his immediate and official counsellors, King William gave, in private, much of his confidence to a clergyman named Carstairs, who was one of his chaplains. This gentleman had given strong proof of his fidelity and fortitude; for, having been arrested in Charles II's time, on account of the conspiracy called Jerviswood's Plot, he underwent the cruel torture of the thumbikins . . . that almost crushed the thumbs to pieces. After the success of the revolution, the magistrates of Edinburgh complimented Carstairs, then a man of importance, with a present of the implement of torture by which he had suffered. The King, it is said, heard of this, and desired to see the thumbikins. They were produced. He placed his thumbs in the engine, and desired Carstairs to turn the screw. 'I should wish to judge of your fortitude,' said the King, 'by experiencing the pain which you endured.' Carstairs obeyed, but turned the screws with a polite degree of attention not to injure the royal thumbs. 'This is unpleasant,' said the King, 'yet it might be endured. But you are trifling with me. Turn the engine so that I may really feel a share of the pain inflicted on you.' Carstairs, on this reiterated command, and jealous of his own reputation, turned the screws so sharply, that William cried for mercy, and owned he must have confessed any thing, true or false, rather than have endured the pain an instant longer.

Sir Walter Scott (1771–1832), Tales of a Grandfather. *William Carstairs became Principal of Edinburgh University, and died in 1715.*

Bonnie Prince Charlie Puts on the Kilt

'Now,' Bonnie Prince Charlie is reputed to have said, on first donning the kilt, 'now I should be a complete Highlander, if only I had the itch.'

G. S. Fraser (1915–1980), Scotland (1955). *On his post-Culloden wanderings, as reported to Robert Forbes, author of* The Lyon in Mourning, *by Patrick Grant who had escorted the Prince for some of the time, he was indeed troubled by lice, and was often 'plashed up to the navel, having no breeches, but a philabeg'.*

King George V at the Butts

You don't need to be musical to recognise a master pianist when you hear one. The authority of absolutism comes through. It was enough to see Walter Hagen swing a club, and he was no stylist, to know you were in the presence of greatness. So it was with King George. Till that morning I had only seen good shots shooting well. But he was something very different. His judgement of speed and distance was flawless. He never had to take a chance. He was so fast that the long shot at the bird which may be just out of range never happened. There was no 'tailoring' and there were no wounded birds. Every bird he hit was stone dead before it hit the heather. Where most guns would be happy to pull off two rights and lefts, one in front of the butt and one behind, the King took five birds and made it look easy. A single shot at long range, change guns, take a right and left; then, with the first gun reloaded, another right and left behind. As for the clean miss, something that happens to the best of shots from time to time, well, he did not miss. I suppose that even he must have had an off day now and again, but it would be hard to imagine it.

Then it was all over. There was shouting in the distance, flags were waved, beaters hove in sight and the dogs went out to do their part. I unfroze. It had been a good beat and birds were plentiful. The head-keeper was happy. Sir John was happy, the King was happy and I was miserable. Because the King was a better shot than my father and I would have to admit it.

The King's pony was led up while the game was being collected and the guns prepared to move on to the next beat. He mounted and signalled to father, who came across to speak with him. Father looked happy too.

'Now, then,' said the King. 'I hope you weren't disappointed with me. Now, tell us. Which of us is the better shot?'

'You, sir.' It was dragged out of me.

Then he was merciful. 'Don't forget, shooting is a matter of practice. And I get much more practice than your father does.'

A great white light dawned on me. Of course that was the explanation. Why hadn't I thought of it sooner?

Donald Sutherland, Butt and Ben (1963)

The Royal Handbag

The coronation of Queen Elizabeth in 1953 aroused controversy in Scotland. Already it had been ordained that the monarch's style was to be Elizabeth II, though no queen of that name had ever before reigned over the kingdom of

Scotland. When in June 1953 the Queen came to Edinburgh to be presented in the High Kirk of St Giles with the crown and other regalia, 'the Honours of Scotland', she was 'wearing not her sovereign robes but a coat and carrying a handbag. . . Sir Stanley Cursiter, the Queen's Limner, recorded the great event. From his painting, which hangs today in Holyroodhouse, he tactfully expunged the handbag.'

Arnold Kemp, The Hollow Drum (1993). *He also notes 'an old* Glasgow Herald *anecdote about the Service of State in St Giles'. Its reporter was waiting in the queue for admission. The befeathered and richly garbed man in front identified himself as the Marchmont Herald and was admitted. Our man of course then said: I am the* Glasgow Herald.'

LAIRDS, LORDS AND LADIES

Borgia-style Doings by the Ord of Caithness

In the year 1565 a tragedy of a striking character was enacted in a more northern district. Actuated by hatred to John , Earl of Sutherland, George, Earl of Caithness, is said to have instigated his cousin, Isobel Sinclair, wife of Gilbert Gordon of Gartay, to poison Sutherland and his Countess and their only son, Alexander Gordon. The Countess was soon to give birth to another child. Had the plot succeeded in its entirety the earldom, it was expected, would have gone to John Gordon, eldest son of Isobel, as being the next heir male. Isobel thus had a substantial inducement to stimulate her to the commission of the abominable deed. Soon an occasion presented itself, and one night when at supper in her house at Helmsdale it was contrived that Earl John and his Countess should partake of a poisoned draught. Alexander Gordon escaped the fate of his parents through having been late for supper, on account of having been out hunting, and when he did appear was sent home supperless by his father, whose suspicions had been, ere this, aroused. Five days thereafter the Earl and Countess died at Dunrobin. But three days ere this had occurred, a similar fate had overtaken him who, by his ambitious mother, had been designed for the earldom; for, on the day on which the unfortunate visitors had been poisoned, a draught of the same liquid had been, unwittingly, given to the young man by one of his mother's servants. This fact served to bring guilt home to Isobel, who was arrested, tried in Edinburgh, and condemned to death. She, however, died from illness on the day appointed for her execution, cursing, ere she departed, the Earl of Caithness as the base instigator of the diabolical act.

Dugald Mitchell, History of the Highlands and Gaelic Scotland (1900)

The Earl leaves Nothing to Chance

The story of how Gilbert, fourth Earl of Cassillis, secured possession of the Abbey lands after the Reformation is told in the *Historie of the Kennedyis*. 'This last Gilbertt was ane particuler manne, and ane wery greidy manne, and cairitt nocht how he gatt land, sa that he culd cum by the samin.' He entered into a conspiracy with the Abbot to obtain a lease of the property; but before the arrangements were completed the Abbot died. The Earl then found an ally in a monk of the Abbey 'quha culd counterfitt the Abbottis hand-writt, and all the haill Conventtis', and caused him to forge their signatures to the necessary document. When this had been done the Earl feared that the monk might reveal the matter, and engaged a knave to murder him. Then, fearing that his hireling might speak, he induced his uncle, Hew of Bargany, to accuse him of theft and hang him at Crossraguel. 'And sa the landis of Glenluse was conqueist.'

C. H. Dick, Highways and Byways in Galloway and Carrick (*1916*). *This was the Abbey of Glen Luce, the time the 1560s. The Earl also acquired the abbey lands of Crossraguel, by roasting the abbey's Commendator on a spit in the 'black vault' of Dunure Castle until he signed a document making over the Abbey's property to Cassillis. For this the Earl was fined by the Privy Council, but allowed to keep the land. As Dick points out, the earl was in charge of dispensing the king's justice in the county.*

Sir Thomas Urquhart is No Sportsman

There happened a gentleman of very good worth to stay awhile at my house, who one day, amongst many others, was pleased in the deadest time of all the winter, with a gun upon his shoulder, to search for a shot of some wildfowl; and after he had waded through many waters, taken excessive pains in quest of his game, and by means thereof had killed some five or six moorfowls and partridges, which he brought along with him to my house, he was, by some other gentlemen who chanced to alight at my gate as he entered in, very much commended for his love of sport; and as the fashion of most of our countrymen is not to praise one without dispraising another, I was highly blamed for not giving myself in that kind to the same exercise, having before my eyes so commendable a pattern to imitate. I answered, though the gentleman deserved praise for the evident proof he had given that day of his inclination to thrift and laboriousness, that nevertheless I was not to blame, seeing, whilst he was busied about that sport, I was employed in a diversion of another nature, such as optical secrets, mysteries of natural philosophie, reasons for the variety of colours, the finding out of the longitude, the squaring of a circle, and wayes to accomplish all trigonometrical calculations by signes, without tangents, with the same comprehensiveness of computation; which, in the estimation of learned men, would be accounted worth six hundred thousand partridges and as many moorfowls. That night past – the next morning I gave sixpence to a footman of mine to try his fortune with the gun during the time I should disport myself in the breaking of a young horse; and it so fell out, that by I had given myself a good heat by riding, the boy returned with a dozen of wildfowls, half moorfowl half partridge; whereat, being exceedingly well pleased, I alighted, gave him my horse to care for, and forthwith entered in to see my gentleman, the most especiall whereof was unable to rise out of his bed by reason of the gout and siatick, wherewith he was seized through his former day's toil.

Sir Thomas Urquhart (1611–1660), Logopandecteison

An Earl in Reduced Circumstances

A remarkable Death this yeare was that of John Steward, the old earl of Traquair, time, place and manner. This man was King James the 6 his cousin and courtier. King Charles the 1 sent him Lord High Commissioner down to Scotland, and sat Viceroy in the Parliament, June 1639. He early cast anchor at Court, the haven of happiness for all aspireing spirits, and this broke him; at last turnd the tennis ball of fortun. What power and sway, place and preferrment, he had then I need (not) mention; onely this copping then with the reverend bishops, and tampering under boord with the Covenanters, he acknowledged to be his bane. But whither by his own malversing, or by paction and resignation of his interest to his sone, or the immediat hand of God upon him, I search not; but he provd a true emblem of the vanity of the world. . . I saw him anno 1661 begging in the streets of Edinburgh. He was in an antick garb, wore a broad old hat, short clock, and pannien breeches; and I contributed in my quarters in the Canongate at that time, which amounted to a noble, which we gave him standing, and his hat off, the Master of Lovat, Culboky, Glenmoriston and myself; which piece of mony he receaved from my hand as humbly and thankfully as the poorest supplicant. It is said that at a time he had not to pay for cobling his bootes, and died as we hear in a poor coblers house. . .

James Fraser (1634–1699), Policratica Temporum, *from the Wardlaw Manuscript. John Stewart, Earl of Traquair, was a victim of politics and his own duplicity and greed. In 1640 he was lampooned by anagrams such as 'John Steuarte: Say No Treuth'; a contemporary pasquil said of him: 'False is thy harte, perfidious plots conceavinge, Thy tounge unfaithfull, and thy looks deceaving.'*

Sir Patrick Hume of Polwarth, and his Daughter Grizel

Sir Patrick Hume of Polwarth, afterwards Lord Marchmont, had a still more narrow escape. The party of guards sent to arrest him had stopped at the house of a friend to the Government to get refreshments, which were amply supplied to them. The lady of the house, who secretly favoured the Presbyterian interest, connected the appearance of this party, and the enquiries which they made concerning the road to Polwarth Castle, with some danger threatened to Sir Patrick Hume. She dared not write to apprize him, and still less durst she trust a messenger with any verbal communication. She therefore wrapt up a feather in a blank piece of paper, and sent it over the hills by a boy, while she detained the military party for as long as she could, without exciting suspicion. In the meantime, Sir Patrick received the token, and his acute apprehension being rendered yet more penetrating by a sense of danger, he at once comprehended that the feather was meant to convey a hint to him that he should fly.

Having long been particularly odious to the Government, Sir Patrick could think of no secure retreat above ground. A subterranean vault in Polwarth churchyard, being that in which his ancestors were buried, seemed the only safe place of refuge. The sole light admitted into this dreary cell was by a small slit at one end. A trusty domestic managed to convey a bed and bed-clothes to this dismal place, and here Sir Patrick lay concealed during the strict search that was made for him in every direction. His daughter, Grizell Hume, then about eighteen years of age, was intrusted with the task of conveying him food, which could only be brought to the vault at midnight. She had been bred up in the usual superstitions of the times, about ghosts and apparitions, but the duty which she was discharging to her father banished all such childish fears. . . But it was not enough to have a faithful messenger; much precaution was also necessary, to secure secretly, and by stealth, the provisions for the unfortunate recluse, since, if the victuals had been taken openly, the servants must naturally have suspected the purpose to which they were to be applied. Grizell Hume used, therefore, to abstract from the table, as secretly as she could, a portion of the family dinner. Sir Patrick Hume was fond of sheep's head (being a good Scotsman in all respects), and Grizell, aware of her father's taste, had slipt into her napkin a large part of one which was on the table, when one of her brothers, a boy too young to be trusted with the secret, bawled out, in his surprise at the disappearance of the victuals, 'Mamma, look at Grizzy – while we were supping the broth, she has eaten up all the sheep's head!'

Sir Walter Scott (1771–1832), Tales of a Grandfather. Polwarth's frustrated arrest was in 1684, year of the Rye House plot against Charles II and his brother.

Lord Belhaven Feigns Death

My Lord Belhaven, without any example I ever heard of in Scotland, with his Ladie a very witty woman's advyce, did faine death, and for seven years was taken by all for dead, yet now appears again safe and sound in his own house. He was much ingadged for Duke Hamilton: fearing the creditors might fall on his person and estate, and knowing, if he were reputed dead, his wife, by conjunct-fie and otherwayes, would keep his estate; he went, with his brother and two servants, towards England. These returned, affirming, that in Solway Sands my Lord was carried downe by the river, and they could no rescue him. His horse and his hatt they got, but when all search was made, his bodie could not be found. His Ladie and friends made great dool for him, and none controverts his death. In the mean time he goes beyond London and farmes a piece of ground, and lives very privatelie there. He had but one boy, a very hopefull youth, and prettie scholer; God strikes him with a fever, as his Mother said, but as others, with a fall from a horse, whereof in a few days he dies. In this reall death, by God's hand, who will no be mocked, the hope of that house perished. So soon as the Duke's debt was satisfied, by selling his own lands, the secret journies of my Lord to his own house were espied, and so much talked of, that he now appears in publict, for his great disrepute; and though he disposes of his estate to his good-son Sillertoun after his death, yet many think both their estates will goe.

  Robert Baillie, Diary (*1661*), *quoted in J. G. Fyfe (ed.)*, Scottish Diaries and Memoirs, 1550–1746 (*1907*)

Viscount Stair and the Source for 'Lucy Ashton'

His wife enjoyed the reputation of a witch during her lifetime, and long after her death. Tradition has preserved a variety of opposite tales about the marriage of the Lucy Ashton of the romance. One was, that the young lady's choice, which had been approved by her father and the friends of the family, did not meet with the sanction of the mother, who told her daughter, 'Weel, ye may marry him, but sair shall ye repent it.' On the nuptial night the bride and the bridegroom were locked in their chamber by her ladyship, who took away the key, to prevent such pleasantries as were not unusual on such occasions. Shrieks and groans were heard to issue from the apartment. The key was reluctantly given up by its keeper. Upon opening the door, the young lady was discovered on the bed bathed in blood, and the husband in a state of insanity, sitting in the chimney with his eyes glaring, and laughing in a hideous manner.

  Another tradition bears some sort of resemblance to the ordinary story. The marriage was a forced one, and after the pair had retired to the chamber where they were to sleep, the young lady attacked her husband with a knife, and wounded him very severely. When the door was opened, the youth was found on the floor weltering in his blood; the wife in a state of madness exclaiming, 'Take up your bonnie bridegroom!' She never regained her senses, and died mad; her husband recovered, but he would give no explanation on the subject, holding any reference, however trivial, to the event, as an affront on his honour.

James Maidment, A Book of Scottish Pasquils, 1578–1715 (1868). *The renown of Sir James Dalrymple, Viscount Stair (1619–1695), author of the* Institutes of the Law of Scotland, *has been clouded by the sensational events within his own family, of which that fictionalised by Scott and set to music by Donizetti was only one. (His daughter's actual name was Janet, and her ill-fated marriage was in 1669.) Another daughter, who became Countess of Dumfries, was also rumoured to be a witch and to have the power of flight. His son, the first Earl of Stair, was the architect of the Glencoe atrocity. His wife, Margaret Ross, 'had the reputation of being on very intimate terms with his Satanic majesty'. On her death she was buried standing upright in her coffin in the family vault at Kirkliston, having foretold that as long as she stood upright the fortunes of the Dalrymples would flourish.*

'Bare Betty'

It was during his college career at Edinburgh that he (Alexander, 4th Lord Elibank) met his future wife, Elizabeth, daughter of George Stirling, an eminent surgeon of Edinburgh, and Member of Parliament for that city. They were married at the ages of twenty-one and sixteen respectively. Elizabeth displayed from her early teens an independence of character which not infrequently led her into eccentricities. . . A somewhat rash Edinburgh minister when conducting 'public examinations' referred to Miss Elizabeth as 'Betty Stirling'. This caused deep offence to the dignity of the young lady: 'Mistress Betty' or 'Miss Betty', she said in tones of scathing rebuke, was the style of address to which she was accustomed, but certainly not 'bare Betty'. Needless to say, after this incident, she was always known in Edinburgh and district as 'bare Betty!'

A. C. *Murray*, The Five Sons of 'Bare Betty' (*1936*)

Masquerading Ladies

In the eighteenth century we find further examples of this craze for 'dressing up'. Anne Mackenzie, who afterwards married Sir William Dick of Prestonfield, and was the daughter of Lord Royston and granddaughter of the famous Earl of Cromarty, used to array herself and her maid in male attire and sally forth into the streets of Edinburgh in search of adventure. This the pair of adventurers generally managed to find, and would not infrequently end the night in the company of a number of intoxicated noblemen in the old Guard House in the High Street.

The Lady Euphemia Montgomerie, daughter of the 9th Earl of Eglinton by his first countess, provides another instance of an inveterate woman masquerader. She married the celebrated 'Union' Lockhart, whose notorious intrigues on behalf of the exiled Stuarts were no doubt furthered by his wife's clever disguises. Dressed as a man, she frequented the taverns and coffee houses of Edinburgh, and thus often obtained political information of the highest value to her husband. On one occasion a budget of important papers destined for the Government was in the hands of a Whig named Forbes. She accordingly disguised her two sons as women, and bade them waylay the guileless messenger and induce him to accompany them to a neighbouring alehouse. Here they speedily drank Mr Forbes under the table, after which they relieved him of his precious papers at their leisure.

Harry Graham, A Group of Scottish Women (*1908*). *See also 'Lady Pitlyal', below.*

An Encounter with Lord Lovat

He had all the atrocity of the oldest and most barbarous times. He began with the rape of his wife . . . there was no outrageous villainy of which he was not capable; yet he joined to the savageness of the worst feudal times the smoothness as well as the cunning of the most civilised hypocrisy. He was indeed proverbially known as a flatterer.

My uncle, Mr Rose of Kilravock, happened to be in Edinburgh when my Lord was passing through to the north, and called on his cousin, for such he was, to enquire after his health. Lord Lovat pressed him to be seated, but my uncle excused himself on the ground of his very short stay in town and having a great deal to do. On Lord Lovat's insisting, however, he took a seat, and at that instant a gentleman, whom the moment before Lord Lovat had embraced as his friend and given a very favourable character, left the room. He had no sooner done so, than Lovat abused him in the most unmeasured terms and said he was one of the greatest scoundrels in the world. Another and another of the company went away with not much better characters from his Lordship. At last, after a pretty long stay, my uncle took his leave. 'My dear Hugh', said Lovat, 'you said you were in a hurry, but if my watch does not deceive me, you have stayed half an hour'.

'That is true,' rejoined my uncle, 'but I took care you should have no audience to give my character to.'

'Ah!' said Lovat with perfect sang froid. 'You are a wag, Hugh; you are a wag.'

Henry Mackenzie (1745–1831), The Anecdotes and Egotisms of Henry Mackenzie

Social Distinctions in 18th-century Montrose

A notion of the stiff manner in which these old ladies could vindicate their principles or their personal dignity is afforded by the various stories told of Mrs Helen Carnegy, of Craigo. On one occasion, as she sat in an easy chair, having assumed the habits and privileges of age, Mr Mollison, the minister of the established Kirk, called on her to solicit for some charity. She did not like being asked for money, and, from her Jacobite principles, she certainly did not respect the Presbyterian Kirk. When he came in, she made only an inclination of the head, and when he said deprecatingly, 'Don't get up, madam,' she at once replied, 'Get up? I wadna rise out of my chair for King George himsel, let abee a Whig Minister.' The same lady had a graduated scale for her courtesies, and which was adapted to different individuals in the town according as she placed them in the scale of her consideration. As she liked a party at quadrille, she sent out her servant every morning to invite the ladies required to make up the game in these terms: 'Nelly, you'll gang to Lady Carnegy's, and mak my compliments, and ask the honour of her ladyship's company and that of the Miss Carnegies, to tea this evening; and if they canna come, gang to the Miss Mudies, and ask the pleasure of their company; and if they canna come, you may gang to Miss Hunter and ask the favour of her company; and if she canna come, gang to Lucky Spark and bid her come.'

John Timbs, A Century of Anecdote, 1760–1860 (1864), *though taken from Dean Ramsay, who notes that the lady died in 1818 at the age of ninety-one. In 1745 she would have been at just the right age to be one of the young ladies whom Duncan Forbes of Culloden sardonically noted as in love with the prince; but she remained true to him.*

Sleep-Walking

The Cromarty family had an hereditary tendency to somnambulism. One of that family, Captain Roderick, who was an intimate of my father's, told us a remarkable instance of this habit in an uncle of his with whom he lived. He happened one night to be awake with his uncle in bed whom he saw at sunrise get up, dress himself, put on his sword, and take some turns through the room, when suddenly he came to the side of the bed where his nephew was lying, who for fear of the consequence drew as far off as the bed would allow, when his uncle plunged the sword into the place of the bed where the boy had lain; then after a certain time returned to bed, and lay quiet till his usual hour of rising. Next morning the boy asked him if he had any frightful dream. 'Indeed I had, Rory, a horrible one; I dreamed that I had killed you.' His nephew told him of the escape which he had made; he bribed him to keep the matter secret, but it was afterwards discovered by his father, Lord Cromarty, who took the lad away from his uncle's.

Henry Mackenzie (1745–1831), The Anecdotes and Egotisms of Henry Mackenzie

The Captivity of Lady Grange

Mrs Erskine, otherwise called Lady Grange . . . was a woman of ungovernable temper, revengeful, and unscrupulous in the accomplishment of her ends. She had, by concealing herself under a sofa in her husband's business chamber, become acquainted with certain circumstances which would certainly, on being publicly divulged, have cost him his office; for during the Rising of 1715, some adherents of the House of Stuart frequently assembled in Lord Grange's mansion to concoct measures in support of the insurrection. Menaces of exposure, which were repeated by Mrs Erskine on every occasion she happened to differ with her husband, rendered the domestic condition of Lord Grange singularly wretched. At length she was induced, in 1730, to accept a separate maintenance. She took lodgings at Edinburgh, but she now proceeded to vex her husband with angry missives containing her wonted threats. . . Lord Grange consulted the members of his family – two adult sons and a daughter, married to the Earl of Kintore – and they unitedly concluded that it was necessary to place their unhappy relative under permanent restraint. Mrs Erskine was accordingly seized in her lodgings on the evening of Saturday, the 22nd April, 1732, and conducted from place to place by night journeys till she reached the Hebrides. For two years she was kept on the lonely island of Heisker, under the care of a peasant farmer. She was then removed to the remote and lonely St Kilda, where she remained seven years. Having succeeded after nine years' captivity in conveying information to the authorities of her detention, her husband and children, who had become aware of her proceeding, caused her to be conveyed to the Isle of Skye. There she died in May, 1745, after a captivity of thirteen years. Her remains were interred in the churchyard of Trumpin, Waternish, Isle of Skye.

C. *Rogers*, Traits of Scottish People (1867). *The author goes on to point out that Lord Grange, however vexed by his wife, was 'one of the most insincere and unscrupulous of his contemporaries. When at his country seat and among the clergy, he professed piety and exhibited the signs of a superior sanctity. In Edinburgh he was known as a debauchee.'*

'Old Q' Puts the Londoners off Milk

Many fabulous stories were circulated and believed respecting him; as, among others, that he wore a glass eye, that he used milk baths, and other idle tales. It is, however, a fact that the duke performed, in his own room, the scene of Paris and the Goddesses. Three of the most beautiful females to be found in London presented themselves before him, precisely as the divinities of Homer are supposed to have appeared to Paris on Mount Ida, while he, habited like 'the Dardan shepherd', holding a gilded apple in his hand, conferred the prize on her whom he deemed the fairest.

J. H. Jesse in George Selwyn and His Contemporaries (1843) says:

> There are still persons living who remember the almost universal
> prejudice against drinking milk which prevailed in the metropo-
> lis, in consequence of its being supposed that this common neces-
> sary of life might have been retailed from the daily lavations of
> the Duke of Queensberry.

*Daniel George, A Book of Characters (1959), quoting, in the first para-
graph, Wraxall's Posthumous Memoirs. William Douglas, Duke of
Queensberry (1724–1810), patron of the turf, was one of the richest men of
his time.*

Lord Buchan Protests

The Earl of Buchan (David Stuart Erskine), who died in his eighty-ninth
year, in 1829, was, in his early years, taken by the hand of Mr Pitt – but,
upon a subsequent occasion, when an election of Scotch Peers took place,
his lordship having, like the other Peers, received a government circular
letter, naming the individuals to be elected, he retired from public life, considering this letter to be an insult to the peerage of Scotland – and upon that
occasion wrote a letter to the minister, in which is this remarkable sentence:
'If the privileges of Scotland are endeavoured to be violated, I shall know
how to make my porridge in my helmet, and stir it with my sword!'

*John Timbs, A Century of Anecdote, 1760–1860 (1864). The Earl of
Buchan (1740–1829), founder of the Society of Antiquaries of Scotland,
was a somewhat eccentric figure. At his funeral the coffin was brought in
wrong way round, feet first; when some of those present suggested it should
be turned, Sir Walter Scott demurred, whispering that as the earl's head had
been turned years ago, he was actually the right way round anyway.*

The Wallace Statue

His essays in statuary were not all equally fortunate. The worst performance
was the erection of a colossal statue of Wallace on a bank above the Tweed on
the anniversary day of Stirling Bridge, a monstrosity which Scott prayed for
lightning to annihilate. On its base was an inscription in Buchan's best style:

In the name of my brave and worthy country, I dedicate this monument
as sacred to the memory of Wallace –

> The peerless knight of Ellerslie,
> Who woo'd on Ayr's romantic shore,
> The beaming torch of liberty;

And roaming round from sea to sea,
From glade obscure or gloomy rock,
His bold compatriots called to free
The realm from Edward's iron yoke.

The unveiling was disastrous. The Earl appeared before the statue with his speech in his hand and destiny on his brow; and at the discharge of a cannon the curtain was dropped. But to the horror of the honest enthusiast and the delight of the audience, the peerless knight of Ellerslie was revealed smoking a huge German tobacco-pipe, which some humourist had stuck in his mouth.

John Buchan (1875–1941), Some Eighteenth-Century Byways (1906). The statue, executed for the thrifty Earl of Buchan by a local man, remains in situ *at Dryburgh.*

Mystifications 1 – 'Lady Pitlyal'

'The cleverest people were the easiest mystified, and when once the deception took place, it mattered not how arrant the nonsense or how exaggerated the costume. Indeed, children and dogs were the only detectives.'
Clementina Stirling Graham, introductory letter to Mystifications.

Mr Russell inquired if she possessed any relics of Prince Charles from the time he used to spin with the lasses:
'Yes,' she said, 'I have a flech that loupit aff him upon my aunty, the Lady Brax, when she was helping him on wi' his short-gown; my aunty rowed it up in a sheet of white paper, and she keepit it in the tea-canister, and she ca'd it aye the King's Flech; and the laird, honest man, when he wanted a cup o' gude tea, sought aye a cup o' the Prince's mixture.' This produced peals of laughter, and her ladyship laughed as heartily as any of them. When somewhat composed again, she looked across the table to Mr Clerk, and offered to let him see it. 'It is now set on the pivot of my watch, and a' the warks gae round the flech in place of turning on a diamond.' Lord Gillies thought this flight would certainly betray her, and remarked to Mr Clerk that the flea must be painted on the watch, but Mr Clerk said he had known of relics being kept of the Prince quite as extraordinary as a flea; that Mr Murray of Simprim has a pocket-handkerchief in which Prince Charles had blown his nose. The Lady Pitlyal said her daughter did not value these things, and that she was resolved to leave it as a legacy to the Antiquarian Society.

Mystifications 2 – The Royal Tooth-Pick

She came as a Mrs Ramsay Speldin. . . She spoke of the 'gude auld times, when the laird of Fintry widna gie his youngest daughter to Abercairney, but tell'd him to tak them as God had gien them to him, or want'.

'And do you mind,' she continued, 'the grand ploys we had at the Midleton; and hoo Mrs Scott o' Gilhorn used to grind lilts out o' an auld kist to wauken her visitors i' the mornin'?

'And some o' them didna like it sair, tho' nane o' them had courage to tell her sae, but Anny Graham o' Duntrune.

'"Lord forgie ye," said Mrs Scott, "ye'll no gae to heaven, if ye dinna like music"; but Anny was never at a loss for an answer, and she said, "Mrs Scott – heaven's no the place I tak it to be, if there be auld wives in't playing on hand-organs."'

Many a story did Mrs Ramsay tell. The party drew their chairs closer to the sofa, and many a joke she related, till the room rung again with the merriment, and the laird, in ecstasy, caught her round the waist, exclaiming 'Oh! ye are a cantie wifie.'

The strangers seemed to think so too; they absolutely hung upon her, and she danced reels, first with the one, and then with the other, till the entrance of a servant with the newspapers produced a seasonable calm. They lay, however, untouched upon the table till Mrs Ramsay requested someone to read over the claims that were putting in for the King's coronation, and see if there was any mention of hers.

'What is your claim?' asked Mr Sandford.

'To pyke the King's teeth,' was the reply.

'You will think it very singular,' said Mr Guthrie, 'that I have never heard of it before; will you tell us how it originated?'

'It was in the time of James the First,' said she, 'that monarch came to pay a visit to the monks of Arbroath, and they brought him to Ferryden to eat a fish dinner at the house o' ane o' my forefathers. The family name, ye ken, was Speldin, and the dried fish was ca'd after them.

'The king was well satisfied wi' a'thing that was done to honour him. He was a very polished prince, and when he had eaten his dinner he turned round to the lady and sought a preen to pyke his teeth.

'And the lady, she took a fish bane and wipit it, and gae it to the king; and after he had cleaned his teeth wi' it, he said, "They're weel pykit."

'"And henceforth," continued he, "the Speldins o' Ferryden shall pyke the king's teeth at the coronation. And it shall be done wi' a fish bane, and a pearl out o' the South Esk on the end of it. And their crest shall be a lion's head wi' the teeth displayed, and the motto shall be weel pykit."'

Mr Sandford read over the claims, but there was no notice given of the Speldins.

'We maun just hae patience,' said Mrs Ramsay, 'and nae doubt it will appear in the next newspaper.'

Some one inquired who was the present representative.

'It's me,' replied Mrs Ramsay Speldin; 'and I mean to perform the office mysel.' The estate wad hae been mine too, had it existed; but Neptune, ye ken, is an ill neighbour, and the sea has washed it a' awa but a sand bunker or two, and the house I bide in at Ferryden.'

. . . Mr Sandford had in his own mind composed a letter to Sir Walter Scott, which was to have been written and despatched on the morrow, giving an account of this fine specimen of the true Scottish character whom he had met in the county of Angus.

We had meant to carry on the deception next morning, but the laird was too happy for concealment. Before the door was closed on the good-night of the ladies, he had disclosed the secret, and before we reached the top of the stairs, the gentlemen were scampering at our heels like a pack of hounds in full cry.

Clementina Stirling Graham, Mystifications (1859). *Her impersonation of 'Lady Pitlyal' fooled many people, including Francis Jeffrey, a sharp legal brain and editor of the* Edinburgh Review, *with whom she once had a lengthy interview.*

Sir Robert Menzies, of Aberfeldy, and Big Sandy, the Gamekeeper

One night Sir Robert thought he would go out himself, and would see whether Sandy was doing his duty. He took his gun with him. He went out above Sandy's house, and on his way past, he fired a shot. Sandy was in, and he heard the shot. He got up and took a big stick with him – he didn't take his dog at all – and went off after him. Sir Robert was going ahead, firing a shot now and again; but Sandy was overtaking him. Then Sir Robert saw Sandy, and when he saw him, he made as if to run away. Sandy was herding him down to the river Tay. When he had nearly caught up with him, Sir Robert turned round and lifted his gun to point it at him, but Sandy came at him with the stick and hit him on the side of the head and knocked him down where he was. Sandy jumped on his back and started beating and kicking him.

Sir Robert started to shout: 'Stop, now, Sandy! It's me! It's me, Sandy! Stop, Sandy!'

'Oh, yes, you b——, I know it's you, but I'll see you won't come again!'

He nearly killed the laird before he realised that it was he. Then he began to ask forgiveness, and he had to go with Sir Robert himself to the castle and leave him there, and Sir Robert spent a fortnight in bed. Sandy went home, and when Sir Robert got better, he sent for him. Sandy arrived.

'Well, here you are, Sandy,' he said.

'Oh, yes,' said Sandy, 'and I'm sure I didn't come here to get crowned'.

'Well, I don't know,' said Sir Robert. 'I was to blame, Sandy, and not you. They were telling me that you weren't looking after game at all, and I was asking you many a time were the poachers troubling you, and you were telling me they weren't; but I don't wonder the poachers weren't troubling you if you were dealing with them the way you were dealing with me.'

Angus MacLellan, The Furrow Behind Me (*1997*)

No Salute for the Laird

In those days we were brought up to salute the pillars of society when we met them on a country road. He told me, 'I've decided to stop saluting the laird. I'll salute the doctor and the minister and the dominie because they contribute to the community. But not the laird.' Then, in a sudden glint of a smile, he would descend from this high seriousness to country humour. 'The laird's nae what you would call very intelligent. There's naething in him except what he puts in with a spoon.'

R. F. Mackenzie, The Search For Scotland (*1989*). *The time was the 1920s, the speaker a friend of the young Mackenzie, 'a railway clerk conducting his own enquiries into the nature of life and society'.*

The Ilk Makes a Pass

The scholarly obsessions were woven up with a personality of endearing silliness or just plain childishness. I never knew why 'Woof, woof,' was his usual greeting (to people rather than to his Afghan hound), nor understood one or two other of his turns of phrase.

He could be difficult, the impossible recalcitrant little boy. He was un-predictable. Sukey Paravicini remembers sitting next to Ian at dinner some-where in Scotland when she was eighteen and being asked whether she was wearing any knickers. Thinking the brave rather than truthful answer was No, she was then told, 'Good, we're going to hold you upside-down by your legs and pour champagne over you.' Years later Iain found himself talking to Mrs Thatcher at some gathering or other and in effect proposi-tioned her (did she really reply that in his condition she didn't think he would be much use? It seems too good to be true?)

Geoffrey Wheatcroft, Absent Friends (*1989*). *Sir Ian Moncreiffe of that Ilk, Albany Herald (1919–1985), was a conspicuous social figure.*

Baron Wigan

Mention should also be made of the Earl of Crawford and Balcarres who really does not only live in but works for Scotland in the Arts. Oddly enough he also holds an English peerage under which he sits in the House of Lords. He is Baron Wigan, and has been known to call himself the original Wigan peer.

Moray McLaren, Understanding the Scots (*1956*)

LOVE, MARRIAGE AND WEDDINGS

Blind Date in Old Kintyre

These two saints – Couslan and Coivin – though both of unquestionable piety, seem to have had ideas on some subjects totally different. Couslan, for instance, inculcated in the strongest manner the indissolubility of the marriage tie ... and if lovers did not find it convenient to marry, their joining hands through a hole in a rude pillar near his church, was held, as it continued to be until almost the present day, an interim tie of mutual fidelity, so strong and sacred that, it is generally believed in the country, none ever broke it, who did not soon after break his neck, or meet with some other fatal accident.

Coivin, in his district, took quite a different course. He proposed that all who did not find themselves happy and contented in the married state should be indulged with the opportunity of parting, and making a second choice. For that purpose he instituted an annual solemnity, at which all the unhappy couples in his parish were to assemble at his church; and, at midnight, all present were sufficiently blindfolded, and ordered to surround the church three times at full speed, with a view of mixing the lots in the urn. The moment that ceremony was over, without allowing an instant to recover from the confusion, the word cabbag (seize quickly) was pronounced; upon which every man laid hold of the first female he met with; whether old or young, handsome or ugly, good or bad, she was his wife till the next anniversary return of the solemnity, when he had as good a chance (if he chose to submit himself to such hazard) of getting a worse or a better bargain.

Statistical Account of Scotland, *Parish of Campbeltown (1792)*

A Diplomatic Marriage That Failed

Kenneth, the eldest son of the chief of the Mackenzies, had married the Lady Margaret, the daughter of John, fourth Lord of the Isles, and it was hoped that by this matrimonial alliance the long feud between the two families would be healed. Like the marriages of so many Highland chiefs, it seems to have been purely a *mariage de convenance*, and the lady was blind of one eye. On the strength of the reconciliation that had taken place, Angus Og came to live in Easter Ross (some accounts say to Balconie and some to Balnagown), and at Christmas time he gave a great feast to all his friends and followers and the leading men of the north. Among the others, his brother-in-law, Kenneth, was invited, but he came without the Lady Margaret, which Angus Og regarded as a slight. Kenneth, on his side, soon also felt slighted: the house was very full, and Kenneth and his forty followers were lodged in the kiln. Kenneth had some cause for thinking that deliberate insult was intended, for a member of the family of Maclean of Dowart was acting as Angus Og's chamberlain, and he and Kenneth had fallen foul of each other some little time previously. Kenneth struck Maclean a blow on the ear which threw him to the ground, whereupon the followers of Angus Og rushed to arms, and Kenneth and his men had to beat a retreat.

He seized some boats lying by the river-bank and crossed over, taking care to sink those he did not need. He found shelter in a house on the opposite shore, but although he was now in no danger he considered it the direst humiliation to be obliged to spend Christmas on land that was not his and staying with a stranger. He therefore persuaded his host, 'who haid no syrnam but a patronimick', to adopt the name of Mackenzie, so that he might be able to say that he had slept under the roof of someone of his own name, and, although the next day was Christmas, he hurried off to interview the Bishop of Ross, who owned the land, and who was at Chanonry, and persuaded him, then and there, to feu him the small piece of land on which the house stood, 'lest Macdonald should brag that he had forced him on Christmas Eve to lodge at another man's discretion and not on his own heritage'.

Kenneth betook himself to Kinellan, where his father was staying. The old man tried to pacify the young one's anger, but, within a couple of days, further cause for quarrel was given, for Angus Og sent a message ordering the Mackenzies to leave Kinellan within twenty-four hours and threatening war to the knife if they did not obey. Kenneth sent back a defiant reply, and declared that as he no longer wished for peace with the Macdonalds he did not desire to have their relations about him, and he sent his wife, Lady Margaret, back, mounted on a one-eyed horse and attended by a one-eyed servant and followed by a one-eyed dog.

I. F. Grant, The Lordship of the Isles (1935). The energetic Angus Og Macdonald (fl. late 15th century) was the bastard son of John, last of the Lords of the Isles. He was murdered in 1490 by his own harper.

The Lady and the Gypsies

John, the sixth Earl of Cassillis, was a stern Covenanter, a man who would never allow anything he said to be misunderstood or misconstrued in any way. There was just one way with him – his own narrow, Cameronian path. A most admirable type, but an uncomfortable man to live with.

Thomas, first Earl of Haddington, the most brilliant lawyer of his day, had by his genius amassed a fortune and been elevated to the peerage.

This Earl of Haddington had a beautiful daughter, Lady Jean Hamilton, who loved and was loved by a gallant knight of about her own years, a Sir John Faa of Dunbar. Picture their consternation when one day the Earl warned his daughter to prepare for her nuptials as he had arranged with the Earl of Cassillis to give her to that nobleman in marriage!

Those were stern days, and the Lady Jean had no option but to bid her lover a last farewell and become the bride of the serious, uncompromising Carrick nobleman.

Some years passed, the Lady Jean had presented her husband with at least three children, and the old romantic attachment to the knight of Dunbar might well be considered a thing of the past. But that was not so, and Sir John Faa at least . . . had never forgotten his true love, and still nursed hopes of claiming her as his own.

Then was held the Assembly of Divines at Westminster, and Cassillis was one of those chosen to attend. Sir John Faa seized the opportunity, and disguising himself as a gypsy, and accompanied by fourteen real gypsies to help him in his mission, he came to Cassillis.

> The gypsies cam' to our gude lord's yett,
> And O but they sang sweetly;
> They sang sae sweet and sae very complete,
> That doun cam' our fair lady.
>
> And she cam' tripping down the stair,
> And all her maids before her:
> As soon as they saw her weel-faured face,
> They cuist the glamourie o'er her.

So much did they 'cuist the glamourie o'er her' that she produced white bread for them to eat, and then, alas! taking off her wedding-ring, she ran off with her old sweetheart.

She was no more than gone when the Earl unexpectedly returned from Westminster. On asking for his lady, the terrified domestics related what had happened.

Tired and fatigued as they were from their long journey, the Earl ordered his retainers to follow, tarrying an impatient moment until fresh horses were saddled, and then galloped off in pursuit of his Countess and her lover.

They had not far to go, and at a spot still called the Gypsies' Steps the band was overtaken, and captured to a man.

The Earl brought them back to Cassillis, and before the lady's horrified eyes hanged the fifteen men on his dule-tree!

D. C. Cuthbertson, Carrick Days (1933). The author notes that there is much to disprove, and nothing to substantiate, this story, which is told also in two different ballads; in one of which the gypsy lover is a real gypsy (Faa or Faw was the name of a leading Scots gypsy clan).

'Droit de Seigneur' on Ulva

The room where the Doctor spent the night is yet shown in the old mansion of the Macquarries. Dr Johnson and the chief, whom he was surprised to find a person of great politeness and intelligence, had a conversation about the usage known by the name of *Mercheta mulierum*, which formerly existed in Ulva, and was a fine paid to the chief by his vassals on the marriage of a virgin. In answer to the Doctor's reference to Blackstone, who has expressed his disbelief that any such claim on the part of landlords ever existed, Macquarrie informed the English sage that the eldest children of marriages were not esteemed among the Gael as among other nations, most of whom adhered to distinct laws of primogeniture, on account of the parentage of the eldest child, from the above-mentioned custom, being rendered doubtful; hence, brothers were very commonly preferred to the proper heirs apparent. He likewise told him that he himself had been in the habit of demanding a sheep, on occasion of every marriage in Ulva, for which he had substituted a fine of five shillings in money.

W. Anderson, Scottish Nation (*1863*). *The story stems from Dr Samuel Johnson's tour of the Western Isles, with James Boswell, in 1773.*

Marriage, Gretna Green Style

In spite of just two witnesses and their signatures being all that was required to authenticate such a marriage, it became usual for there to be a celebrant who was often termed a 'priest' who was in fact anyone who did not let the disapproval of the church prevent him earning money by giving a sought-after service which many people regarded as legal. These priests were seldom, as is sometimes thought, unfrocked clergy although there were a few. One was Rev. Thomas Blair, known as the 'curate of Cornwall', who was ejected in 1689 from the parish of Lennel, Berwickshire, for not praying for King William and Queen Mary and who thereafter not only performed irregular marriages but compounded his offence in several cases by backdating the marriage lines to conceal ante-nuptial fornication. All sorts of people became 'priests' – blacksmiths, shoemakers, bakers, anyone at all could, if they wished, put a couple through a ceremony in the presence of the required two witnesses and then provide a short certificate, the marriage lines, which set forth the particulars of the event.

Anne Gordon, Candie for the Foundling (*1992*)

Robert Burns – a Married Man

Shortly after my last return to Ayrshire, I married 'my Jean'. This was not in consequence of the attachment of romance, perhaps; but I had a long and much-loved fellow-creature's happiness or misery in my determination, and I durst not trifle with so important a deposit. Nor have I any cause to repent it. If I have not got polite tattle, modish manners, and fashionable dress, I am not sickened and disgusted with the multiform curse of boarding-school affectation; and I have got the handsomest figure, the sweetest temper, the soundest constitution, and the kindest heart in the county. Mrs Burns believes, as firmly as her creed, that I am *le plus bel esprit, et le plus honnete homme* in the universe; although she scarcely ever in her life, except the Scriptures of the Old and New Testament, and the Psalms of David in metre, spent five minutes together in either prose or verse. I must except, also, from this last, a certain late publication of Scots poems, which she has perused very devoutly; and all the ballads in the country as she has (O the partial lover! you will cry) the finest 'wood-note wild' I ever heard.

  Robert Burns (1759–1796), letter to Miss Peggy Chalmers, 16 September 1788, from The Letters of Robert Burns, *edited by R. Brimley Johnson (1928)*

An Unsuitable Match

I met the Lovats in their drawingroom; it was after their evening dinner, about 9 p.m. Lord Lovat said, 'I hear you have been keeping company with our son. It is causing a great deal of concern to his mother and I.' He spoke of the seriousness of marriage, and how it could not be entered upon lightly. Then Lady Lovat said, 'You know we are of the Roman Catholic faith'. She asked if I was old Kirk or Free Kirk. I replied,

  'I am a Jew; all who believe in and worship Christ are Jews, for he was born a Jew and brought up a Jew, baptised a Jew, practised the rites of the Jewish faith, died and rose triumphantly from the grave a Jew, the one and only mediator between God and Man.'

  I told them I respect their beliefs in the same way as I would those of a Hindoo or Moslem, but personally I did not believe the virgin Mary had divine power any more than Mary Stuart or Mary Tudor. I also do not believe the Pope is infallible. Tam said, 'A good point, which more than demonstrates how unsuitable you are to each other.'

  Mormond Tam now spoke of his son's noble birth and background. I told him there is only one kind of birth, natural or caesarean, and a pretty painful business it is. The tinkie wife on Strichen moss and Mrs Fraser in her fine bedroom went through the same process; twice I had acted as necessary girl to Benffs Kitta the howdie wife and saw at first hand the agony women endure. Lady Cauldock kept glancing at me, then said, 'I hope you have not got yourself into trouble.'

  'I am a virgin woman,' I replied, 'and your son tells me he is a virgin man and I believe him.' Tam said to think sensibly of what might only be a passing fancy. The best of all this, Shemmy had never asked me to marry or even actually suggested it, I do not know what he had said to them but obviously they were determined to end our friendship. Tam said one should think well from every angle, and it might end in marriage. I knew what he meant, but the wifie took him up wrong and in an unguarded moment of weakness, showed her true colours. 'Tam, how could you say such a thing, it is unthinkable for Simon to marry the fishwife's daughter.'

She was beautifully attired in cream silk; the heavy piping and large buttons of her dress were covered in a fine check Fraser tartan. I decided 'Now I shall let you have it, I will take the wind out of your sails.' I asked what she thought she was. He replied one must maintain standards; I told them they would be in a bonny mess if the poor disappeared overnight, and 'it will be a bad day for you when they decide to maintain standards'. He said, 'This is a democracy, with reasonable opportunity for all'; I said, 'That is the biggest load of dirt since the dung cart went round the Broch gathering the dry closets yesterday.' He was excited and started to habber.

'Please do not talk such vulgarity in the presence of my wife.'

. . . I said to the wifie, 'As for you, madam, your heart is as cold as your backside is reputed to be.' Tam rang for the butler. He said, 'N-n-n-never has anybody sp-sp-sp-spoken to her ladyship in such a manner.' He said to the butler, 'Show Miss Watt to the door.'

Christian Watt (1833–1923), The Christian Watt Papers, *edited by David Fraser (1983). Lady Lovat found the Buchan climate cold and even in summer was reputed to wear two pairs of flannel drawers, hence her local nickname 'Lady Cauldock' (Scot. cold backside). 'The Broch' is Fraserburgh.*

MERCHANT VENTURERS

Darien – First Impression of the Promised Land

November 4th, 1698: – We came into the great Harbour of Caledonia. It is a most excellent one, for it is about a league in length from N.W. to S.E. It is about half a mile broad at the mouth, and in some places a mile and more farther in. It is large enough to contain 500 sail of ships. The greatest part of it is land-lock'd, so that it is safe, and cannot be touch't by any Wind that can blow. The Harbour and the Sea makes the Land that lyes betwixt them a Peninsula. There is a point of the Peninsula at the mouth of the Harbour, that may be fortify'd against a Navy. This Point secures the Harbour, so that no Ship can enter but must be within reach of their Guns. . . In short, it may be made impregnable, and there is bounds enough within it, if it were all cultivated, to afford 10,000 hogsheads of sugar every year. The Soil is rich, the Air good and temperate, the Water is sweet, and everything contributes to make it healthful and convenient. . .

We are certainly much bound to Providence in this affair; for as we were searching for the place we were directed to, we found this, and though the Privateers had been so often at Golden Island, and though English, Dutch and French had been all over this coast, from Portobelo to Cartagena, yet never one of them made the discovery; even the Spanish themselves never knew of this place. Besides, for as great a secret as we thought the project, it was known all the West Indies over, and yet it was not in their power to crush it. At Madera they seemed to know it; at St Thomas I'm sure they knew it; at Portobelo their intelligence was so good that they knew the names of all our Councillors and Captains of Ships before we landed, and had that particular observation that there were four Roberts among them . . . I have already seen Dutch, French and English all at the same time in our Harbour, and all of them wonder what the rest of the world have been thinking on, when we came hither to the best Harbour of America, in the best place of it.

From the journal of one of the colonists aboard the Endeavour, *quoted in* J. G. Fyfe (ed.) Scottish Diaries And Memoirs, 1550–1746 (1907)

A Rising Man

Mr Miller was a man of few words, but his words were to the point and he spoke as a man who thoroughly understood the business to be done. There was little or no geniality in his manner and I must say the truth that the impression he made on me was not prepossessing. I perceived at once the delicacy of our position towards each other and the wide difference between the life of a dependence under countrymen abroad and a life at home. A young man may be a clerk or manager of a counting house in Liverpool or Glasgow without any personal or social contact with his employer. He has a given work to do and a given time in which to do it, and his domestic home is his castle against the world, and an asylum from capricious tempers he may find in his place of business employment. According to the custom of British mercantile establishments in foreign cities the employers and the employed live together under the same roof and sit at the same table – hence the difficulty to draw and preserve the line which marks the separation between the two parties.

My employer was then about thirty or thirty three-years of age and one of the handsomest men I ever saw. He dressed with taste suited to the climate, and as he had two of the finest horses in Buenos Ayres his gracefulness as a horseman was admired. He came originally from Aberdeenshire, as an adventurer to Brazil, and after Buenos Ayres had gained its independence by the overthrow of the British forces in 1808 he had entered into partnership with Mr Eyes from Liverpool and together they had created a large business.

To a superficial hearer his language was free from the Scottish accent; he spoke as if he wished to conceal his northern Scottish origin – but as soon may the Ethiopian change his skin, or the leopard his spots as a Scottish man the peculiar drawl of his mother tongue! These remarks give the clue to his characteristic passion of pride, and its converse a sense of shame. I had been informed, and my own quick observation confirmed, the report that pride was his ruling passion, and that nothing mortified it more than an allusion to his humble social origin. It was said that his father was a working shoemaker who had given his sons superior education to enable them to rise in the world and acquire fortune. When I joined him he had Alexander Miller, a brother a few years younger than himself, and a second brother was expected from the north of Scotland before the end of the year. He was thus not only realising a fortune for himself, but also putting his two brothers in a position to assist him and raise themselves. What a weakness to be ashamed to acknowledge the honest industry of a hardworking father! especially when the fruit of that labour is applied for the benefit of the sons.

James Macintyre, A Merchant's Tale: Life and Adventures of a Nineteenth-Century Scottish Trader, *edited by Jocelyn Hemming and Nancy Thurley* (1994)

MOUNTAINS

Ben Nevis in Winter

We were in a curious situation, for we had never enjoyed a single ray of sunshine throughout the day. It was always above us and elsewhere. Now we were only spectators of the reflection of a sunset, but our elevation enabled us to gaze on the brilliant rose-pink of the snows on Carn Mor Dearg, the Aonachs, and the more distant ranges, tints as brilliant as those of any Alpine sunset and even more varied and delicate. As the moment of sunset approached the changes became more rapid – from golden to delicate rose-pink, then to full-blooded crimson, and finally, quite suddenly, to a ghostly pallor. The visibility extended to the Cairngorms, which seemed to be floating in a luminous golden haze; and the line of the horizon was marked by a pale blue band. Just before sunset this band developed a semi-circular and darker protuberance about the apex of the shadow of Ben Nevis. As the sun went down this 'anti-sun' rose and swelled out more and more. About a minute later the blue band along the horizon again became level and darker in colour. Then it gradually broadened, shading from purple through violet to brilliant heliotrope, above which the sky was bright green slowly merging into grey-blue higher up – an intensely cold sunset, typical of fine weather and hard frost. This was the first time I had experienced the Scottish counterpart of the phenomenon so graphically described by Sir Leslie Stephen in connection with a sunset viewed from the summit of Mont Blanc.

Meanwhile Murray was leading in a gingerly manner round a corner and the rope was running out by inches at a time. For long periods nothing whatever seemed to be happening; then there came a thunderous roar of great slabs of hard snow falling clear past an overhang into the depths of Observatory Gully. At length Murray pulled in the slack and summoned me to join him. As I proceeded I ceased to wonder at the time taken by the leader. There had been much step-cutting on small and insecure ledges, and it was a fine piece of leadership. A further short run-out of rope saw Murray on the crest of the ridge where we eventually joined him. It was very late indeed, but we hardly troubled about that, for the sight held us spellbound. We looked across the depression between Nevis and Carn Dearg as if through a 'magic casement' to a golden-orange sea of cloud stretching away over the Atlantic, and still fringed on the horizon by the fiery line of retreating day. The sea was perfectly level but delicately moulded into orange wavelets. It was lapping against the walls of Ben Nevis itself, creeping up the valley of the Allt a'Mhuillinn, breaking in torn waves against the Carn Dearg Buttress – peacefully but inexorably advancing like the sweep of night. We felt that we were looking 'on the foam of perilous seas, in faery lands forlorn', and it was not difficult to enter into the imaginative soul of the old Gaelic bards who gazed across the western seas at sunset with the assurance that somewhere amidst these distant fiery wavelets must lie the Tir-nan-Og, the isles of the blest and the ever-young.

But there were hard realities to be faced, and a sweep of icy wind soon set us moving along the crest. It was easy to lower ourselves into the Tower Gap, but the far side was sheathed in ice and frost crystals, menacing and impossible-looking. Murray made the first attempt to scale the wall by means of the groove overlooking Glover's Chimney, but he could make nothing of it; then I had a look at the flank above Tower Gully, but I fared no better. There was no longer any rhapsodising about nature, for the keen wind whistled through the Gap, and our one thought was to avoid benightment in such inhospitable regions. We had 180 feet of line, and we thought of retreating down the ice slope into Tower Gully: but the long descent of Observatory Gully would have taken hours in the darkness, especially by three dispirited and defeated men. There must surely be some other way. Then someone hit upon the idea of throwing the rope over the rocky bulge above us. This was not altogether easy on account of the wind, but eventually it was done. It just happened that it was my end of the rope which drew up tight against the icy groove, so up I had to go like a sack of corn, with much undignified clawing and scrabbling, but, of course, I retained the naive illusion that I was only receiving moral support from the rope. Later on, when I was securely anchored above and was helping the others, I revised this first impression although it must be admitted that the whole manoeuvre did not take a long time to execute.

One lesser difficulty followed at a little groove between some huge blocks, and the way was clear to the steep, shallow chimney to the top. The snow was very deep and powdery, and it was necessary for the party to anchor carefully as the leader clambered up the final short wall on to the level snowfield. There was no cornice. As we took off the rope on the summit plateau and shook hands on our hard-earned victory the time was about a quarter to six.

As becomes Scottish mountaineers, heirs to the Munro tradition and no mere rock or ice gymnasts, we advanced to the summit of the Ben. There was still a faint orange glow in the west and one bright, twinkling light at the edge of that cloudy sea. Murray thought it was a lighthouse, but the idea was fantastic. The light shone out brightly for about a minute and then vanished for good. It was our first sight of the planet Venus as an evening star. The night was brilliant with moon, stars and planets. Jupiter, Mars and Saturn shone brightly, almost in a straight line. The moon was about first quarter and the crests of the cloud waves shone like silver. Except for two rocky islets, the summits of Sgurr a'Mhaim in Mamore and Bidean nam Bian in Glencoe, the cloud sea was unbroken. Perhaps it was the spiritual exuberance of victory, but we all felt supremely fit and light of foot; the air was no longer chill but invigorating, like wine. The frost was actually keen, for the knees and seats of our breeches were hard as boards. I think we all wished that we could go on climbing for ever in that cheerful moonlight and limpid atmosphere.

J. H. B. Bell, Ben Nevis, Tower Ridge, *from the* Scottish Mountaineering Club Journal, 1940. *Murray was W. H. Murray, himself a notable writer on mountaineering.*

'Ferlas Mor'

The Great Grey Man of Ben Macdhui, or Ferlas Mor as he is called in the Gaelic, is Scotland's Abominable Snowman. . . I know two men who claim to have heard Ferlas Mor. The first was alone, heading over Macdhui for Corrour on a night when the snow had a hard, crisp crust through which his boots broke at every step. He reached the summit, and it was while he was descending the slopes which fall towards the Larig that he heard footsteps behind him, footsteps not in the rhythm of his own, but occurring only once for every three steps he took.

'I felt a queer, crinkly feeling in the back of my neck,' he told me, 'but I said to myself, "This is silly. There must be a reason for it." So I stopped and the footsteps stopped, and I sat down and tried to reason it out. I could see nothing. There was a moon about somewhere, but the mist was fairly thick. The only thing I could make of it was that when my boots broke through the snowcrust they made some sort of echo. But then every step should have echoed, and not just this regular one-in-three. I was scared stiff. I got up and walked on, trying hard not to look behind me. I got down all right – the footsteps stopped a thousand feet above the Larig – and I didn't run. But, man, if anything had as much as said "Boo!" behind me, I'd have been down to Corrour like a streak of lightning.'

The second man's experience was roughly similar. He was on Macdhui, and alone. He heard footsteps. He was climbing in daylight, in summer; but so dense was the mist that he was working by compass, and visibility was almost as poor as it would have been at night. The footsteps he heard were made by something or some one trudging up the fine screes which decorate the upper parts of the mountain, a thing not extraordinary in itself, though the steps were only a few yards behind him, but exceedingly odd when the mist suddenly cleared and he could see no living thing on the mountain, at that point devoid of cover of any kind.

'Did the steps follow yours exactly?' I asked him.

'No,' he said, 'that was the funny thing. They didn't. They were regular all right; but the queer thing was that they seemed to come once for every two and a half steps I took.'

He thought it queerer still when I told him the other man's story. You see, he was long-legged and six feet tall, and the first was only five-feet-seven!

Alastair Borthwick, Always a Little Further (1947)

Sensitivity About the Paps of Jura

Northward lie Islay and the fine Island of Jura with its two beautiful rounded hills which are called the Paps of Jura: they are like the magnificent breasts of some giantess lying outstretched on the ocean-bed. The unambiguity of these two hemispheres rising from the level plain of the sea adds a touch of human pathos to their majesty, and evokes with peculiar force the feeling that everyone must have had at moments in looking at nature: that it is a dumb living thing which has suffered for long ages an unjust but ordained imprisonment. . . I wanted to preserve some memento of them and went over to a stationery booth to buy a postcard of the Paps of Jura.

Gentility may spring from misdirected or thwarted natural sensibility as well as from social fear or snobbishness, and the Highlanders are a peculiarly sensitive people. Machrihanish is an artificial eruption on a Highland shore where it is difficult for a Highlander to know what the social and moral code is. The two hills are there in any case for anyone to look at if he wishes. To come to the point, I could not buy nor beg a single picture-postcard of the Paps of Jura. At last I managed to find a postcard with the legend: 'Machrihanish, with a distant view of the Jura Hills', a triumph of trick photography in which by some inexplicable manipulation of perspective two tiny non-committal almost invisible mounds were shown in the extreme right-hand corner. I bought this postcard and still treasure it.

Edwin Muir (1887–1959), Scottish Journey (1935)

Neophytes in Bothy Society

I was one of a motley collection of Gordon's College schoolboys who had chosen to spend Hogmanay in the Cairngorms, using as our base camp Bob Scott's bothy at Luibeg. We discovered that more than forty climbers were housed in various outbuildings and that we had been relegated to the stick shed as befitting our lowly station. Minor snowdrifts formed inside the building and an indoor thermometer recorded 40 degrees of frost. Next door in the bothy, which was reserved for the hierarchy and where the heat from a blazing fire drove one back to the farthermost corners, were two very celebrated mountaineers – Bill Brooker and Mac Smith. We soon guessed their identity by the excited buzz of conversation that signalled their return from a climb, the sudden hush as they entered the bothy, and the easy grace with which they accepted the seats of honour nearest the fire. Mac Smith was the . . . chieftain of the Luibeg Clan – an all-round mountaineer who had taken part in almost every important summer or winter event in recent years. He knew the Cairngorms better than any of his contemporaries, and they would have been the first to admit it. The bothy armchair, which has only recently been vacated and converted to firewood, was Mac's prerogative – a rustic throne. Bill Brooker, (the young Lochinvar), cut a more dashing figure, the complete counterpart to Mac's slightly reserved manner. To all outward appearances he was merely another pimply-faced schoolboy like ourselves, full of wild talk. But then who could forget that this was the same young heretic who had but recently burst into the climbing arena with a series of routes which had defied the best efforts of preceding generations?

. . . These were the real mountaineers – not mere 'hill-bashers' like ourselves who had that day tramped many an endless mile in search of a minor 3,000-foot Munro top away out in the middle of the Great Moss. We had built a little cairn on what appeared the most elevated undulation and had been well satisfied with our day's achievement. These men spoke of icy vigils and gigantic ice-falls; routes that finished long after dark; remote bivouacs in faraway corries; riotous nights in bothies . . . these were the very elements missing from our scholarly conception of mountaineering which had led us with mathematical precision up and down the weary lists of Munro's Tables.

I do not know what impression we left behind. A few of our number were kilted and this earned us the title of the 'Horrible Heelanders', a name which stuck. I remember listening with envy to the two demi-gods as they planned the first winter ascent of Crystal Ridge, success already a foregone conclusion. Late next night when they did not return at the appointed hour, we spoke hopefully of a search party, but this merely earned for us the derision of the company. Their confidence was soon rewarded by the arrival of the victors, eyebrows caked with frozen drift, faces glowing with the heat of battle. . .

Tom Patey, Cairngorm Commentary, The Scottish Mountaineering Club Journal, 1962

Suilven – 'the Monster'

For two years, since my first sight of it, I had been haunted by the mountain – an astonishing pillar, seen endways from the Oykell road; from the shores of Loch Assynt, a crouching monster. . .

This day, to put off the moment of seeing it face to face, I chose to climb first on the easy Canisp, which blocks the view; then, grasping the summit cairn firmly, I turned to look at Suilven across the gash of Glen Dorcha. A monster indeed, but at the moment passive. I started up its gentle slopes at the south-east end in sun; but once embarked on the long ridge, down came the mist. Suilven is made up of three humped masses connected by very narrow *bealachs*; as I came over the top of Meall Bheag, the first hump, I could dimly see the slopes of Meall Mheadhonach, the second, but I could not see down to the *bealach* in between; when I had groped my way down I found that it consisted of one rock, across which you could straddle – a nice place, and by some freak of wind the mist cleared to the south-west as I sat there a minute, and though I could not see the top I had left five minutes ago, I could see the hills of Skye forty miles away. On the second and broader *bealach*, connecting Meall Mheadhonach with Caisteal Liath, the highest, I met a party of three coming back from the top, and realised from their sad and dripping mackintoshes just how wet I must be myself. An easy forty minutes took me to the top of Caisteal Liath – the Grey Castle that faces the sea, more majestic and less terrifying than the monster seen from Canisp or the spike from the road to Lairg. But I could not see the sea, or Lochinver, or the little lochans starring the moor all round the base of Suilven; and I was beginning to tire of walking along the wet spine of the monster enclosed in mist. How dull it would be, I told myself, to retrace my steps to the *bealach* where I had met the other party, and take the usual route down the gully. When my other voice remarked that the dull thing was the only sensible thing on a day like this, I dismissed it as the devil's guile. Quite wrongly; the devil in fact was busy at my elbow as I peered over the edge of the castle ramparts, pointing out to me that there was green nearly all the way down, and suggesting that I should save time and energy by descending straight to the string of lochans on Suilven's northern base.

Gaily I started down. In a quarter of an hour I realised three things. First, that this north face of the Grey Castle is made up of continuous rock bands, ten to fifteen feet high, with grassy terraces between (from above, of course, only the terraces are visible); second, that these terraces slope outwards; third, that it would be difficult and lengthy to retrace my steps because I had zigzagged down a good deal, finding the weak place in each rock band. Although I knew now which voice had been the devil's, this last consideration made me decide to go on, scrambling somehow down the rock band, then prowling along the grass terrace to find the best place to attack the next band. This worked all right for a dozen rounds or so; then came an unfairly high band, perhaps twenty feet, with no visible cracks, and wet tufts of grass the only apparent holds. I scouted along the terrace, and finally saw a small ledge about seven feet down, and a possible foothold about six feet lower. I swung cautiously on to the ledge, did a complicated doubling-up to shoot my feet down to the hold – it was wet and slimy; I had to make up my mind quickly, and I did so by praying hard and jumping for the grass terrace below. I landed square, and everything would have been perfectly all right but for my rucksack, which I had entirely forgotten, and which now swung outwards and twitched me down over the next band. It was a moderate one, only about twelve feet, and the terrace below was flatter than most. So I stopped after one bound, and for two minutes sat and laughed in a loud and silly way at my extremely humiliating but very funny situation. 'Here is one calling herself a mountaineer', I mocked, 'fancying her judgment, her eye for a good route, her caution on rock, reduced to falling off a mountain to get down it!'

Janet Adam Smith, Mountain Holidays (1946). *A bealach is a hill pass.*

Climbing Ben Ledi

The ascent is no' an extremely difficult thing, an' it's no very easy aither. I've been twice on the tap, an' took the easiest way, first by gain wast to a farmhoose aboot three miles or so fae Callender, an' up a cart-road the fouk tak for peats. Gaen this way, ye haud up the sooth wast ridge, an' the climb is no sae steep as the way we took this year. This time we began to climb just aboon the brig across the Lubnaig water, an' had aboot an oor's hard wark thro' boggie grund afore we got to the real mountain. There's nae less than seven great high shoulders to climb this way, an' when ye're at the fit o' ony ane o' them, you're like to think, noo, if I was up here I'm at the tap. But na, my boy, you've a lot to do yet: tak' it easy, you'll win up some time, so dinna be disappointed when you get up there if ye see anither as high, an' after that anither, an' anither. Sit ye doon an' tak' a rest here at this stream, and gies a drink. There's nae hurry – you'll fag i' the end o'd if ye tak na' care.

The truth is, if you're to gae up Benledi, you maun mak' up your mind to do'd. It's no to be trifled wi'. The tap o'd lies a gude bittie north yet, an' canna be seen fae Callender even. Yon that ye thocht was the head yestreen is the third ridge fae the tap only. I dare say if you'd kent this ye wadna been here ee'noo.

'*Tammy Trampalot*', Nine Days in the Highlands, *from the* People's Journal (1858), *quoted in William Donaldson*, The Language of the People (1989)

Blaeberries

Climbing towards the summit of the Cobbler one July day, I was hot and thirsty, but the sun, hotter and thirstier, had been there before me and drunk the runnels dry. Lying flat in a bed of Blaeberries I thrust handfuls of the purple fruit into my mouth, and, greatly refreshed, gained the summit. An hour or so later, having descended from the hill, I was walking along the road that runs round the head of the loch to Arrochar. Meeting people who smiled pleasantly to me, I smiled pleasantly to them. But they seemed unusually pleasant, and I began to wonder what was wrong. Though I knew it was nothing about my dress, for I always climb mountains in my ordinary clothes, I adjusted my tie. Their pleasantness at last became unbearable, and I darted into the Arrochar hotel. 'Who have you been kissing today?' asked the barman. 'Blaeberries,' I replied, seeing in the mirror at his back the large purple stain on my mouth.

Andrew Young (1884–1971), A Prospect of Flowers (*1945*)

MUSIC AND MUSICIANS

Stone Age Singing: a Speculation

It even seems possible that the traditional music of the Hebrides and of other parts of Scotland, based upon the pentatonic scale (the normal seven-tone scale but without the semi-tone intervals), may have very early origins, well before the arrival of the first Celts in the Islands. This scale, particularly associated with vocal rather than instrumental music, has a limited distribution in modern or recent Europe, where the few areas in which it survives are on the extreme fringes of the north and north-west, including Lapland and Scotland, and to a less extent Ireland, Finland and the Faeroes: in northern Asia it extends through Siberia to Mongolia and beyond. Such a survival-pattern suggests that we are dealing with the remnants of an ancient tradition, elsewhere submerged by later musical scales of seven-note type, and the rarity of the pentatonic scale in Ireland, and still more in Wales and Brittany, implies that it is not to be associated with the Celtic-speaking peoples. Such things are in their very nature incapable of proof, but we may have here a vocal tradition surviving from remote prehistory, and when we sing 'Auld Lang Syne' we may be perpetuating the melodic conventions of the Circumpolar Stone Age.

Stuart Piggott, Scotland Before History (*1958*)

The Gairloch Pipers

In 1609 an ancestor of mine . . . John Roy Mackenzie, paid a visit to the laird of Reay in Sutherland . . . on John Roy's return from his visit to Tongue House, Mackay accompanied him as far as the Meikle Ferry, on the Kyle of

Sutherland. On their arrival at the ferry it seems there was another gentle-man crossing, accompanied by a groom, who attempted to prevent anyone entering the boat but his master and his party. Mackay had his piper with him, a young, handsome lad of only seventeen summers. A scuffle ensued between the piper and the groom, the former drew his dirk, and with one blow cut off the groom's hand at the wrist.

The laird of Reay at once said to his piper: 'Rory, I cannot keep you with me any longer; you must at once fly the country and save your life.' John Roy said: 'Will you come with me to Gairloch, Rory?' And the piper was only too glad to accept the offer.

. . . Rory was piper in succession to four of the Gairloch Lairds. . . Rory did not marry till he was sixty years old. He had just the one son, the cel-ebrated blind piper. . . He was not blind from birth, as has been errone-ously stated, but was deprived of his sight by smallpox when about seven years old. He was known as Iain Dall (Blind John) or *an Piobaire Dall* (the Blind Piper). After mastering the first principles of pipe music under his father's tuition, he was sent to the celebrated Macrimmon in Skye to finish his musical education. He remained seven years with Macrimmon, and then returned to his native parish. . . When he was with Macrimmon there were no fewer than eleven other apprentices studying with the master piper, but Iain Dall outstripped them all, and thus gained for himself the envy and ill-will of the others. On one occasion, as Iain and another apprentice were playing the same tune alternately, Macrimmon asked the other lad why he did not play like Iain Dall. The lad replied, 'By St Mary, I'd do so if my fingers had not been after the skate,' alluding to the sticky state of his fin-gers after having eaten some of that fish on which Macrimmon had fed them at dinner. And this has become a proverbial taunt which northern pipers to this day hurl at their inferior brethren from the south.

One of the Macrimmons, known by the nickname of Padruig Caogach, composed the first part of a tune called *Am port leathach* (the half tune), but was quite unable to finish it. The imperfect tune became very popular, and, as it was at the end of two years still unfinished, Iain Dall set to work and completed it. He called it *Lasan Phadruig Chaogach*, or 'The Wrath of Padruig Caogach', thus, whilst disowning any share in the merit of the com-position, anticipating the result which would follow.

Osgood Mackenzie (1842–1922), A Hundred Years in the Highlands. Caogach means squint-eyed. It was said that Padruig had the blind piper pushed over a cliff, but he survived. Four generations of Mackay pipers, starting with Rory, served eight generations of Mackenzie lairds.

There were two families at the head of the profession – viz. the McRimins and the McAslans, both of the Isle of Skye. One of the former is said to have composed a song well known in the Highlands, the burden of which is:

Oh for three hands!
One for the claymore, and two for the pipes!

... The following anecdote, which a friend of mine had from Lord John Drummond soon after the circumstance happened, shows how much veneration was paid a celebrated piper by his scholars. In the last rebellion a body of loyal Highlanders was defeated at Inverury, and the laird of McLeod's chief piper, one of the McRimins, taken prisoner after a stout resistance. Next morning the rebel pipers did not play through the town as usual; upon which Lord John, who commanded, sent for them, and asked the reason of their neglect. They answered, that whilst McRimin, their master, was in captivity, their pipes were *dumb*, and nothing but his release could make them do their duty.

John Ramsay of Ochtertyre (1736–1814), Scotland and Scotsmen in the Eighteenth Century

The Origin of the Hebrides Overture

It was said that this was the manner in which the overture, The Hebrides, took its rise: Mendelssohn's sisters asked him to tell them something about the Hebrides. 'It cannot be told, only played,' he said. No sooner spoken than he seated himself at the piano and played the theme which afterwards grew into the overture.

W. A. Lampadius, Life of Mendelssohn, *quoted in F. Marian McNeill*, An Iona Anthology *(1971)*

Chopin at Hamilton Palace

... perhaps the most unique visit he paid was to the Duke of Hamilton at Hamilton Palace. . . His description of the musical guests at Hamilton Palace is both amusing and sarcastic. Little wonder.

> Art here means painting, sculpture and architecture. Music is not art, and is not called art. . . These queer folk play for the sake of beauty, but to teach them decent things is a joke. . . One day after my piano playing, and after various songs by other Scottish ladies, they brought a kind of accordion, and his hostess (who was regarded locally as a great musician) began with the utmost gravity to play on it the most atrocious tunes.

This picture of the Duchess roaring out raucous music on an accordion after Chopin had played the piano is surely enough to make the gods laugh. No wonder Chopin added, 'What will you have? Every creature here seems to me to have a screw loose.'

T. Ratcliffe Barnett, Scottish Pilgrimage in the Land of Lost Content (1949).
Chopin's visit to Scotland took place shortly before his death in 1849.

Neil Gow Speaks His Mind

. . . in Athol house, after supper was announced, a portion of the fashion-able party lingered in the ball room, unwilling to forsake the dance. Neil, who felt none of the fashionable indifference about supper and its accom-paniments, soon lost patience, and addressing himself to the ladies, cried out, 'Gang doun to your supper, ye daft limmers, and dinna haud me reelin' here, as if hunger and drouth were unkent in the land – a body can get naething dune for you.'

Robert Chambers, Scottish Biographical Dictionary. Neil Gow (1727–1807), the Perthshire violinist, was the most popular musician in the country.

The Reticence of Lady Nairne

At the head of the musical society of Edinburgh were the Misses Hume. They were consulted by Mr Purdie, music dealer, when he proposed, about 1821, to bring out a collection of national airs with suitable words. The Misses Hume consulted in their turn their friend Mrs Nairne, with whose own aspirations the scheme fitted in admirably. The result was the forma-tion of a ladies' committee, the proceedings of which were meant to be shrouded in mystery, and were really kept long in concealment. The mem-bers of this committee either supplied Mr Purdie's songs or revised them. It is almost unnecessary to say that the presiding genius was Carolina Nairne. No doubt literary puzzles were the fashion of the era, but this well-born and accomplished little clique, who professed, and in general were fully disposed, to despise fashions which they themselves did not set, strike the work-a-day men and women of the present generation as being half-super-cilious, half-childish, in their mummery. Mrs Nairne assumed the not very euphonious name of Mrs Bogan of Bogan, and used the non-aristocratic alliterative initials of B. B., in her dealings with the publisher. (Perhaps there was a little humorous hit at her own conscious predilections in the choice of name and initials.) Even this *nom de plume* was whispered charily to Mr Purdie under seal of utmost secrecy. Its owner was so much in earnest in her disguise, that she wrote in a feigned hand, and employed other feigned hands to transcribe her MSS. These MSS she signed variously 'B. B.', or 'sent by B. B.', or merely 'S. M.', the initials of 'Scottish Minstrel', the title which Mr Purdie and the ladies of the committee had given to the collection. At a later date she wished to shake the evidence that it was a woman who had composed her songs, and writes to one of the committee: 'As you observed, the more mystery the better, and still the balance is in favour of "the lords of the creation". I cannot help in some degree undervaluing beforehand what is said to be a feminine production. . .' She ventured, however, on personal interviews with Mr Purdie, at his place of business, as Mrs Bogan of Bogan. On these occasions she was carefully got up for the occasion as an old country lady of a former generation. One can imagine the dash of fun and frolic with which the former country belle and beauty would engage in this species of masquerading, whether or not she borrowed the idea from the clever mystifications practised with success by Miss Graham Stirling on Scott and Jeffrey. Mrs Nairne was likewise so successful that Mr Purdie never dreamed of Mrs Bogan of Bogan being a lady resident in the same town with himself. . .

Sarah Tytler and J. L. Watson, The Songstresses of Scotland, Vol. II (1871). Carolina Oliphant (1766–1845), born in Gask, Perthshire, married Major, later Lord, Nairne. She is the author of many celebrated songs, including 'Caller Herrin',' 'The Laird o' Cockpen', and 'Will Ye No' Come back Again?' which were published in The Scottish Minstrel.

Music in the Field

The author of this noble ballad ('Aiken Drum') was William Nicholson, the Galloway poet, as he was, and still is, called in his own district. He was born at Tanimaus, in the parish of Borgue, in August 1783; he died circa 1848, unseen, like a bird. . . Poor Nicholson, besides his turn for verse, was an exquisite musician, and sang with a powerful and sweet voice. . . There is one story about him which has always appeared to me quite perfect. A farmer, in a remote part of Galloway, one June morning before sunrise, was awakened by music; he had been dreaming of heaven, and when he found himself awake he still heard the strains. He looked out, and saw no-one, but at the corner of a grass-field he saw his cattle, and young colts and fillies, huddled together, and looking intently down into what he knew was an old quarry. He put on his clothes, and walked across the field, everything but that strange wild melody, still and silent in this the 'sweet hour of prime'. As he got nearer the 'beasts', the sound was louder; the colts with their long manes, and the nowt with their wondering stare, took no notice of him, straining their necks forward entranced. There, in the old quarry, the young sun 'glintin' on his face, and resting on his pack, which had been his pillow, was our Wandering Willie, playing and singing like an angel – 'an Orpheus; an Orpheus'. What a picture! When reproved for wasting his health and time by the prosaic farmer, the poor fellow said: 'Me and this quarry are lang acquant, and I've mair pleesure in pipin to thae daft cowts, than if the best leddies in the land were figurin away afore me.'

John Brown (1810–1882), The Black Dwarf's Bones, from Horae Subsecivae (1858)

Taking 'Young Scotland' in Hand

Sir Alexander Campbell Mackenzie tells an amusing recollection of his early training. His harmony master was Charles Lucas, who took him in hand when he was ignorant of counterpoint. 'Whenever there was anything startling in my composition-exercise, he would remark, "That is all very well for young Scotland," punctuating the remark with a pinch of snuff, "but it won't do; take it out, sir, take it out".'

Frederick J. Crowest, Musicians' Wit, Humour and Anecdote (*1902*). *Mackenzie (1847–1935) was a highly regarded composer in his day and his works are still played.*

'Sour Plums in Galashiels'

There is concern for music in the Borders. Ruskin told about a local man, who, as he lay dying, realized that maybe he was the only one who still knew the notes of the old tune of 'Sour Plums in Galashiels' and he sent for someone skilled in musical notation to write it down from his playing. Ruskin said, 'Is not this strange that a man, setting out on his heavenly journey, should be concerned to see that the tune "Sour Plums in Galashiels" should not cease from the earth?'

R. F. Mackenzie, A Search for Scotland (*1989*).

Mary Garden's First Triumphs

A brave little slip of a woman – she was only 5' 4" in height but everybody who saw her on stage thought of her as tall, and she kept her weight steady at 112 pounds – she had what Shaw would have seen as the Life Force within her. She wanted to be at the top, and so she was, throughout her professional life. She arrived with the new century and with the opera which, at that time, seemed to embody it. Charpentier's *Louise* – the story of working-class people and the teenage couple who defy parents and convention in the pursuit of free love – had its premiere at the Opéra-Comique on 2 February 1900 and on 13 April (a Friday) the heroine fell ill half-way through. The unknown, untried understudy took over – with the big aria, 'Depuis le jour', immediately ahead of her. She, 'la petite Garden', became the talk of Paris and followed Louise with *La Marseillaise*, a short-lived opera in which she played the fiancée of Rouget de l'Isle, making everyone laugh – though good-naturedly – when she suddenly stood up and cried, 'Je suis française!'

J. B. Steane, Singers of the Century, Vol. 2 (*1998*). *Mary Garden (1874– 1967) described in her autobiography her audition for Debussy's 'Pelléas et Mélisande'. He played the piano and said not a word. Then she was called into the office, where he was sitting. He rose, took both of her hands in his and asked where she was born. 'Aberdeen, Scotland.' 'To think', he said,*

'that you had to come from the cold, far North to create my Mélisande,
because that is what you are going to do, Mademoiselle.'

Young Sydney McEwan Wins a Prize

At Kirn pier there was always a pierrot show, and once a week the professional entertainers augmented their own song and dance by way of a Grand
Talent Contest.

The season was coming close to its end, and this was the day of the
cream of the talent – the day when the finalists of the fading summer reas-
sembled in competition for the championship of champions.

My brother it was who had entered my name. He'd heard my soprano at
school and sometimes in the parish hall. He knew I was good. And he had
his eye on the prize that he knew would be shared.

I was at the age of indifference. I had my boats, and that was enough –
paltry, moored cobles that developed in my child's imagination into pirate
ships and handsome, salt-sprayed brigantines, edging their way through the
seven seas.

I was still busy at the business of ships when my brother shouted: 'The
concert's started!'

And I came running to the pier where the pierrots had their stage. There
were lots of other ambitious youngsters there. The girls had on their Sunday-best
frocks and their heads were dressed with ribbons. The boys looked uncomfortably clean, with their hair slicked down and their boots reflecting the sun.

I bore the mark of my boats. Their tar had rubbed off on my hands and
knees, and the jersey I'd started the day with was sadly the worse for wear.

I sang without effort or nervous concern. I suppose my main idea was to
get the thing over with and back to my sailing of the seas.

But even at this early age the Lord had blessed me with an exceptional
voice. None of the embellishments of silk and lace could alter the fact that
I was the obvious winner. Its confirmation was the audience applause that
echoed along the pier.

The prize was a five-shilling piece and a shining half-crown. Such wealth!
We were off to spend that half-a-crown – the five-shilling piece was for
taking home.

We spent it, of course, on the hire of a boat, and my notions of piracy
became more real. We were out there rowing when my mother appeared on
the beach, and she yelled and waved and looked anxious – not for our
safety, but as to how we'd come by the money for the hire.

We ran up the shingle, and my brother dropped out the words excitedly
as he ran: 'Sydney won the talent competition!'

By the time I reached her, I'd worked up a certain sense of pride and
confidently held out the five-shilling piece.

I was assaulted with abuse. My brother got it also. Imagine her son appearing on a public stage in the sort of state that West Coasters sum up picturesquely as 'having the erse hangin' oot o' his breeks!'

Sydney McEwan, On the High C's (*1973*). *He went on to become 'Father Sydney', a much-loved Catholic priest as well as a celebrated singer.*

Playing the Pibroch

We stood under the branches of a tree on the Balmoral Estate waiting for the rain to moderate. A blackie sang from another tree, and there were cushie doos making their presence known from the other side of the clearing. The rain went off. Mist hung about the trees in still air and blanketed the hills. Pipe Major Robert U. Brown walked into the clearing, tuned his pipes, and began to play 'Lament for the Children'. It seemed all other sounds had stopped. Could the blackies and the doos be listening too, as the music left the piper, and lifted itself into the hills. No other music could pay such respect to the nativity of the land as it made the past present nor record with such sadness the originating event.

For a time nothing was said until I asked the piper:

'How long does it take to learn to play a pibroch?'

He answered: 'It takes seven years to learn to play the pipes, and seven years to learn to play a pibroch, and then you need the poetry.'

George Bruce (1909–), interview with Pipe Major Robert U. Brown, from The Land Out There (*1991*)

Jazz and Violence

The three gangs were Golly's, Naz's, and the Val d'Or boys. There was actually a Golly, who always smelled of gelignite – it has quite a strong, unmistakable smell – a Naz, a portly little chap called William Nisbet, and the Val d'Or was a café. Sometimes the leadership and even the names would become blurred or changed; but at every dance there was violence. We coined the phrase 'faces are changing at the Jazz Band Balls', some of them regrettably, almost unrecognisably. We tried a different venue to give the gangs the slip, but this attempt, held at the Palace Ballroom at the foot of Leith Walk, generated the most spectacular fracas of all. At one point Golly threw Naz down a flight of steps which ended in the centre of the dance floor. Al Fairweather, Sandy's trumpet player, tried unwisely to separate them and was lucky to escape injury. The Naz lifted Golly and threw him against a mirror that covered one wall. One minute there were these two identical chaps hurtling towards each other back to back with a complete circle of onlookers, open-mouthed and with alarmed, frozen expressions: then crash! Half of them disappeared and the floor was covered with shards of silver. I found a pocket book before the police came, with eight pence and a card proclaiming that a William Nisbet was unfit for army service. I threw it out of the window.

After that we hired two bouncers, both jazz fans, and things got quieter. One was Jackie McFarlane who was five feet tall, insisted on singing 'Frankie and Johnnie' in a nasal Dalkeith accent, and learned his brawling in the International Brigade in Spain. The other was Tom Connery, who became Sean. None of his 007 crap years later matched the mayhem available from Golly and Naz.

Sandy Brown, The McJazz Manuscripts (1979)

The Clyde Valley Stompers

A typical itinerary for this band's week was Bristol, Glasgow, Dover, Aberdeen, Penzance, London, Edinburgh; so they lived in the wagon. They had a unique way of retaining sanity: about every three days they would stop the wagon, go into a field and punch each other senseless. By an evolutionary mechanism that requires more study than I can afford, some fine musicians came out of the band.

Sandy Brown, The McJazz Manuscripts (1979)

PHILANTHROPISTS

Miser and Benefactor

During the latter part of his life, he carried his parsimonious habits to the utmost extreme. He is said to have lived in a small apartment, which he rented, denying himself all the comforts and conveniences of life, and even using its necessities in the most sparing manner; insomuch, that his whole general expense, room rent included, did not exceed £5 sterling annually. Many of the anecdotes which have been handed down by tradition, respecting the habits and privations of this singular individual, seem to be nearly the same as are related of certain English misers of celebrity. It is told of him, for instance, that he used to keep himself warm by walking backwards and forwards in his room with a bag of coals on his back, judging, no doubt, that this was a more economical method of procuring heat, than burning the coals. Also, that he sometimes contrived to satisfy the cravings of appetite by going to the market, and tasting a little of the various articles of provision, such as meal, butter, cheese, etc., by way of ascertaining their qualities before he should make any purchase. . . A particular friend of his who was in the way of spending an evening with him occasionally (for he was naturally of a social disposition) was so highly honoured that, as often as the meeting took place, a small rush-light was produced to enliven the scene. One evening, however, the same friend perceiving the rays of the moon shining brightly into the apartment, observed, no doubt with the purpose of ingratiating himself more with his host, that it was a pity to waste the candle when the moonlight was quite sufficient. The hint was not lost, and afterwards when the two friends met, the moon was laid under contribution to furnish the necessary light, as often as she could afford it.

Robert Chambers, Scottish Biographical Dictionary. Robert Gordon (c.1665–1732) left a substantial fortune to endow Robert Gordon's Hospital in Aberdeen.

A Sceptic Visits New Lanark

All is here arranged with great skill; and everything that you behold, dwelling places of the people (about fourteen hundred in number), their dresses, their skins, all bespoke cleanliness and well being; all savoured of the Quaker. I have never been into any manufacturing place without reluctance, and I positively refused to go into any of them here. . . Being at NEW LANARK, however, I was rather curious to know whether there was any reality in what we had heard about the effects of the Owen 'feelosophy'. I had always understood that he had been the author of his own great fortune, and the founder of this village; but I found, that the establishment had been founded by a Mr DALE, who had two or three daughters with great fortunes; that Mr OWEN had got one of these daughters, and one of these fortunes; that Mrs OWEN had been dead for some years; that the concern had long been in other hands; that the only part of it which was ever of his invention, was a large building, in which the 'feelosophical' working people were intended to eat and drink in common; that they never did this. . . The building, in NEW LANARK, which OWEN erected for the 'feelosophers' to carry on their community of eating and drinking, is used as a school room; and here I saw boys in one place, and girls in another place, under masters appointed for this purpose, carrying on what is called 'education'. There was one boy pointing with a stick to something stuck up upon the wall, and then all the rest of the boys began bawling out what that was. In one large room they were all singing out something at the word of command. . . In another great apartment of this house, there were eighteen boys and eighteen girls, the boys dressed in Highland dresses, without shoes on, naked from three inches above the knee, down to the foot, a tartan plaid close about the body, in their shirt sleeves, their shirt collars open, each having a girl by the arm, duly proportioned in point of size, the girls without caps, and without shoes and stockings; and there were these eighteen couples, marching, arm in arm, in regular files, with a lock-step, slow march, to the sound of a fiddle, which a fellow, big enough to carry a quarter of wheat, or to dig ten rods of ground in a day, was playing in the corner of the room, with an immense music book lying open before him. There was another man who was commanding officer of the marching couples, who, after having given us a march in quick step as well as slow step, were disposed of in dancing order, a business that they seemed to perform with great regularity and elegance; and it was quite impossible to see the half-naked lads of twelve or thirteen, putting their arms round the waists of the thinly-clad girls of the same age, without clearly perceiving the manifest tendency of this mode of education, to prevent 'premature marriages', and to 'check population'.

William Cobbett (1763–1835), Cobbett's Tour in Scotland and in the Four Northern Counties of England in the Autumn of the Year 1832 *(1833)*

Carnegie at Home in Skibo Castle

Each day at eight Carnegie was awakened by his piper, a morning harbinger who started his notes at a distance, gradually approaching the castle, which he circled, pausing and skirling beneath the windows of the guests. All went to breakfast to the tones of the organ, which discoursed also throughout the meal. 'My morning devotions', Carnegie called this music. . . No prospect delighted him so intensely as a waterfall. Old-time visitors to Skibo still remember the little poem, 'The Burnie' – 'it drappit from a gray rock upon a mossy stane' – which their host was fond of reciting – a ballad that expressed an abiding phase of his temperament – his fondness for tinkling water. 'I am building a new loch', he wrote, 'to give us a reserve for the castle waterfall, which is a grand success – and I'm so happy. Dabbling in water seems a necessity.'

Burton J. Hendrick, The Life of Andrew Carnegie *(1933)*

Formative Experiences of a Food Scientist

I got more permanent impressions of Glasgow, which have affected my whole life, by prowling round the city on Saturdays to see the tenement slums which, like every other industrial city in Britain, formed about half the housing and were indescribably gloomy and filthy. Having been brought up in the country where almost all the people, even the poorest, lived in single houses with a front and back door and a garden, and where one could go out at night and see the moon and the stars, the thought of life in these slums was most depressing. One Saturday night I went up to see the Salt Market in the middle of the slums. I wandered round it till about ten o' clock when the pubs were emptying out crowds of drunken men, many of them spoiling for a fight. One scene which still sticks in my memory is of a woman lying dead drunk in the road, her head on the pavement and her skirts thrown up, with nobody taking the slightest notice of her.

On one or two Saturdays I went to the Free Breakfast Mission in a hall in the east end. There all the down and outs could come in and have a big mug of coffee and a slice of bread and butter provided they were willing to sit through some hymn singing and one or two speeches by fervent evangelistic laymen urging them to have their souls saved. These experiences gave me an intense hatred of unnecessary hunger and poverty and affected my subsequent life much more than any lectures I listened to on philosophy.

Lord Boyd Orr (1880–1971), As I Recall (1966). At that time a Glasgow University student, John Boyd Orr later became first head of the UN Food and Agriculture Organisation and winner of the Nobel Peace Prize (1949).

PHILOSOPHERS AND SCHOLARS

George Buchanan Despairs of Michel de Montaigne

Buchanan chuckled with delight as he recounted with merriment how he had chastised Michel de Montaigne. He did not spare the rod and spoil the lad who was a pampered child at home. Such nonsense as waking him up with soft music was ignored in college. . . When Montaigne was made Gentleman-of-the-Bedchamber to Henry II, he met Mary as a favourite daughter-in-law of that King, who enjoyed his company. This caused Buchanan to exclaim: 'Look at him! He can talk with monarchy as an equal! That is the result of a well-born soul, a well-filled purse is my opinion. Such lads should have no means, like myself, for egotism will ruin the most promising career ever launched from any college. All he wishes to do is to draw himself as a painter does his portrait with a crayon. He cares nought for worldly prospects, nor fame. . . His one desire is to be Master of the Arts of Life. What is the rising generation coming to?'

Arnold Fleming, The Medieval Scots Scholar in France (1952). George Buchanan (1506–1582), Scotland's leading humanist of his generation, born to a cottar's family in Killearn, taught for seven years in the Collège de Guienne, Paris. Later, as young James VI's tutor, he applied the same robust teaching methods to the king as he had to Montaigne.

Edward Dwelly on Compiling a Gaelic Dictionary

No-one who has always spoken a language like Gaelic from the cradle can ever realize the extraordinary difficulties presented to a stranger who wishes to acquire it. First, the majority of Gaelic speakers only a very few years ago could neither read nor write it, so when one heard an unfamiliar word or phrase and the first instinct was of course to write it down lest it should be forgotten, the question was how to spell it – of course the speaker could not tell! I was baulked in this way times without number, and my progress with the language immensely retarded in consequence. Next, the great difficulty of inducing a Gael to engage in a Gaelic conversation if he thinks he can make himself understood at all by means of indifferent English, or even if there is anyone present who cannot understand Gaelic, makes the acquisition of a knowledge of colloquial Gaelic much more difficult than is the case with other modern tongues, for it is only by posing as a Highlander and one who knows Gaelic that one can ever hope to hear it spoken habitually and without restraint.

Edward Dwelly (1864–1939), preface to The Illustrated Gaelic–English Dictionary, *Second Edition, 1920. Dwelly was a Londoner but if anyone deserved to be an honorary Scotsman, it was he. At the age of 17 he joined the London Scottish Regiment and a lifelong attachment to things Gaelic followed, culminating in his great* Dictionary, *which he not only compiled but set in type himself. It was published in instalments between 1901 and 1911, and in a second edition in 1920.*

Young David Hume

> . . . as a Boy he was a fat, stupid, lumbering Clown, but full of sensibility and Justice – one day at my home, when he was about 16 a most unpleasant odour offended the Company before dinner. . . 'O the Dog. . . the Dog', cried out everyone, 'put out the Dog; 'tis that vile Beast Pod, kick him downstairs. . .'
>
> Hume stood abashed, his heart smote him. . .
>
> 'Oh do not hurt the Beast', he said, 'it is not Pod, it is Me!'
>
> How very few people would take the odour of a stinking Conduct from a guiltless Pod to wear it on their own rightful shoulders.

Told by Lady Dalrymple to her granddaughter, Lady Anne Lindsay; quoted in E. C. Mossner, The Life of David Hume *(1980)*

Dr John Leyden and English

When he arrived at Calcutta in 1805, I was most solicitous regarding his reception in the Indian capital. 'I entreat you, my dear friend,' I said to him the day he landed, 'to be careful of the impression you make on your entering this community; for God's sake learn a little English, and be silent upon literary subjects, except among literary men.' 'Learn English!' he exclaimed, 'no, never; it was trying to learn that language that spoilt my Scotch; and as to being silent, I will promise to hold my tongue, if you will make fools hold theirs.'

General John Malcolm, letter to the Bombay Courier. *John Leyden (1775–1811), son of a Teviotdale shepherd, became a distinguished scholar in literature, linguistics and anthropology*

Andrew Melville's Greek

When, some years afterwards, he became Professor of Latin at Geneva, his Scottish stubbornness, in defending his own pronunciation of Greek, roused the wrath of the Professor of that language, who was a native of Greece. 'Vos Scoti, vos barbari!' he indignantly exclaimed, 'docebitis nos Graecos pronunciationem linguae nostrae, scilicet?'

John Edgar, History of Early Scottish Education *(1893). ('You Scots, you barbarians! Just think, will you teach us Greeks how to pronounce our own language?') Andrew Melville (1545–c.1622) took up his post at Geneva in 1568. Later he returned to become Principal of Glasgow University and a leading Reformer.*

Napier of Merchiston, Diviner

He often walked abroad in the evening, in a long mantle, and attended by a large dog; and these circumstances, working upon minds totally unable to appreciate the real nature of his researches, raised a popular suspicion of his being addicted to the black art. It is certain that, no more than other great men of his age, was he exempt from a belief in several sciences now fully proved to have been full of imposture . . . as yet, the bounds between true and false knowledge were hardly known. Napier, therefore, practised an art which seems nearly akin to divination, as is proved by a contract entered into, in 1594, between him and Logan of Fastcastle. . . This document states it to have been agreed upon, that, as there were old reports and appearances that a sum of money was hid within Logan's house of Fastcastle, John Napier should do his utmost diligence to search and seek out, and by all craft and ingine (a phrase for mental power) to find out the same, or make it sure that no such thing has been there. For his reward he was to have the exact third of all that was found, and to be safely guarded by Logan back to Edinburgh.

Robert Chambers, Scottish Biographical Dictionary. *John Napier of Merchiston (1550–1617), was the discoverer of logarithms.*

Thomas Reid's Bad Dreams

About the age of fourteen, I was almost every night unhappy in my sleep from frightful dreams; sometimes hanging over a dreadful precipice, and just ready to drop down; sometimes pursued for my life, and stopped by a wall, or by a sudden loss of all strength; sometimes ready to be devoured by a wild beast. How long I was plagued by such dreams, I do not recollect. I believe it was for a year or two at least; and I think they had quite left me before I was sixteen. In those days, I was much given to what Mr Addison, in one of his Spectators, calls castle-building: and in my evening solitary walk, which was generally all the exercise I took, my thoughts would hurry me into some active scene, where I generally acquitted myself much to my own satisfaction; and in these scenes of imagination, I performed many a gallant exploit. At the same time, in my dreams, I found myself the most arrant coward that ever was. Not only my courage, but my strength failed me in every danger; and I often rose from my bed in the morning in such a panic, that it took some time to get the better of it. I wished very much to get free of these uneasy dreams, which not only made me unhappy in sleep, but often left a disagreeable impression in my mind for some part of the following day. I thought it was worth trying whether it was possible to recollect that it was all a dream, and that I was in no real danger, and that every fright I had was a dream. After many fruitless attempts to recollect this when the danger appeared, I effected it at last, and have often when I was sliding over a precipice into the abyss, recollected that it was all a dream, and boldly jumped down. The effect of this commonly was, that I immediately awoke. But I awoke calm and intrepid, which I thought a great acquisition. After this my dreams were never very uneasy, and, in a short time, I dreamed not at all.

Quoted in Robert Chambers, Scottish Biographical Dictionary. *Thomas Reid (1710–1796) elaborated the philosophy of 'Common Sense' in opposition to what he saw as the sterile scepticism of his contemporary David Hume. At the time he describes, he was already an undergraduate at Marischal College, Aberdeen.*

At Dinner with Michael Scott

Michael Scott, the 'wondrous wizard', about whom historians have fought doughtily, was born in 1195 near Kelso. He was a precocious pupil in the local school at Roxburgh. All agree that his fame spread all over Europe, and that he returned to his native land to die. Border folk still keep his memory as green as the lawn around his old Tower of Oakwood. Many believe that his books on The Black Arts exist, although it is risky for anyone to find them because the fiends of Hell would be aroused if these grim parchments were disturbed.

He enjoyed the questionable reputation of having the power of hypnotism. On one occasion he invited some friends to dinner to show his conjuring feats. The time was in mid-winter, yet he had sprays of fresh sprouting vine shoots and bunches of luscious grapes on the same branch adorning his table-centre. The company sat around and were invited to select a bunch for themselves, but their host forbade them to stretch forth their hands until he gave permission. When Scott said 'cut!', the vine with the grapes mysteriously disappeared and the guests found themselves with a knife in one hand and his neighbour's sleeve in the other.

Arnold Fleming, The Medieval Scots Scholar in France (1952)

Adam Smith Carried off by Gypsies

A singular accident happened to him when he was about three years of age. As he was amusing himself one day at the door of his uncle Mr Douglas's house in Strathenry, he was carried off by a party of gypsies. The vagrants, however, were pursued by Mr Douglas, were overtaken in Lesliewood, and his uncle, as Mr Stewart remarks, was the happy instrument of preserving to the world a genius who was destined not only to extend the boundaries of science, but to enlighten and reform the commercial policy of Europe.

Robert Chambers, Scottish Biographical Dictionary. *Adam Smith (1723–1790) wrote* The Wealth of Nations.

Adam Smith in Trouble at Oxford

Something having excited the suspicion of his superiors with regard to the nature of his studies in private, the heads of his college entered his apartment one day without any previous notice, and unluckily found the young philosopher engaged in reading Hume's *Treatise of Human Nature*. The offender was of course severely reprimanded, and the objectionable work seized and carried off.

Robert Chambers, Scottish Biographical Dictionary

Adam Smith's Library

The library which Dr Smith had collected during his life though small was valuable. The books were well selected, and he was particularly careful that the bijous which he admitted into his collection should be in excellent order. Mr Smellie, in his life of Dr Smith, says, 'The first time I happened to be in his library, observing me looking at the books with some degree of curiosity and perhaps surprise, for most of the volumes were elegantly, and some of them superbly bound. "You must have remarked," said he, "that I am a beau in nothing but my books".'

Robert Chambers, Scottish Biographical Dictionary. *Mr Smellie was William Smellie (see Writers).*

Adam Smith as a Person

The Founder of the science of business was one of the most unbusinesslike of mankind. He was an awkward Scotch professor, apparently choked with books and absorbed in abstractions. He was never engaged in any sort of trade, and would probably never have made sixpence by any if he had been. His absence of mind was amazing. On one occasion, having to sign his name to an official document, he produced not his own signature, but an elaborate imitation of the signature of the person who signed before him; on another, a sentinel on duty having saluted him in military fashion, he astounded and offended the man by acknowledging it with a copy – a very clumsy copy no doubt – of the same gestures. And Lord Brougham preserves other similar traditions. 'It is related,' he says, 'by old people in Edinburgh that while he moved through the Fishmarket in his accustomed attitude – that is with his hands behind his back, and his head in the air – a female of the trade exclaimed, taking him for an idiot broken loose, "Hech, sirs, to see the like o' him to be aboot. And yet he is weel eneugh put on"' (dressed). It was often so too in society. Once, during a dinner at Dalkeith, he broke out into a lecture on some politics of the day, and was bestowing a variety of severe epithets on a statesman, when he suddenly perceived the nearest relative of the politician he was criticizing, sitting opposite, and stopped; but he was heard to go on muttering, 'Deil care, Deil care, it's all true.'

Walter Bagehot (1826–1877), Adam Smith as a Person, *in* Biographical Studies. *The 'sentinel' was the doorkeeper of the Custom House. Smith did not merely return the 'salute' but, imagining himself back in the 'trained band', of which he was an officer, insisted on marching with the discomfited doorman up the street.*

Dugald Stewart's Fertility of Mind

In the year 1778, during which Dr Adam Ferguson accompanied the commissioners to America, he undertook to supply his place in the moral philosophy class; a labour that was the more overwhelming, as he had for the first time given notice, a short time before, of his intention to add a course of lectures on astronomy to the two classes which he taught as professor of mathematics. Such was the extraordinary fertility of his mind, and the facility with which it adapted its powers to such inquiries, that, although the proposal was made to him and accepted on Thursday, he commenced the course of metaphysics the following Monday, and continued, during the whole of the season, to think out and arrange in his head in the morning (while walking backwards and forwards in a small garden attached to his father's house in the college), the matter of the lecture of the day. The ideas with which he had thus stored his mind, he poured forth extempore in the course of the forenoon. . . To this season he always referred as the most laborious of his life; and such was the exhaustion of the body, from the intense and continued stretch of the mind, that, on his departure for London, at the close of the academical season, it was necessary to lift him into the carriage.

Robert Chambers, Scottish Biographical Dictionary. *Dugald Stewart (1753–1828) developed the 'Common Sense' theories of Thomas Reid and had immense influence on English and American philosophical thinking in the early nineteenth century.*

A Self-Taught Mathematician

Stone was the son of a gardener in the employment of John, Duke of Argyle, at Inverary, in the early part of the eighteenth century. . .

> He attained the age of eight years before he learnt to read; but a servant having taught him the letters of the alphabet, he soon made a rapid progress with very little assistance. . . The duke of Argyle, who to his military talents united a general knowledge of every science that can adorn the mind of a great man, walking one day in his garden, saw lying upon the grass a Latin copy of Newton's *Principia*. Having called someone to carry it back to his library, the young gardener told him that it belonged to himself. The duke was surprised, and asked him whether he was sufficiently acquainted with Latin and geometry to understand Newton. Stone replied, with an air of simplicity, that he knew a little of both. The duke then entered into conversation with the young mathematician, asked him several questions, and was astonished at the force and accuracy of his answers. The duke's curiosity being redoubled, he sat down on a bank, and requested to know by what means he acquired such knowledge. 'I first learnt to read', said Stone: 'the masons were then at work upon your house: I went near them one day, and saw that the architect used a rule and compass, and that he made calculations. I inquired what might be the meaning and use of these things; and I was informed that there was a science named arithmetic. I purchased a book of arithmetic, and I learnt it. I was told there was another science, called geometry: I bought books, and learnt geometry also. By reading, I found there were good books on these two sciences in Latin: I bought a dictionary, and learnt Latin. . . It seems to me that we may learn anything, when we know the twenty-four letters of the alphabet.'

Robert Chambers, Scottish Biographical Dictionary, *quoting a letter written by the Chevalier de Ramsay to Father Castel. Edmund Stone (c.1700–c.1738)*

*became a Fellow of the Royal Society and wrote several books on math-
ematical subjects.*

D'Arcy's Doos

D'Arcy also became a member of the Homeric Club, a society of classical
enthusiasts who met to read Greek plays and poetry. Once a year they went
for an expedition to the country, and upon one occasion they visited the
village of Glenfarg in Perthshire, and lunched at the Inn. As they stood
about the yard, two of the local lads approached D'Arcy and asked who the
distinguished and bearded company might be. He replied that they were the
Homeric Club from Dundee.

'Oh!' said the fellow. 'Is that so? Whaur's yer doos?'

Ruth Thompson, D'Arcy Wentworth Thompson 1860–1948 *(1958). Sir
D'Arcy Wentworth Thompson, author of* On Growth and Form, *born in Edinburgh, was Professor of Zoology first at Dundee and then at St Andrews.*

Douglas Young Draws Tears in Kirriemuir

The other example I would like to quote is something that happened in the
most matter-of-fact little town of Kirriemuir in the East Lowlands. That ami-
able and highly scholarly eccentric, Mr Douglas Young, Classics Lecturer at
St Andrews University, was in some small public hall where a number of
business men and farmers had gathered, and he was being cross-questioned
by them. The subject of his cross-questioning was the fact that he wrote his
poetry deliberately in the Old Scots Tongue. Was not this, so it was put to
him, an affectation for a polyglot scholar whose normal speech was English?

For an answer Douglas, black-bearded, thin, attenuated, rather odd-look-
ing (just the sort of figure the average dour Lowlander might have dismissed
as a poseur) rose to his full six-and-a-half feet and recited a few lines. The
lines he spoke were those of the 23rd Psalm, 'The Lord is my shepherd', but
he spoke them in his Scots version, or translation as you will, which he
himself had made.

Now there is no Psalm, indeed it would be difficult to think of any other
piece of prose, more familiar to the Scottish ear and heart than 'The Lord is
my shepherd'. All these Lowland farmers and country town business men
had heard and repeated the 23rd Psalm since their earliest childhood, but
they heard and repeated it in Church or Sunday School in English. Now, for
the first time, they heard this most familiar Psalm repeated in what was to
them really familiar language, the language of their families in childhood.
The effect, so an onlooker told me, was immediate. These hard, matter-of-
fact Scotsmen from the Lowland town of Kirriemuir were touched to the
heart and showed it. There were tears in some eyes.

Moray McLaren, Understanding the Scots (1956). *Such a gathering, for such a speaker, might seem unlikely; but Douglas Young did speak in public for the Nationalist cause, which in the 1930s was closely linked with the revival of creative writing in Scots.*

POLITICS AND POLITICIANS

The Trial of Robert Baillie of Jerviswood

Baillie was a Lanarkshire laird, of strong Presbyterian sympathies, who more than once fell foul of the government of Charles II. In 1683 he was falsely implicated in the conspiracy to assassinate Charles and his brother, later James VII, was arrested, maltreated and while seriously ill, brought to trial, where he conducted his own defence, and drew a remarkable admission from the Lord Advocate.

'My lord, I think it very strange that you charge me with such abominable things; you may remember that when you came to me in person, you told me that such things were laid to my charge, but that you did not believe them. How then, my lord, did you come to lay such a stain on me with so much violence? Are you now convinced in your conscience that I am more guilty than before? You may remember what passed betwixt us in prison.'

The whole audience fixed their eyes upon the advocate, who appeared in no small confusion, and said,

'Jerviswood, I own what you say. My thoughts there were as a private man; but what I say here is by special direction of the privy council. And', pointing to Sir William Paterson, clerk, 'he knows my orders.'

'Well,' said Baillie, 'if your lordship have one conscience for yourself, and another for the council, I pray God forgive you; I do. My lords', he added, 'I trouble your lordships no further.'

The assize was empannelled at midnight, and sat till nine in the morning of the succeeding day, when a verdict of guilty was returned against Mr Baillie, and he was sentenced to be executed that afternoon, at the cross, and his limbs to be afterwards exhibited on the jails of four different Scottish towns. The reason for such precipitation was the fear of his judges that a natural death would disappoint the wishes of the government, which called imperatively at this moment for a public example to terrify its opponents.

Robert Chambers, Scottish Biographical Dictionary. *This judicial murder happened in 1684.*

A Victim of the 'Radical War'

I kent Jeems Wilson lang afore he was a prominent Radical. He

was a noble weever, and mony a time made stockings and drawers for my guidman. He was often in our hoose in Kilbride, and
had dinner with us twenty times. He was hightly respeckit a'
roun' the kintra side. On the morning o' the 'rising' Wilson on
reaching Kilbride cam to the hoose. I never remember sic a mornin'
o' thunder, lichtening, and rain. He was fair drookit, and his claes
were dreepin' wi' wat. I speered at him where he was goin' and
he said – 'Didna ye hear: we're goin' to overturn the Government.' 'O ye idiots!' I said, 'ye may as weel try to overturn God
Almighty. If ye go to the Cathkin Braes the sodgers'll blaw ye up
like the peelins o' onions.' Wilson looked as if he was clean de-
mented, and stood afore the fire shiverin' and his teeth chattering.
I offered him a dish o' tea but he wadna tak it. He was quiet for
some time, and then said, 'Did ye hear what happened in my
hoose the day? Spae Matty fell doon deid before we left. She was
askin' us a' not to leave, and got very excited and fell doon deid.'
Wilson when leaving my house left what he ca'd his sword standing up against the hearthstane, and the last words he said, 'I'm
gaun up to see Jock Tamson', a weaver in the village. Mrs Hamilton, of the Avondale Hotel, cried at him, and she gave him a
glass of whisky. It was quite true about Matty fa'an dead. She
was a body that went about the kintra and telt fortunes and things
o' that sort, and she said to Wilson that morning that when he
would come hame again his heid wad be aff. The sword lay in
oor house for mony a day, but some o' the Hamilton folk claimed
it. There was a man ca'd M'Intyre alang with Wilson that day,
and his wife cam after him to take him back. He refused, and she
grippit his hat and took it from him, but that didna dae ony
good. He got a twalmonth in gaol.

*Mrs Hunter, an eyewitness, recording her memories of the 'Radical War'
of 1820 in the Glasgow* Weekly Mail, *3 December 1887 (when she was 96
years old), quoted in William Donaldson,* The Language of the People *(1989).
Wilson was one of three men to be executed for taking part, on 30 August
1820; Mrs Hunter went to see his end and recorded that after being hanged,
Wilson's head was cut off as had been foretold by the spae-wife.*

Electoral Put-Down

At a late election for Perthshire, Sir John Campbell solicited a Mr MacGregor
to use his influence with his son, to give his vote for Sir George Murray. Old
MacGregor said it was useless, as his son had pledged himself to support
the opposite party; at which Sir John gave expression to his displeasure, by

saying, 'He was not a true MacGregor, there was some bad blood in him.' 'I wouldna doubt but there is', replied the old man, 'for his mother was a Campbell'.

'The Laird of Logan' (*1863*)

First MP in a Cloth Cap

On Hardie's first day at the House of Commons, the policeman at the gate took one look at the former miner, dressed in his ordinary working clothes and cloth cap, and asked suspiciously, 'Are you working here?'

'Yes', replied Hardie.

'On the roof?'

'No', said the new MP. 'On the floor.'

Attributed to James Keir Hardie (1865–1915) in Clifton Fadiman, The Little, Brown Book of Anecdotes (1985)

Another View of Keir Hardie (and his Cap)

From the year 1889, when he went to Paris to take part in the foundation of the second International, Hardie was a fully-fledged Socialist waging inexpiable war against the Liberal party. But it was no part of his plan in those early days to take the Red bonnets over the Border. The Scottish Labour party was conceived, not as the nucleus of a British Labour party, but as a movement for the emancipation of Scotland from the tyranny of English political ideas as expressed in Liberalism. Like all anti-English movements in Scotland, it was obliged to look to the Continent for its ideas. Hence the aggressive Socialism that it preached from the beginning. . .

It was well for Keir Hardie – whether it was to the advantage of British politics is another question – that he was not permitted to continue in the political career he had planned for himself, which consisted in perambulating Scotland with the Red flag in one hand and the 'blue blanket' in the other. His fellow-countrymen were deplorably apathetic. No Scottish constituency seemed to think that Mr Cunninghame Graham needed his or anyone else's company at Westminster. When at the General Election of 1892 this Scottish patriot and sworn foe of Liberalism did get into Parliament, it was for a London constituency and with the support of a Liberal party organisation. There was a 'cave' of South-West Ham Radicals who were not satisfied that the official Liberal candidate shared their enthusiasm for the economics of Henry George. Why they should have thought of Keir Hardie as a suitable person to explain the beauties of the Single-tax to the West Ham electors does not appear, but choose him they did. He travelled from Old Cumnock to South-West Ham comforted by the assurance that he was practically certain to keep the Liberal out. As it happened, the Liberal did not need any keeping out. He went out flatly and finally in the middle of the campaign by dying. Keir Hardie, in the language of the day, was on velvet. The local Liberals, being unable to put a new candidate in the field with any chance of success, had no option but to concentrate on the 'Labour' candidate, who at least could be relied on to go into the Liberal lobby on all vital occasions. The result was the celebrated bit of clowning by which the member for South-West Ham saw fit to advertise his arrival at Westminster. Wearing a cap instead of his customary bowler, he drove up in a two-horse charabanc with a bugler on the box. And is it not written of those who disfigure their faces and sound a trumpet before them that they have their reward?

Donald Carswell, Brother Scots (1927). *The blue blanket was King James VI's term for the tradesmen's banner which signified a Labour dispute.*

The Treatment of Scottish Suffragettes

The third woman . . . was Maude Edwards, who had slashed the picture of the King in the Royal Scottish Academy. The report of her trial at Edinburgh Sheriff Court was headlined 'STORMY COURT SCENES' in the *Edinburgh Evening Despatch* (3 July). At the beginning of the trial she shouted to the Sheriff, Lord Maconachie, 'I will not be tried. I am not going to listen to you or anyone whatever.' The Sheriff took this as a plea of not guilty. When suffragettes applauded he ordered the court to be cleared. 'This was an operation attended with some difficulty and no little amusement', reported the *Evening Dispatch*. Many women resisted the attempts of the police to eject them, especially Dr Grace Cadell who 'required three officers to remove her'. From the dock Maude Edwards kept up a running fire of commentary, making so much noise that some witnesses had to cross the court to give evidence where the jury could hear them. She was sentenced to three months' imprisonment.

Dr Ferguson Watson examined Maude Edwards on 4 July. She was in a somewhat hysterical state; the medical officer reported that 'she did not behave like a sane person'. One reason why she braved such a public act which she knew must result in her arrest and imprisonment, in spite of English precedents for forcible feeding, was because she had armed herself with a medical certificate stating that she had a cardiac condition and could not be forcibly fed without mortal risk.

From remarks which she made to Dr Ferguson Watson at the outset she clearly felt safe from forcible feeding, but although he did not consider her 'a very good case for feeding' he saw no reason why he should not try. He placed little credence in the medical certificate 'because it was written by a lady doctor [his emphasis] who is not now able to judge whether forcible feeding will do any harm'.

Leah Leneman, The Women's Suffrage Movement in Scotland (*1981*, revised *1998*)

Lord Rosebery and His Guests

His moods were always varied and frequently disconcerting throughout his life and became increasingly perplexing as he grew older. He was known to ignore guests almost entirely, and his secretary vividly recalls one weekend party at Dalmeny who only saw their host once – when he had to go into the library to get a paper-knife. Conversation stopped at once, and the male guests rose from their chairs; Rosebery walked to his desk, got his paper-knife, and withdrew. Some visitors to his houses noticed that in spite of the splendour, in each room there was only one chair which could be called comfortable, and which was exclusively reserved for Rosebery.

Robert Rhodes James, Rosebery (*1963*)

Andrew Bonar Law's Speech Technique

He never made the same speech twice, but on analysis nearly every speech he made was the same speech. He had his thoughts in little blocks, like a child's box of bricks. On a speaking campaign the blocks would be laid in one order, say A.B.C.D.E.F., and so on, for the first speech, and in quite a different order for the next and succeeding speeches, say X.B.C.L.M. for the second, A.Y.J.P.Q. for the third and so on. Slight changes of introductory phrase, the introduction of local allusions, the new juxtaposition of topics made each speech to those who accompanied him seem a new speech, but with a haunting air of familiarity about it. He was able to speak without notes, though he borrowed from Lord Randolph Churchill the trick of searching his pockets for a written note of an important set of figures, or a specially important quotation, which he then discarded. When the note was retrieved by some admirer it was found to be blank paper.

Collin Brooks, More Tavern Talk (*1952*)

John McLean – Orator

Not long before his last arrest I heard him speaking in Cathedral Square. Again, needless to say, it was raining. I had a chat with him while he waited for the crowd to gather. He had a beautiful voice and a most modest and sincere courtesy. He knew that sooner or later he would be re-arrested and that he would not come out of jail alive. But he bravely mounted his little platform to bear his burning witness, and highly peculiar witness it was. By this time unemployment had come to Clydeside like the plague, and he asked his audience to join with him there and then in a demonstration.

They were to demand that great wooden shelters should be erected in Glasgow Green to give the unemployed cover for their heads, and that very night they were to occupy the crypt of the Cathedral to shelter from the wind and the rain.

It was sad to listen to this silver-voiced and silver-haired man spinning his fantasia. The wall of Duke Street prison was on his left, the dark mass of the Cathedral loomed behind him and on his right the gross bulk of the Royal Infirmary loomed even larger. The rain kept falling with the dreary persistence of a conversational bore. With an equally dreary persistence John McLean developed his theme of the down-trodden proletariat stretching themselves on the pavement for the night to be trodden down even more thoroughly. The audience listened with the genuine respect they always felt for John McLean, but when he called upon them to march over to the Cathedral, there were no takers. They did not fancy sleeping in a draughty crypt when they all had warm beds to go home to, and so home they went.

Colm Brogan, The Glasgow Story *(1952). John McLean (1879–1923), prominent among the 'Red Clydesiders', was appointed Consul to Great Britain by Lenin's Soviet Government, a post ignored by the British Government. In 1918 he was sentenced to jail for five years, the period later reduced to six months after widespread protest.*

James Maxton – Entertainer

He not only preached the revolution; he looked it. Once – he told me the story himself – he had been induced to go to Inverness and act as best man at a friend's wedding; he had, he said, got for the first and last time a tall hat, and he was seated gloomily hunched up in a corner of the tearoom at Buchanan Street Station with his tall hat, and his long hair, awaiting the early morning train for the north. Enter an effusive, garishly dressed gentleman, and addressed Maxton:

'Hallo, chum, waitin' on the train?'

'Yes.'

'Where are you playing?'

'Playing?'

'Yes, old man. I see you're one of us. I'm on the halls myself!'

Thomas Johnston (1881–1965), Memories *(1925). James Maxton (1885–1946) was one of the 'Red Clydeside' MPs, who conspicuously failed to turn rhetoric into action. A man of strikingly cadaverous appearance, he was described by Colm Brogan in* The Glasgow Story *thus: 'His long lank and greasy hair made him look like an Indian squaw who had lost interest in life and had decided to let everything go.' His visit to Inverness was made before he accused its inhabitants of coming to Glasgow with the hayseed in their boots and the heather sticking out of their ears (Hansard, 1934). He*

attracted stories. When jailed for agitation in 1918, he was asked by a more
conventional sort of convict what he was in for. 'Sedition', replied Maxton.
The other man looked most disapproving. 'Why didna ye marry the lassie?'
he asked.

The Right Sort of Pacifist

[Ramsay] MacDonald nervously asked Shinwell if there was an escape-route
to the rear, and quickly shied away when a burly six-footer wielding a heavy
piece of lead pipe jumped up next to him.

'Who's this?' MacDonald stammered.

'Oh, you've no need to worry about him,' replied Shinwell. 'It's only
McGovern. He's a pacifist.'

'He's the sort of pacifist I much prefer on my side,' declared MacDonald.
Peter Slowe, Manny Shinwell (1993)

Campaigning for Nationalism in Aberdeen

I went, that day, to a home where the door swung open and the tiny room
seemed filled with the gaunt figure of a man. He towered above me with a
malevolent glare as he leant over the table. The open cupboard contained
a half loaf, an opened tin of condensed milk, a small pat of margarine, and
a packet of powder sold as tea. Behind him, on the box bed, two tiny children cried among the straw that had escaped from the remnants of the
mattress, while an older one, too scared to make a sound, determinedly
tried to cover their bare limbs with bits of clothing that served in place of
blankets. The man bolted the door and flung the breadknife point downwards into the table. 'Ye're no' goin' oot o' here alive.' Normally, perhaps,
I should have been afraid, but I was too wrought up to gather any such
sensation. 'Keep that for the landlord,' I said, 'and sign for Scotland's freedom, so's we can give the bairns the same chance as the King's bairns.'

'Haud oot yer haun' flat', he commanded. While he looked at my outstretched palm I took the opportunity to study him. Starvation, the ravages
of red-biddy and rage overmasked a finely modelled face, and madness glared
from his eye. There was no fire in the grate, and he shivered.

'Ye're no' feart. Yer haun's no' shakin,' he said.

'No, I'm no feart.'

'I'd cut yer thrapple for twopence,' and he grabbed my wrists; but my
anger was still uppermost.

'If it would clear these filthy dens they dare to call houses, if it would
show the world the conditions imposed on such as you in order that men
may make money – Good God man! – cut my throat by all means; but that
would do no good, so help me instead towards the remaking of Scotland.

Come on, sign the paper, and gie's yer haun', and we'll right the wrongs of our people.'

Wendy Wood (1893–1981), I Like Life (1938). Wendy Wood, born in England, became a passionate nationalist. In 1972 she set out to fast unto death in order to compel the Government to honour its commit-ment to publish plans for a Scottish Assembly, and was dissuaded with some difficulty.

Electioneering in Orkney

I never canvassed. To ask anyone how they were going to vote would have seemed impudent to many of my constituents. Laura once approached the subject obliquely by asking a man how he thought his Papa Westray parish would vote. She got a terse and dusty answer. 'The folk in this parish will vote as they think fit. They will vote Liberal if they be of that mind.'

Jo Grimond (1913–1993), Memoirs (1979)

An Egg for Mrs Thatcher

. . . we got a tip-off from the media that Thatcher was touring the Volvo plant in Irvine, Ayrshire. She could flaunt herself all over Poland, but daren't announce she was coming to Scotland. Her visits were always kept secret. A whole bunch of us decided to combine a day trip doon the watter to Ayr-shire with an impromptu debate on the merits of the Poll Tax. Our prob-lem, as usual, was lack of funds. We were completely brassic when we got on the train. We made a class appeal to the ticket collector to let us travel for free. When he heard the nature of our mission he was only too happy to pass us by. 'Just give her all the best from me!'

We passed a market on the way to Volvo and Jack said, 'C'mon, we'll take some rotten fruit.' Someone else suggested eggs and I ended up with one in each pocket. When we got to the plant and saw the battalions of police, it was clear we'd get arrested for blowing our noses. But Jack hurled an egg and solidarity bid me follow. Unfortunately, I missed and only hit her car, but they still nabbed me. I was shoved onto the floor of the meat wagon, face down with my arms up my back. All I could think of was this other egg in my pocket. What if they frisked me and the evidence smashed? When they finally allowed me to sit up, I made a contorted effort to dispose of the thing without being seen. I hid it in the folds of a polis raincoat stuffed down the back of the seat. Fortunately it was dry when we got out and the guy left his coat behind. I wonder what happened to that hidden egg. . .

All the police in the station were really positive. They were fuming about the Poll Tax because their rates had previously been paid for them. Anyway,

Thatcher provoked a special vitriol in Scotland, even among some polis. . .
I don't think the sheriff in Kilmarnock had much time for her either. When
the egg case came to court I was refused legal aid and played at being a
lawyer by defending myself. After listening patiently to my cross examina-
tion and summing up, he said he did not wish to question the sincerity of
my case or my witnesses. But he had no alternative than to find me guilty.
He fined me £100 for aiming an egg at the Prime Minister of the day. It was
a pretty good deal.

Tommy Sheridan, with Jean McAlpine, A Time to Rage *(1994). Mrs
Margaret Thatcher's government, at the behest of her Scottish lieutenants,
had used Scotland as a 'test-bed' for its ill-fated Poll Tax in 1993.*

PORTENTS AND PROPHECIES

The Dream of King Alexander II

When King Alexander lay in Kerrera sound, he dreamed a dream and he
thought three men came to him. He thought that one wore royal apparel;
this man was very frowning, and red-faced, and stout in figure. The second
man seemed to him tall, and slender, and youthful; the fairest of men, and
nobly dressed. The third was by far the largest in figure, and the most frowning of them all. He was very bald in front. He spoke to the king, and asked
whether he intended to go plundering to the Hebrides. He thought he
answered that that was certain. The dream-man bade him turn back, and
said to him that they would not hear of anything else.

The king told his dream; and men begged him to turn back, but he would
not do that. And a little later he fell ill, and died. Then the Scots broke up
the levy, and conveyed the king's body up into Scotland. The Hebrideans
say that these men who appeared to the king in his sleep must have been St
Olaf, king of Norway; and St Magnus, earl of the Orkneys; and St Columba.

Sturla Thordarsson, Hakon's Saga, *translated by G. W. Dasent (1894).*

The Linlithgow Hermaphrodite

It is said that thair was many marvellis about this tyme, that prognosticat
the kingis death. The night befoir his deceas thair appeared ain cleir comet.
In the yeir preceiding thair was one borne, quhilk had the members of both
male and female, called in oure language ane scratch, in whom manes
nature did prevail, bot becaus his dispositioun and proportion of bodie
represented ane voman, he being in ane manes hous, in Linlithgow, and so
associating in bedding with the guidman of the hous his dochter, maid hyr
to conceive with chyld; quhilk being devulgit throw the countrie, and the

matrones understanding this damosell deceived in this manner, being offendit that this monster tratour should sett him forth as ane voman, being ane verrie man, they gatt him accused in judgment, to be brunt quick for his schamfull behaviour.

Robert Lindsay of Pitscottie (c.1532–1580), Chronicles of Scotland. *The king referred to is James II (killed by an exploding cannon, 1460).*

A Warning to King James IV Before Flodden

At this time the king came to Lithgow, where he was at the counsall verrie sad and dollorous, makand his prayers to God, to sen him ane guid success in his voyage. And there cam ane man clad in ane blew gowne, belted about him with ane roll of lining, and ane pair of brottikines on his feet, and all other things conforme thereto. But he had nothing on his head, but side hair to his shoulders and bald before. He seemed to be ane man of fifty years, and cam fast forwards, crying among the lords, and specially for the king, saying that he desired to speak with him, whill at the last he cam to the desk where the king was at his prayers. But when he saw the king he gave no due reverence nor salutation, but leaned him doun, gruflings upon the desk, and said, 'Sir King, my mother has sent me to thee, desiring thee not to go where thou art purposed, whilk if thou do, thou shall not fare weill in thy journey, nor none that is with thee. Farder, scho forbade thee not to mell nor use the counsell of woman, whilk if thou do thou wilt be confoundit and brought to shame.'

Be this man had spoke thir words to the king, the evensong was near done, and the king paused on thir words, studying to give him ane answer. But in the meantime, before the king's eyes, and in presence of the whole lordis that were about him for the time, this man evanisched away, and could be no more seen. I heard Sir David Lindsay, lyon-herald, and John Inglis, the marchell, who were at that time young men and speciall servants to the king's grace, thought to have taken this man, but they could not, that they might have speired further tidings at him, but they could not touch him. But all their uncouth novells and counsall could not stay the king from his purpose and wicked interpryse, but hasted him fast to Edinburgh to mak him ready, and to mak provision for himself and his army against the said day appointed.

Robert Lindsay of Pitscottie, Chronicles of Scotland. *Tytler in his* History of Scotland *ascribes the happening to a stratagem of James's English queen, anxious to avoid war with her native country.*

The Union of the Crowns

We are told that when King James was preparing to go and take possession of his crown of England, his subjects of Scotland came to take their leave of him, and convey him part of the way thither, with all the state and magnificence imaginable; but amongst these numerous attendants, deck'd up in their finest apparel, and mounted on their best horses, there appeared an old reverend gentleman of Fyfe, cloathed all over in the deepest mourning; and being asked why, whilst all were contending to appear most gay on such an occasion, he should be so singular? Why truly, replied he, there is none of you congratulate his Majesty's good fortune more than I do . . . but since I look upon this procession, as Scotland's funeral solemnity, I'm come to perform my last duty to my deceased and beloved country, with a heart full of grief and in dress correspondent thereto.

George Lockhart of Carnwath (1673–1731), Memoirs Concerning the Affairs of Scotland in May 1707. *Lockhart was a Jacobite and against the Union of 1707; interestingly, his* Memoir *was published in Dublin in 1799 on the eve of the similarly controversial parliamentary Union of Great Britain and Ireland.*

Capture of a Sturgeon

The 7 of August a sturgion fish was taken in the Yarr of Drumchardeny, within our paroch of Wardlaw. It was 12 foot in length, a monstruous creatur. In all my travels I never saw so big. Severall English came out from Inverness, who had not seen such another. They bought it at a very great rate, to preserve it pickled, this fish being meat and medicin; they barrelled it, and sent it to London, wher it will sell very deare. The report is that such fishes coming ashore is ominous, and presages the death of some eminent person.

James Fraser (1634–1699), Policratica Temporum *(from the Wardlaw* Manuscript*) (1905). The best example of an eminent person Fraser could provide was the second brother of the Laird of Cawdor, who accidentally shot himself some weeks later.*

Richard Cameron, The First Cameronian

On the 20th of June, 1680, in company with about twenty other persons, well-armed, he entered the little remote burgh of Sanquhar, and in a ceremonious manner proclaimed at the cross, that he and those who adhered to him renounced their allegiance to the king, on account of his having abused his government, and also declared a war against him and all who adhered to him, at the same time avowing their resolution to resist the succession of his brother the Duke of York. The bulk of the presbyterians beheld this transaction with dismay, for they knew that the government would charge it upon the party in general. The privy council immediately put a reward of five thousand merks upon Cameron's head, and three thousand upon the heads of all the rest; and parties were sent out to waylay them. The little band kept together in arms for a month, in the mountainous country, between Nithsdale and Ayrshire. But at length, on the 20th of July, when they were lying in a secure place on Airsmoss, Bruce of Earlshall approached them with a party of horse and foot much superior in numbers. Cameron, who was believed by his followers to have a gift of prophecy, is said to have that morning washed his hands with particular care, in expectation that they were immediately to become a public spectacle. His party, at sight of the enemy, gathered closely around him, and he uttered a short prayer, in which he thrice repeated the expresssion – 'Lord, spare the green, and take the ripe' – no doubt, including himself in the latter description, as conceiving himself to be among the best prepared for death. He then said to his brother, 'Come, let us fight it out to the last; for this is the day which I have longed for, and the day that I have prayed for, to die fighting against our Lord's avowed enemeies; this is the day that we will get the crown.' To all of them in the event of falling, he gave the assurance that he already saw the gate of heaven open to receive them. A brief skirmish took place, in which the insurgents were allowed even by their enemies to have behaved with great bravery; but nothing could avail against superior numbers. Mr Cameron lying among the slain, his head and hands were cut off, and carried to Edinburgh, along with the prisoners . . . It happened that the father of Cameron was at this time in prison for non-conformity. The head was shown to the old man, with the question, 'Did he know to whom it had belonged?' He seized the bloody relics with the eagerness of parental affection, and, kissing them fervently, exclaimed, 'I know, I know them; they are my son's, my own dear son's; it is the Lord; good is the will of the Lord, who cannot wrong me or mine, but has made goodness and mercy to follow us all our days.' The head and hands were then fixed upon the Netherbow Port, the fingers pointing upwards, in mockery of the attitude of prayer. The headless trunk was buried with the rest of the slain in Airsmoss, where a plain monument was in better times raised over them.

  Robert Chambers, Scottish Biographical Dictionary. *Richard Cameron (c.1648–1680) was a leader of the extreme Covenanting party.*

The Prophet Peden

Alexander Peden, the celebrated Covenanter, enjoyed the reputation of being gifted as a prophet. The ascription of supernatural powers to those eminent for their sagacity and piety was not uncommon in ancient Scotland. The prophecies assigned to Peden are generally unimportant, or such as a shrewd person might readily vaticinate without supernatural assistance. One of his prophecies was sufficiently remarkable. Discoursing to his people from Amos vii. 8, he used these words – 'I'll tell you good news. Our Lord will take a feather out of Antichrist's wing which shall bring down the Duke of York, and banish him out of these kingdoms. And there shall never a man of the House of Stuart sit upon the throne of Britain after the Duke of York, whose reign is now short.' Peden died in 1686, two years before the dethronement of James VII, and the event of the Revolution.

C. Rogers, Traits of Scottish People *(1867). In* The Scottish Covenanters *James Barr records Peden's remarks to Isabel Weir when she married John Brown in 1685: 'Isabel, you have got a good man, but you will not enjoy him long. Prize his company and keep linen by you to be his winding-sheet, for you will have need of it when you are not looking for it, and it will be a bloody one.' Brown was shot by Claverhouse's men on 1 May 1688. Peden died a natural death, but his newly buried body was exhumed and strung up on a gibbet by government dragoons. His reputation lived on and fathered a minor industry; in his* Autobiography *the Rev. Alexander Carlyle (1722– 1805) noted that in 1744, 'we were alarmed with the howling and weeping of half-a-dozen of women in the kitchen, which was so loud and lasting that I went to see what was the matter, when, after some times, I learned from the calmest among them that a pedlar had left a copy of Peden's* Prophecies *that morning, which having read part of, they found that he had predicted woes of every kind to the people of Scotland; and in particular that Clyde would run with blood in the year 1744, which now being some months advanced, they believed that their destruction was at hand'.*

The Mermaid of Loch Slin

Loch-Slin is a dark sluggish sheet of water, bordered at every side by thick tangled hedges of reeds and rushes; nor has the surrounding scenery much to recommend it . . . its appearance at this time in the quiet of the Sabbath morning, was one of extreme seclusion. The tall old castle of Loch-Slin, broken and weather-worn, and pregnant with associations of the remote past, stood up over it like some necromancer beside his mirror; and the maiden, as she tripped homewards along the little blind pathway that went winding along the quiet shore – now in a hollow, anon on a height – could see the red image of the ruins heightened by the flush of the newly-risen sun, reflected on the calm surface that still lay dark and grey under the shadow of the eastern bank. All was still as death, when her ear suddenly caught at a low indistinct sound as of a continuous knocking, which heightened as she went, until it was at last echoed back from the old walls, and which, had she heard it on a week morning, she would have at once set down as the knocking of clothes at a washing. But who, she thought, can be 'knocking claes' on the Sabbath? She turned a projecting angle of the bank, and saw, not ten yards away, what seemed to be a tall female standing in the water immediately beyond the line of flags and rushes which fringed the shore, engaged apparently in knocking clothes on a stone, with the sort of bludgeon still used in parts of the north country for the purpose. The maiden hurried past, convinced that the creature before her could be none other than the mermaid of Loch-Slin; but in the midst of her terror she was self-possessed enough to remark that the beautiful goblin seemed to ply its work with a malignant pleasure, and that on a grass plot directly opposite where it stood, there were spread out as if to dry, more than thirty smocks and shirts, all horribly dabbled with blood.

Hugh Miller (1802–1856), Scenes and Legends of the North of Scotland. *This observation, by a country girl in 1742, was said to have occurred on the day the roof of the nearby Fearn Abbey church collapsed, killing many of the congregation.*

The Woman of Revelation

The Buchanites . . . possessed considerable property, which all enjoyed alike, and though several men were accompanied by their wives, all the responsibilities of the married state were given up. Some of them wrought gratuitously at their trades, for the benefit of those who employed them . . . they scrupulously abjured all worldly considerations whatsoever, wishing only to lead a quiet and holy life, till the commencement of the Millennium, or the day of judgement, which they believed to be at hand. Observing, they said, how the young ravens are fed, and how the lilies grow, we assure ourselves that God will feed and clothe us. Mrs Buchan, who was said to have given herself out to be the Virgin Mary, at first denied that she was so. Instead of being the mother of Christ, she said, after the flesh, she was his daughter after the spirit. The little republic existed for some time, without anything occurring to mar their happiness, except the occasional rudeness of unbelieving neighbours. At length, as hope sickened, worldly feelings seem to have returned upon some of the members; and, notwithstanding all the efforts which Mrs Buchan could make to keep her flock together, a few returned to Irvine. It would seem that as the faith of her followers declined, she greatly increased the extravagance of her pretensions, and the rigour of her discipline. It was said that when any person was suspected of an intention to leave the society, she ordered him to be locked up, and ducked every day in cold water, so that it required some little address in any one to get out of her clutches. In the year 1786, the following facts were reported by some of the seceding members on their return to the west.

> The distribution of provisions she kept in her own hand, and took special care that they should not pamper their bodies with too much food, and every one behoved to be entirely directed by her. The society once being scarce of money, she told them she

had a revelation, informing her they should have a supply of cash from heaven: accordingly, she took one of the members out with her, and caused him to hold two corners of a sheet, while she held the other two. Having continued for a considerable time, without any shower of money falling upon it, the man at last tired, and left Mrs Buchan to hold the sheet herself. Mrs Buchan, in a short time after, came in with £5 sterling, and upbraided the man for his unbelief, which she said was the only cause that prevented it from coming sooner. Many of the members, however, easily accounted for this pretended miracle, and shrewdly suspected that the money came from her own hoard. That she had a considerable purse was not to be doubted, for she fell on many ways to rob the members of every thing they had of value. Among other things, she informed them one evening, that they were all to ascend to heaven next morning; therefore it was only necessary that they should lay aside all their vanities and ornaments . . . Next morning she took out all the people to take their flight. After they had waited till they were tired, not one of them found themselves any lighter than they were the day before, but remained with as firm a footing on earth as ever. She again blamed their unbelief – said that want of faith alone prevented their ascension; and complained of the hardship she was under, on account of their unbelief, to continue with them in this world. She at last fell on an expedient to make them light enough to ascend: nothing less was found requisite than to fast for forty days and forty nights. The experiment was immediately put in practice, and several found themselves at death's door in a very short time. She was then obliged to allow them some spirits and water; but many resolved to submit no longer to such regimen, and went off altogether. 'We know not', thus concludes the statement, 'if the forty days be ended; but a few experiments of this kind will leave her, in the end, sole proprietor of the society's funds'.

. . . After her death . . . it was a long time before her votaries would straighten or dress the corpse; nor would they coffin her, until obliged by the smell; and after that they would not bury her, but built up the coffin in a corner of the barn, always expecting that she would rise again from the dead, according to her promise. At last the neighbouring country people, shocked with these proceedings, went to a justice of peace, and got an order that she should be buried; so that the famous Mrs Buchan was at length reduced to a level with all the dead generations of her kind.

Robert Chambers, Scottish Biographical Dictionary. Elspeth Buchan lived from 1738–1791.

Second Sight – The Priest's Tale

Father McCrimmon and I had been out rabbit-shooting, and, tired of the sport, we sat down to rest on a grassy knoll. The ghostly island stories had taken possession of my mind, and as we sat and smoked I inquired if the priest was a believer in ghosts generally, and in the second sight in particular. The gaunt, solemn-voiced, melancholy-eyed man replied, that he believed in the existence of ghosts just as he believed in the existence of America – he had never seen America, he had never seen a ghost, but the existence of both he considered was amply borne out by testimony.

'I know there is such a thing as the second sight,' he went on, 'because I have had cognisance of it myself. Six or seven years ago, I was staying with my friend Mr McIan, as I am staying now, and just as we were sipping a tumbler of punch after dinner, we heard a great uproar outside. We went out, and found all the farm-servants standing on the grass and gazing sea-wards. On inquiry, we learned that two brothers, McMillan by name, who lived down at Stonefield, beyond the point yonder, fishermen by trade, and well-versed in the management of a boat, had come up to the islands here to gather razor-fish for bait. When they had secured plenty of bait, they steered for home, although a stiff breeze was blowing. They kept a full sail on, and went straight on the wind. A small boy, Hector, who was employed in herd-ing cows, was watching the boat trying to double the point. All at once he came running into the kitchen where the farm-servants were at dinner. "Men, men," he cried, "come out fast; McMillan's boat is sinking – I saw her heel over." Of course the hinds came rushing out bareheaded, and it was the noise they made that disturbed my friend and I at our punch. All this we gathered in less time than I have taken to tell you. We looked narrowly seaward, but no boat was to be seen. Mr McIan brought out his telescope, and still the sea remained perfectly blue and bare. Neither McIan nor his servants could be brought to believe Hector's story . . . Hector, still persist-ing that he had seen the boat capsize and go down, got his ears soundly boxed for his obstinacy, and was sent whimpering away to his cows, and enjoined in future to mind his own business. . .

'But, although Hector got his ears boxed, it turned out that he had in all probability spoken the truth. Towards the evening of next day the McMillan sisters came up to the house to inquire after the boat, which had never reached home. The poor girls were in a dreadful state when they were told that their brothers' boat had left the islands the previous afternoon, and what Hector the cow-herd averred he had seen. . .

'Days passed, and the boat never came home, nor did the brothers. It was on Friday that the McMillans sailed away on the fresh breeze, and on the Wednesday following the bay down there was a sorry sight. The missing sailors were brave, good-looking, merry-hearted, and were liked along the whole coast; and on the Wednesday I speak of no fewer than two hundred and fifty boats were sailing slowly up and down, crossing and re-crossing, trawling for the bodies. I remember the day perfectly. It was dull sand sultry, with but little sunshine; the hills over there (Blaavin and the others) were standing dimly in a smoke of heat; and on the smooth, pallid sea the mournful multitude of black boats were moving slowly up and down, across and back again. In each boat two men pulled, and the third sat in the stern with the trawling-irons. The day was perfectly still, and I could hear through the heated air the solemn pulses of the oars. The bay was black with the slowly crawling boats. A sorry sight', said the good priest, filling his second pipe from a tobacco pouch made of otter's skin.

'I don't know how it was,' went on the Father, holding his newly filled pipe between forefinger and thumb, 'but looking on the black dots of boats, and hearing the sound of their oars, I remembered that old Mirren, who lived in one of the turf huts yonder, had the second sight; and so I thought I would go down and see her. When I got to the hut, I met Mirren coming up from the shore with a basket of whelks, which she had been gathering for dinner. I went into the hut along with her and sat down. "There's a sad business in the bay today," said I. "A sad business," said Mirren as she laid down her basket. "Will they get the bodies?" Mirren shook her head. "The bodies are not there to get; they have floated out past Rum to the main ocean." "How do you know?" "Going out to the shore about a month ago I heard a scream, and, looking up, saw a boat off the point with two men in it, caught in a squall, and going down. When the boat sank the men still remained in it – the one entangled in the fishing net, the other in the ropes of the sails. I saw them float out to the main sea between the two wines" – that's a literal translation', said the Father, parenthetically . . . 'Mirren told me that she saw the bodies float out to sea between the two wines, and that the trawling boats might trawl for ever in the bay before they would get what they wanted. When evening came the boats returned home without having found the bodies of the drowned McMillans. Well,' – and here the Father lighted his pipe – 'six weeks after, a capsized boat was thrown on the shore in Uist, with two corpses inside – one entangled in the fishing-net, the other in the ropes of the sails. It was the McMillans' boat, and it was the two brothers who were inside. Their faces were all eaten away by the dog-fishes, but the people who had done business with them in Uist recognised them by their clothes. This I know to be true,' said the Father emphatically, and shutting the door on all argument or hint of scepticism. 'And now, if you are not too tired, suppose we try our luck on the copses down there? 'Twas a famous place for rabbits when I was here last year.'

Alexander Smith (1830–1867), Summer in Skye. 'Between the two wines' was acknowledged by Smith as a mistranslation of the Gaelic eadar dha lionn, 'between two fluids', referring to the bodies suspended beneath the surface of the sea.

Second Sight – The Poet's Tale

The houses in the village were scattered at intervals along a road stretching towards the sea but ending in a blind alley some way short of it. One winter towards the end of the great War, John was returning home from a ceilidh at two in the morning, walking in the direction of the sea, when he saw a great glow of light coming down the road towards him at the rate of about forty miles an hour. In the middle of the glow was a man without a head and with only one arm, moving effortlessly forward as if he were skating. When he came level with the Hopper's house he turned sharp at right angles and shot through the gates like an arrow.

John was so terrified that he dared not go past the Hopper's house, so he took a long detour through the bogs to reach his own house, which was fifty yards further down the road. When he got inside the door he fainted, as was recorded next morning by his family. Next day, which was a Wednesday, John's adventure was the talk of the village.

During the night following a Norwegian boat with a cargo of combustible chemicals ran on the rocks beyond the village and was blown to pieces. On Thursday morning all the villagers went out to look for the bodies but none could be found till John and another man came across one in a crevice in the rocks. It was headless and had only one arm. 'That', said John, 'is the man I saw in the night.'

It was the only body found. As the war was on, timber was scarce for coffins, so they buried him in a large wooden box which they found in the Hopper's outhouse. That was why he had gone in at the Hopper's gate. He was looking for his own coffin.

Louis MacNeice (1907–1963), I Crossed the Minch (*1938*)

SCHOOLS AND SCHOOLMASTERS

Barring-Out

The most famous case of a barring-out, through its fatal result, was a sixteenth-century one at the High School of Edinburgh. Some years earlier there had been an insurrection of the kind, its cause not stated, but as it happened in August, it was probably provoked by some denial of 'play', a term preferred by Presbyterians to 'holy days'. That time the rebels were overcome and punished, all they got for their pains being the offer of a scrimp week in May. In September, 1595, they again had to complain of stinted holidays and claimed their 'privilege' by a march to the council chamber. The magistrates' refusal of their petition provoked a scholastic strike in the usual form. Some ardent spirits armed themselves with swords, halberds and pistols; even armour is mentioned among the equipment of these young fire-eaters, who garrisoned the school, laying in provisions for a siege. The master had to appeal to the municipal authorities for aid; then the ministers, we are told, advised starving the rebels out; but the magistrates had no patience with a mob of 'bairns'. What force made the police of that period came to the attack under Bailie MacMoran, a leading citizen, whose house, now restored as a University Settlement, is one of the relics of Old Edinburgh. The scholars refusing to surrender, he set his *posse comitatus* to force open the door; but before a breach had been made in their defences one of the ringleaders, William Sinclair, firing out of a window, killed the doughty magistrate with a pistol shot through his head.

This tragedy drove the horror-struck boys into submission; and a number of them were carried off to the Tolbooth, Sinclair having been arraigned forthwith, and he might have been hanged off-hand by the law of the red hand. But the dispensers of justice had to think twice before venturing on a feud with a powerful clan, who threatened revenge against the citizens of Edinburgh for their young kinsman's blood. Lord Sinclair, their chief, got King James to interfere; and though several of the boys were brought to some sort of trial, whatever the verdict they presently went free, the only explanation being that they were 'gentlemen's bairns', a quality to cover a multitude of sins in these good old times.

A. R. Hope-Moncrieff, A Book About Schools (*1923*)

A Native Son of Elgin

About 1750, when Elgin vegetated in its quiet, local solitude, there was little communication with the outside world, and little trade, beyond supplying the neighbouring lairds and farmers with the commodities they required. The ruins of the cathedral lay where they had fallen. The considerable space about them, appropriated as the burying-ground of the parish, was without enclosure, and at night the superstitious inhabitants avoided the precincts, under the conviction that it was haunted.

A poor maniac woman called Gilzean, a soldier's widow, who after suffering many troubles abroad returned to Elgin with her child, made the cathedral her resting-place, and excited the awe of the inhabitants by her wanderings and incoherent ravings in the solitudes of the night. The font in the cathedral was the baby's cradle, and she seems to have appropriated the chapter-house as her home. She wandered about the town in the daytime getting food from the charitable, and ultimately they procured her a home in the town.

The child grew up an idle, wayward lad. In the parish schools of Scotland, however, with the consent of the master, children whose parents were unable to pay their fees got their education gratis. The lad being sharp and intelligent acquired considerable instruction in this manner. When he came to man's estate he enlisted as a soldier, and was soon carried off to the wars. The maniac died, and both she and her son were long forgotten.

Some fifty years had passed away, when a carriage drove up to the door of the Gordon Arms hotel, from which alighted an elderly gentleman of active, military bearing. He remained for two or three days in Elgin, gave his name as General Anderson, put himself in communication with the Provost and other officials of the place, called on various old people, visited the old haunts of the town, and wandered up and down on the banks of the Lossie.

Nothing more was heard of him until 1826–27 when a letter reached the magistrates of Elgin intimating that General Anderson had died, and had by a will, dated November 22, 1815, bequeathed the whole of his means and estate, after the payment of certain annuities, to the sheriffs and magistrates and the clergy of the established church in Elgin as trusteees, for the purpose of building and endowing an hospital and schools, to be called the Elgin Institution. . .

The generous donor was the maniac's son, who had gone to the East Indies as a soldier, and by his bravery and admirable conduct had raised himself to the distinguished rank of General in the army, and had accumulated this fortune – £16,000 being prize-money from the siege of Seringapatam.

Joseph Mitchell (1803–1883), Reminiscences of My Life in the Highlands

Young Henry Brougham is Vindicated

Henry Brougham, when at the High School in Edinburgh, made 'his first public explosion', as Lord Cockburn calls it. 'He dared to differ from Luke Fraser, a hot but good-natured old fellow, on some bit of latinity. The master, like other men in power, maintained his own infallibility, punished the rebel, and flattered himself that the affair was over. But Brougham reappeared next day, loaded with books, returned to the charge before the whole class, and compelled honest Luke to admit that he had been wrong. This made Brougham famous throughout the whole school.' 'I remember', adds Cockburn, 'as well as if it had been yesterday, having had him pointed out to me as "the fellow that beat the master".'

John Timbs, A Century of Anecdote (1864). Brougham (1778–1868) went on to become Lord Chancellor, and the subject of many anecdotes (see Theatricals). He invented the carriage named after him, of which Sydney Smith, seeing it go by with Brougham's monogram on the door, said: 'There goes a carriage with a "B" on the outside and a wasp within it.'

The School Cock-Fight

The school, like almost all the other grammar-schools of the period in Scotland, had its yearly cock-fight, preceded by two holidays and a half, during which the boys occupied themselves in collecting and bringing up their cocks. And such always was the array of fighting birds mustered on the occasion, that the day of the festival, from morning till night, used to be spent in fighting out the battle. For weeks after it had passed, the school-floor would continue to retain its deeply-stained blotches of blood, and the boys would be full of exciting narratives regarding the glories of gallant birds, who had continued to fight until both their eyes had been picked out, or who, in the moment of victory, had dropped dead in the middle of the cock-pit. The yearly fight was the relic of a barbarous age; and, in at least one of its provisions, there seemed evidence that it was that of an intolerant age also: every pupil at school, without exemption, had his name entered on the sub-scription list, as a cock-fighter, and was obliged to pay the master at the rate of twopence per head, ostensibly for leave to bring his birds to the pit; but, amid the growing humanities of a better time, though the twopences con-tinued to be exacted, it was no longer imperative to bring the birds; and availing myself of the liberty, I never brought any.

Hugh Miller (1802–1855), My Schools and Schoolmasters. The school was in Cromarty, around 1812. The perquisite not only of the fees, but of the dead fighting-cocks for their table, encouraged the ill-paid schoolmas-ters throughout the country to maintain this Shrove Tuesday ritual, doubt-less encouraged by the majority of their pupils.

In the Rector's Study

Every now and then the Rector sends for me to come to his study.

Oooh Anne Gillies you're for it. I ham up extreme terror for their ben-efit, and then I go along to the study to learn another Gaelic song. They just come back to him without warning when he's in the middle of something else, and he has to pass them on to me quickly before he forgets about them again. He only has to sing a few verses through and I've got them. Then he writes out the words for me, and I jot down the first note or two in sol-fa at the top of the page to remind myself how they start. Once you get started the rest comes back no bother. He has given me some songs nobody outside his own family in Raasay knows, in addition to some from other islands he's heard from his brother Calum the collector. Also he writes Gaelic verse himself – translations from Pindar and *The Aeneid*. He composes them in the morning while he's shaving himself in the mirror and when he gets to school he wants to hear how they will sound to the tune of waulking songs. He's not much of a singer himself mind you. Sometimes I have to guess what he means. Sometimes I have to be careful not to laugh, but sometimes it's impossible.

'Ah, Anne, isn't it an aawfully funny thing, Gaelic singing,' he says. 'It strikes straight at the emotions. It was George Campbell Hay that explained it. Strikes straight at the emotions, he said. Laughing and crying – such a narrow margin between them. Aawfully funny things the human emotions.'

Yes sir, I croak, tears streaming down my face. I love him so much. He is the most exasperating man I've ever met.

Anne Lorne Gillies, Song of Myself (1991). *The Rector of Oban High School at the time was John Maclean, translator of* The Odyssey *into Gaelic.*

The Gaelic Teacher's Kilt

The Gaelic teacher wears a kilt all the time. They say that one day he went to an education meeting wearing a suit and this wifie came up to him in front of all the other teachers and said, 'Why, Mr Thompson, this is the first time I've seen you with your trousers on.'

Anne Lorne Gillies, Song of Myself

SCIENTISTS AND ENGINEERS

Putting Scotland on the Map

There were at this time (1608) only three maps of Scotland in existence, all of them so rude and inaccurate as to be wholly useless. The infidelity of these sketches had long been known, and was the subject of great and universal complaint. Urged on by this, and by the general dissatisfaction, Mr Gordon employed himself in making geographical surveys by actual mensuration; a labour which none of his predecessors had ever subjected themselves to. . . In 1641, King Charles was applied to by the celebrated map and atlas publishers, the Blaeus of Amsterdam, for his patronage of an atlas of Scotland, which they were then contemplating, and requesting his majesty to appoint some qualified persons to assist them with information for the intended work; and in especial, to arrange and amend certain geographic sketches of one Timothy Pont, of which they had previously been put in possession, but in a confused and mutilated state. This task, King Charles . . . devolved upon Mr Gordon.

. . . The work consists of 46 maps, general and particular, with ample descriptions and detached treatises on the antiquities of Scotland. Of such importance was this undertaking considered, that, wild and disordered as the times were, Mr Gordon was during its progress made a special object of the care and protection of the legislature. An act of parliament was passed exempting him from all new taxations, and relieving him from the quartering of soldiers. To carry this law into effect, orders were issued from time to time by the various commanders of the forces in North Britain, discharging all officers and soldiers, as well horse as foot, from troubling or molesting,

or quartering on Mr Robert Gordon of Straloch, his house, lands, or tenants, and from levying any public duty on the said Mr Robert Gordon, or
on any of his possessions.

Robert Chambers, Scottish Biographical Dictionary. *Robert Gordon of
Straloch (1580–1661) was a pioneering geographer. Timothy Pont (c.1560–
1630), son of an Edinburgh minister, was the first projector of an atlas of
Scotland. With the aid and encouragement of Sir John Scot of Scotstarvit,
the atlas was first published in 1648.*

Mr Gregory's Barometer

The peculiarity of Mr Gregory's pursuits caused him to be noted throughout the whole country, and he being the first person in Scotland who possessed a barometer, from which he derived an extensive knowledge of the
weather, it was universally believed that he held intercourse with the beings
of another world. So extensive had this belief been circulated, that a deputation from the presbytery waited on him, and it was only one fortunate
circumstance that prevented him from undergoing a formal trial for witchcraft. He had from choice obtained an extensive knowledge of the healing
art, his opinion was held in the highest estimation, and as he practised in all
cases without fee, he was of great use in the district where he lived.

Robert Chambers, Scottish Biographical Dictionary. *David Gregory
(1661–1701), of a notable Aberdeen scientific family who were also kinsmen of Rob Roy MacGregor, became Professor of Astronomy at Oxford.
H. Grey Graham, in* Scottish Men of Letters in the Eighteenth Century *(1908)
makes the subject of this story Lewis Reid, minister of Strichen (and father
of Thomas Reid the philosopher). He was given the barometer by Gregory,
who was his brother-in-law.*

The Stirling Pint

In the year 1750, having occasion to visit Stirling, and knowing that by an
act of the Scottish parliament, this borough had the keeping of the Pint Jug,
the standard, by special statute, for weight and for liquid and dry measure
in Scotland, he requested a sight of it from the magistrates. Having been
referred to the council house, a pewter pint jug which had been kept suspended from the roof of the apartment, was taken down and given to him;
after minutely examining it, he was convinced that it could not be the standard. The discovery was in vain communicated to the magistrates, who were
ill able to appreciate their loss . . . resolved, if possible to recover this valuable antique, he immediately instituted a search; which, though conducted
with much patient industry during part of this and the following year, proved
unavailing. In the spring of 1752, it occurred to him, that this standard

might have been borrowed by some of the braziers or coppersmiths, for the purpose of making legal measures for the citizens; and having learned that a person of this description, called Urquhart, had joined the rebel forces in 1745, that his furniture and shop utensils had been brought to public sale on his not returning; and that various articles which had not been sold, were thrown into a garret as useless, he obtained permission to inspect them; and to his great satisfaction, discovered, under a mass of lumber, the precious object of his long research. Thus was recovered the only legal standard of weight and measure in Scotland; after it had been offered, in ignorance, for public sale, and thrown aside unsold as trash, and long after it had been considered by its constitutional guardians as irretrievably lost.

Robert Chambers, Scottish Biographical Dictionary. *The persevering researcher was the Rev. Alexander Bryce (1713–1786), minister of Kirknewton and a practical scientist and engineer of great accomplishment.*

James Watt, Inventor

When Watt went to reside at Soho, Birmingham counted among the inhabitants of its vicinity several men of celebrity, among whom were Priestley, Darwin, Withering, and the father of Maria Edgeworth. These and other learned men, with Watt and Boulton, met once a month, on the evening of full moon, a time chosen in order that the members might see their way home; and on that account their association was called the Lunar Society.

Each sitting of the Lunar Society was for Watt an opportunity for showing the fecundity of invention with which nature had endowed him. One day Darwin said to his companions, 'I have imagined a double pen – a pen with two beaks, by the aid of which we may write everything in duplicate.' Watt replied, 'I hope to find a better solution of the problem.' Next day the copying machine was invented. It has since received various modifications, but its present form as used in counting houses is described and drawn in Watt's patent of 1780.

W. Anderson, Scottish Nation (1863). *The Darwin mentioned is Erasmus, grandfather of Charles Darwin.*

William Murdock's Wooden Hat

He had heard a great deal about the inventions of James Watt; and he determined to try whether he could not get 'a job' at the famous manufactory at Soho. . . When William arrived at Soho in 1777 he called at the works to ask for employment. Watt was then in Cornwall, looking after his pumping engines; but he saw Boulton, who was usually accessible to callers of every rank. In answer to Murdock's enquiry whether he could have a job, Boulton replied that work was very slack with them, and that every place was filled up. During the brief conversation that took place, the blate young Scotchman, like most country lads in the presence of strangers, had some difficulty in knowing what to do with his hands, and unconsciously kept twirling his hat with them. Boulton's attention was attracted to the twirling hat, which seemed to be of a peculiar make. It was not a felt hat, nor a cloth hat, nor a glazed hat: but it seemed to be painted, and composed of some unusual material. 'That seems to be a curious sort of hat,' said Boulton, looking at it more closely; 'what is it made of?'

'Timmer, sir,' said Murdock, modestly.

'Timmer? Do you mean to say that it is made of wood?'

'Deed it is, sir.'

'And pray how was it made?'

'I made it mysel, sir, in a bit laithey of my own contrivin'.'

'Indeed!'

Boulton looked at the young man again. He had risen a hundred degrees in his estimation. William was a good-looking fellow – tall, strong and handsome – with an open intelligent countenance. Besides, he had been able to turn a hat for himself on a lathe of his own construction. This, of itself, was a sufficient proof that he was a mechanic of no mean skill. 'Well!' said Boulton at last, 'I will enquire at the works, and see if there is anything we can set you to. Call again, my man.'

'Thank you, sir,' said Murdock, giving a final twirl to his hat.

Samuel Smiles (1812–1904), Men of Invention and Industry (1884). William Murdoch (1754–1839), who anglicised his name to Murdock, born near Auchinleck in Ayrshire, was the inventor of the process of using coal gas for lighting. Matthew Boulton (1728–1809), an Englishman, was Watt's partner at the Soho works in Birmingham.

Why the Hydrometer Was Invented

In 1787 bleaching with the new element chlorine was carried out commercially in Aberdeen. A new constellation of enquirers glittered in the Scottish and English skies – Watt, Boulton, Roebuck, Wedgwood, Macintosh, Gordon, Cochrane. To make a violet dye, Gordon got lichens from the West Highlands and sent people to collect human urine. As they went round the houses they found that greedy suppliers were offering a watered-down product and it was to circumvent them that the hydrometer was invented. The urine collectors carried pocket hydrometers.

R. F. Mackenzie, The Search For Scotland (1989). For generations before, rural householders had kept a urine tub at the door, to use in the fulling of cloth. The new scientific processes were closely guarded: Charles Macintosh (1776–1843), inventor of rubberised waterproofing, imported monoglot Gaelic speakers to work in his new Glasgow factory, to foil industrial espionage.

The Imperceptible Bridge

The bridge of Musselburgh is on a smaller scale, but equally perfect in its construction. A remarkable testimony to its merits was paid in Mr Rennie's presence by an untutored son of nature. He was taking the work off the contractor's hands, when a magistrate of the town, who was present, asked a countryman who was passing at the time with his cart, how he liked the new bridge.

'Brig,' answered the man. 'It's nae brig ava: ye neither ken when ye're on't, or when ye're aff't.'

Robert Chambers, Scottish Biographical Dictionary. *Sir John Rennie (1761–1821), who designed bridges at Musselburgh, Kelso and many other places, including the old Waterloo Bridge in London, was one of the most eminent civil engineers of his time.*

The Rivalry Between Rennie and Telford

Although they were fellow-countrymen and although later in life we find their names occasionally coupled, there is little evidence of any personal collaboration between the two most eminent engineers of their day and they were certainly not friends. A curious letter written by Telford from Chester in April 1805 to James Watt at his home in Heathfield helps to explain the reason for this. Watt had evidently sent Telford news of the death of Rennie's wife and Telford replies:

'I am truly sorry to find that Mr Rennie has suffered so serious and distressing a loss and I am only sorry to inform you that his conduct prevents me from benefiting by his acquaintance. Altho' I never had any connection with him in business or ever intentionally did anything to injure or interfere with him, I, in every quarter, hear of his treating my character with a degree of illiberality not very becoming. This is so marked a part of his conduct that I really believe it does him a serious injury and proves serviceable to me.'

L. T. C. Rolt, Thomas Telford *(1958). Telford (1757–1834), constructor of the Caledonian Canal and many roads, bridges and harbours, founded the Institution of Civil Engineers. The elder Sir John Rennie, another 'self-made' man, had risen to eminence earlier and may have been professionally jealous. His sons did not join the Institute until after Telford's death and when the younger Sir John Rennie became its President, Rolt notes that he took the opportunity in his address to 'subtly disparage Telford and his work'.*

J. B. Neilson and the Hot Blast

He proceeded to make a series of experiments at the Gas-works, trying the effect of heated air on the illuminating power of gas, by bringing up a stream of it in a tube so as to surround the gas-burner. He found that by this means the combustion of the gas was rendered more intense, and its illuminating power greatly increased. He proceeded to try a similar experiment on a common smith's fire, by blowing the fire with heated air, and the effect was the same; the fire was much more brilliant, and accompanied by an unusually intense degree of heat.

Having obtained such marked results by these small experiments, it naturally occurred to him that a similar increase in intensity of combustion and temperature would attend the application of the process to the blast-furnace on a large scale; but being only a gas maker, he had the greatest difficulty in persuading any ironmaster to permit him to make the necessary experiments with blast-furnaces actually at work. Besides, his theory was altogether at variance with the established practice, which was to supply air as cold as possible, the prevailing idea being that the coldness of the air in winter was the cause of the best iron being then produced. Acting on these views, the efforts of the ironmasters had always been directed to the cooling of the blast, and various expedients were devised for the purpose. Thus the regulator was painted white, as being the coolest colour; the air was passed over cold water, and in some cases the air pipes were even surrounded by ice, all with the object of keeping the blast cold. When, therefore, Mr Neilson proposed entirely to reverse the process, and to employ hot blast instead of cold blast, the incredulity of the ironmasters may well be imagined. What! Neilson, a mere maker of gas, undertake to instruct practical men in the manufacture of iron!

Samuel Smiles (1812–1904), Industrial Biography (1863). It took several years before James Beaumont Neilson (1792–1865) was able to fully demonstrate his idea at the Clyde Iron Works. The new process had an immediate and dramatic influence on the development of the Scottish steel industry and the Scottish economy. But Neilson had wanted in his youth to be a preacher, following the example of the Haldane brothers, who traversed the countryside giving open-air sermons. His father refused to hear of his son 'preaching at the back o' dikes', and James dutifully settled down to a mechanical career with the Glasgow Gas-works.

Kirkpatrick Macmillan's Bicycle Ride

Kirkpatrick Macmillan, a blacksmith who lived at Courthill in Dumfriesshire, is believed to have built the first pedal-driven bicycle, in 1839. According to legend, a customer brought in a 'Swiftwalker' or hobby-horse, for repair, and Macmillan, intrigued by the machine, made a copy of the machine for himself, adding to it treadles, rods and cranks of his own invention to drive the rear wheel. No version of his machine has been preserved, but it is recorded that in 1842 Macmillan rode upon his bicycle from his home to Glasgow, a round trip of 140 miles. In the city his arrival caused a stir, and he accidentally knocked down a small boy. Arrested for causing a public nuisance, he was fined five shillings, although the magistrate is said to have paid the fine for him. On his homeward route, Macmillan placed a bet with the coachman of the Glasgow–Carlisle coach that he would beat the coach to Sanquhar. Macmillan did so, thus winning the first bicycle race ever held. He does not seem otherwise to have profited from his invention.

A photograph in the Transport Museum in Glasgow shows a man believed to be Macmillan, perched not on a bicycle but a tricycle, with double front wheels; the museum also has a restored treadle-drive bicycle made by a local blacksmith for Gavin Dalzell, a tea merchant of Lesmahagow, in 1849.

James Clerk Maxwell's Laboratory

I have regularly set up shop now above the wash-house at the gate, in a garret. I have an old door set on two barrels, and two chairs, of which one is safe, and a skylight above, which will slide up and down.

On the door (or table) there is a lot of bowls, jugs, plates, jam pigs, etc., containing water, salt, soda, sulphuric acid, blue vitriol, plumbago ore; also broken glass, iron, and copper wire, copper and zinc plate, bees' wax, sealing wax, clay, rosin, charcoal, a lens, a Smee's galvanic apparatus, and a countless variety of little beetles, spiders, and wood lice, which fall into the different liquids and poison themselves. I intend to get up some more galvanism in jam pigs; but I must first copper the interiors of the pigs, so I am experimenting on the best methods of electrotyping. So I am making copper seals with the device of a beetle. First I thought a beetle was a good conductor, so I embedded one in wax (not at all cruel, because I slew him in boiling water in which he never kicked), leaving his back out, and pressed wax into the hollow, and black-leaded it with a brush; but neither would that do. So at last I took my fingers and rubbed it, which I find the best way to use the black lead. Then it coppered famously. I melt out the wax with the lens, that being the cleanest way of getting a strong heat, so I do most things with it that need heat. Today I astonished the natives as follows. I took a crystal of blue vitriol and put the lens to it, and so drove off the water, leaving a white powder. Then I did the same to some washing soda, and mixed the two white powders together; and made a small native spit on them, which turned them green by a mutual exchange, thus: 1. Sulphate of copper and carbonate of soda. 2. Sulphate of soda and carbonate of copper (blue or green).

James Clerk Maxwell (1831–1879), letter to Lewis Campbell, 5–6 July 1848, from P. M. Harman (ed.), The Scientific Letters and Papers of James

Clerk Maxwell (1990). *The 'natives' were Maxwell's family at Glenlair. He was seventeen at the time. For some years the family had been in the habit of referring to his experimenting as 'Jamsie's durts'.*

Sir James Young Simpson Makes a Successful Experiment

Seeing he was ever recklessly rash in regard to himself, it is not unlikely he may have had a private trial of chloroform, and laid it aside again, to start fair with his two assistants, who had worked so unflinchingly with him. Some other compounds were tried that night, and then chloroform, which was lying in its little phial among some papers, was unearthed, and the result of this, its first trial as an anaesthetic, 4th November 1847, is best described in Professor Simpson's own words in a letter to Mr Waldie, who had previously drawn his attention to this heavy-smelling 'perchloride of formyle'.

> I am sure you will be delighted to see part of the good results of our hasty conversation. I had the chloroform for several days in the house before trying it, as, after seeing it such a heavy, unvolatile-like liquid, I despaired of it, and went on dreaming about others. The first night we took it, Dr Duncan, Dr Keith, and I all tried it simultaneously, and were all 'under the table' in a minute or two.

Dr George Keith, writing to me in 1891, says . . .

> it is pretty correct, only he says we all took the chloroform at once. This, with a new substance to try, would have been foolish, and the fact is, I began to inhale it a few minutes before the others. On seeing the effects on me, and hearing my approval before I went quite over, they both took a dose, and I believe we were all more or less under the table together, much to the alarm of your mother, who was present.

Professor Miller, his neighbour, who used to come in every morning to see if the experimenters had survived, says:

> . . . On awakening, Dr Simpson's first perception was mental. 'This is far stronger and better than ether,' said he to himself. His second was to note that he was prostrate on the floor, and that among the friends about him there was both confusion and alarm. Of his assistants, Dr Duncan he saw snoring heavily, and Dr Keith kicking violently at the table above him. They made several more

trials of it that eventful evening, and were so satisfied with the results that the festivities of the evening did not terminate till a late hour, 3 a.m.

Evelyn Blantyre Simpson, The Life of Sir James Young Simpson (1896). The author was Simpson's daughter.

Sir Ronald Ross Makes a Breakthrough

The afternoon was very hot and overcast and I remember opening the diaphragm of the substage condenser of the microscope to admit more light and then changing the focus. In each of these cells there was a cluster of small granules, black as jet and exactly like the black pigment granules of the plasmodium (malarial parasite) crescents. As with that pigment, the granules numbered about 12 to 16 in each cell and became blacker and more visible when more light was admitted through the diaphragm. . .

Next day I went to hospital immensely excited. The last survivor of the batch fed on the 16th, mosquito 39, was alive. After looking through yesterday's specimen I slew and dissected it with a shaking hand. There were the cells again, 21 of them, just as before, only now much larger! Mosquito 38, the seventh of the batch fed on the 16th, was killed on the fourth day afterwards – that is, on the 20th. This one was killed on the 21st, the fifth day after feeding, and the cells had grown during the extra day. The cells were therefore parasites and, as they contained the characteristic malarial pigment, were almost certainly the malaria parasites growing in the mosquito's tissues.

The thing was really done. We had to discover two unknown quantities simultaneously – the kind of mosquito which carries the parasite and the form and position of the parasite within it. We could not find the first without knowing the second nor the third without knowing the first. By an extremely lucky observation I had now discovered both the unknown quantities at the same moment. The mosquito was the anopheles and the parasite lives in or on its gastric wall and can be recognised at once by the characteristic pigment. All the work on the subject which has been done since then by me and others during the last 25 years has been mere child's play which anyone could do after the clue was once obtained.

Sir Ronald Ross (1857–1932), Memoirs

Charlie Macintosh's Cryptogamic Feast

Two notable scientific functions in which he took a prominent part were the 'Fungus Shows' which were held in Perth and Dunkeld in the autumns of 1875 and 1877 respectively, under the auspices of the Cryptogamic Society of Scotland. The first of these was a specially memorable occasion, for it was the first gathering of its kind ever held in this country, and probably the most successful. One of the functions in connection with the conference was a banquet in the Salutation Hotel, at which some seventy gentlemen nobly hazarded their lives in the cause of science by partaking of a repast consisting almost entirely of fungi, prepared by a chef brought specially from London for the purpose. The menu, which has been preserved, provides amusing reading. It is as follows:

> Stewed Pigeons, with Chantarells. Curried Fungi
> Dressed Calf's head, with Fungi. Turkeys stuffed with
>   Truffles
> Cavaliers Broil. Fistulina hepatica à l'Anglaise
> Hydnum repandum à la President
> Boletus edulis à la Dhonuil Dhu
> Arabicus rubescens à la Grevillea
> Polyporus intybaceus à la MM. les Curés
> Boletus scaber à la Société Cryptogamique
> Marasmius oreades à la Reine des Fées
> Sparassis crispa à la Scottish Naturalist

. . . The present writer, although he was present at the banquet, does not recall any dire results following, so it may be presumed that the species chosen for experimentation really were all edible.

Henry Coates, Charlie Macintosh, Post Runner, Naturalist and Musician (1924). *Charlie Macintosh, the post runner for a great tract of Perthshire, was a man of many parts, much loved and admired.*

Alexander Graham Bell Makes the First Telephone Call

On March 10, 1876, Bell made the first telephone communication over a line set up between two rooms in a building in Boston. The epoch-making words recorded by Mr Watson, Bell's assistant, were simply: 'Mr Watson, come here; I want you.'

J.J. Carty, Smithsonian Report for 1922

Alexander Fleming Cultivates a Mould

Fleming transferred several spores to a dish containing agar and left them for four or five days to germinate at room temperature. He soon obtained a colony of the mould similar to the first one. Then he planted in the same agar different bacteria in isolated streaks, forming, as it were, the radii of a circle with the mould as centre. After incubation, he noticed that certain microbes survived in close proximity to the fungus – the streptococci, the staphylococci and the diphtheria bacillus, for instance, whereas the typhoid and influenza bacteria were not affected in the same way.

The discovery was becoming tremendously interesting. Unlike lysozome, which acted more especially upon the inoffensive microbes, this mould seemed to produce a substance which could inhibit the growth of microbes which caused some of the most serious diseases. It might, therefore, have an immense therapeutic value. 'Here', said Fleming, 'it looks as though we have got a mould that can do something useful.' He cultivated his *penicillium* in a larger receptacle containing a nutritive broth. A thick, soft, pock-marked mass, at first white, then green, then black, covered the surface. At first the broth remained clear. After several days, the liquid assumed a vivid yellow colour. What mattered now was to find out whether this liquid also possessed the bactericidal properties of the mould.

The methods perfected in 1922 for lysozome suited Fleming's purposes admirably. He hollowed out a gutter in a dish of agar, and filled it with a mixture of agar and the yellow liquid. Then microbes were planted in streaks, perpendicularly in the gutter, up to the very edge of the dish. The liquid appeared to be just as active as the original mould. The same microbes were affected. There was therefore in the broth a bactericidal (or bacteriostatic) substance produced by the mould. How great a strength did it have? Fleming experimented with weaker and weaker solutions – a 20th, a 40th, a 200th, a 500th. Even this last still arrested the development of the staphylococci. The mysterious substance contained in the golden liquid appeared to be endowed with quite extraordinary power. Fleming at that time had no means of knowing that the proportion of the active substance in the 'juice' was scarcely more than one in a million. The proportion of gold in the sea is greater than that.

André Maurois, The Life of Sir Alexander Fleming, *translated by Gerard Hopkins (1959). The ultimate discovery of penicillin was very close. Maurois notes that Fleming's friends remembered how he 'would stare at every mouldy surface, his eyes glinting with curiosity, and be for ever asking whether they hadn't got any rotting old shoes to give him'.*

THE SEA AND SEAFARING

The Story of Alexander Selkirk

Alexander Selkirk, who was rendered famous by Mons. de Foe, under the name of Robinson Crusoe, was born in Largo, 1676. His history, divested of fable, is as follows:

Having gone to sea in his youth, and in the year 1703, being sailing master of the ship *Cinque Ports*, Captain Stradling, bound for the South

Seas, he was put on shore on the island of Juan Fernandez, as a punishment for mutiny. In that solitude he remained for four years, from which he was at last relieved and brought to England by Captain Woods Rogers. He had with him in the island his clothes and bedding, with a firelock, some powder, bullets and tobacco, a hatchet, knife, kettle, his mathematical instruments, and Bible. He built two huts of Pimento trees, and covered them with long grass, and in a short time lined them with skins of goats which he killed with his musket, so long as his powder lasted (which at first was but a pound); when that was spent he caught them by speed of foot. Having learned to produce fire by rubbing two pieces of wood together, he dressed his victuals in one hut and slept in the other, which was at some distance from his kitchen. A multitude of rats often disturbed his repose by gnawing his feet and other parts of his body, which induced him to feed a number of cats for his protection. In a short time these became so tame that they would lie about him in hundreds, and soon delivered him from the rats, his enemies. Upon his return, he declared to his friends that nothing gave him so much uneasiness as the thoughts, that when he died his body would be devoured by those very cats he had with so much care tamed and fed. To divert his mind from such melancholy thoughts, he would sometimes dance and sing among his kids and goats, at other times retire to his devotions. His clothes and shoes were soon worn, by running through the woods. In the want of shoes he found little inconvenience, as the soles of his feet became so hard that he could run everywhere without difficulty. As for his clothes, he made for himself a coat and a cap of goats' skins, sewed with little thongs of the same cut into proper form with his knife. His only needle was a nail. When his knife was worn to the back, he made others as well as he could of some iron hoops that had been left on shore, by beating them thin and grinding them on stones. By his long seclusion from intercourse with men, he had so far forgot the use of speech, that the people on board Captain Rogers's ship could scarce understand him for he seemed to speak his words by halves. The chest and musket which Selkirk had with him on the island are now (1790) in the possession of his grand-nephew John Selkirk, weaver in Largo.

The First Statistical Account of Scotland, *Parish of Largo (1790)*

Sir Walter Scott Buys a Wind, and Hears about a Pirate

Off Stromness, 17th August 1814 — Went on shore after breakfast. We clomb, by steep and dirty lanes, an eminence rising above the town, and commanding a fine view. An old hag lives in a wretched cabin on this height, and subsists by selling winds. Each captain of a merchantman, between jest and earnest, gives the old woman sixpence, and she boils her kettle to procure a favourable gale. She was a miserable figure; upwards of ninety, she told us, and dried up like a mummy. A sort of clay-coloured cloak, folded over her head, corresponded in colour to her corpse-like complexion. Fine light-blue eyes, and nose and chin that almost met, and a ghastly expression of cunning, gave her quite the effect of Hecate. She told us she remembered Gow the pirate, who was born near the House of Clestrom, and afterwards commenced buccaneer. He came to his native country about 1725, with a snow which he commanded, carried off two women from one of the islands, and committed other enormities.

At length, while he was dining in a house in the island of Eday the islanders made him prisoner, and sent him to London, where he was hanged. While at Stromness, he made love to a Miss Gordon, who pledged her faith to him by shaking hands, an engagement which, in her idea, could not be dissolved without her going to London to seek back again her 'faith and troth', by shaking hands with him again after execution.

We left our Pythoness, who assured us there was nothing evil in the intercession she was to make for us, for we were only to have a fair wind through the benefit of her prayers. She repeated a sort of rigmarole which I suppose she had ready for such occasions, and seemed greatly delighted and surprised with the amount of our donation, as everybody gave her a trifle, our faithful Captain Wilson making the regular offering on behalf of the ship. So much for buying a wind. Bessy Millie's habitation is airy enough for Aeolus himself, but if she is a special favourite with that divinity, he has a strange choice. In her house I remarked a quern, or hand-mill.

... On board at half past three, and find Bessie Millie a woman of her word, for the expected breeze has sprung up, if it but last us till we double Cape Wrath. Weigh anchor to bid farewell to Orkney.

Sir Walter Scott, Journal (1814)

Last Voyage of the *Comet*

By 1816 she was definitely outclassed on the Clyde. Bell thereupon tried her on the Firth of Forth, but again she was a failure. In what now wears a suspicious look of being a last despairing effort, he put her on the long run up and down the west Highlands from Glasgow to Fort William by way of the then nearly new ... Crinan Canal. Her first voyage in these perilous seas began on March 31, 1820.

It proved at first an adventure of brilliant promise. Perhaps the Highland folk were flocking to pick up their share of the new wealth of the industrial Lowlands; perhaps it was all due to the art of Donald McDougall, who was hired – just as the Cunard White Star company took Mr Henry Hall on the maiden voyage of the *Queen Mary* – to delight the passengers with the music of the bagpipe: his emoluments being six shillings a week 'and his meat'. At all events, Bell was cheerfully declaring a dividend of thirty-seven and a half per cent by December.

It was almost certainly never paid. On the fourth of that month the *Comet* arrived at Fort William in poor shape, and good Captain Bain would have laid her up at Corpach for the winter. Bell would have none of this caution, however, and ordered the skipper to keep his schedule. The ship was leaking when she got back to Oban; it was in a snowstorm that she set off to face the fierce tides of the inner isles and find the sheltered waters of the Firth of Clyde. And she failed to get there. Between the islands of Jura and Scarba and the mainland the currents of Corryvrechan rage powerfully. To get through that Dorus Mhor, the Great Door, is still a matter of navigational anxiety. The worn *Comet* took the rocks at Craignish Point.

She broke up, of course, the after end coming away at the point where she had been lengthened; the forward part, including the engines, remaining attached to the County of Argyll. In all probability the fat dividend went in the attempts to salve her ... We know at least that the sum of £5 18s 6d was expended on whisky alone, the beverage served out to the helpful natives of the Craignish peninsula. It was all in vain.

George Blake (1893–1961), Down to the Sea (1937). Henry Bell (1767–1830) launched the Comet, *first passenger steamboat in Europe, in 1812.*

The Building of Dhu Heartach Lighthouse

In fine weather, when by the spy-glass on the hill the sea was observed to run low upon the reef, there would be a sound of preparation in the very early morning; and before the sun had risen from behind Ben More, the tender would steam out of the bay. Over fifteen sea-miles of the great blue Atlantic rollers she ploughed her way, trailing at her tail a brace of wallowing stone-lighters. The open ocean widened upon either board, and the hills of the mainland began to go down on the horizon, before she came to her unhomely destination, and lay-to at last where the rock clapped its black head above the swell, with the tall iron barrack on its spider legs, and the truncated tower, and the cranes waving their arms, and the smoke of the engine-fire rising in the mid-sea. An ugly reef is this of the Dhu Heartach; no pleasant assemblage of shelves, and pools, and creeks, about which a child might play for a whole summer without weariness, like the Bell Rock or the Skerryvore, but one oval nodule of black-trap, sparsely bedabbled with an inconspicuous fucus, and alive in every crevice with a dingy insect between a slater and a bug. No other life was there but that of sea-birds, and of the sea itself, that here ran like a mill-race, and growled about the outer reef for ever, and ever and again, in the calmest weather, roared and spouted on the rock itself. Times were different upon Dhu Heartach when it blew, and the night fell dark, and the neighbour lights of Skerryvore and Rhu-val were quenched in fog, and the men sat prisoned high up in their iron drum, that then resounded with the lashing of the sprays. Fear sat with them in their sea-beleaguered dwelling; and the colour changed in anxious faces when some greater billow struck the barrack, and its pillars quivered and sprang under the blow. It was then that the foreman builder, Mr Goodwillie, whom I see before me still in his rock-habit of undecipherable rags, would get his fiddle down and strike up human minstrelsy amid the music of the storm. But it was in sunshine only that I saw Dhu Heartach; and it was in sunshine, or the yet lovelier summer afterglow, that the steamer would return to Earraid, ploughing an enchanted sea; the obedient lighters, relieved of their deck cargo, riding in her wake more quietly; and the steersman upon each, as she rose on the long swell, standing tall and dark against the shining west.

Robert Louis Stevenson (1850–1894), Memoirs of an Islet, *from* Memories and Portraits

The Blue Men of the Minch

The Blue Men of the Minch, according to Hebridean legend, sprang up from the sea in the Sound of Shiant and put to the skipper of every passing ship two lines of Gaelic poetry. Unless he could quote the next two lines of the text, they light-heartedly sank his ship. It meant that he was not of the blood. The Blue Men were artists who did not want the island culture to be contaminated, and perhaps it was their pranks that held off for such a long time the influence of the outside world.

Hector MacIver, The Outer Isles, *from* Scottish Country, *edited by George Scott-Moncrieff (1935)*

The Boats Come Homeward

In Eilean a' Cheo, the Isle of Mist, as the folk of the Hebrides call Skye, there is a certain headland which ought to be named, but is not, the Headland of Waiting. Many years ago, and yet not so many either, on one of those beautiful nights which have passed away with the fairies, a young maiden, tempted by moonlight and love of the sea, found her way to the furthest point of that same headland, and also found when there that she was not alone. Sitting on the rocks were the women of the township, waiting and listening till the dip of the oars and the sound of the iorram, the boat-song, should foretell the return of the men from the fishing-banks and the luck of their catch. By-and-bye, there came across the waves the sound of a light airy iorram (perhaps the sea-reivers' song) accompanied by short quick strokes. 'Och! och!' said the women, 'light is the fishing tonight, but lighter still are the hearts of our men, and warm the welcome before them be their luck what it may.' Later on came other sounds, fainter this time, the tired thud of long laborious strokes and the rising and falling of the slow-

rowing iorram, Iùraibh o hì, iùraibh o hó. 'Isn't it the beautiful sound!' said
the women, 'there is luck on someone tonight, and the luck of one is the
luck of all'.

Kenneth Macleod (1871–1955), The Sounds of the Sea, from The Road
to the Isles

Hiring a Third Mate – Glasgow Style

Meeting my father in Union Street in Glasgow when on these unproductive
rounds of the shipping offices, I began to tell him about my latest disappointment. As we talked, a well-built and smiling man came down the steps
from the Anchor Line office, and gave my father a hearty good-day then
stopped to chat.

I had not met Captain McFee before, but knew of him as an important
figure in Clydeside shipping circles. He was the Marine Superintendent of
the Anchor Line, the very man I had long sought to meet. I had tried to gain
his ear on many occasions without success, for there was always a self-
assured young clerk at the outer desk who told me how busy his principal
was and adding – as he regarded me – that there were no vacancies for a
deck officer at the moment, but he would take my name.

It was not of the sea and ships that the talk ran. I was briefly indicated as
'M'son, David' and their common interest in literature was quickly resumed.
It came out that Captain McFee was the author of a narrative poem that
had just been published in Glasgow. My father spoke well of it. He thought
Norman: A Poem in Five Duans a very special effort for an Ayrshire seaman
to compose. How strange it was that I should then consider an indulgence
in imaginative verse unfitting in a hardy follower of the sea!

The Captain was surprised to learn that his old acquaintance should
have bred a sailor son, and particularly one at a loss for employment. To
his inquiry as to why I had not come to see him about a job, I could only
explain that I had just come from his office, where a clerk had told me
there were no vacancies, but he would take my name. The Captain did
not seem in the least nettled by his clerk's method of fending off casual
applicants, but he did say something about counter-jumpers, then asked
me what my qualifications were. It then appeared that the junior's information was incorrect. A third mate was needed in a hurry for the SS
Australia, which was due to sail from Glasgow that very afternoon. It
was then about twelve noon and the tide served at three. Could I be
ready in time to get aboard? I could, and I did. It was thus as a 'pier-
head jump' I joined the Anchor Line, in whose service I remained for
nearly fifty years.

David Bone (1874–1956), Landfall at Sunset (1955). Brother of Sir
Muirhead Bone and the journalist James Bone, David Bone too was knighted

and retired as Commodore Master of the Anchor Line. He wrote The
Brassbounder *(1910), among other nautical novels.*

The Departure of the Empress of Britain

The launching of the *Queen Mary* was ruined by all kinds of false symbol-
ism; the end of a fine bit of engineering and craftmanship was debased into
a stunt by the merchants of sensationalism. Let us forget it. But I would like
to remember Glasgow and the Clyde on a Sunday morning when the
Empress of Britain went down the water.

It was a serene day with a light mist before the sun. As we stood at the
top of a brae near Old Kilpatrick we could see a line of people waiting
quietly along the river-side. Beyond them the dull water had a milky whiteness; and the distant banks faded into nothing. Then the great white ship
came towards us out of the haze, all comely and innocent, like a child of the
mist and the morning sun. Little tugs went before and after her, fussy and
anxious, like mortal nursemaids tending an immortal child. She passed us
very slowly, with just the thinnest trail of smoke from one of her stacks. I
noticed then that a curious thing happened. As she came abreast of us,
through the diffused and milky light of the morning, she gleamed in her
whiteness as though she had not borrowed from the sun but possessed a
radiance of her own. It was an illusion born out of sentiment perhaps; but
the illusion was perfect. Nor would I have been the only person who thought
he had seen a wonder. The people watched her go by not quite in silence but
with a subdued and murmuring excitement that showed a deeper emotion
than silence or cheers. So the lovely white ship, wrought in the unlovely
town, passed down the river and out of our sight.

John R. Allan, Summer in Scotland *(1938). Interestingly in view of
J. R. Allan's comments, George Blake, an eyewitness, wrote that there was a
'curious lack of ostentation' about the launch of the Queen Mary.*

Launching Liquids

The liquid in the launching bottle for Ben Line ships built by Charles Connell
was cold tea. The owners stipulated that the bottle should contain whisky,
more appropriate for a Scottish ship than the traditional champagne. However at Connell's yard the task of shrouding the bottle's nakedness in red,
white and blue ribbon was entrusted to the youngest apprentice who had
helped build the ship, and it was an open secret that his elders and betters
made sure that the contents were not wasted.

Michael Strachan, The Ben Line, An Anecdotal History *(1992). Charles
Connell's shipyard was at Scotstoun, Glasgow; they built many of the Ben
Line steamships.*

SPORTS, GAMES AND PASTIMES

Edinburgh Bowlers in the Eighteenth Century

The first bowling green in Edinburgh . . . was in the centre of Argyle Square, the first square in Edinburgh, and was well frequented by some of the citizens of respectable middling rank. . . A little later, the bowling-green most played at was that of Heriot's Gardens, which continued to flourish for many years and produced several excellent bowlers, the diversion becoming quite a rage among the lawyers, and being also honoured with the company of some of the most fashionable gentlemen of the town, among whom was . . . Mr Hay, better known afterwards as Lord Newton, his judicial title, who used to mix business with his amusement, his clerk often attending and writing to his dictation between the ends of the game. On him in his lifetime, his friend and fellow-bowler at an after period, Mr H. Erskine, wrote an excellent epitaph all in bowling terms, and strictly applicable to the character of the man. I don't know if any copy of it was reserved; I only remember the first lines:

> Beneath his much-loved turf, ah, well-a-day,
> Lies the dead length of honest Charles Hay

Dead length, in the language of the bowling-green, means an exact length, parallel latitudinally to the Jack.
   Henry Mackenzie (1745–1831), The Anecdotes and Egotisms of Henry Mackenzie

Golfing Exploits – 1

Golf, a favourite amusement of Edinburgh, was played on Bruntsfield Links, tho' the crack players preferred those of Leith. I recollect a wager laid by a celebrated golfer, that he could strike a ball from one of the windows in the building at the end of the Luckenbooths looking down the street, in six strokes to the top of Arthur's Seat, the first stroke to be from the bottom of a stone basin. He won his bet; the first stroke striking the ball to the Cross, and the second reaching the middle of the Canongate.
   Henry Mackenzie, The Anecdotes and Egotisms of Henry Mackenzie

Tennis Debacle

Tennis was formerly a good deal played at Edinburgh, where there was a tennis court within the precincts of Holyrood House, and another at Leith . . . now a warehouse for salt and other merchandise.

Sir John Steuart, who had attained abroad much reputation and considerable proficiency in games of all sorts, was one of the tennis players. There was in the tennis court here a marker, an uncommon good player; at London a Frenchman had the reputation of being the best in England. Sir John thought the Edinburgh marker a better player than this Frenchman; he suggested to some of his companions a profitable speculation of betting largely on the Edinburgh against the French marker, and offered to go to London to conduct it. He carried the Edinburgh marker with him, who going incognito to the tennis court in Westminster, told Sir John he might double the proposed bets, for he was sure of winning. Acting on this information, Sir John made very large bets which he would probably have won but for an accident by which the match went off. Soon after the commencement of the play, the ball of the Frenchman (whether from accident or design) struck the Scotsman on the face with such force as to cause him to suffer considerable pain. The *perfervidum ingenium Scotorum* took fire on this, and in a stroke soon after, wifully misdirected his ball so as to strike the Frenchman on the face and put out one of his eyes, on which the umpires decided that the match was off; and so Sir John returned with his marker re infecta.

Henry Mackenzie, The Anecdotes and Egotisms of Henry Mackenzie. Re infecta: *the thing unaccomplished.*

Ladies' Bathing Customs . . .

The ladies' bathing is conducted on the genuine Scotch principle of not being at all ashamed of it, as why should they? Is it not pure? and healthy? and ordered by the doctor? and anything wrong in it? So the ladies emerge, in full day, from their flats, in their bathing-dresses, attended by a maid, and a sister or aunt, the maid carrying a small bundle containing a towel and some dry clothes, the friend tittering. The bather crosses the road, and goes to the sea, which is never more than a few yards, or inches, beyond the road's edge. She then enters the water, and shivers, or splashes, according to her taste, conversing or laughing or screaming all the while, with her attendants ashore. But it is on coming out that the delicate part of the operation begins; for, as they don't walk home wet, and then dress in their own rooms, they must change their whole raiment before the public. For this purpose the maid holds a portion of the dry vestment over the dripping lady's head, and as the soaked gown descends to the heels, the dry is supposed to descend over the head as fast, so that the principle is, that, between the two, the lady is never seen. Ignorance is sometimes bliss, and it is very wise in the assistants never to tell the patient anything about it. But I wonder how, when they happen to be looking at a fellow-exhibitor, and observe the interest taken from every window, and by all the street, they can avoid discovering that such feats are seldom performed without revelations, and that a single fold of wet linen adheres too accurately to the inner surface to require any other revelation.

Lord Cockburn (1779–1854), Circuit Journeys (1888). Cockburn was writing about Ardrossan, where in the 1840s many people rented upstairs flats for the summer.

. . . and Nudism at Nairn

More bathing machines for ladies are urgently needed. Bathing from the unprotected shore, in full view of the promenade, seems a trifle uncivilised to Southern minds, and can only be safely practised by ladies in very strong health and with very strong nerves. Finally some arrangement by which ladies might be enabled to ramble by the sea-shore at any time after breakfast without exposing themselves to the intolerable nuisance of nude men and lads bathing from the sands at all hours.

Letter to the Nairn newspaper, August 1871, quoted in Isobel Rae and John Lawson, Dr Grigor of Nairn (1994). They go on to note that it took the town council another ten years to outlaw nude bathing on part of the beach; and to recall 'a lady guest at the Marine Hotel who preferred a room overlooking the beach, the better to observe "parties while undressed bathing". One gentleman correspondent objected strongly to being made "to adopt the detestable custom of bathing in drawers. If ladies don't like to see men naked why don't they keep away from the sight?"'

Boaty's Revenge

Boaty, who long acted as Charon of the Dee at Banchory, was a first-rate salmon-fisher, and was much sought for by amateurs. One day he was in attendance with his boat on a sportsman, who caught salmon after salmon, and between such fish-catching took a pull at his flask, without offering Boaty any participation in the refreshment. Boaty got annoyed, and seeing no prospect of amendment, deliberately pulled the boat to shore, shouldered the oars, rods, landing-nets and fishing apparatus, which he had provided, and set off homeward. His companion, keen for more sport, was amazed, and peremptorily ordered him to come back. But all the answer made by the offended Boaty was, 'No, no; them 'at drink by themsells may just fish by themsells.'

John Timbs, A Century of Anecdote (1864)

Waste Land Football

The same attraction to squalor drew me to the football matches on Saturday afternoon. Crosshill was a respectable suburb, but there were vacant lots scattered about it, chance scraps of waste ground where the last blade of grass had died, so that in dry weather they were as hard as lava, and in wet weather a welter of mud. On these lots teams from the slum quarters of the south side played every Saturday afternoon with great skill and savage ferocity. Fouls were a matter of course, and each game turned into a complicated feud in which the ball itself was merely the means to an end which had no connexion with the game. Some of the teams had boxers among their supporters; these men stood bristling on the touchline and shouted intimidations at the opposing players. I first saw one of these games shortly after I came to Glasgow; a brown fog covered the ground, and a small, tomato-red sun, like a jellyfish floating in the sky, appeared and disappeared as the air grew thicker or finer. I found later that more civilized football teams played in the Queen's Park recreation ground, and I began to attend them instead, and later still, when I was earning enough money to spare a sixpence on Saturday, I attended the matches of the Queen's Park Football Club. But there was a grimy fascination in watching the damned kicking a football in a tenth-rate hell.

Edwin Muir (1887–1959), Autobiography

'Pitching Toss'

Gambling ran deep in the industrial tradition. It was endemic among immigrant Irish navvies and rural mining communities. This was how Abe Moffat described 'pitching toss' at Lumphinnans:

> One would throw two pennies up in the air, and all the other members of the group would bet they would come down as tails. If they came down as heads, then the person who threw them up in the air would win all the stakes that were laid down on the ground . . . It reminds me of the visitor who came to a mining village and said the miners had a queer kind of religion; a group of miners stood in a ring every Sunday morning and they all looked up at the sky and looked down on the ground and together they would say, 'Jesus, tails again.'

T. C. *Smout*, A Century of the Scottish People, 1830–1950, *quoting Abe Moffat*, My Life with the Miners (1965). *Presumably in the latter case, tails lost.*

Golfing Exploits – 2

A more singular episode at the first hole I recall from September 1927, when the town was full of visitors and a great many spectators were hanging about the first fairway. A foursome was on the tee, ready to drive off, when there debouched from Grannie Clarke's Wynd an elderly white-bearded man, wearing a top hat, and pedalling a tricycle. He progressed slowly across the fairways towards the sea. Everybody shouted at him, 'Fore!' – a monosyllable very salutary for filling the lungs with salt-laden air. But the veteran paid no attention. Perhaps he was deaf. Finally, one of the foursome swung his club and drove. The ball was hooked somewhat, and impinged upon the tricyclist's lum hat, knocking it off. With astonishing agility the old man dismounted, his white beard bristling. After grasping the lum hat with one hand, and brandishing the clenched fist of the other, he re-mounted and rode off towards the sands, amid loud cheers. Not many golfers in future are likely to run a risk of dislodging the top hat of a white-bearded tricyclist. It is doubtful too if any will repeat Major Chiene's feat of killing a swallow on the wing. He had the poor bird stuffed, and mounted on the ball that slew it, to sit as a talking-point in the clubhouse.

Douglas Young (1913–1973), St Andrews (1969), describing incidents on the Old Course at St Andrews.

The Rise of a World Champion . . .

One time when I was in Glasgow on football business I killed a couple of hours by dropping into one of the frowstier boxing clubs, on the south side of the river, and found a new world champion. The highlight of the evening's fighting was an exhibition by a very good boy who was tipped to become a considerable figure in British, if not world, boxing, and when he stepped into the ring there was some understanding of the opinion of his supporters. He was tall and good-looking and there was such a buzz of admiration for him that hardly anyone bothered to look at his opponent until the bell went for the first round of their spar. Then I saw him . . . a little compact fellow, with a baby face and dark, neatly parted hair. He wore pale-blue shorts and, as he shifted and moved about the ring with lithe grace and a sense of power, I had to check with my neighbours that the big fellow was the prospect. 'Oh, that's just wee Benny Lynch', they told me. 'He'll come on . . .'

Lynch went through three rounds with the big fellow and hardly once raised his hands above the level of his waist. He used his feet, his uncanny sense of balance, the most delicately timed movements of his head and his body to keep out of distance and all the time you could see, behind that expressionless little face, a spirit that, if unleashed, would have cleared not only the ring in which he was cavorting like a dancer, but also the hall.

'Can he punch?' I asked them.

'Oh, aye,' they said. 'Wee Benny's got the dig all right.'

That was all I had to know. When, a few weeks later, the Ring, Blackfriars, people announced that Lynch would appear in the ring to take a bow – and any old challenges that were flying around – I wrote in my Sunday column that London fight fans would have the opportunity of seeing the next fly-weight champion of the world. I didn't have long to wait for justification. He went through the existing Scottish flyweights like a knife through butter and eventually he was matched – some said he was overmatched – with that classy champion Jackie Brown at Belle Vue, Manchester in September 1935, with the Manchester boys betting heavily on Brown to retain his title against the comparatively unknown boy from Glasgow. Lynch flattened Brown in the second round with as lovely a punch as I ever saw and pipers played him in triumph from the ring.

John Macadam, The Macadam Road (*1955*)

. . . And His Fall

Never have I seen such a mob as got round him in his hotel that night . . . big-shots and small-shots and a great number of damp squibs, all came into the room that had been set aside for the new world champion and all of them wanted to buy a drink for him. He stood them off manfully that night, but you could see the way it was going to go if they didn't put an armed guard outside his door thereafter. Alas! They never got round to the armed guard.

. . . Around eighteen months later I heard this-and-that about his prepa-ration at a quiet countrified spot outside Glasgow for another defence of his title against the American Jackie Jurich, and I went up to see for myself . . . He was, I was happy to see, with Puggy Morgan, his old trainer and one of the grandest handlers in the business. Puggy was devoted to Benny and was happy as a sandboy at his condition. 'Oh,' said Puggy, in that fantastic bass Glasgow drawl of his, 'Oh. If nothing happens to upset the wee man.' Benny had locked his car and handed over the key to Puggy. They spent all their time on the road, in the gym and on the moors. They were like a couple of brothers together on a holiday.

'Look at him', said Puggy. 'He's got me oot there in the heather like a ghillie and him wae a wee airgun . . . shootin' rabbits . . . an' it no the Twelfth yet.'

That was the atmosphere two weeks before the fight, and when Benny came on the scales on the day there was a gasp of horror that almost took the roof off the hall when they announced his weight. He was so far over eight stones, the flyweight limit, that they would have to perform an ampu-tation. . . He forfeited his title.

. . . the last I heard of him was when they were running a benefit boxing show for one of the former champions who was in bad health. When the appeals and the speeches were at their height a little, tubby figure came up to the ringside, stuffed something into the auctioneer's hand and said, 'Get him what you can for that,' and disappeared into the shadow. It was his red robe, with Benny Lynch, World Champion, proudly blazoned across the back.

It was the last gesture. Two years later he was dead.

John Macadam, The Macadam Road

The Ancient Art of Football Prose

There is an old Charlie attached to every football ground in Britain. He does a running story for the local evening paper. He does a story for one or more Sunday papers. He does another story or stories for one or more Monday morning papers ... on this day, old Charlie, flustered a little at being late, wheezed and panted along the line of newspapermen until he came to his seat ... From an upper layer of waistcoat pockets he took anything up to half a dozen already sharpened pencils which he laid alongside the programme. He selected one of the notebooks and drew it towards him portentously. Only then did he look up.

'Which side,' he said to the next man, 'kicked off with a rush?'

Old Charlie – all the old Charlies – had been using the sacred soccer jargon so long in his numerous reports that he even talked it. This jargon is worth a little attention by the philologists. Its principal feature is the avoidance of the obvious and the simple. Also it is derivative and the more highfalutin the source, the better the effect. Hence, the net attached to the goal – which, by the way, is the Citadel – is invariably the Rigging. . . The admitted master of this form of writing was John Dunlop, known to millions of soccer fans as 'Waverley' of the *Glasgow Record*. John could not write any other way, and his best effort is conceded to be the final words of a description of a centre-forward who broke through and scored a goal. John wrote, '. . . and with his parthian shot suspended the spheroid in the rigging'.

John Macadam, The Macadam Road (*1955*)

A Sporting Gesture

Tully produced a complimentary admission ticket from the waistband of his playing shorts during a game in which he was getting the better of his immediate opponent, the fearsome full-back Don Emery. He handed it to Emery, with the observation, 'Here, would you not be better watching from the stand?'

Peter Burns and Pat Woods, Oh, Hampden in the Sun (*1997*), *on Charlie Tully, Celtic star of the late 1940s, and central figure of many other tales.*

A Magisterial Put-down

As a young Rangers player, Alex Ferguson, now manager of Manchester United, was unhappy at being left out of the first team. He stormed into the office of legendary manager Scott Symon. 'Why have I been in the second team for three weeks?' he asked. The magisterial Mr Symon replied, 'Because we don't have a third team.'

Tom Shields, Tom Shields Too: More Tom Shields's Diary (*1993*)

THEATRICALS

Digges and Debts

Digges was of good descent . . . and was first in Edinburgh as an officer of dragoons, and much admired by the ladies; but some ill conduct, in the nature of swindling, blew up his character, and obliged him to leave the army in disgrace. Some time after, he began his theatrical career, and visited Edinburgh, first as actor, and latterly as manager. He was the original Young Norval in Douglas, a character which he afterwards exchanged (very wisely) for Old Norval . . . A person had called very often to dun him for payment of a debt; at last he got access to the manager, and after stating the amount of the debt said that considering the length of time it had been owing, and the many times he had called about it, it would be but fair to allow interest. 'My good sir,' answered Digges, 'I must fairly tell you, it is not my interest to pay the principal, and not my principle to pay the interest.'

Henry Mackenzie (1745–1831), The Anecdotes and Egotisms of Henry Mackenzie. *David Stewart of Garth, writing later (1822), puts an identical phrase into the mouth of Rob Roy MacGregor, when dunned by the Duke of Montrose* (Sketches of the Character, Institutions and Customs of the Highlanders of Scotland).

End of the Performance

Brougham went one day with a lad named Pillans (later rector of the High School and one of Scotland's greatest educationists) to the Edinburgh Theatre to see a new play. It proved to be dull. Every attempt at fun missed fire. Four acts dragged out. The curtain went up on the fifth with the stage set for a dinner party. The gentleman in the chair flourished his glass and asked for a toast. Young Henry Brougham stood up in the pit and said, 'I humbly propose, "Good afternoon",' which was then the customary toast for concluding a party. He turned, walked toward the door, and waved his hat for the audience to follow him. With laughter and cries of 'Good afternoon', they streamed out of galleries, pit, stalls and boxes. That was the first of Henry Brougham's countless *public* speeches. Many of them were to be equally successful, but few had the same merit of brevity.

Chester W. New, The Life of Henry Brougham *(1961). Henry Brougham (1778–1868), a notable prankster in his young day, became Lord Chancellor of Great Britain.*

William Leitch's Practical Use of Props

. . . the scene painter, along with Macklin the machinist, were sent off to Ayr one Saturday to get the theatre there ready for *Bluebeard* for Monday night. Under the impression that their expenses had been paid by the manager, they set off with empty pockets . . .

> We got to Ayr about nine o' clock, and I got off the coach cold, stiff, and faint, for I had eaten nothing since eight in the morning. Our lodging had been provided at the house of a baker, whose wife Macklin knew, and who gave us a simple Scotch supper, for which we were both very thankful. About ten o' clock Macklin came to me and said, 'My dear boy, get to bed, for although tomorrow is Sunday, we must be up at six o'clock, and get into the theatre before people are up, otherwise there is a possibility of our getting into trouble for desecrating the Lord's Day.' I didn't like this at all, but there seemed to be no help for it. I was awakened in the morning by old Mack, and we were soon at the stagedoor of the theatre. When we opened it and got on the stage, I shall never forget the look of desolation it had. . . The wretched paltry pieces of set scenery, broken and torn, lying about, the hazy light of a misty morning hardly showing the tackle overhead, the dirt and dust and confusion, with the intense silence, were all very depressing. We began our work, and the old bluechamber was got out and the 'flats' put together. They were sadly faded, and looked very bad, and I had but a poor stock of materials; but I worked away as well as I could, though I felt very weak and stupid; and poor Macklin was in a still worse condition. About nine o'clock we heard a peculiar tapping at the door, and then a low whistle. Macklin immediately got up, and staggered to the door, saying, 'That must be Jamie.' I had not heard of Jamie before, but it appeared that he was a half-witted creature, who always made his appearance to Macklin when he came to Ayr. I asked Jamie if he had any money, but he had not a farthing. I had left my watch at home, and neither of us had anything else which we could have pledged, even if a pawnshop had been open on Sunday. Something, however, had to be done; so Jamie and I got a bit of candle lighted, and descended to an apartment under the stage, where, after a long search among dust and dirt, we

discovered four empty beer-bottles covered in grease. They had evidently been used as candlesticks. Having cleaned them as well as we could, Jamie was sent off with directions to sell them, and to spend what he could get for them on something to eat. It was getting on for twelve o'clock when he came back. He had got threepence ha'penny for the bottles, and this he had expended in a few potatoes and three small salted herrings. . . A new difficulty arose. How were they to be cooked? for there was neither pot nor pan on the premises. We searched everywhere, and were returning in a hopeless state, when, in a dark place under the stage, my foot struck against something sharp, and on stooping to ascertain what it was, I brought up a dilapidated white iron theatric helmet. I was about to throw it away, when it occurred to me that if it could hold water it might serve our purpose. To test this, we clambered up to a cistern kept in readiness in case of fire, when to our great joy we found the old helmet was watertight. A fire was speedily made in the green-room; the potatoes were washed and peeled, packed into the helmet, and the herrings placed on top, and all cooked together.

William Leighton Leitch (1804–1883) in a memoir given to his friend A. Macgeorge in 1879, recorded in Robert Brydall, Art in Scotland *(1889)*

Mumford's Geggy

The area of the Fair was also the home of Mumford's Geggy, which stood at the corner of the Saltmarket and Greendyke Street. It seems however that the name 'geggy' was only added as a nostalgic afterthought when the theatre had closed. It had been opened as a puppet show in 1835 by Mr Mumford, a drunken Englishman much given to lecturing his patrons on the evils of drink. He is also said to have been responsible for a spurious and much-recycled retort when his audience accused him of being a little under the weather in the title role of a performance of Rob Roy. 'If you think I'm drunk,' he said, 'wait till you see Bailie Nicol Jarvie.'

. . . The most famous actor in Mumford's Geggy was Geordie Henderson, who was renowned for his 'dying fall' and his habit of issuing challenges to fight the sometimes rowdy audience or stagehands or whoever was handy. Informality on stage was a Glasgow tradition in all types of theatres. . . After a particularly affecting dying fall as Romeo, the audience requested a repeat performance. When he had complied three times and the audience was still unsatisfied, Henderson got up, strode to the edge of the stage, and pointed to the floor which was carpeted with the discarded shells of nuts and whelks (the contemporary equivalent of our – or rather your – popcorn) thrown onto the stage by the audience. 'Giffe ye think ahm goin tae dee oan a' they whulks again, ye've goat anither think comin,' he said, and stalked back to his tomb.

Alasdair Cameron, Popular Entertainment in Nineteenth-Century Glasgow *(1995). The 'geggy' was a dismountable theatre, though its origin, like the present-day showbusiness 'gig', perhaps, comes from the Glasgow verb 'gag', meaning tour from point to point.*

The Bosjesmans

Some idea of the [Glasgow] Fair's scope can be gleaned from a report of 1865 which mentioned that the central area of the Fair held nine exhibitions, six peep-shows, two waxworks, a circus, twelve shooting galleries and five acting theatres, in addition to a host of peripheral events. We also know, for example, that in 1844 a total of 96,000 people paid 1d (a penny) to see the 'Bosjesmans'. These were advertised as primitive tribesmen from Africa, though they were rumoured to be Irish labourers dressed in feathers and rabbit skins and whose primitive language was Gaelic. It was also said that one of the Bosjesmans ate live rats as part of their performance. This certainly outdid another showman who merely bit off their heads and skinned them with his teeth, managing to skin twenty in as many minutes until the police reluctantly intervened on behalf of the tender-stomached.

Alasdair Cameron, Popular Entertainment in Nineteenth-Century Glasgow

'Gang Hame an' Practise, Harry'

There was a famous old music-hall in Glasgow at this time called the Scotia. It was run by a most competent woman, Mrs Baylis. She believed in giving local talent a chance. One evening a week, several trial 'turns' were put on. This was easily the most popular night of the week at the Scotia – the patrons got free rein for their criticisms and for a peculiarly mordant type of humour which I have never come across anywhere else in the world. If a newcomer could 'get it across' with the Scotia audiences on a trial night he had the right stuff in him. Several reputations were made in the Scotia on such nights; thousands were blasted irretrievably. Taking advantage of a half-holiday, I went up to Glasgow and asked Mrs Baylis for a trial turn. She looked me up and down and said, 'What are ye?' 'I'm a comic,' I replied. 'Well, all I can say is that you don't look like one,' was her only comment. Then she turned to her desk and went on working. 'I'm really no' bad, Mrs Baylis,' I pleaded. 'Gie me a chance an' I'll mak' them laugh.' Probably the doleful expression in my words and on my face moved dear old Mrs Baylis to a reconsideration of my request. At all events, she turned around smilingly and remarked, 'Laddie, you're makin' me laugh already;

come up a fortnight tonight an' I'll let ye loose among them for a minute or two. Ye'll maybe be sorry ye were so persistent!'

When the time came for me to go on the stage at the Scotia I was shaking in every limb. The trial turns preceding mine had all got short shrift. Most of them were 'off' in less than half a minute, and those that didn't willingly retire of their own accord were promptly hauled off by the stage-manager by the aid of a long crooked stick which he unceremoniously hooked round their necks. The oaths and blasphemy employed by some of the disappointed would-be stars in the wings were only equalled by the riotous mirth of the audience in front. . . I 'got over' pretty well, being allowed to sing two songs with a minimum of interruption and caustic comment. This was really a triumph for any trial run at the Scotia. Before I left, Mrs Baylis came round and congratulated me. 'Gang hame an' practise, Harry,' she said. 'I'll gie ye a week's engagement when the winter comes round.' I took Mrs Baylis's advice.

Harry Lauder (1870–1950), Roaming in the Gloaming *(1928)*

Show-business Priorities

The show went a bomb and Roma and George did seven minutes, we did a minute over our time, so the whole company was called for the Saturday morning for discussion.

We all turned up on the Saturday morning and I was called up to Mr Frutin's office. He was extremely nice. He said, 'George, how did you like it last night?' I said, 'It was great. I thought the show was marvellous, thoroughly enjoyed it.' He said, 'That's fine. Hey George, you did a minute over your time.' I said, 'I know, Mr Frutin, but we'll tighten up, I'm sure.' He said, 'No, George, you won't tighten up, you'll take it out. One minute per house is two minutes per night – it's twelve minutes per week. Do you know how much whisky I can sell in twelve minutes?' And I said, 'I haven't a clue.' 'Well,' he said, 'I can sell a lot of whisky in twelve minutes. So, George, you get that minute out tonight and', he said, 'if you don't, I will sack you.'

George Johnstone, Roma Derry and George Johnstone – Scotland's Musical Vocal Act Supreme, *from* Those Variety Days, *edited by Frank Bruce, Archie Foley and George Gillespie (1997). Alec Frutin was owner-manager of the Glasgow Metropole Theatre.*

A Gentleman in the Audience

Another English artiste, a male impersonator making one of several farewell appearances, also met with hostile uproar as soon as she appeared.

But she had a gallant champion. A tall gent rose from his seat in the front row of the stalls and faced the howling mob.

'Aw, come on,' he appealed to them. 'Gi'e the poor auld coo a chance.' This unexpected intervention brought a brief period of silence during which the lady artiste walked to the footlights and rebuked the noisy mob with the heartfelt words, 'Thank goodness there's one gentleman in the audience.'

Stanley Baxter, Stanley Baxter's Bedtime Book of Glasgow Humour (*1986*). *This is one of many anecdotes about the heyday of the Glasgow Empire; an institution of which the English comedian Arthur Askey once remarked, 'I've never performed before a non-English speaking audience, except at the Glasgow Empire.'*

TRANSPORT AND TRAVEL

Booking a Seat on the Buchan Line

It would be though a mistake to think that the lack of small talk means that the Aberdeenshire farmers are inarticulate or pushovers. Take the solicitor who was going back from Fraserburgh to London. It was about time for luncheon so he decided to go along to the dining car. There was no one in the compartment but just in case anyone joined the train at one of the many stations on the Buchan line, he left his bowler hat to claim his nice corner seat by the window.

This worked fine until the train arrived at Ellon. It was Friday and the carriage was invaded by farmers set for the mart at Aberdeen. The first man into the compartment saw the hat, fancied the seat in the corner, lobbed the bowler into the luggage-rack and sat down.

By the time the solicitor came back the compartment was blue with the smoke of Bogey roll and bluer still with descriptions of the weather. But the air wasn't so thick that he didn't see that his seat had been taken. He entered confidently.

'Excuse me, my man,' he said, 'that's my seat, you know.'

'Oh aye,' said the farmer, moving his pipe to the other side of his mouth. 'How's that?'

'Well, goodness me, didn't you notice? I booked that seat with my bowler hat there.'

'Ah, well, mannie,' said the farmer, 'ye may as weel ken – it's erses that books seats on the Buchan line.'

Charlie Allan, The Buchan Line, *from* Neeps and Strae (Ardo Publishing Co., Methlick, *1996*)

Border Incident

One day a mutual friend of ours, a great democrat, was travelling there third class, and two men got in. One lit a pipe, and in a few minutes deposited a fearful spit close to our friend's toe. He became infuriated and launched forth: 'Good heavens, sir, you, an educated Scotsman, perform this filthy act. Let me tell you that not only is it a dirty habit, but one which may infect our lungs, and therefore dangerous. Never do it again while I am in the carriage!' The spitter had never been spoken to like this before. He gazed blankly, and apparently abashed, knocked the ashes out of his pipe, but never said a word until they came to the next station, when he turned to his pal and remarked: 'We'll get oot here, John, and leave yon puir earrl to his lonely grandeur!'

W. G. Elliott, In My Anecdotage (*1925*). *The author gives John Buchan as the source of the tale.*

The Skipper of the *St Ola*

When I first went to Orkney the journey was made in one of several generations of *St Ola's*, a steamboat of old-fashioned design on to which cars were driven over planks and in whose saloon burnt a coal fire. She rolled and bucketed and wallowed. But my memory is that she got across the Firth in weather which now causes her far larger and more sophisticated successors to skulk in port. Her skipper, Captain Swanson, was a man of independence and character, red of face and large of body. It was said that he had many brushes with the military who ran the harbours during the war. One story runs that having taken his ship out of Scrabster more or less in defiance of the Guards' officer in charge of the port, he picked up his megaphone and bawled at the exquisite but slightly absurdly turned out figure on the pier, who must indeed have looked rather like a commissionaire, ' I have seen better dressed and more capable dummies than you outside cinemas.'

Jo Grimond (1913–1993), Memoirs (*1979*)

An Unfortunate Mix-up

'The Chief of Raasay was in one respect a most fortunate man, for he had ten daughters born to him, and beautiful ladies they were . . . When he was going to Edinburgh Lady Raasay asked him to buy a piano. For the girls must be taught music, else how can they take their rightful place in the world of fashion when the time comes?

'So the Chief bought a piano in Glasgow – a spinet mounted on four legs. The legs were taken off, and the spinet was packed in a crate and put on a steamer at the Broomielaw in Glasgow to be delivered in Raasay.

'On the same steamer was placed another crate, very much the same as the crate containing the spinet. But inside this crate was a coffin containing the body of Finlay the Piper, who had laid it as a last command upon his family that his body be buried with his ancestors at Portree . . .'

'But why did they put the coffin in a crate?' asked Mary, who had stopped spinning, entranced by this tale though she had been wearied by the previous talk. 'I never heard of a coffin in a crate. It sounds a fairy-tale.'

'No so,' answered Alasdair. 'It was put into a crate right enough, and the reason was this: before the schoolmasters came to the Island and taught the people that the world is round and goes rushing round the sun instead of the sun round it, the people were full of idle superstitions. One of these was that it was most unlucky to carry a dead man in a ship. As the sailors on the steamer were mostly from the Island, they would refuse to sail with a coffin in the ship, so the dead man in the coffin was hid by a crate.

'Now what happened at Clachan, Raasay, when the steamer arrived would never have happened were it not for the time of the year. It was the last night of the year when the ferry boat came out to meet the steamer. And you know in those days it was not considered right that anyone should bid farewell to the old year without many a *deoch slainte*. It was the right thing, and everybody in those days was careful to do the right thing.

'The last night of the year is specially dangerous to ships sailing among the Isles. If you hear of ships driven on rocks, of drowned passengers and lost seamen, it most often happens on the last night of the year. I find no fault with the sailors; but at any rate, when the crate that was supposed to contain the piano was opened in the big room in the Chief's house at Clachan the young ladies fainted and Lady Raasay was carried to her bed in a fit. But the future Lady Hastings, who ruled as a Queen over India, soon rallied her nine sisters and bore them off to a room at the top of the house, where she set them to play a game . . .'

'What had happened?' asked Red William.

'Need you ask?' was the reply. 'The sailors, celebrating the old year as they were right in doing, handed down into the ferry-boat the wrong crate.'

'And what happened to the piano?' asked Mary.

'I am just coming to that,' resumed Alasdair. 'You are so impatient. You are like my grandson who when he gets a story-book reads the first few pages and then the last few pages. He can't wait; he must know at once how the story ends. The end of the story is just as you might expect. The friends of Finlay the Piper assembled in Portree for the funeral. The steamer was late. It was the last day of the year, as I have said, and it hung heavy on their hands. But the Caledonian Hotel was there. They spent much of the day under its hospitable roof. That was a grand place in its day. The third cousin of my wife, Bean a Chaledonian, was hospitality and kindness itself. When in the gloaming the steamer came, the mourners found that Wentworth Street was not quite so broad as it used to be. They never so much as noticed anything different from the usual shape in the supposed coffin. There really wasn't much difference in shape. They bore it, in as good an order as could be expected on the last night of the year, to the churchyard and lowered it in the grave which had been prepared.

'Then the first spade of soil was thrown in on the coffin. . . And out of the grave there came a musical sound . . . bing . . . bing. The sexton dropped the spade. The mourners stepped back from the grave.

'"Heaven help us," cried Calum Uisdean, "Finlay is playing the pipes in his coffin."

'"Oh, you amadan," cried a mourner, "that wasn't the sound of the pipes. It was a wail of agony."

'They rushed to the Caledonian to renew their courage. One said one thing and one another. The policeman was summoned; he brought the doctor; they went back to the graveyard. The doctor took charge, and got the coffin brought up out of the grave. In the light of a lantern dimly burning the coffin was prised open. And there was the piano of the last Chief of Raasay . . . '

'What happened to Finlay the Piper?' asked Mary.

'Need you ask? A boat with four oars brought Finlay the Piper on the first day of the New Year to Portree. The Chief of Raasay sent his best boat with the coffin. And in the evening they buried him beside his ancestors with all due honour and respect. And that night there was in Portree a funeral celebration such as the Island had not known since the day when no funeral was deemed respectable unless there were half a dozen good fights after it. When the new dispensation came to the Island and all sorts of good old customs were put under the ban, including even the music of bagpipes, fighting after a funeral came to an end. Peggie Nighean Uisdean, when they told her that there wasn't a single fight after the burial of her husband, exclaimed, 'John is buried and not a single bloody head in the churchyard. Shame is on me, for they will say of me that I spared the whisky at my husband's funeral.' That's how times change. What is an honour with one generation becomes a disgrace with the next. But the funeral of Finlay the Piper was long remembered: for that night six slept soundly in the cells of the new prison in Portree.'

Finlay J. Macdonald, Crotal and White

An Intolerable Fellow-traveller

Falconer of Phesdo in Kincardineshire, MP for that county, used to journey to London to attend Parliament in that stage coach. He had travelled much abroad, was a humourist, and fond of talking. A gentleman who knew him told me that at the beginning of one of these London journeys he addressed the companions of his journey in the following terms: 'Ladies and gentlemen! We are going to be companions for three weeks; it will add much to the comfort of our society to know something of each other; I am Falconer of Phesdo, going to London to attend my duty in Parliament; if you gentle-men and ladies will be as communicative as I, it will point our conversation to the topics which each person is best qualified to speak on, and may instruct or amuse the rest of the company.' – But the Scottish shyness pre-vented all but one other gentleman from following his example.

Henry Mackenzie (1745–1831), The Anecdotes and Egotisms of Henry Mackenzie

The Carlisle Goods

. . . many an evening my father was to be its train guard. Although this was an arduous duty involving thirty-six hours away from home it was, I know, his favourite task. Like a similar duty to and fro from Berwick it meant traversing his beloved Border country, an act which though mostly accom-plished in darkness in these circumstances never failed to delight him. . . . The knowledge that my father occupied the van made me long to accom-pany him on his journey, but of course there was no question of my being allowed to complicate his duties and I kept my distance on the bridge. Soon the Carlisle got right of way and with a sharp high-pitched NB whistle the superheater got easily on the move. As she chuffed gently under the bridge my eyes would focus hopefully on the guard's van. Father, however, was a Scot and I understood his native distrust of demonstration. Prolonged cheer-ing and waving were out. His habit was to wait until the van approached the bridge, lean out nonchalantly to see if I were present, acknowledge my greeting with one wave of his arm, and promptly retire inside. In view of what I considered to be the seriousness of his duties his gravity of manner never seemed inappropriate. I thought he was wonderful.

Thomas Middlemas, Mainly Scottish Steam *(1973). The 'NB whistle' was the characteristic toot of the North British Railway's engines.*

The Lagg Ferry

On arriving at the ferry, we found every corner of the inn crowded with drovers who had been detained by the weather for several days, and were passing their time, as was their wont, in riotous and continuous drinking.

We felt it was no agreeable sojourn to stay in the inn with these half-intoxicated and noisy people, for the very air was impregnated with the odour of whisky.

We appealed to the ferrymen to take us across. At first they positively refused on account of the storm, but with some persuasion, and a handsome douceur, their scruples were overcome, and they prepared for the voyage.

No sooner had the drovers, who had been so long detained, heard that the boat was to cross at our instigation, than they got excessively angry, talked in Gaelic long and loud, and insisted that we should take at the same time a cargo of their cattle. This the boatman could not refuse, and eighteen cattle were put on board.

The boat was of great width of beam, and the cattle were fastened with their heads to rings on the gunwale on each side. We also had the chief drover's pony, which stood in the middle of the boat.

The wind was quite in our favour, but it blew furiously, and the sea was high, but its severity we did not so much notice in the shelter of the harbour.

At last we cleared the land, and got into the channel. How the wind did roar, and how the cattle struggled to get their heads free! The extent of sail we carried was forcing the bow of the boat too deep into the sea, and there was fear of being swamped.

The men tried to lower the sail, which, in their agitation, they could not effect, and all looked helpless.

On this the drover seized the helm, and with sharp and decisive words took command of the boat. By his admirable steering he relieved her a good deal, and enabled the men to lessen sail. Still the boat flew before the wind and rolled heavily; every moment we expected would be our last. I grasped the stirrup of the saddle on the pony, in the hope that if we did go the creature might swim ashore.

How admirably the drover steered! We had to take the narrow and rocky entrance of Lagg harbour, a most difficult navigation; but the drover's sharp and distinct orders were promptly obeyed, and in no time he landed us in shelter within the little bay. . . The time we took to effect the crossing, nine miles, was little more than half an hour.

Joseph Mitchell (1803–1883), Reminiscences of My Life in the Highlands. *To get from Islay to the mainland, he and his companions crossed to Jura, and walked the entire length of that island in a rainstorm to reach the ferry. Most nineteenth-century travellers in the Islands have similar tales to tell.*

UNIVERSITIES

A One-Man University

. . . the remarkable progress of his pupils, with the public applause he received at their laureation, induced the magistrates of Edinburgh to fix upon Mr Rollock as a fit person to open their university, for which they had received a charter from King James the previous year. This invitation Mr Rollock was persuaded to accept, and in the beginning of winter 1583 he entered, with all his accustomed zeal upon his laborious office, being the sole teacher, and in his own person comprising the character of principal and professors in the infant establishment.

Robert Chambers, Scottish Biographical Dictionary. *Robert Rollock (1555–1598) was a young professor at St Andrews when he was appointed Edinburgh University's first Principal.*

A College Librarian

In the College of Edinburgh about the middle or latter part of the seventeenth century there was a strange, vain, pedantic librarian, whose name, I think, was Henderson. He knew Latin well, but little of his own tongue, if that might be called English. When Oliver Cromwell was in Scotland, he visited the library of Edinburgh College, accompanied by the librarian, whom he cautioned that in the confusion of the times he must be very attentive and take care that none of the books were embezzled. After some minutes of rumination, his conductor hoped his Highness would allow him to ask if that word embezzled was derived from the Latin *imbecillis*.

. . . The North wall of the College then, as it continued to do even in my life-time, like the Tower of Pisa leaned very much outwards off the perpendicular; and there was a traditionary prediction that it was to fall on the wisest man in the College. Henderson would never pass this wall for fear of its falling on him.

Henry Mackenzie (1745–1831), The Anecdotes and Egotisms of Henry Mackenzie

Student Pranks, 1680-style . . .

December 25th, being Zooll day, the youths of the Colledge of Edinburgh having caused make the pope's effigies of timber, with a painted face, lyke a man, the head covered with a lyert pirewig, on his head a triple crown of timber, in his ryght hand a key and piece of money, in his left hand a cross and a lighted candle, and his body covered with a gown of stamped calligo, the belly bosse, and filled with powder, mounted on a chaire, was carryed by them up Blackfrier-wind, and burnt in the high town. This the Duke of York took ill, as a reflection on him, being then in the Abbay of Halyrudhous . . . 22nd January 1681, there was a proclamation at the Cross of Edinburgh, commanding all the students of the Colledge to remove off the town fifteen myles. This was done for burning the pope's effigies.

Robert Law, Diary, *quoted in J. G. Fyfe*, Scottish Diaries and Memoirs, 1550–1746 (1907)

. . . and a Few Years Later

Two episodes of disorderliness which took place under Principal Alexander Monro, who was elected in 1685, are described. In one, a student named

Robert Brown fixed a placard on the College gates threatening to kill the regents and ordering the Principal to recant a sermon which he had preached. Despite this, no action was taken against Brown. However, when he and some friends went to the house of Sir George Lockhart, Lord President of the Court of Session, who was away from home, and frightened his wife, Monro's patience gave way: 'I confess I could no longer forbear,' he relates, 'I went to the class where Brown was, and called him to the Upper Gallery, and gave him all his proper names, and threatened him, if he did not immediately beg my Lady Lockhart's pardon, I would break his bones. All these big words I said to him, and the day thereafter extruded him with the usual solemnities. Upon which he frequently swore he would be revenged, and told the under Janitor that he had bought a pair of pistols to shoot me (one might have served).' On another occasion a Mr Gourlay, although not a regent himself, had been employed to do the work of one of the regents, Herbert Kennedy. 'The boys found him out of his element,' reports Monro, 'and drove him out of the schools with snow-balls.' After this Gourlay probably ceased to teach, but continued to live in the College until the students, learning that he had been licensed to preach by the Presbyterians (who were at that time nonconformists), 'beat up his chamber door and windows with stones; and pulling off his hat, cloak and periwig, and reproaching him with "Fanatic", forced him to remove from the chamber which he had possessed peacefully before.'

Christine Shepherd, University Life in the Seventeenth Century, *from Gordon Donaldson (ed.),* Four Centuries: Edinburgh University Life, 1583–1983 (1983). *The reference to 'boys' is a reminder of how young students were: equivalent to the upper years of secondary school pupils. They appear to have adhered to a stoutly Episcopalian middle way between Catholics and Presbyterians.*

A Youthful Professor

At fifteen years of age, Mr Maclaurin took his degree of master of arts . . . The subject he selected for his thesis was the 'Power of Gravity', and this, according to the custom of the times, it was necessary for him to defend publicly. It may be necessary to observe, for the information of those who are not acquainted with the manner in which such disputations were conducted in Scotland, that the candidate was left free to select for this ordeal any literary or scientific subject he thought proper. The depth and boldness of the topic proposed by young Maclaurin at once revealed what kind of studies had engaged his attention while at the university, and excited the wonder and admiration of all present. In most instances, the subjects of disputation were of a trifling kind, and adapted chiefly to afford the candidate an opportunity of displaying his ingenuity and acquaintance with the

mood and figure of the school of logic. But the mind of our youthful philosopher disdained to stoop to anything puerile or commonplace, and the
sublimity of his subject showed at once the nature of his studies and the
depth of his erudition. At that time the philosophy of Newton was comparatively unknown, and even men the most distinguished in science were
slow to comprehend the great and important truths it contained. . .

When Mr Maclaurin was only nineteen years old, in the autumn of 1717,
a vacancy occurred in the professorship of mathematics in the Marischal
college of Aberdeen. For this he presented himself as a candidate. . . A very
able competitor appeared in the field against him, but after a competition,
or comparative trial of excellence, which lasted for ten days, Mr Maclaurin
was declared the successful candidate.

Robert Chambers, Scottish Biographical Dictionary. *Colin Maclaurin
(1698–1746), born on Tiree, later became Professor of Mathematics at
Edinburgh and was one of those responsible for the dramatic raising of the
standards of intellectual life in the eighteenth century.*

Academic Innovation

Hutcheson's first step was to discipline his class, 'by keeping the students to
rules, catalogues, exact hours &c. wherein there is certainly a very great
decay', and then to organise the class work. This was altogether a new
departure, as under the Regent system, much time was spent in elementary
work. Hutcheson, instead of confining himself to an oral commentary in
Latin upon some scholastic text-book, inaugurated a new method of lecturing in English, and he covered the whole field of 'Natural Religion, Morals,
Jurisprudence and Government', in the five daily lectures he gave each week.

William Robert Scott, Francis Hutcheson *(1900). Hutcheson (1694–1746)
became Professor of Moral Philosophy at Glasgow in 1729. His teaching
methods, including his walking up and down the lecture room while talking, startled his students and outraged some of his more traditionally minded
colleagues.*

Academic Conservatism

Professors of Scottish Universities are mostly 'celestial bodies'; but 'there is
one glory of the sun and another glory of the moon, and another glory of
the stars'. Not all of them are always revered by all their pupils. Caird . . .
delighted at rare intervals to refer to one or two of the more quaint and
antique of the theological Professors. One of them, he said, was engaged for
the greater part of his life upon a book which, according to the author,
'began with the Infinite and Absolute and went right on', but it did not get
beyond the first sentence. The same Professor used to object to all proposals

for the increase of scientific teaching in the College on the ground that 'it was not consistent with the idea of a University as it existed in the Divine Mind'. And he held the medical faculty in horror and fear – as 'an exacting and expensive Faculty, not only of doubtful benefit, but a detrimental and deteriorating influence in the history of this University'.

   Sir Henry James and John Henry Muirhead, The Life and Philosophy of Edward Caird (1921). *Caird was a student at Glasgow in the mid-nineteenth century.*

Moral Philosophy from the Soap Factory

The greatest joke in Wilson's life was his appointment to the Chair of Moral Philosophy at Edinburgh in 1820. It was an unashamedly political appointment. By far and away the best candidate for the position was Sir William Hamilton, but Hamilton was a Whig, and the Town Council, which made the appointment, had a large Tory majority. The Whigs did not give up without a fight. 'The Chaldee Manuscript' and other indiscretions of *Blackwood's* were cast up against him and his moral character impugned, much to Wilson's anguish, for, fierce though his own critical attacks could be, he could not bear the slightest touch of adverse criticism himself. Scott and other influential Tories bestirred themselves on his behalf. In the end, Wilson won easily, by twenty-one votes to nine. . .

   When Wilson learned that he had got the Chair, jubilation soon gave way to panic. He had now to give regular lectures on moral philosophy, and what did he know of moral philosophy? He sat down and wrote an impassioned plea to his old college friend Alexander Blair, a critic and philosopher who later became Professor of Rhetoric and Belles Lettres at University College, London, but who was now working at his father's soap factory near Birmingham. After telling Blair of his appointment, and describing the anguish he had suffered during the campaign of defamation against him, he went on:

> God only knows what is to be the ultimate issue. One thing is certain, that if I can get through the *first course of Lectures* with reputation, my future life may glide on usefully and respectably. I therefore, my best friend, conjure you by all that is holy beneath the heavens to listen, now, to my words – and, if you can do what I now implore, you will confer upon me the greatest blessing one human being ever conferred upon another, and, ultimately, be no sufferer in anything yourself. . . Whatever subjects you propose to me, let them be tolerably easy.

. . . Blair could not come to stay with Wilson in Edinburgh, but he helped his friend by writing a series of long impersonal letters which contained the substance of a course in moral philosophy. This set the pattern that was to continue for years. Wilson depended absolutely on Blair's letters, and could not lecture at all without them. Sometimes the expected letter did not arrive until the morning of the lecture, and he read it on the way to the university. Wilson's appeals to Blair make the most extraordinary reading. When a student asks a question or proposes an objection, Wilson has him put it in writing and forwards it to Blair for his answer. Here is a typical extract from a letter to Blair: 'I enclose a letter from one of my students. If the objections in it appear good and worthy of answer I wish you to state them as general objections to our Theory, and to refute them.' Or this: 'Could you send me a good letter-full on the effects of passion on association? Anything you chuse bold and eloquent.'

David Daiches, Christopher North, *from* Literary Essays *(1956). John Wilson (1785–1854) is better known under his pseudonym Christopher North (see also the Writers section). Daiches notes that despite his ignorance of the subject, Wilson as a lecturer was a huge success: 'Few remembered what he said, but all agreed that he was wonderful.'

Professors at Play

With the meeting on Friday, 2 April 1875 the symposium moved to the Balmoral Hotel, 91 Princes Street, which remained its venue for the rest of its recorded existence. The Lord Provost sang 'The Bonny House o' Airlie', and Blackie, after mystifying his colleagues with a Gaelic song, *'Mairi Laghach'*, gave his own Jenny Geddes to the tune of 'The British Grenadiers', beginning:

> Some praise the fair Queen Mary, and some the good Queen Bess,
> And some the wise Aspasia, beloved by Pericles,
> But o'er all the world's brave women, there's one that bears the rule,
> The valiant Jenny Geddes that flung the three-legged stool,
> With a row-dow-at-them-now! Jenny fling the stool!

The song gave rise to an animated discussion as to 'whether the stool hurled at the head of the Dean in St Giles had three or four feet.' Professor Wallace even doubted the historical existence of such a person as Jenny Geddes, but found no-one to back up his theory. 'There being likely to be no agreement among the respective supporters of the quadruple and tripedal theories of Jenny Geddes' missile, Sir Robert Christison remarked that as the Symposium had by a committee been the means of settling the difficult geographical question as to the existence of the island of Eig, there was good hope that by the same agency the historical question as to Jenny Geddes might be definitely settled.

... The committee appointed to investigate the Jenny Geddes question reported on 31 March 1876. The stool said to have been hers had been inspected in the Antiquarian Museum. It had four legs and was so heavy that the Dean would not have survived a blow on the head from it. The committee was inclined to favour a statement by Robert Mein in his pamphlet 'The Cross removed, prelacy and patronage disproved' [1756] that it was his grandmother, Barbara Hamilton, who had led the disturbance in St Giles. Masson begged leave, as a minority of one, to present a separate report: the main report 'concedes too much to the wretched spirit of scepticism prevalent in this day. Jenny Geddes and her stool are precious articles of our national belief not to be given up without danger of sapping the foundations of society in our beloved Scotland.'

C. P. Finlayson, The Symposium Academicum, *from Gordon Donaldson (ed.), Four Centuries: Edinburgh University Life, 1583–1983 (1983)*

Lord Kelvin Does Not Shine

When Kelvin, then plain Mr Thomson, went off to lay the Atlantic cable, his place was taken by a Mr Day, much inferior in scientific genius, but much superior as a teacher. Just before the great man came back, burdened with celebrity and a brand-new knighthood, a student wrote on the blackboard, 'Work while the Day liveth, for the Knight cometh wherein no man may work.'

Colm Brogan, The Glasgow Story (1952). *Kelvin taught at Glasgow University, and according to Brogan his classes 'resembled a disorderly political meeting'.*

Student Pranks, circa 1910

A music hall entertainer and magician had got himself into trouble with the police by printing the letters MD after his name in some of his advertisements. He said in court that the letters did not mean Doctor of Medicine, but Merry Devil, and waved the matter aside with a light laugh. He was punished by a small fine. But we, who could not become MDs without at least seven years of hard work, did not so easily forgive him. When he came to Glasgow to give his entertainment a handful of medical students in the gallery hissed and booed him. The magician came down to the footlights and delivered himself very aptly on the subject of the medical profession in general and of medical students in particular. He wound up by quoting the poet Burns to the effect that, 'They gang in stirks and come oot asses.'

He then proceeded with his entertainment ... I have no recollection that he pretended to be anything other than a showman, and what followed seems to me to be beyond his deserts.

On a certain Thursday morning a Jewish medical student wrote on the back of an envelope 'Meet at the first house of the Coliseum tonight.' Not more than fifty men can have seen the notice, and the Jewish student was quite an obscure person. But by half past six that evening the Coliseum music hall was packed with students. Their pockets were bulging with missiles and grim determination was written on their faces. The atmosphere was electric enough to provide the magician with free current for the rest of his life. The turns preceding his were galloped through at top speed and greeted with thunderous applause. The fatal number went up. There was a dead silence. After a pause the curtain rose on a sort of woodland glade in which a prominent structure was the Cage of Death, an alarming structure of polished metal connected with miles of flex. There was no magician. The orchestra struck a few chords, and a lady in blue appeared tentatively from the wings, followed by the doctor himself. The mob had somehow been unprepared for a mixed target. They shouted to the magician to take the woman off. There was a short, irresolute interval. And then an ungallant potato hit La Belle Electra on the knee. Down came the fireproof curtain and the audience surged forward to the orchestra, shouting, yelling and swearing. My own experience of what happened next is a little limited. A drunken lad in my neighbourhood produced a revolver, announcing that it was loaded and he was going to shoot the buzzard. I reached over, took the revolver from him and kicked it below the seats. I then tripped him up and sat on his head. When I looked over the seat-back I saw the stage occupied by five students, who were giving an impromptu music-hall turn of little merit. They were capering, singing, and waving sticks. They were joined by a more determined figure, a broad, prognathous man called Alexander Garvie. He took the stick from the nearest student and thrust it through the fireproof curtain. Most of us were very much astonished, for we had believed the fireproof curtains to be made of wrought iron; but Garvie pulled the stick upwards and downwards till he had made a six-foot rent in the curtain and through this rent he boldly entered.

I had got my murderer into a chastened mood and now held him on a plush seat with his arm twisted behind his back. The students were now charging down the corridors and over the backs in the seats, making for the rent in the curtain. The circles and the gallery were standing up shouting for the magician at the tops of their voices.

After he had passed the rent, disarmed a stage-hand with a broom, Garvie saw an unco sight. On the stage were two hundred policemen. I have checked the figures and know them to be accurate. He had never seen so many policemen before. He was seized and thrown through the rent his own hands had made.

We saw Garvie perform a back somersault, hit the stage and fall over into the orchestra. He was there seized by the throat by a plain-clothes man and removed rapidly from view. Then through the hole in the curtain poured the police, with batons drawn and battle in their eyes. Except for that one potato, our ammunition was intact, and we let them have it. They came bravely one by one, and on each was registered at least a dozen hits. Peasemeal bombs, bags of maize, eggs, potatoes, tomatoes, herring, soot, thickened the air, and policeman after policeman leapt from the stage over the orchestra railing and into the eel-pit. They were blinded and angry and they laid about them with their batons. The mob hit back with ash sticks and knuckles, but were being driven back slowly to the entries, and it looked highly probable that someone would be killed when Williamson, an ex-President of the Union, rushed up to the police lieutenant and seized him by the lapels, shrieking at him, 'Call your men off or I hold you responsible for anything that happens.'

The word responsible penetrated the angry lieutenant's consciousness, and he blew a shrill blast on his whistle. Everything became astonishingly quiet. The policemen stopped bludgeoning, and the students stopped fighting and swearing. Williamson, the lieutenant and the President of the SRC made their way to the stage. Williamson shouted in his little, thin voice that he would make the magician apologise and then we must all go home quietly; and the party then disappeared through the rent and shortly the fireproof curtain rose. In the meantime there had been a good deal of skilful and unostentatious shouldering of students out into the street. The platform party consisted of the three before mentioned and the magician. The last-named appeared to say something, a tomato hit Williamson on the chest, the platform party began to argue with one another, the fireproof curtain fell, a few shots were fired, but the police 'had the matter well in hand' . . .

. . . On Monday five students appeared in the police court on various charges arising out of the incident. A bewildered bailie sat on the bench; the prosecuting counsel was a police officer in uniform; for the defence there appeared two magnificent King's Counsel, one of them a sheriff, and two or three distinguished juniors. This array of wigs and gowns had a striking effect upon the bailie and the police witnesses. A few leading liars were put up to testify to the impeccable behaviour of the five martyrs. One was fined a pound, another was admonished, and the other three left the court without a stain on their characters.

J. M. Bridie (Osborne Henry Mavor, 1888–1951), One Way of Living (1939)

WITCHES AND WARLOCKS

Major Weir's Cane

Major Weir . . . was a distinguished warlock of his time, and a very particular friend of 'Sathan'. This intimacy was productive of fatal results, as it led to his being burnt for crimes, of which witchcraft was the least, in the year1670. 'He was dreaded for his sorceries, and admired for his gift of prayer.' Weir's reputation for sanctity and his facility of praying had for a number of years rendered his presence a comfort to those who were sick and in trouble. Upon occasion of his visits he always took his cane, without which he was unable to give religious consolation, and he uniformly leant upon it when in the act of praying. Common report asserts that this cane was his familiar spirit, and the devil had told him that so long as he had it in his hand no earthly power could hurt him. When carried from prison for execution, he held it in his hand; and when the fagots were attempted to be set on fire which were placed around him, they would not burn, although every effort was made to raise a flame, to the astonishment of the crowd assembled to witness his death. The executioner was told to remove the major's cane. It was forcibly wrenched from his grasp, and the torches applied to the wood, which instantly ignited, and in due time the unhappy wretch was reduced to ashes. The stick, when removed from Weir, flew up in the air and disappeared.

James Maidment, A Book of Scottish Pasquils, 1568–1715 (1868). *Thomas Weir was born at Kirkton, Carluke, in 1599. He became captain of the Edinburgh City Guard (and in that capacity abused and insulted Montrose before his execution) as well as being a leading Presbyterian. In the end he confessed publicly to a string of crimes and necromantic activities. His sister Jean was implicated in his activities, which included the admission that they had driven in a fiery coach from Edinburgh to Leith, with Satan at the reins; and was also accused of incest with him. She was hanged a few days after he was burned to death. In popular legend, his pact with the devil made him free of all dangers, except for 'one burn'. He was always very careful when crossing streams, but the 'burn' turned out to be of a different nature. It was recorded that no one dared to live in the Weirs' house in the West Bow, Edinburgh, for almost a hundred years after their deaths.*

Silver Bullets Needed

But especially the scattered Covenanters believed firmly that their chief persecutors received from the Evil Spirit a proof against leaden bullets – a charm, that is, to prevent their being pierced or wounded by them. There were many supposed to be gifted with this necromantic privilege. In the battle of Rullion Green, on the Pentland Hills, many of the Presbyterians were willing to believe that the balls were seen hopping like hailstones from Tom Dalziel's buff-coat and boots. Silver bullets were not supposed to be neutralized by the same spell; but that metal being scarce among the persecuted Covenanters, it did not afford them much relief.

. . . To John Graham of Claverhouse, a Scottish officer of high rank, who began to distinguish himself as a severe executer of the orders of the Privy

Council against nonconformists, the Evil Spirit was supposed to have been still more liberal than to Dalziel ... He not only obtained proof against lead, but the devil is said to have presented him with a black horse, which had not a single white hair upon its body. This horse, it was said, had been cut out of the belly of its dam, instead of being born in the usual manner. On this animal Claverhouse was supposed to perform the most unwonted feats of agility, flying almost like a bird along the sides of precipitous hills, and through pathless morasses, where an ordinary horse must have been smothered or dashed to pieces. It is even yet believed that mounted upon this steed, Claverhouse (or Clavers, as he is popularly called) once turned a hare on the mountain named the Brandlaw, at the head of Moffatdale, where no other horse could have kept its feet.

Sir Walter Scott (1771–1832), Tales of a Grandfather. *It was widely believed that it had taken a silver bullet to kill Claverhouse, by then Viscount Dundee, at Killiecrankie in 1689.*

The Flying Countess

I am weel assured that the Countess of Dumfreice, Stair's daughter, was under a very odd kind of distemper, and did frequently fly from the one end of the room to the other, and from the one side of the garden to the other; whither by the effects of witchcraft upon her, or some other way, is a secret. The matter of fact is certain.

Robert Wodrow (1679–1734), Memoirs.

The Hag of the Cràach

The HAGS and GOBLINS that haunted certain localities were almost as much dreaded as the Devil. The worst of these was CAILLEACH A' CRATHAICH, the Hag of the Cràach – a wild and mountainous district lying between Corrimony and Glenmoriston. This being rejoiced in the death of men, the Macmillans being especially the objects of her fierce malice. Her manner was to accost some lonely wayfarer across the wilds, and secretly deprive him of his bonnet. As he travelled on in ignorance of his loss, she rubbed the bonnet with might and main. As the bonnet was worn thin by the friction, the man grew weary and faint, until at last, when a hole appeared in it, he dropped down and died. In this way fell at least five Macmillans within the last hundred and twenty years – and all were found in the heather without a mark of violence. One evening Donald Macmillan, Balmacaan, met her at Cragan a' Crathaich, and exchanged a passing salutation with her. He went on his way unaware of the fact that she had taken his bonnet. His eyes were, however, soon opened, and he hastened back to the Cragan, where he found her rubbing his head-gear with great vigour. A terrible struggle took place for its possession, in which he in the end prevailed; but as he hurried away from her she hissed into his ear that he would die at nine o'clock on a certain evening. When the evening arrived, his family and neighbours gathered around him, and prayed and read the Scriptures. The hag's words were, however, to be fulfilled, and, as the clock struck the fatal hour, he fell back in his chair and expired.

William Mackay, Urquhart and Glenmoriston: Olden Times in a Highland Parish (*1914*)

Conversation with a Witch

Jean Roy (Red Jean) was a sensible, industrious old woman, and was by no means a bogey to anyone in the parish, yet she was, by all her neighbours, regarded as 'uncanny' . . . One day Jean had no milk, and went to a neighbour's house to ask for some. This neighbour, who had heard all about Jean, curtly refused, as she believed that the milk was asked for, not because it was really needed, but that Jean should get a 'foretaste' of it, and then she would be able to bewitch the cow and get all the milk for herself. Jean was indignant at the unexpected refusal and said, 'Weel, you cannot expect your cow to be a blessing to you when you refuse a drop of milk to a poor widow.' Within a week that cow was choked on a turnip. A few days after this she asked a fisherman for a piece of rope, and he gave her thirty yards. When she measured it she said, 'You will bring thirty crans of herring in tomorrow.' He did, and Jean's reputation as a witch was established.

With all this knowledge of Jean, half a pound of tea, and two pounds of sugar, I ventured to call on her. She had seen me coming and courteously met me at the door and invited me in. I followed her, muttering the usual Gaelic salutation, 'Peace be here.' When she got me seated, it was a case of being interviewed. I had to tell her all I could of my forebears, where I had been since I left the parish, what I did, whether married, etc., etc. She told me that her father and my grandfather were once nearly caught red-handed in a smuggling bothy, and that the two of them quickly jumped into a peat bog, and with blackened bodies and faces they chased away the excisemen, and that my grandfather lost his situation as precentor in the church because of this escapade. All this and much more that she told me was news to me, and I felt that it was about time that I should turn the tables and get her to talk about herself. . .

'I am glad you like tea,' I said, 'as I have brought you some.'

'Now that was very kind of you.'

'Not at all,' I answered, 'because I wish to ask you a favour.'

'Weel?'

'I want you to cure my toothache.'

'O, poor man, do you suffer from that? I never thought you would come to me to do that.'

She then became cautious, and added, 'Weel, some people say that I can cure it, but perhaps yours is not of the kind that I can cure.'

After being assured that her cure would be tried, and that people had been telling me of cures wrought by her, she went 'ben' the house, and during the next quarter of an hour I could hear muttered spellings. At length she came out with a paper carefully folded, and told me it was to be worn over my heart and under my waistcoat for seven days. 'You must not tell that you got it or the toothache will come back.'

But I – heretic that I am – opened it ere I had been half an hour away from her, and this is what was written on it in a very shaky hand:

> Petter sat on a marable ston weaping. Jesus cam by and said 'What ales ye petter?' Petter answered and said 'Oh Lord the tuack.' Jesus answered and said 'Be ye weel from the tuack Petter, and not only ye but all that believe on me.' May the Lord bless his own words and unto him the praise. Amen.

'You can do two or three other things,' I said – 'Oh, well, not much. People sometimes say that I can take things out of people's eyes, but it was my good father that told me how to do that; but I will tell you. I need to know the name and surname of the sufferer, and then after the sun sets, and before it rises, I go to a well opening to the north, and at the well mouth I say words in Gaelic which my father told me on his death bed. I then take a mouthful of the water and carry it back to the house, and when I put it out I always find the troublesome speck.'

'But how can that be,' I queried, 'when you haven't been near the sore eye?'

'Oh, well, I don't know; but I could give you the names of three or four folk who will tell you that I took things out of their eyes, and I do it because my father said, 'Freely ye have received, freely give,' and then she added with a trace of bitterness in her voice, 'Perhaps that is why so many people ask me to do this for them, but I never do harm to anyone.'

'That is not what Effie Macleod says,' I ventured to say. 'She thinks you choked her cow on a turnip.'

'Oh, no, I didn't. How could she expect any good to happen when she wouldn't give a poor creature a drop of milk, and me a friend of hers? The cow wouldn't choke if she were not too lazy to cut the turnips as she ought to do.'

'But didn't you give thirty crans of herring to Sandy Macfarlane?'

'Oh, no, I didn't; but everyone wishes well to poor Sandy, as he would give a body anything. The fish were sent into his nets that he might have more to give to the like of me. It's those that give that get.'

'But you could give good luck, though. They all say that', I contended.

'Oh, well, there are kind people to whom I wish well, and I wish them well openly, and it often happens as I wish; that's how. Sometimes they wish some token of my good wishes, and I give them a threepenny bit with a hole in it, and they think if they put it in the bottom of the churn they will have more butter, or a fisherman ties it in his nets and thinks he will get on better, but it is only a sign that Jean Mackay wishes them well. The old folk said that if this were done when the moon was growing it is better, and the old folks knew a lot.'

'Isn't it nonsense they say about wise women taking the shape of cats and worrying their enemies?'

'Oh, indeed, yes. Did you ever hear of the man at Thurso who said he was worried by black cats, and slashed right and left with a sword among them and cut off one of their hind legs, and the woman sent for the leg in the morning? He gave it back, and cats never bothered him after that. Didn't the folk laugh at him when the minister asked him what part of the body the woman would have sent for if he had cut off a cat's tail.'

Alexander Polson, Scottish Witchcraft Lore *(1932). The conversation took place in the 1890s.*

WITS

Punsters at Play

Lord Kelly, a determined punster, and his brother Andrew were drinking tea with James Boswell. Boswell put his cup to his head, 'Here's t'ye, my Lord.' – At that moment Lord Kelly coughed. – 'You have got a coughie,' said his brother. – 'Yes,' said Lord Kelly, 'I have been like to choak o' late.'

Henry Mackenzie (1745–1831), The Anecdotes and Egotisms of Henry Mackenzie

Sydney Smith Reflects on the Scots, Their Habits and Their Climate

They are so imbued with metaphysics that they even make love metaphysically. I overheard a young lady of my acquaintance, at a dance in Edinburgh, exclaim, in a sudden pause of the music, 'What you say, my Lord, is very true of love in the *abstract*, but –' here the fiddlers began fiddling furiously, and the rest was lost. No nation has so large a stock of benevolence of heart: if you meet with an accident, half Edinburgh immediately flocks to your door to inquire after your pure hand or your pure foot, and with a degree of interest that convinces you their whole hearts are in the inquiry. . . Their temper stands anything but an attack on their climate. They would have you even believe they can ripen fruit; and, to be candid, I must own in remarkably warm summers I have tasted peaches that made most excellent pickles; and it is upon record that at the siege of Perth, on one occasion, the ammunition failing, their nectarines made admirable cannon balls.

Sydney Smith (1771–1845), quoted in Lady Holland, Memoir of the Rev.
Sydney Smith *(1878)*

The Founding of the Edinburgh Review

Towards the end of my residence in Edinburgh, Brougham, Jeffrey and myself
happened to meet in the eighth or ninth storey or flat in Buccleuch Place,
the then elevated residence of Mr Jeffrey. I proposed that we should set up
a Review. This was acceded to with acclamation. I was appointed editor,
and remained long enough in Edinburgh to edit the first number of the
Review. The motto I proposed for the Review was, 'Tenui Musam meditamur
avena' – 'We cultivate literature on a little oatmeal.' But this was too near
the truth to be admitted; so we took our present grave motto from Publius
Syrus, of whom none of us had, I am sure, read a single line . . .

Sydney Smith, quoted in Lady Holland, Memoir of the Rev. Sydney Smith

Petrie of *The Clincher*

The editor of *The Clincher*, Alexander Wyllie Petrie (born c.1853, probably
in Kilmarnock, died 1937), was a Glasgow hairdresser fallen on hard times
who became one of the best-known street characters in the city round the
turn of the century. As 'The Glasgow Clincher' (he wore the name pasted
on his hat) he would cruise around Buchanan Street, mild-eyed, immacu-
lately dressed, dapper Paw Broon moustache, selling his small quarto
paper, and keeping up a continuous stream of impromptu wit on the topics
of the day. He was one of the last, and ablest, of the old 'street patterers'.
He was continually harassed by the police and the burgh courts; they shut
him up at least twice as a pauper lunatic; but Petrie, buoyant and irrepress-
ible, could seldom be kept off the streets for long. He had himself diagnosed
as sane, and then proclaimed he was the only certified sane man in Glasgow. . .

The Clincher had few advertisements, and any small return it made came
from the editor personally selling it in the city centre. The paper was entirely written by Petrie under a number of pseudonyms, and it supported a
large, imaginary staff, including a typewriter (female typist), reporters, office
boy, and lion tamer, all of whom commented trenchantly on their creator's
bêtes noires in the Scotland of his day.

Petrie regarded himself as an inspired fool lashing the corruptions of the
age

'. . . the only Editor in the Universe who has manifested the Golden
Sun Splendour of Transcendental Concentrated Race Experience.
Yes, I am also the inventor of Petrie's Golden Petals for the Hair,

and the Author of "Not Getting Old" and "Out on Bail". Yes, I am the Elect Dramatist of the age and last (but not least) the Creator of *The Glasgow Clincher* – The clinching *Clincher* that clincheth.'

William Donaldson, The Language of the People: Scots Prose From the Victorian Revival (*1989*)

WORK

The Spey Loggers

In order to have a run of water at command, the sources of the little rivers were managed artificially to suit floating purposes. Embankments were raised at the end of the lakes in the far-away glens, at the point where the different burnies issued from them. Strong sluice-gates, always kept closed, prevented the escape of any but a small rill of water, so that when a rush was wanted the supply was sure.

The night before a run, the man in charge of that particular sluice set off up the hill, and reaching the spot long before daylight opened the heavy gates; out rushed the torrent, travelling so quickly as to reach the deposit of timber in time for the meeting of the woodmen, a perfect crowd, among whom it was one of our enjoyments to find ourselves early in the day. The duty of some was to roll the logs into the water; this was effected by the help of levers . . . The next party shoved them off with long poles into the current, dashing in often up to the middle in water when any case of obstruction occurred. They were then taken in charge by the most picturesque group of all, the youngest and most active, each supplied with a clip, a very long pole thin and flexible at one end, generally a young tall tree; a sharp hook was fixed to the bending point, and with this, skipping from rock to stump, over brooks and through briers, this agile band followed the log-laden current, ready to pounce on any stray lumbering victim that was in any manner checked in its progress. There was something graceful in the action of throwing forth the stout yet yielding clip, an exciting satisfaction as the sharp hook fixed the obstreperous log. The many light forms springing about among the trees, along banks that were sometimes high, and always rocky, the shouts, the laughter, the Gaelic exclamations, and, above all, the roar of the water, made the whole scene one of the most inspiriting that either actors or spectators could be engaged in.

Elizabeth Grant (*1797–1885*), Memoirs of a Highland Lady 1797–1827 (*1898*). Clip *is Gaelic for hook.*

Fishwives on the Road

The most essential part of a fishwife's equipment was her plaid. In Inverallochy and Cairnbulg they wore a black and red dice of a different check. St Combs was blue and black, Broadsea black and white, Pitulie grey and white, Rosehearty natural and brown.

Often you were glad to dry your plaid at a tinkies fire. We always had a friendly relationship towards the tinkies, who lived in hoop tents on Strichen and New Deer moss. My mother aye smoked a pail of whitings to give to these folk, also they got our old clothes. As solitary women on the road we had a certain amount of protection from the tinkies. I have been glad on a dark night to walk from New Deer to Strichen in the company of old Foly Stewart, who told me much of the misery of their hard life. His great grand-father had fought with Stewart of Appin, and fled to Buchan from Culloden; they had no wish to settle in houses. My mother also gave a fishie to several mannies who lived in slab-built shelters, with a fire between a circle of stones on the side of the road. They broke stones into road mettle. They were glad of any titbit – 'He that giveth to the poor lendeth to the Lord'. Fishwives were often attacked both for money and carnal knowledge. All carried sharp gutting knives. I would not have hesitated to plunge it into anybody who attempted to molest me. The fisherwomen met at Strichen and came home in a bunch. An old iron pot and kettle lay in a sheltered corner above the Ugie; here the group would often brew tea and boil an egg. . . We sat down in a circle round a fire, and one of the number gave thanks before we ate; Old Mab from St Combs would ask the Almighty to bless our feet on our way home.

   Christian Watt (1833–1923), The Christian Watt Papers, *edited by David Fraser (1983)*

Bones

The job I took up in Fairport and kept for two years was a job in a bone factory. This was a place where fresh and decaying bones, gathered from all over Scotland, were flung into furnaces and reduced to charcoal. The char-coal was sold to refineries to purify sugar; the grease was filled into drums and dispatched for some purpose which I no longer remember. The bones, decorated with festoons of slowly writhing, fat yellow maggots, lay in the adjoining railway siding, and were shunted into the factory whenever the furnaces were ready for them. Seagulls, flying up from the estuary, were always about these bones, and the trucks, as they lay in the siding, looked as though they were covered with moving snowdrifts. There were sharp complaints from Glasgow whenever the trucks lay too long in the siding, for the seagulls could gobble up half a hundredweight of maggots in no time, and as the bones had to be paid for by their original weight, and the maggots were part of it, this meant a serious loss to the firm. After one of these complaints the foreman, an Irishman, would go out and let off a few shots at the seagulls, who would rise, suddenly darkening the windows. But in a little while they would be back again.

  Edwin Muir (1887–1959), Autobiography

Snowed Up

Monday, 28th December, 1908. The snow had started about midday. By early evening it was very bad. Even down at Girvan on the sea-shore it was whirling and drifting. The 4.15 express Glasgow to Stranraer was standing in Girvan station. The Stranraer engine backed on – 126, one of Smellie's Wee Bogies, Driver Willie McEwan and Fireman Charlie Robison. Out of the blizzard to the south came the train *from* Stranraer. They had had a terrible crossing of the moors. 'Run,' cried its driver Cuthbertson to his fireman, Geordie Thomson. 'Tell them for God's sake don't let the 4.15 away!' But officialdom shillied and shallied – there was no precedent – the 4.15 was let go.

Up at Barrhill it was worse. Surfacemen were out digging. There was a light engine lying in the station. But still no restraining hand was laid on the 4.15. In the appointed manner she left Barrhill and battled out into the storm. There were no snow fences then, and the cuts were filling. Up about The Gunners they got into a deep one, stuck, backed out, charged again, got through. Another mile they struggled on. Then in the cutting about Milepost 14 3/4 they stuck fast. All attempts to set back were unavailing.

Charlie Robison the fireman got the tablet and set out for Barrhill. He took the engine headlamp with him, but as he plunged and floundered among the drifts it was more bother than it was worth and as he passed the Gunner's Cut he hung it *on a telephone pole cross-bar,* so high had the drifts risen! And there, for many a day, it hung, a mute witness to that terrible journey. Robison got to Barrhill, gave up his tablet, and walked back to his train upon the moor!

It was an awful night. I remember it, up in our village at the head of the Doon Valley. There was illness in our family and my parents were up half the night. The carpet was billowing on the bedroom floor. The snow was of a strange powdery kind I'd never seen before; it was creeping through every seam; in the morning the dressing-table was festooned with it. The storm-bound train soon drifted up. It was *non-corridor.* There was no steam heating. In the compartments the snow seeped in till it was over the passengers' knees!

All night came no succour. The light engine from Barrhill had tried it, but had got only half-way and was lying abandoned in a drift. It was eleven o'clock next morning when a party from Barrhill made its way to them. By that time the only way they could get food to most of the passengers was by the lamp-holes in the carriage roofs. So passed another day. The water in the tender became exhausted. The enginemen threw out their fire, then when the remaining heat had faded out, they retreated to a surfacemen's hut at the north end of the cut. 'Why did you abandon the engine?' Manson railed at them at the enquiry. 'Why did you abandon the engine?'. . . Tuesday night went by.

Meanwhile from the north the work of rescue had been going on. Tragedy and comedy jostled one another. Early on Tuesday morning a train left Ayr with a squad of dock labourers from Troon. Just below Kilchoan they went slap into a big drift in the cutting. Out sprang the dockers with their shovels. But they left the doors open, and by the time they got a way cleared ahead she was drifted up solid, outside and *in*! So all day Tuesday they were working single-road past *that*. Then it was a time of bad unemployment, so they got a train-load of unemployed gathered at Kilmarnock and brought them down to Barrhill. The poor souls, ill-clad, ill-shod, took one look at the arctic wilderness and fled back into the train again!

The snow-plough got down. No 242A of Ayr shed was on it – an old Stirling 0–4–2 – Johnnie McGarva and Tam Young. She was no match for the drifts. So they brought out more and more engines to push her, till they had *seven* of them laying at it, and of course up about the Gunner's Cut instead of shoving her round the curve they put her straight out on to the moor! Up at the plough, Inspector Guinea, of St Enoch, was running about with a bottle of whisky in his pocket. A big Girvan driver removed it adroitly, then most earnestly helped Guinea to look for it.

On the Wednesday they got the doors on the lee-side of the train cleared and the passengers out. A relief train came up as far as it could and they got them transferred and taken down to Barrhill station. There they were lodged for the night. There was at least one child among them. On the Thursday they got the line cleared round by Dumfries, and the Stranraer passengers got home that night. One, a dairyman's wife from Kirkcolm, died the following morning.

On the Thursday afternoon they got the train out. Black and cold, the engine was brought back to Girvan shed with its crew, and, do you know, not a soul looked near them. The driver drifted away, probably to a public-house; the fireman was standing about, irresolute and shivering. Geordie Thomson was a young man, not long married. His house was nearby and he was just going off duty. 'Come hame wi' me,' he said to the fireman. 'We hinna much, but you're welcome to a share.' They brought him in and seated him at the kitchen table. With that peculiar effect of snow and smoke, the man was blacker than any negro, and as she hurried off with a meal, Mrs Thomson filled a basin of hot water and set it in front of him that he might wash. Next moment they heard a cry, and the fireman, his face buried in his arms, lay sobbing his heart out on the table . . .

For a man who, clad only in the poor garments of a fireman of those days, with bare hands and probably with no food, had fought and beaten the blizzard on the heights of the Chirmorie, had come pretty near the Edge.

David L. Smith, Tales of the Glasgow and South-Western Railway (*1937*). *James Manson was Locomotive Superintendent of the line; Hugh Smellie his predecessor.*

The Building of the *Nerissa*

At the beginning of November 1925 Sir James happened to encounter in London the Lord Mayor of Liverpool, Sir Frederick Bowring, whose firm managed the Red Cross Line (New York, Newfoundland and Halifax Steamship Company). Sir Frederick told him that the company would have liked to have a new cruising ship for the following year, which in winter would maintain their service between New York and Bermuda. They had failed, however, to place an order in time.

Sir James suggested that the work could, in fact, be done at Port Glasgow in seven months. This was an almost unheard-of undertaking in the case of a high-quality passenger ship of almost 6,000 tons, but a contract with William Hamilton and Company was signed on the 3rd of November. A night-shift was organized in the drawing-office and orders for steel were passed out, morning by morning, as the plans were completed. The keel was laid on the 10th. The workers in the yard undertook to do the necessary overtime. In a corner of the drawing office an artist prepared designs for the decoration of cabins and public rooms. The ship was launched on the 31st of March 1926. She completed her trials and was delivered to the owners on the 5th of June. The cost of the *Nerissa* had been £164,000.

For James Lithgow this was a demonstration to the world and to the industry itself that in spite of all its troubles British shipbuilding retained its efficiency and its workers their willingness and skill.

'The ordinary man in the street', he said at the launch, 'imagines that America is the place for hustle and that we on this side muddle along, that our equipment is not good, and that our manufacturers spend their time arguing points of wages with the men instead of getting on with the job. We never open a paper but we are advised to copy American methods and spend more money on plant. It seems to me that, so far, the *Nerissa* is rather a contradiction of that idea.'

J. M. Reid, James Lithgow: Master of Work (*1964*). *Not the least remarkable aspect of the story is that the building took place at a time of high industrial discontent, including the General Strike of February 1926.*

WRITERS

Dr Walter Anderson and Croesus, King of Lydia

Dr Walter Anderson . . . is a remarkable specimen of that class of authors who, without the least power of entertaining or instructing their fellow-creatures, yet persist in writing and publishing books, which nobody ever reads, and still, like the man crazed by the lottery, expect that the next, and the next, and the next, will be attended with success. Perhaps Anderson's *cacoethes scribendi* received its first impulse from the following ludicrous circumstance. His parish comprehending the house of Ninewells, he was often entertained there, in company with the brother of the proprietor – the celebrated David Hume. The conversation having turned one day on the successes of Mr Hume as an author, Anderson said, 'Mr David, I dare say other people might write books too; but you clever fellows have taken up all the good subjects. When I look about me, I cannot find one unoccupied.' Hume, who liked a joke upon an unsuspecting clergyman, said, 'what would you think, Mr Anderson, of a history of Croesus, king of Lydia? – that has never yet been written'. Mr Anderson was delighted with this idea, and, in short, 'upon that hint he wrote'. In 1755 was published, 'The History of Croesus, king of Lydia, in four parts' one of the most curious productions recognised in the history of literary mania.

  Robert Chambers, Scottish Biographical Dictionary. Cacoethes scribendi: *itch to write*.

Sir James Barrie Looks Specially Small

The pallbearers at Thomas Hardy's funeral included distinguished writers (Rudyard Kipling, G. B. Shaw, A. E. Housman) and politicians (Stanley Baldwin, Ramsay Macdonald). Shaw, the tallest and most obviously impressive, later remarked that he himself had looked well at the ceremony, but 'Barrie, blast him! looked far the most effective. He made himself look specially small.'

  C. Asquith, Portrait of Barrie, *quoted in C. Fadiman*, The Little, Brown Book of Anecdotes (*1985*)

James Bone, or was it Robert Lynd?

Bob Lynd lean and lank, James Bone rotund and heavy, Bob with his almost woebegone face and James with his eyes always at the point of twinkle and his lips curved in an anticipatory understanding smile. They seemed to linger over their whiskies as their forebears might have done in Belfast or Edinburgh. It has long been canvassed in Fleet Street whether it was Lynd who said to Bone or Bone to Lynd, 'Have you ever realised that we have grown into the kind of men our parents warned us against?'

Collin Brooks, More Tavern Talk (1953). *James Bone, brother of Sir Muirhead and Sir David Bone, was a distinguished journalist and author of* The Edinburgh Perambulator.

James Boswell Conducts Research

He obtruded himself everywhere. Lowe (mentioned by him in his *Life of Johnson*) once gave me a humorous picture of him. Lowe had requested Johnson to write him a letter, which Johnson did, and Boswell came in, while it was writing. His attention was immediately fixed, Lowe took the letter, retired, and was followed by Boswell. 'Nothing', said Lowe, 'could surprise me more. Till that moment he had so entirely overlooked me, that I did not imagine he knew there was such a creature in existence; and he now accosted me with the most overstrained and insinuating compliments possible. "How do you do, Mr Lowe? I hope you are very well, Mr Lowe. Pardon my freedom, Mr Lowe, but I think I saw my dear friend, Dr Johnson, writing a letter for you?" – "Yes, sir." – "I hope you will not think me rude, but if it would not be too great a favour, you would infinitely oblige me, if you would just let me have a sight of it. Everything from that hand, you know, is so inestimable." . . . I was overcome', said Lowe, 'by this sudden familiarity and condescension, accompanied with bows and grimaces. I had no power to refuse; we went to the coffee-house, my letter was presently transcribed, and as soon as he had put the document in his pocket, Mr Boswell walked away, as erect and proud as he was half an hour before, and I ever afterwards was unnoticed. Nay, I am not certain . . . whether the Scotchman did not leave me, poor as he knew I was, to pay for my own dish of coffee.'

Thomas Holcroft, Memoirs (1798)

George Douglas Brown and his Father

His mother, Sarah Gemmell, was Irish of the second generation, a dairy-worker on his father's farm. Yet this was no question of boy-and-girl light-of-love, or an affair between the village Lothario and a dairymaid. She was thirty-eight, a mature, capable woman, and this was her first child; he, a travelled man; with two brothers at one time or another professors of English in Paris, and a sister who had married money from Australia. It was the family, by all accounts, who stopped the marriage, and though the fact of George Douglas Brown's illegitimacy burned itself into his whole life, there was a curiously lasting association between Sarah Gemmell's son and his father. And it is on record that young Brown, overhearing, as he sat on top of the station waggonette, the characteristic Ayrshire comment 'Aye, auld Broon's bastard – ye ken – Drumsmudden', burst out: 'I'd rather be auld Broon's bastard than the son o' any man in this brake.'

James Veitch, George Douglas Brown (*1952*). *As George Douglas, he wrote* The House with the Green Shutters.

The Sarcasm of Robert Burns

He indulged his sarcastic humour in talking of men, particularly if he thought them proud; or disdainful of Persons of inferior rank; his Observations were always acute and forcibly expressed. I was walking with him one day, when we met a common Acquaintance not remarkable for Ability or intellectual Endowments. I observed how extremely fat he had lately grown. 'Yes,' said Burns, 'and when you have told that you have exhausted the subject of Mr ——. Fatness is the only quality you can ascribe to him.'

Henry Mackenzie (1745–1831), The Anecdotes and Egotisms of Henry Mackenzie. *There is a less authenticated anecdote of Burns being present at Greenock harbour when a well-off merchant fell into the water and was rescued by a seaman. The rescuer was offered a shilling, and the bystanders protested at the meanness. Burns intervened: 'Surely', he said, 'the gentleman best knows the value of his own life.'*

The Meeting of Burns and Scott

I saw him one day at the late venerable Professor Ferguson's, where there were several gentlemen of literary reputation, among whom I remember the celebrated Mr Dugald Stewart. Of course, we youngsters sat silent, looked and listened. The only thing I remember which was remarkable in Burns's manner, was the effect produced upon him by a print of Bunbury's, representing a soldier lying dead on the snow, his dog sitting in misery on one side – on the other his widow, with a child in her arms. These lines were written beneath:

> Cold on Canadian hills, or Minden's plain,
> Perhaps that mother wept her soldier slain;
> Bent o'er her babe, her eye dissolved in dew,
> The big drops mingling with the milk he drew
> Gave the sad presage of his future years,
> The child of misery baptised in tears.

Burns seemed much affected by the print, or rather by the ideas which it suggested to his mind. He actually shed tears. He asked whose the lines were; and it chanced that nobody but myself remembered that they occur in a half-forgotten poem of Langhorne's called by the unpromising title of

'The Justice of Peace'. I whispered my information to a friend present; he mentioned it to Burns, who rewarded me with a look and a word, which, though of mere civility, I then received and still recollect with very great pleasure.

His person was strong and robust; his manners rustic, not clownish; a sort of dignified plainness and simplicity, which received part of its effect perhaps from one's knowledge of his extraordinary talents. His features are represented in Mr Nasmyth's picture: but to me it conveys the idea that they are diminished, as if seen in perspective. I think his countenance was more massive than it looks in any of the portraits. I should have taken the poet, had I not known who he was, for a very sagacious country farmer of the old Scotch school, i.e., none of your modern agriculturists who keep labourers for their drudgery, but the douce gudeman who held his own plough. There was a strong expression of sense and shrewdness in all his lineaments; the eye alone, I think, indicated the poetical character and temperament. It was large, and of a dark cast, which glowed (I say literally glowed) when he spoke with feeling or interest. I never saw such another eye in any human head, though I have seen the most distinguished men of my time. His conversation expressed perfect self-confidence, without the slightest presumption. Among the men who were the most learned of their time and country, he expressed himself with perfect firmness, but without the least intrusive forwardness; and when he differed in opinion, he did not hesitate to express it firmly, yet at the same time with modesty. I have only to add, that his dress corresponded with his manner. He was like a farmer dressed in his best to dine with the laird. I do not speak in malam partem, when I say, I never saw a man in company with his superiors in station or information more perfectly free from either the reality or the affectation of embarrassment.

Sir Walter Scott (1771–1832). The words spoken by Burns, as related by Sir Adam Ferguson, were: 'You'll be a man yet, sir.'

Thomas Carlyle's Manuscript Destroyed

Mill (John Stuart Mill) had borrowed that first volume of my poor French Revolution. . . Well, one night about three weeks ago, we sat at tea, and Mill's short rap was heard at the door: Jane rose to welcome him; but he stood there unresponsive, pale, the very picture of despair; said, half-articulately, gasping, that she must go down and speak to Mrs Taylor. . . After some considerable additional gasping, I learned from Mill this fact: that my poor manuscript, all except some four tattered leaves, was annihilated! He had left it out (too carelessly); it had been taken for waste-paper: and so five months of as tough labour as I could remember of, were as good as vanished, gone like a whiff of smoke. – There never in my life had come upon me any other accident of such moment; but this I could not but feel to be a sore one. The thing was lost, and perhaps worse; for I had not only forgotten the structure of it, but the spirit it was written with was past; only the general impression seemed to remain, and the recollection that I was on the whole well satisfied with that, and could hardly now hope to equal it. Mill, whom I had to comfort and speak peace to, remained injudiciously enough till almost midnight, and my poor Dame and I had to sit talking of indifferent matters; and could not till then get our lament freely uttered. She was very good to me; and the thing did not beat us. I felt in general that I was as a little schoolboy, who had laboriously written out his Copy as he could, and was showing it not without satisfaction to the Master; but lo! the Master had suddenly torn it, saying: No, boy, thou must go and write it better. What could I do but sorrowing go and try to obey? That night was a hard one; something from time to time tying me tight as it were all round the region of the heart, and strange dreams haunting me: however, I was not without good thoughts too that came like healing life into me; and I got it somewhat reasonably crushed down, not abolished, yet subjected to me with the resolution and prophecy of abolishing ... and so, having first finished out the piece I was actually upon, I began again at the beginning. Early the day after tomorrow (after a hard and quite novel kind of battle) I count on having the First Chapter on paper a second time, no worse than it was, though considerably different.

   Thomas Carlyle (1795–1881), letter to his brother in Rome, 23 March 1835. John Stuart Mill (1806–1873), political philosopher and Carlyle's friend, had lent numerous books to Carlyle to help him write The French Revolution *and had taken a keen interest in the project. By late September 1835, Carlyle had finished rewriting the first volume.*

The Reality of Sherlock Holmes

That Sherlock Holmes was anything but mythical to many was shown by the fact that I have had many letters addressed to him with requests that I forward them. Watson has also had a number of letters in which he has been asked for the address or the autograph of his more brilliant confrère. A press-cutting agency wrote to Watson asking whether Holmes would not wish to subscribe. When Holmes retired several elderly ladies were ready to keep house for him, and one sought to ingratiate herself by assuring me she knew all about bee-keeping and could 'segregate the queen'. I had considerable offers also for Holmes if he would examine and solve various family mysteries. Once the offer – from Poland – was that I should myself go, and my reward was practically left to my own judgement. I had judgement enough, however, to avoid it altogether.

   Sir Arthur Conan Doyle (1859–1930), Memories and Adventures *(1930)*

'Don Roberto' Gives an After-dinner Speech

After dinner, Cunninghame-Graham addressed the assemblage. What a noble figure he was, this 'Don Roberto', with his beautiful countenance – enhanced to my mind by the beauty of age: his snow-white hair brushed back from his serene brow, his Van Dyck moustaches and peaked beard, his graceful, slender figure! His address was, without exception, the most masterly after-dinner speech I have ever heard. Without a note to aid his memory, he held his audience under a veritable spell for half an hour. His theme was the power of the *pen*. When he came to the descriptive power at a writer's disposal, his eloquence rose to a *crescendo* of genius: with him the spoken word rivalled the splendid written prose of his great book, *The Horses of the Conquistadors*. He had loved horses, as the Arabians of the desert love them. He was himself a superb horseman. He described a great herd of wild horses in the heart of South America, that region of large spaces and wild nature that he knew so well. As he spoke, you could hear the countless hoofs of untamed horses on the soft earth; you could hear the splash of the water as the herd waded into a wide, still mere, to drink. It was a piece of real witchery. He closed his oratory on another and solemn note. The world was on its way to perdition. Everywhere you read and heard men say: We need practical men, business men, to govern us. 'Practical men,' he cried, his voice rising like a trumpet-call! 'Business men! Why, we have had these practical men, these men of business, to rule us for two generations. And where have they led us? For God's sake let us have no more of them!' He paused, and then spoke his last words. 'It is not the practical men we need to govern us: it is the Poets: for only by the light of Imagination do men see Truth!'

Charles Richard Cammell, Heart of Scotland (*1956*). *The occasion was the International PEN Congress in Edinburgh, in 1934.*

The Meeting of Hogg and Tannahill

. . . he detailed to me his interview with Robert Tannahill, immediately prior to the melancholy fate of the author of 'Gloomy Winter' and many of our finest Scotch songs. Hogg . . . was an ardent disciple of Izaak Walton. In his piscatory excursions I often accompanied him, and carried a fishing rod, though usually I killed more time than fish, and was especially dexterous in hooking trees. The last trout – a fine, large, yellow fin – I brought to land, I dragged out of a deep sluggish pool, twenty yards below Mount Benger bridge. As the poor trout lay gasping on the bank, Hogg looked in the water and said to me, 'That pool aye reminds me o' the pool of the Cart in which poor Tannahill drowned himself. Do you mind the story?' I remarked, 'No; he died before I was born.' 'Well,' he continued, 'I once travelled all the way from Edinburgh to Paisley allenarly [that was an old Scotch word

Hogg used often] to see him. I supposed that when I arrived in Paisley I had only to ask for Tannahill the poet, but to my astonishment nobody knew who he was. I was sent from one Tannahill to another, and many others, but none of them the object of my search. At last I found him on his loom, one of a long range; he was a swarthy man, bearing no external indication of the intellectual lava tide that slumbered in his soul. I told him my nom-de-plume, and I have never forgotten the look of absolute bewilderment with which he regarded me, as I told him how far I had come just to look upon him, and that now I was before him with the same feelings as when

> Jonson sat in Drummond's classic shade.

During the whole of that night we sat together, and he sang many of his choicest melodies. . . In the morning, I was about to start by the coach for Glasgow on my way home. Being somewhat late, I required to run some distance. Tannahill ran by my side. When about to part, he grasped my hand convulsively, and burst into tears. I said, "Hoot, Robert, dinna tak' things so serious; we shall often meet again; and if you'll no come to Edinburgh to visit me, I'll come to Paisley to see you." "No, Hogg," he replied, "this has been the proudest day of my life; but it cannot be" – and with this sobs choked his utterance. I had scarcely reached Edinburgh before I read in the newspapers an account of his sad end.'

　　Dr Charles Marshall, recorded in Mrs Garden, Memorials of James Hogg, the Ettrick Shepherd. *Robert Tannahill (1774–1810) drowned himself in the River Cart.*

Hugh MacDiarmid Passes out in the Bath

[Edwin and I] found Peggy at her wits' end, Christopher having come home from some farmers' junketing and locked himself in the bathroom, since when there had been neither sound nor movement from him. Peggy was sure he had passed out. Edwin managed to scramble from outside through the high, narrow bathroom window, and found Christopher lying mother-naked, cold, insensible but alive in a completely dry bath, and unlocked the door at once. We lugged the poet into the living-room, where we laid him on the hearth-rug by the fire, covered him with blankets and left him to Peggy's ministrations in that respectable council house.

　　Willa Muir, Belonging (Hogarth Press, London, 1968). *This recollection from the mid-1920s records a visit by the poet Edwin Muir and his wife Willa to Hugh MacDiarmid (Christopher Murray Grieve) at a time when they were all living in Montrose. Grieve was then a journalist on the local paper, hence his attendance at the farmers' revel.*

A Drunk Man Looks at the Thistle

Christopher usually wrote his poetry in snatches: he never had any sense of form and after some months of scribbling on the back of envelopes and odd bits of paper, he sent to Glasgow an urgent call for me to come for a week-end and see the litter (and mess!) he'd been making out of my bright idea, as Blackwood's were asking for the MS and there was no MS. It was late at night when I reached Montrose and after his wife and youngsters went off to bed, we sat down to a table, a great heap of scribbled bits of paper and a bottle of whisky. I can still see Christopher's face when I was indicating the shape the poem, or for that matter a musical composition, ought to take – he was literally flabbergasted either by the extent of my knowledge or by the whisky – it's anybody's guess! We spent until day-break sorting out the items worth keeping, Christopher arranging them on the table like a pack of cards in the order that I indicated as likely to give the best sequences, climaxes, etc. My plans necessitated a pianissimo close, after so much bus-tle ('the Stars like thistle's Roses flower') to be followed by ('Yet ha'e I silence left, the croon o' a') and I'm pretty certain I supplied the last two lines to bring the thing to some sort of conclusion.

Francis George Scott (1880–1958), autobiographical letter, 1945, quoted in Maurice Lindsay, Francis George Scott and the Scottish Renaissance. A Drunk Man Looks at the Thistle *was suggested by Scott, to whom the work is dedicated, and he provided a framework for the poet to follow, but this bid for virtual ownership of the most significant Scots poem of the twentieth century is critically dissected by Alan Bold in his biography* MacDiarmid (1988).

Hugh MacDiarmid Visits William Soutar

About 3.30, C.M.G. came striding in, resplendent in full Highland rig-out. He had been celebrating his descent on the South – but hadn't reached the blethering stage, so we had a hearty time, with much loud laughter. He had a number of MSS with him and read part of his Red Scotland, which sounded quite convincing. As he read, he supported himself at an angle over my table, and the angle increased with the reading till he was literally dropping cigarette-ash and dialectical materialism all about me. I thought it might relieve the congestion if he removed his plaid – but discovered that it was part of the regalia.

William Soutar (1898–1943), Diaries of a Dying Man. *At this time (April 1937), MacDiarmid was living on the Shetland island of Whalsay; Soutar was bedridden at his home in Perth.*

William McGonagall Discovers his Vocation

The most startling incident in my life was the time I discovered myself to be a poet, which was in the year 1877. During the Dundee holiday week, in

the bright and balmy month of June, when trees and flowers were in full
bloom, while lonely and sad in my room, I sat thinking about the thousands
of people who were away by rail and steamboat, perhaps to the land of
Burns, or poor ill-treated Tannahill . . . Well, while pondering so, I seemed
to feel as it were a strange kind of feeling stealing over me, and remained so
for about five minutes. A flame, as Lord Byron has said, seemed to kindle
up my entire frame, along with a strong desire to write poetry; and I felt so
happy, so happy, that I was inclined to dance, then I began to pace backwards and forwards in my room, trying to shake off all thought of writing
poetry; but the more I tried, the more strong the sensation became. It was
so strong, I imagined that a pen was in my hand, and a voice crying, 'Write!
Write!'

   *William McGonagall (c.1825–1902), Brief Autobiography. He proceeded
to write his first poem, on his friend the Rev. George Gifillan:*

>   Rev. George Gilfillan of Dundee,
>   There is none you can excel;
>   You have boldly rejected the Confession of Faith,
>   And defended your cause right well.
>
>   The first time I heard him speak,
>   'Twas in the Kinnaird Hall,
>   Lecturing on the Garibaldi movement
>   As loud as he could bawl.
>   etc., etc.

The Discovery of 'Ian Maclaren'

. . . he did not discover Barrie – Frederick Greenwood has that honour –
and he did not discover Crockett, though he was quick to appropriate them
both to his own purposes. The only member of the Kailyard trio that he did
actually unearth was 'Ian Maclaren', and his manner of doing so was characteristic. The Rev. John Maclaren Watson, minister of Sefton Park Presbyterian Church, Liverpool, enjoyed a high reputation as a preacher. Nicoll
asked him to contribute some articles to *The Expositor* and, never having
met him, invited him to Hampstead to discuss the matter. First impressions
were not favourable. 'He stayed with us three nights,' Nicoll wrote to a
friend, 'and was very pleasant, but somehow I did not take to him as much
as I expected; he was too cynical for me.' But the cynical fellow could tell a
good sentimental story, and his host took to him enough to leave him no
peace until he promised to write some articles on the same lines for the
British Weekly. The result (after one or two false starts) was the profitable
welter of sentiment known in book-form as *The Bonnie Brier Bush*. After

that Nicoll ceased to have qualms about Watson's cynicism. Other people may find it less easy to forgive Nicoll his charity.

Donald Carswell, Brother Scots (1927). *He was writing of Sir William Robertson Nicoll, founder and editor of the* British Weekly. *Of 'Ian Maclaren's'* The Bonnie Brier Bush *and similar works, the critic Kurt Wittig wrote: 'Whatever their merits, they have nothing to add to the Scottish literary tradition.'*

Hugh Miller Discovers his Scottishness

I first became thoroughly a Scot some time in my tenth year; and the consciousness of country has remained tolerably strong within me ever since. My uncle James had procured for me from a neighbour the loan of a common stall-edition of Blind Harry's *Wallace,* as modernized by Hamilton . . . I was intoxicated with the fiery narrative of the blind minstrel, with his fierce breathings of hot, intolerant patriotism, and his stories of astonishing prowess; and, glorying in being a Scot, and the countryman of Wallace and the Graham, I longed for a war with the Southron, that the wrongs and sufferings of these noble heroes might yet be avenged.

Hugh Miller (1802–1856), My Schools and Schoolmasters

The Amorous Exploits of 'Christopher North'

He could have been no common young man, so far as personal interest and the power of ingratiating go . . . In some one of the recesses, between university term-times, must have taken place, if at all, the reported extravagance of his joining himself to a party of strolling players, enjoying the disguise with its accompaniments of hardship or joviality, and taking the leading parts, both in tragedy and in comedy, at country fairs throughout England, no doubt under grotesque vicissitudes of popular acceptation. . . He was said to have become temporary waiter at an inn for the sake of some fair stranger there resident, and to have been so great a favourite with all and sundry, as the humorous and eccentric young 'John', that the establishment would scarce part with him. These histories are really traceable to very slight occasion in fact. A still odder tale used to be circulated of him, apparently dependent on impulses of a more serious kind; how having been smitten with the outlandish charms of a beautiful jet-eyed gipsy daughter of the king of that mysterious tribe, he followed the gang in secret, and preferring his suit, succeeded in it – was allowed to assume the gipsy garb – to marry the dark maiden, or at least settle for some time in their encampment, a sort of adopted heir to the Egyptian princedom, till discovered and reclaimed to civilized life by his friends.

C. Rogers, Traits of Scottish People (1866). *The subject is John Wilson (1785–1854), author as 'Christopher North' of the* Noctes Ambrosianae *described in successive issues of* Blackwood's Magazine.

Isobel Pagan at Home

For thirty years Isobel Pagan lived in a wretched little hovel by the banks of Garpel Water, on the property of Lord Dundonald. Her house was nothing but an improvised shelter erected beneath a low arch, which had originally been built as a brick-store in connection with some local tar-works, and was scarcely fit for human habitation. But she seems to have been perfectly satisfied with so squalid a residence.

> When I sit in my cottage,
> I may be well content,
> The Lady she is kind to me,
> The Laird will pay my rent,

is the drift of one of her songs, and so long as she was kindly treated and paid no rent, she was quite resigned to such a life.

In this hovel of hers Isobel Pagan entertained all the worst characters of the neighbourhood . . . Her cottage was the scene of nightly orgies indulged in not only by the local peasantry, but also by gentlemen of the neighbourhood. Attracted to Isobel's bacchanalian concerts by her ready flow of wit, they made up parties to visit the strange old woman and be entertained by the clever impromptu rhymes and the indifferent whisky for which she was notorious . . . Isobel was not a woman who could safely be made a butt of, and many who came to laugh at her physical peculiarities found the tables turned on themselves. She was in the habit of satirising those who annoyed or offended her in verse which was not marked by any delicacy or the desire to spare the feelings of her victims.

Harry Graham, A Group of Scottish Women (*1908*). *Isobel Pagan (1741– 1821) never learned to write, but published a collection of her songs in 1803. A typical barb of hers runs:*

> Mr —— , in the Kyle,
> Ca'd me a common —— ;
> But if he hadna tried himsel',
> He wadna be so sure.

Allan Ramsay's Library

Now prosperous, in 1726 Ramsay quitted the dingy old shop near the Tron Kirk, and established himself in the Luckenbooths – a row of 'lands' standing in the High Street fronting St Giles', and blocking the street to a narrow entry. Above his door he placed the busts of William Drummond of Hawthornden and Ben Jonson, instead of the dilapidated figure of Mercury which had adorned the door of the wig-shop – for the poet had abandoned the trade in periwigs, razors and curling-tongs, and become a bookseller, as befitted his dignified literary position. He started the first circulating library in the kingdom, and lent out books at a penny a night, sometimes of a description which made the godly weep. Instead of soul-guiding works like . . . *The Groans of Believers,* or *The Balm of Gilead,* there were the works of Congreve, Wycherley, Dryden, and Matt Prior: yea, the scandalous *Atlantis* of Mrs Manley, which was found in the hands of young ladies. One knows how the Reverend Robert Wodrow wrote his lamentation that 'all the villainous, profane, and obscene books and plays, as printed at London, are got down by Allan Ramsay and lent out, for an easy price, to young boys, servant women of the better sort, and gentlemen . . . by these wickedness of all kinds are dreadfully propagat among the youth of all sorts.' Magistrates, who were pious elders, examined the shelves to see if ugly rumours which the pious hypocrite Lord Grange had reported were true, but the pawky librarian had hidden the worst before they looked. . .

H. Grey Graham, Scottish Men of Letters of the Eighteenth Century (1908). At this time, Ramsay (1686–1758), formerly a wig-maker, had had his first success, with The Gentle Shepherd. *There is more of Lord Grange under* Lairds, Lords and Ladies.

Sir Walter Scott as a Boy

I last night supped in Mr Walter Scott's. He has the most extraordinary genius of a boy I ever saw. He was reading a poem to his mother when I went in. I made him read on; it was the description of a shipwreck. His passion rose with the storm; he lifted up his eyes and hands –

'There's the mast gone,' says he; 'crash it goes: they will all perish!'

After his agitation he turns to me.

'That is too much melancholy,' says he; 'I had better read you somewhat more amusing.'

I preferred a little chat, and asked him his opinion of Milton and other books he was reading, which he gave me wonderfully indeed. One of his observations was: 'How strange it was that Adam, just new come into the world, should know everything. That must be the poet's fancy,' says he.

But when told he was created perfect by God Himself, he instantly yielded.

When at last he was taken to bed last night he told his aunt he liked that lady.

'What lady?' says she.

'Why, Mrs Cockburn; for I think she's a virtuoso like myself.'

'Dear Walter,' says his aunt, 'what is a virtuoso?'

'Don't you know? Why, it's one who will know everything.'

Now, sir, you will think this is a very silly story. Pray what age do you suppose that boy to be? Name it now before I tell you.

'Why, twelve or fourteen.'

No such thing; he is not quite six, and he has a lame leg, for which he was a year at Bath, and has acquired the perfect English accent, which he has not lost since he came, and he reads like a Garrick. You will allow this an uncommon exotic.

From a letter of Alison Cockburn (1712–1794)

Sir Walter Scott's Bankruptcy

On the failure of Messrs Constable and Company, in January, 1826, Messrs Ballantyne and Company, printers, of which firm Sir Walter Scott was a partner, became insolvent, with debts of £102,000, for the whole of which, Sir Walter was, of course, liable, in addition to his liabilities for the bookselling house. It thus appeared that the most splendid literary revenue that ever man made for himself, had been compromised by a connection, partly for profit, and partly otherwise, with the two mechanical individuals concerned in the mere bringing of his writings before the world. . .

The blow was endured with a magnanimity worthy of the greatest writer of the age. On the very day after the calamity had been made known to him, a friend accosted him as he was coming from his house, and presented the condolences proper to such a melancholy occasion.

'It is very hard,' said he, in his usual slow and thoughtful voice, 'thus to lose all the labours of a lifetime, and be made a poor man at last, when I ought to have been otherwise. But if God grant me health and strength for a few years longer, I have no doubt that I shall redeem it all.'

. . . His creditors proposed a composition; but his honourable nature, and perhaps a sense of reputation, prevented him from listening to any such scheme. 'No, gentlemen,' said he, quoting a favourite Spanish proverb, 'Time and I against any two. Allow me time, and I will endeavour to pay all.'

Robert Chambers, Scottish Biographical Dictionary

Susan Ferrier Assists Sir Walter Scott in Decline

To assist them (the family of Scott) in amusing him in the hours which he spent out of his study, and especially that he might be tempted to make these hours more frequent, his daughters had invited his friend the author-ess of *Marriage* to come to Abbotsford; and her coming was serviceable; for she knew and loved him well, and she had seen enough of affliction akin to his to be well skilled in dealing with it. She could not be an hour in his company without observing what filled his children with more sorrow than all the rest of the case. He would begin a story as gaily as ever, and go on, in spite of the hesitation in his speech, and tell it with highly picturesque effect, but, before he reached the point, it would seem as if some internal spring had given way; he paused, and gazed round him with the blank anxiety of look that a blind man has when he has dropped his staff. Unthinking friends sometimes pained him sadly by giving him the catch-word abruptly. I noticed the delicacy of Miss Ferrier on such occasions. Her sight was bad, and she took care not to use her glasses when he was speaking; and she affected to be also troubled with deafness, and would say, 'Well, I am getting as dull as a post; I have not heard a word since you said so-and-so,' being sure to mention a circumstance behind that at which he had really halted. He then took up the thread with his habitual smile of courtesy, as if forgetting his case entirely in the consideration of the lady's infirmity.

J. G. Lockhart (1794–1854), Memoirs of the Life of Sir Walter Scott. Before Susan Ferrier abandoned anonymity as an author, Scott himself was often believed to have written Marriage.

William Smellie and the *Encyclopedia Britannica*

Amongst Mr Smellie's many literary undertakings, one of the earliest was the compilement and entire conducting of the first edition of the work just named (*Encyclopedia Britannica*), which began to appear in numbers at Edinburgh in 1771, and was completed in three volumes in quarto. The plan, and all the principal articles were devised and written or compiled by him, and he prepared and superintended the whole of that work, for which he only received the sum of £200, from its proprietors, Mr Andrew Bell, engraver, and Mr Colin Macfarquhar, printer. Had Mr Smellie adhered to this literary project, there is little doubt that he would ultimately have realised an ample fortune, as both the proprietors did in great affluence, arising solely from the labours of Mr Smellie in the original fabrication of the work. Unfortunately, however, when applied to by the proprietors to undertake the second edition, he fastidiously refused to meddle with it on account of their desiring to introduce a plan of biography into it, which Mr Smellie imagined would detract from its dignity as a Dictionary of Arts and Sciences.

Robert Chambers, Scottish Biographical Dictionary. William Smellie (c.1740–1795) was one of the impecunious freelance writers in whom, since the eighteenth century, Scotland has abounded; he was more of a polymath than most.

Tobias Smollett Fails to Surprise his Mother

Smollett now revisited his native country for the first time since he had left it. On arriving in Scotston, in Peeblesshire, where his mother resided with her daughter, Mrs Telfer, it was arranged that he should be introduced to the old lady as a gentleman from the West Indies, who was intimately acquainted with her son. The better to support his assumed character, he endeavoured to preserve a very serious countenance, approaching to a frown; but while his mother's eyes were rivetted with the instinct of affection upon his countenance, he could not refrain from smiling: she immediately sprang from her chair, and, throwing her arms round his neck, exclaimed 'Ah! my son, my son!'

   Robert Chambers, Scottish Biographical Dictionary. *Tobias Smollett (1721–1774), celebrated novelist, left Scotland in 1739 and returned on this visit in 1755.*

Muriel Spark's Metamorphosis

One of the great mysteries that emerges from the cuttings file is the way her looks have changed dramatically over the years. The first publicity photographs in the 1950s, when she was in her thirties (she was born in 1918), show a sturdy, bun-faced woman with tight, ugly curls and mannish clothes. Then when she moved to Rome, in her late forties, she suddenly emerged as a startling beauty – svelte, slim, elfin, dressed in couture clothes and chattering away about her jewellery. (She had the habit then of buying herself an 'important' piece, a Cartier watch or a diamond brooch, to commemorate each novel. She doesn't any longer, because 'there's no call for it in Tuscany. It just stays in the bank'.) The late sixties and early seventies were her Roman Spring: she moved in high society and occupied a flat as big as a football pitch in the centre of Rome. A friend who knew her then, Eugene Walter, said that the transformation happened quite suddenly: 'I saw her off on the plane to New York one day, a dumpy middle-aged Scottish woman, and met her off the plane two weeks later, a teenager in a full-length mink coat.'

   How did she suddenly become a beauty in middle life? 'Oh, really?' She gives a fluttery sort of feminine-genteel laugh. 'Well, I don't know. I had hairdos and all sorts of things. I think I was quite pretty when I was young, and then I went through a very bad period in my thirties. And then in my forties it sort of cleared up. But I was never a great beauty. A lot has to do with having a bit of money, to buy some clothes and have my hair done.' But in your thirties, you were?. . . 'I was fat, yes, I don't know why: I just was. I went up and down a great deal. Then I lost weight and I felt very much better and looked very much better.' Success obviously suited her. 'It suits everybody', she says with sudden firmness. 'If it's deserved; if they've worked for it.'

   Lynn Barber, Mostly Men *(1991)*

An Exchange Between Stevenson and Lang

One of the poems in Robert Louis Stevenson's sequence *Underwoods* refers to his friend Andrew Lang, a famously keen angler (see Anglers and Stalkers, above):

> Dear Andrew, with the brindled hair,
> Who glory to have thrown in air,
> High over arm, the trembling reed,
> By Ale and Kail, by Till and Tweed.
>   (No. XIV, *To Andrew Lang*)

Lang however took, or pretended to take, umbrage:

> Dear Louis of the awful cheek!
> Who told you it was right to speak
> Where all the world might hear and stare,
> Of other fellows' brindled hair?

Gilbert Stuart Over-indulges

During his labours for this magazine (*The Edinburgh Magazine and Review*), Stuart did not neglect his pleasures. He is said one night to have called at the house of his friend Smellie, in a state of such complete jollity, that it was necessary he should be put to bed. Awakening, and mistaking the description of place in which he was lodged, he brought his friend in his night-gown to his bedside, by his repeated cries of 'house! house!' and, in a tone of sympathy, said to him, 'Smellie, I never expected to see you in such a house. Get on your clothes, and return immediately to your wife and family: and be assured I shall never mention this affair to anyone.'

Robert Chambers, Scottish Biographical Dictionary. *Gilbert Stuart (1742–1786) was a writer and journalist who never fulfilled his early promise.*

James Thomson, Poet of Indolence

Every body is aware of the indolent character of the author of 'The Seasons'; of his being found once in a garden, eating fruit off a tree with his hands in his pockets, etc. A friend one day entered his room, and, finding him in bed, although the day was far spent, asked him in the name of wonder why he did not get up? 'Man, I hae nae motive', replied the poet.

Robert Chambers, Scottish Jests and Anecdotes (*1832*)

James ('BV') Thomson Recalled

Stuart was a tall, lean, yellow-faced very quiet man, with two boasts: one was that he was the oldest subaltern in the Italian Expeditionary Force, if not in the whole British Army, and the other was that in his youth, as a regular soldier, he had been the only one of his name in the Army List, the others all being Stewarts. Both boasts were probably wrong, but he made them good-humouredly. To me, it was much more interesting that he had been an early admirer of James Thomson – I mean, 'BV' – and had tried to find him in BV's last terrible phase, only to come belatedly upon Philip Bourke Marston, the blind poet, in whose rooms BV had his last fatal haemorrhage and collapse. BV had once said to him a casual thing which he and I were both to remember, a trite enough sentence but, for some reason or no reason, memorable. Stuart had grown indignant about some injustice, and BV, whom life had treated so harshly, said 'don't grow angry, Stuart; it wears away the tissues of the soul'. . . . BV with so much reason for anger kept his perpetual temper, even though he kept it in perpetual gloom.

Collin Brooks, More Tavern Talk *(1953). Thomson (1834–1882), the author of* The City of Dreadful Night, *also took the name Bysshe Vanolis, in honour of Shelley (Bysshe) and the German Romantic writer Novalis.*

Alexander Trocchi Organises 'Sexual Training' in Paris

. . . excited by the theme of *The Story of* O and the idea of a 'specialist brothel', Alex decided to train some women on the finer points of sexual technique and either wanted to encourage wide-spread promiscuity, or make some money, or was it something else? It is hard now to know precisely what his motives were, but the facts are he did 'sign up' a few women – friends, girlfriends, even wives, and at least one 'training session' took place. Trocchi watched while a nominated male made love to a female. He could not afford a leather whip and stood ready to correct any 'defects' with a wooden ruler! . . . On another occasion, at a party, Trocchi was greatly excited by the wife of a Dutch friend and stalked round the room with a French bread at his crotch, imitating a giant erection, extemporising in great detail on what he intended to do for this lady in a sexual way. His diatribe, accomplished with much leering, ended with the line; 'I'm going to get my little finger into her cunt!' Suddenly, the Dutchman, who had not, until that point, understood what Trocchi was saying, leapt at him, causing a shower of sparks as several marijuana joints were knocked out of several pairs of hands. Trocchi came off very much second-best from the fracas, and later remonstrated with his friends. 'Like, why did he attack me?' He genuinely seemed mystified.

Andrew Murray Scott, Alexander Trocchi: The Making of the Monster (Edinburgh, Polygon *1991*)

Raymond Vettese Experiences an Illumination

I was a message boy for Bob Mackenzie, a grocer in North Street. I pedalled his elderly, creaking bicycle through the streets of Montrose and even across the bridge that spans the South Esk to deliver to Rossie Island and the community beyond, Ferryden.

One Saturday in June (a few weeks after discovering Dylan) Montrose changed – or I did. As I pushed the pedals down it was as if I had suddenly cycled into an alternative town, a place existing parallel to Montrose and yet fundamentally different. This town, this Montrose, was charged with gold, streamed with light. Everything glowed. Even the douce grey concrete lamp-posts were surrounded by radiance. And people were enveloped by that same radiance. I knew that I also shone and I felt a mighty surge of love and compassion for all that I saw. And what I saw had slowed down. People inched along the street. My limbs pedalled in fractions. In Christie's Lane I understood everything. I knew absolutely, yet without any words of explanation, the whole purpose. I knew the joy and sorrow of things, the littleness and hugeness of our briefness and immortality. I said aloud OF COURSE. As if this had just been waiting to be found and I had been absurdly stupid not to recognise it before.

. . . A few days later I cycled into eternity again, but this time my visit was accompanied by language. I had just delivered groceries to Mrs Gunn, an elderly crippled woman of whom I was very fond. She was a trusting soul who left her front door unlocked. I was to put the groceries away in the kitchen (she was upstairs in bed often) and then I was to take a three-penny bit from her purse, which she left on the table. As I rode away from her house in Mount Road I re-entered that other Montrose. Everything was radiant again but this time there was a strange, high-pitched sound in my ears, a sound I would liken to amplified cicadas, and there were words in my head. It was as if I were being spoken to:

> Our span, not worth spitting on,
> is almost over you
> and carries with it
> all the cruelties

So it began, the first poem I had ever written.

Raymond Vettese, The Seeds of Poetry, *in W. G. Lawrence (ed.),* Roots in a Northern Landscape *(1996). Another Scottish writer, Fionn MacColla, had earlier experienced such a satori, again in Montrose, whilst gazing at a vase of flowers.*

John Wilson's Muse is Muzzled

. . . should you chance to come across an eighteenth century poem entitled 'Clyde', written in the heroic style by John Wilson, who went to school in

Lanark and taught later in Lesmahagow and Greenock, you may be surprised at the tribute therein paid to the accommodation of the people.

> As shines the moon among the lesser fires,
> Unrivalled Glasgow lifts her stately spires:
> For commerce, glorious with her golden crown,
> Has marked fair Glasgow for her favourite town:
> She makes her stately edifices thrive,
> And merchants rich in princely splendour live;
> Extends her spacious streets on every side,
> And bids her poor in palaces reside.

The last line will strike many Glaswegians as rather more than astonishing. Poor Wilson was compelled to abandon his stately Muse, so respectably embellished with the kindly sentiments of local patriotism. The magistrates and minister of Greenock, when the poet was admitted to a headmastership there in 1767, would have none of that. These solemn tyrants were horrified by what they called 'the profane and unprofitable art of poem-making' and made Wilson swear to abjure the vice. He did so because he had a large family to keep and the job was precious. His biographer, John Leyden, MD, who wrote a prose as copious as Wilson's couplets, described his surrender:

> To avoid the temptation of violating this promise, which he esteemed sacred, he took an early opportunity of committing to the flames the greater part of his unfinished manuscripts. After this, he never ventured to touch his forbidden lyre again, though he often regarded it with the mournful solemnity, which the harshness of dependence, and the memory of its departed sounds, could not fail to inspire.

It did not pay to be a song-bird in the austere groves of Scottish Presbyterian piety.

Ivor Brown (1891–1974), Summer in Scotland (1952). A contemporary poet, Douglas Dunn, has made an elegant apologium for Wilson:

> But know, I worked, and tried;
> And hope still for a small posterity
> And, through a chink in time, to hear men say,
> That, wasting these best talents of my life,
> I fed my children and I loved my wife.

John Wilson in Greenock (1786), from St Kilda's Parliament

ACKNOWLEDGEMENTS

The compiler and the publishers acknowledge their gratitude to those copyright-holders or agents who have given permission for extracts to be reproduced in this anthology. Whilst every effort has been made to identify copyright owners, in some cases we have not been able to do so. We will be pleased to hear from copyright owners in such cases.

The compiler is also grateful for the facilities extended by the Edinburgh Central Library, the Mitchell Library, Glasgow, and by the London Library.

Thanks are due to the following for allowing extracts to be included: Charlie Allan for John R. Allan, *Summer in Scotland*; Ian Allan Publishing, for David L. Smith, *Tales of the Glasgow & South-Western Railway*; Ardo Publishing Co. for Charlie Allan, *The Buchan Line*; Birlinn Ltd, for Angus MacLellan, *The Furrow Behind Me*, Tom Patey, *One Man's Mountains*, and Donald Sutherland, *A Highland Childhood* (reissued as *Butt and Ben*); A. & C. Black, for Kenneth Macleod, *The Road to the Isles*; Cambridge University Press, for J. A. Lovat-Fraser, *Erskine*; Canongate, for Duncan Williamson, *The Horsieman*; Cassell & Co., for Douglas Young, *St Andrews*; Curtis Brown, for André Maurois, *The Life of Sir Alexander Fleming*; Dunlugas Publishing for Isobel Rae and John Lawson, *Dr Grigor of Nairn;* Faber & Faber, for J. Forsyth Hardy, *John Grierson: A Documentary Biography*; Floris Books for Iain Macdonald (ed.), *Turgot: Life of St Margaret, Queen of Scotland*; Dairmid Gunn, for Neil Gunn, *Highland Pack*; Robert Hale, for A. A. MacGregor, *Somewhere in Scotland*; David Higham Associates for Louis MacNeice, *I Crossed the Minch*; Hodder & Stoughton, for Norman Maclean, *The Former Days*; Gerald Laing, for *Kinkell: The Reconstruction of a Scottish Castle*; the Rev. Brooke Kingsmill-Lunn, for Hugh Kingsmill, *Skye High*; Mainstream Publishing, for Bob Crampsey, *The Young Civilian*; Ronald Mavor, for *Dr Mavor and Mr Bridie* (Canongate) and James Bridie, *One Way of Living*; Thomas Middlemas, for *Mainly Scottish Steam*; PFD, for Eric Linklater, *A Year of Space* (Copyright © Eric Linklater 1954); Polygon, for Camille Dressler, *Eigg: Story of an Island*; Random House Group Ltd for J. M. Reid, *James Lithgow, Master of Works,* and for Don Whyte, *The Lonely Shore*; Michael Russell (Publishing) for Michael Strachan, *The Ben Line*; The Society of Authors, for Compton Mackenzie, *My Life and Times, Octave vii*; A. P. Watt, for Hesketh Pearson, *Skye High*; The Wellcome Trust, for J. D. Comrie, *History of Scottish Medicine*; Neil Wilson Publishing, for Alastair Dunnett, *The Canoe Boys*.

INDEX OF PROPER NAMES

Authors quoted are listed in bold type